Hans Hörmann

To Mean –
To Understand

Problems of Psychological Semantics

Translated from the German by
Bogusław A. Jankowski

With 5 Figures

Springer-Verlag
Berlin Heidelberg New York 1981

Professor Dr. Hans Hörmann
Ruhr-Universität Bochum
Psychologisches Institut
P. O. Box 10 21 48
D-4630 Bochum-Querenburg
Federal Republic of Germany

Bogusław A. Jankowski
Tamka 33A/16
00-355 Warszawa, Poland

Translated from the German:
Hans Hörmann: Meinen und Verstehen
Grundzüge einer psychologischen Semantik

© Suhrkamp Verlag, Frankfurt am Main 1976
Alle Rechte vorbehalten

ISBN 3-540-10448-8 Springer-Verlag Berlin Heidelberg New York
ISBN 0-387-10448-8 Springer-Verlag New York Heidelberg Berlin

Library of Congress Cataloging in Publication Data

Hörmann, Hans, 1924 – To mean, to understand. Translation of Meinen und verstehen. Bibliography: p.   Includes index. 1. Psycholinguistics. 2. Semantics. 3. Languages – Philosophy. I. Title.
P37.H613 1981   401'.9   80-29125
ISBN 0-387-10448-8

© Springer-Verlag Berlin Heidelberg 1981.
Printed in Germany.

Typesetting and Bookbinding: Appl, Wemding. Printing: aprinta, Wemding
2125/3140-543210

82-787

Contents

This book is dedicated to NIAS, the Netherlands Institute for Advanced Studies, in gratitude for a year of peace and tranquillity, unobtrusive stimulation, and excellent service.

Preface

It is not uncommon in science that following a period of turbulent growth, a skeptical mood builds up and doubts begin to be expressed as to the rationale of progress achieved and the extent to which the position reached coincides with the original goals. This kind of discomfort is felt today by linguists and their close companions, the psycholinguists.

Despite its growing intensity, this discomfort is not readily verbalizable. Still, we will try to characterize it tentatively with a few angry assertions, each of which taken separately is perhaps untenable in its extreme form, but which together convey a sense of the malaise that seems to afflict the area in question.

For one thing, the models and theories current in linguistics tend to approach a level of complexity at which extreme sophistication borders on folly.

Further, the present inflation of macro- and microsystems testifies to the growing arbitrariness of theorizing – in spite of the abundance of publications specifying the criteria by which to evaluate these systems against a metatheory of science; thus we are made aware of the widening gulf between linguistic theory and the realities of language.

Finally, the developments in linguistics and the affiliated psycholinguistics since the mid-1950s have contributed very little to a clarification of the problems of language use. For instance, have they helped us in understanding how language is acquired or learned so that our insights might be of any practical significance? The plain statement that a person understands a sentence has been replaced by the formulation that syntactic descriptions are mapped by the hearer upon the linguistic input and thereupon receive their semantic interpretations. Do not such formulations require – in addition to an appreciable intellectual effort – a great amount of good will to be acknowledged as tokens of progress?

If we want to go beyond a mere diagnosis of the discomfort by suggesting, in rough outline, a more agreeable solution, we must delve into the genesis of the problem at hand.

The human mode of existence and coexistence is dominated by two basic acts which are in need of scientific investigation; these are the acts of meaning and of understanding. Being in possession of language, every human being is aware of the fact that language is the vehicle and medium through which and in which something is meant and understood. But attempts at a scientific interpretation of what is involved in these processes have yielded either terminologically well-integrated conceptual frameworks which, however, cannot do justice to the manifold aspects of the phenomenon, or quite disparate, heterogeneous approaches and procedures which tend to ignore evidence contributed from other quarters (whether linguistic, philosophical, or psychological).

All these approaches have come to nothing, and not a minor reason for their failure has been their "isolationism" with respect to what are kindly called the neighboring disciplines – called so and blissfully ignored. This isolationism is often justified with rationalizations like "linguistics (psychology) requires a linguistic (psychological) way of thinking". The argument is of course untenable, just as would be the assertion that the acts of meaning and of understanding are purely psychological phenomena and as such can be accounted for only by psychology. The fact is that in order to gain significant insights into language processes, the psychologist cannot renounce the aid of either linguistics or the philosophy of language. Indeed, without such aid, psychology is apt to veer off into aimless empiricism or empty conceptual exercises. At the same time, neither linguistics nor the philosophy of language can be expected to arrive at satisfactory solutions single-handed: they both need psychology to avoid excessive speculation by exposing themselves to the resistance of reality.

Thus, in the present volume an attempt is made to transcend disciplinary divisions. The book does not propose any single system or model of meaning and of understanding, let alone of language or speaking. The author's assumption is that the available evidence could only serve to construct a model that is either extremely speculative and removed from reality or one that is veridical but without explanatory value.

The aim of the book is to ply back and forth between linguistics, psycholinguistics, and language philosophy in order to bring to the reader's attention all that is worth considering in an inquiry into the processes of meaning and of understanding, and also what deserves to be discarded as misleading.

Not a few of these suggestions are negatively phrased. The tenor of "that can't be so" definitely prevails at the beginning, in the discussion of generative grammar, and there are valid historical grounds for this attitude: scarcely any other science has been so successful over such a short period of time as has generative linguistics since 1956. It is definitely the most coherent theoretical system in the realm of linguistics; but precisely its sense of mission, the frequent claim to convey *the* truth, makes us marvel why it has nothing (or practically nothing) to tell us about the actual processes of meaning and of understanding.

There is one more reason for the negative phrasing of many of the arguments brought forth in these pages. When reflecting upon the acts of meaning and of understanding we might try to start with defining these processes, but this would

VIII

only show that we are not even sure how large the gaps in our knowledge are, i. e., how much more we would have to know about these acts to arrive at definitive statements. In our search for valuable insights we must be prepared to pursue a variety of trains of thought, many of which may end up in blind alleys or drain out in the sands of vagueness. If we are too specific in our contentions, we run the risk of being disproved by reality; if we are too general, we cannot hope to go beyond banalities. For the time being, the only chance of defining the approximate location of meaning and of understanding (as the two basic acts of language use) in the framework of our present knowledge seems to be by marking out the places at which the various attempts at coping with the problem have run aground.

However, the reader may find his knowledge enlarged by the evidence and arguments presented in this volume, although some of the new knowledge will be of the kind noticed by Saint Augustine: I know as long as you don't ask me; as soon as you ask me, I don't know. What the actual value of such knowledge is must be decided not in the light of any theory of science but by each of us for himself.

*

The book starts with a discussion of the concept of 'sign' (Chap. 1), where we dwell on the implications and historical background of the concept. The next chapter contains a brief outline of the development of psycholinguistics in the 1950s and 1960s.

Thus the scene is set for the introduction of the generativists' key concept: competence. Those who enlarge upon competence do not necessarily go into performance, as we know.

In Chap. 4 we outline the manner in which generative grammar has come to hold sway over psycholinguistics: as syntax dragging behind its poor relation, semantics.

Chap. 5 is devoted to the linguists' own attempt to vindicate the poor relation with the construction of the lexicon (or dictionary) and its dimensions. The psychological overtones discernible in this discussion gain in strength in the next chapter, where we review the various attempts at describing and explaining the uses of language in terms of semantic dimensions and features, and where the limitations of these models are pointed out.

On the basis of this analysis, Chap. 7 puts forward the concept of sense constancy as a global description and rough approximation of the processes underlying the acts of meaning and of understanding.

Chap. 8 surveys the various contributions made by the recent trend in linguistics know as generative semantics. The next two chapters are likewise devoted to auxiliary evidence made available by the philosophy of language from Wittgenstein to Searle (Chap. 9), and by Russian psychology of language and speech physiology (Chap. 10).

This evidence reveals the intrinsic directedness of the components of verbal actions, also focusing our attention on the way language processes are embedded in the preverbal situation. The nonverbal roots of language are thus explored in the light of the findings of communication psychology and sociolinguistics (Chap. 11).

The origins of language can be traced an any of three levels: phylogenetic, ontogenetic, and microgenetic (generation of the utterance). In Chap. 12, the emergence of the acts of meaning and of understanding is explored on all three levels, notably in language acquisition.

The processes of language are invariably centered on the ego; Chap. 13 examines the consequences of this ego-enteredness and the ways and means by which the internal states of the ego are communicated to the hearer.

All this gives rise to the idea that the utterance may be seen as a series of instructions intended to modify the hearer's consciousness. These instructions are arranged in the form of the sentence, hence Chap. 14 inquires into "what goes on in a sentence".

The hearer enjoys a certain freedom in processing an utterance: he may follow one or other of many different strategies. His overall goal is to "look through" the sentence and the words to what is meant by the speaker. Chap. 15 deals accordingly with the levels and vectors of understanding.

The conception put forward in this book has substantially benefited from discussions conducted in our work group for language psychology and information processing at Ruhr University; the contributions by Michael Bock, Hans-Georg Bosshardt, Johannes Engelkamp, Gerda Lazarus-Mainka, and Gregor Terbuyken are gratefully acknowledged.

I am indebted to the translator of the book, B. A. Jankowski, for suggesting some minor revisions of the German text.

Bochum, January 1981   H. Hörmann

Chapter 1

The Problem of Signs

Relatively early, both linguists and psychologists of language came to realize that the scientific analysis of language needed, or would heuristically thrive on, a pivotal concept encapsulating what is unquestionably the fundamental characteristic of language: the ability to make the not-here and the not-now available to discourse and hence accessible to our consciousness, thinking, planning, and reporting. Such a central concept is that of *sign*. A language can function as language precisely because it operates with signs.

The concept of sign is thus in the first place a distinctive characteristic of the *function* of language. From this angle we may explore phylogenetically, for example, when and to what purpose signs were brought into play. The same approach happens to underlie the concept of sign in information theory – a matter to be taken up later on. The clearest exposition of the sign concept to date is contained in Bühler's (1934) *organon* model. The sign is what allows us, under the influence of speech sounds, and somehow "right through" them, to comprehend, become aware of, and possibly perform, what the speaker has in mind when uttering the sounds.

It has to be realized, however, that the functionalist concept of sign has not been agreeable to linguistic science, or at any rate to the majority of contemporary schools of linguistics. This – for non-linguists – rather disturbing fact becomes comprehensible when we bear in mind the linguists' conception of their science; at this point the matter will be dealt with only in passing.

General linguistics is concerned with the exploration of what might be called *language-in-itself* rather than with language (speech) as used in the process of communication, i. e., putting it in Saussurian terms, with the analysis of *langue* rather than *parole*.

With this conceptual dichotomy linguistics arrived at a major crossroads in its evolution. Conceived as an abstract language system, *langue* exists in the brain of every member of the particular speech community much like a dictionary distributed far and wide in countless identical copies. That is to say, being present in each individual, *langue* – according to Saussure – constitutes an inter-individual phenomenon. *Parole,* on the other hand, is being constantly recreated in the process of language use under the prescriptive influence of *langue.*

Obviously, this kind of division has served to detach the object of inquiry from the actual flow of language processes, as something that persists as an underlying agent[1] (at any rate from a synchronic point of view, which is the only relevant one in this context) throughout those highly variable and largely incidental processes.

As we see, ever since Saussure, if not earlier, linguists have conceptualized a static structure as the object of their investigations, a structure removed one step behind the language processes of which we have first-hand experience.

We might note in passing that the idea of attributing to language as an object of inquiry a mode of existence that could be separated from language's use and therewith studied in isolation, would scarcely have arisen were it not for the invention of writing. Indeed, the written word strongly suggests a static, product-like character of language – and even today it is precisely the product, not the production, as Hartmann (1974) puts it, into which the linguist inquires.

The concept of sign changes inevitably as we turn from *language as function* to *language as a static system.* Rather than conceptualizing the characteristic *function* of language, the sign has become for modern linguistics the supportive *element* of language[2].

Sign as *element* of language: this position cannot fail to affect the next question in the course of our analysis: whereas Bühler (and also Schaff, a Marxist semiologist) would want to know what man *does* with signs when using language, the linguist inquires into what a sign *is.* The sign has become autonomous – something for which linguistics has to pay a high price today, being compelled to construe a special "science of the use of signs", that is, pragmatics.

The autonomization of the sign, i. e., its separation from the flow of actual linguistic (and extralinguistic) processes, has made possible those grandiose inquiries upon which modern linguistics as a *langue*-centered science looks back in pride. The sign as element of language is at the same time congenial to an approach that conceptualizes language in terms of information sharing: the speaker offers part of what is at his disposal to the hearer who had not shared it before.

The autonomization of the sign and the concomitant neglect of *parole* have at the same time paved the way toward the construction of those systems of signs–

---

[1] One reason for this particular approach is presumably the *Psychologismus-Verdikt* – as named by Apel (1973) – which goes back via Husserl to Frege; this view asserts that all the problems involved in the *discovery* of possible linguistic structures might be of interest at best to the psychologist, whereas, in scientific-logical terms, only the logical *substantiation* or justification of structures has a legitimate status.

[2] In fact, this kind of shift could not be avoided in the sentence used earlier in this text, where language was described as operating "with signs". When using the deceptive term *sign,* one should perhaps say: language operates through the medium of signs, or, the user of language operates with signs.

in-themselves and systems of concatenations of signs-in-themselves that contribute greatly to the discomfort noted at the outset of the present discussion.

Once the sign has been granted the status of a thing, it is possible to approach the problem of its definition from two angles, not necessarily mutually exclusive; let us call them simply the referential and the structuralist approaches.

The referential conception, many centuries old and therefore less constrained by the aesthetic ideal of the formalists, continues to bear traces of its derivation from the representational function of language. The sign is under this conception most adequately characterized by the Scholastic phrase *stat aliquid pro aliquo*.

Even if no translation of the phrase is needed, we can only profit from considering its possible meaning. A sign *stands for something other than itself,* i. e., for the referent. And it is this relation of standing one for another that causes us to assume that signs have some meaning.

If we pause for a moment, we cannot fail to notice how very difficult it is to resist the psychological tendency to turn everything into things. We just experienced a case of reification when passing from "what it could mean" or "refer to" to "a sign". Now the *sign* carries something more, namely, meaning. A more careful wording would probably reveal the tautology involved in the statement *A sign has meaning*.

Once we are aware of the alarming imprecision that afflicts this kind of jargon, we may proceed to discuss the three problems that come up at this point:

1) How is it that a sign is endowed with *meaning?* (More appropriately: How does a sign form turn into a sign?)

2) What does *referent* mean?

3) What does *standing for something else* mean?

In respect of the first problem, it might be expedient to illuminate the phylogenetic horizon of the sign in its most relevant form of the human language sign[3]. Of course, we cannot be expected to demonstrate the continuity of the evolutionary sequence culminating in human language. However, both the necessity and feasibility of *the sign in the course of an activity* becomes perfectly clear on examining all the evidence available on the "use of signs" in the animal kingdom (it suffices to recall the investigations by Frisch, Heinroth, Lorenz, Sebeok, and many others) and the evidence of what man's intervention renders possible to achieve in this domain and what has been found impossible (consider here Köhler's work, Premack's research, and the Gardners' chimpanzee Washoe)[4].

Something may become the sign for something else. This transformation may well be brought about through a specific modification in the hereditary equipment of the species. Thus the capacity for using some particular perceptual or kinesthetic pattern as "the sign for another (particular) thing" is present in an

---

[3] Strangely enough, Chomsky refuses to consider the phylogenetic or biological evidence in the discussion of essential features of human language; we shall take up this question, as well as Toulmin's arguments on the competence issue, in Chap. 3 (pp 18 ff.).

[4] The issue is discussed in some detail in Hörmann (1971a, pp 7 ff. and 20 ff.).

individual from birth. For man – and presumably also for the higher primates – there is however an incomparably more important capacity: the much more general faculty of generating signs and establishing or acquiring conventions. Before any learning can take place this faculty of turning things into symbols must be present (as underlined by Cassirer). A cogent argument is the randomness and instability of the isolated act of learning. Establishing the meaning of signs across individuals (GH Mead) is conceivable solely in the framework of a communicative experience that reaches far beyond individual acts of learning. The phenomenon of transparency for meaning: the perception of a greeting by and through the sound of "good morning" is certainly present, in essence at least, in the perception of the higher-order species. This has been pinpointed by Bruner in the not quite adequate phrase *going beyond the information given*. It is indeed a case of information *generation* as we go beyond the (retinal, aural, etc.) sensory data. To understand therefore means to become aware – right through the medium of language – of what is meant or referred to. Analogously, to become aware of and to appreciate a work of art means to perceive the intended aesthetic object right through the medium. Understanding is thus a manifestation of that general ability which seems to have attained its peak in human language. According to Husserl (1970, pp 522ff.), any perception is an act of interpretation, and it was under the influence of the philosopher that this view gained ground, also in non-behavioristic psychology, over the old, elementarist way of thinking that percepts arise by stringing together bits of sensory data. Back in 1909 it was claimed by von Allesch that

> what we actually do is round off shapes into configurations *(Gestalten);* we experience them as being human, we imagine human beings in them, and there is a human element in every gesture ... This kind of comprehending and complementing is tantamount to interpreting percepts in terms of available knowledge. The complementing seems to proceed step by step, and we are guided closely by the subjective need to round off our perceptions (1909, p 498).

Forty years later Arnheim (1947, p 69) wrote in much the same vein:

> Perception consists in the application, to the stimulus material, of perceptual categories ... which are evoked by the structure of the given configuration. These categories are the indispensable prerequisites which permit us to understand perceptually[5].

Going beyond the sensory data is thus indispensable even in the perceptual registration of an object; the phenomenon of shape constancy demonstrates the domination of the *intended* object over the evidence obtained from retinal data alone.

The manifestations of this particular faculty differ in depth of coding. Between the nature-induced symptom as construed by Bühler[6] and the quite arbitrarily

---

[5] These views – which are very close to the currently popular analysis-by-synthesis model of perception – are reviewed here in considerable detail since they keep threading through the present volume in diverse ways.

[6] In his organon model, Bühler distinguishes three *modi significandi* of the sign: it is a *symbol* in its reference to things and states of nature, it is a *symptom* in its dependence on the sender (speaker), it is a *signal* via its appeal to the receiver (hearer).

conventionalized symbol there extends a gradation in terms of both communicative reliability and availability (which is by no means the same thing!) of whatever might be used as a socially effective signal. A ritualization at the transmitting end (Huxley) is contrasted with growing semantization at the receiver end (Wickler). But in the light of the foregoing arguments the latter should not be viewed as marking the sudden appearance of a qualitatively new dimension of behavior. How much fundamental insight on the very subject of human language behavior can be gained from an examination of the prelinguistic modes of communication becomes evident from two outstanding examples: Ploog's (1972) studies of communication in ape communities and Efron's (1941) investigation of tradition as affecting the gesticulation of Italian and Jewish immigrants in the United States.

Our assumption that there is a basic ability to construe one thing as a reference to another, a faculty that is a prerequisite for the use of signs, is by no means opposed – as claimed by Schaff (1962) – to the view, also shared by Marxist theorists, that signs result from cooperation. The postulated faculty of "seeing through" the sensory data and comprehending what they mean is but a precondition for the emergence and functioning of signs. Which particular sensory datum (or sign-to-be, in Osgood's terminology, to be discussed later) is eventually chosen, in the process of code formation, to stand for some other thing, depends on: biological factors (Lenneberg 1967; Ploog 1972; Toulmin 1971), occasionally on acoustic predilection (as expressed in sound symbolism: Werner 1957; Ertel 1969), and in many cases on its particular genesis as described by learning theory (from Pavlov to Osgood). Be that as it may, cooperative activity is discernible at the root of any communication system, though not in the case of each and every sign. Such a system begins to emerge as soon as guidelines of action have been elevated to the level of signification as the only medium. Wittgenstein (1953) has offered a lucid outline of how the first language game comes into being: an instruction is framed in symbolic terms in the course of joint action.

Our first question about how a sign (to abide by the nominal form) comes into being has made us aware both of the general ability of going beyond sensory data and of the importance of the cooperative factor. These are both dynamic rather than static relationships – a realization which should accompany us as we approach the next question: What is meant by *referent?*

Saussure's initial standpoint becomes clear when he says: The link between sound form *(signifiant)* and content *(signifié)* is as strong as if these were "two sides of one sheet of paper". Bierwisch (1966, p 57) rightly notes that Saussure's idea

has greatly affected linguistic theory, leading to numerous attempts at assigning each linguistic phenomenon to one of the two sides. Numerous misunderstandings have arisen along the way.

And this is not the least of the reasons why the question deserves to be discussed here.

This distinctly static conception may be suitable for the paradigm of referencing in its most narrow sense: I may use the name of my friend as a kind of representation of his person.

In the case of most other signs, and especially a majority of the language signs, Saussure's reference to *signifiant* as locked up with *signifié* creates a problem. What does *content* mean, and what is the *referred* thing? From Titchener and Bloomfield to Osgood and Brown investigators have endeavored to resolve this question. What we know today is that the simple answer "The referent is the object associated with the sign", is as confusing as the suggestion to substitute for referent the image invoked by the sign; what is for instance the image of *but* or *equitable?* The view that the referent is a disposition activated by the sign is helpful in overcoming an excessively static conception of the connection between sign and content.

All conceptions postulating some connection between sign and referent that enable the sign to stand for the referent owe at least some of their plausibility to the fact that for twenty centuries there has existed a suitable concept, and about a century ago a mechanism was proposed in an effort to interpret this connection. The concept is *association*.

Ever since Thorndike and Pavlov it has been possible to demonstrate convincingly how such a connection comes into being. Pavlov conceptualized a second signal system (signal of signals) to make room for the two tiers of the relevant processes; Osgood has described with fascinating precision the point at which the mediation between sign and referent takes place. Still, in one respect – and one of special interest to us – none of those theories has proved satisfactory: they all operate in the framework of a stimulus-response (S-R) psychology which essentially assigns just one response to any one stimulus. Yet what proceeds in the hearer in response to the stimulus *rain,* and what is discernible as his overt response, may vary across a spectrum of enormous breadth (fetch the coat, open the umbrella, bring in the laundry, take off shoes and stay in, cancel plans) and cannot be thought of as a generalized response or class of responses, if the notion of response is to retain the meaning that made it so apparently useful in S-R psychology. The presumably crucial move by which *response* would be replaced by *knowledge* or *consciousness* (in line with, say, James or Ach) could not be accomplished within the behavioristic psychology of the time.

Among the earliest opponents of the underlying conception of sign as a substitute stimulus for the "natural" stimulus – which leans heavily on behaviorism and Pavlovism – was Susan Langer (1942) who approached symbols as vehicles for the conceptions of objects rather than as substitutes for objects (pp 57 ff.). But even here the perplexing question persists as to what *conception* of an object means and how it is turned into a vehicle.

Thus the problem of what is referred to by the sign remains open. The difficulty involved in a precise and at the same time meaningful interpretation of referent as part of the duality *signifiant* and *signifié* has given a strong impetus to the structuralists' search for a radical solution. Before delving into the issue, let us examine the difficulties involved in the use of the term *sign* as a static concept in nominal form, with respect to our third question, which is closely related to the second one.

The statement *stat aliquid pro aliquo,* in addition to *aliquid* and *aliquo,* has one more doubtful component, *stat*. What does it actually mean, to stand for something else?

Does the sign, e. g., the word *apple*, really *stand* for the apple? Certainly not when I feel like eating an apple: then it is rather a pear *(horribile dictu)* that could substitute for an apple. The sign *apple* does stand for an apple when uttered to the fruitseller, who may respond by either selling the apple or by saying "sold out". Thus, to stand for another thing turns out, upon closer scrutiny, to be a highly dynamic relationship, rather than a static representation of one *(apple)* for the other (apple). Some of the dynamic forces at work between two people in any situation, while originating from an intention and guided by knowledge and reality, are effected through the medium of language as embodied in signs. Whether or not one thing stands for another, what exactly it does stand for and what it means to *stand for,* cannot be decided in isolation from the particular situation in which signs are used in a dialogue. (Bloomfield was perfectly aware of this function of the speech act as a link between practical events but failed to reap the fruits of his insight by clinging to a behavioristic definition of meaning in terms of stimulus and response; cf. Hörmann 1971 a, p 267.)

In an experiment involving naming wooden blocks (which is discussed in detail in Chap. 13), Olson (1970) showed that people tend to modify their term of reference to a block according to what other block is next to it: a round one, a white one ... Obviously, sign and referent are not as intimately interrelated as are the two sides of a sheet of paper. What exactly a sign stands for and what *standing for something* means is determined by the dynamics of the situation. This is where we ought to heed Schaff's (1967, pp 1745–46) advice:

> It is language which is the point of departure for the conception and interpretation of the sign – and not vice versa ... It is only by beginning with the process of human communication as a certain type of relationship that we can understand the meaning of such categories ... as *sign, meaning,* etc.

There can be no doubt that with their competent treatment of the problem, both Olson and Schaff have moved beyond the range of *langue,* and this is one more reason for disregarding the rather artificial boundary of linguistics. Being a strictly static verb, the Latin *stare (stat aliquid pro aliquo)* – just as the expression *to have meaning* – is singularly unsuited to drawing our attention to the dynamic aspect of the issue. Probably a better approximation could be obtained with such verbs as *to refer to, to have in mind, to mean.*

Looking back at the difficulties which beset the static, nominalized notion of sign, as revealed in the analysis of our three questions, we can more fully appreciate this particular developmental trend in linguistics (which has also received impetus from other sources). Indeed, the reified sign is singularly suited to be linked with other signs according to combinatorial rules – which explains the domination of syntax in modern linguistics. It took several decades, from Peirce via Ogden and Richards to Morris, before it was realized that a sign conceived in the Saussurian way could hardly serve as a convenient tool for establishing with equal precision the connection with what is being talked about and to what purpose. The tendency to treat the sign primarily and principally as an entity that could be combined with other entities of the same kind according to complex rules was extremely difficult to overcome. It was much later that consideration was accorded to the question of what a referent was and how to interpret the process of reference itself, a process manifested in the interrelation between sign and referent and registered in our consciousness as the phenomena of *meaning* something and *understanding* something.

Characteristically, it was postulated, even after Morris, that syntax should be merely *supplemented* with semantics (and, in more extreme cases, with pragmatics). This reflects the view that first there are signs which secondly carry meaning and thirdly can even be used.

Although to supplement syntax with semantics and eventually also pragmatics is a necessary consequence of the separation of *langue* from *parole,* the triad syntax–semantics–pragmatics alone gives no guarantee that the *langue/parole* distinction, with its inadequate concern for the function of language, would yield new insights into the *processes* of language.

Let us note in passing that the semantics to which the subtitle of the present book refers is by no means a triplet of syntax and pragmatics as described above.

Reverting once more to Saussure's notion of sign, we shall quote Bierwisch (1966, p 59) by way of a summary:

> There does not seem to be much sense in replacing Saussure's image with some other. If we were to insist on this, the relationship between *signifiant* and *signifié* could be more aptly likened to that between the leaves and roots of a tree; these are likewise interdependent, but their relationship consists of a complex system of connections and branches ... And precisely this system of interconnections ought to be studied by linguistics.

Let us supplement this with the question: Is this a task for linguistics alone?

This basic, function-ignoring position of linguistics has been upheld in an otherwise seminal redefinition of *sign*. We owe this again to Saussure, who proposed to define a sign by what makes it different from everything else. This retreat to a formal approach has led to substantial progress.

In adherence to the Saussurian dictum, "in language there are only differences without positive terms" (1959, p 120), the entire edifice of structural linguistics, including Chomsky, is squarely founded on the mechanism of difference-finding. The structural linguists set out to feed the primary data into that mechanism and proceeded to apply the same/different razor to increasingly complex evidence. Placing their difference-finder at sentence level, the generative linguists assigned it a specific task: rather than discovering differences in general, they focused on exploring the differences between the grammatical and the ungrammatical. But we should not anticipate.

The search for differences yielding evidence of linguistic structures has been particularly successful in phonology: sounds which a native speaker cannot tell meaningfully apart are considered one phoneme, even though their particular versions (allophones) may differ acoustically.

At this point it becomes obvious that differences have no objective existence but have to be ascertained by a decision maker who knows within which activity the particular identification is being made. As Chomsky (1965, pp 21–22) put it: "It may be necessary to guide and draw out the speaker's intuition in perhaps fairly subtle ways".

In order to "draw out" intuition, the linguist typically presents the native speaker with some words or sentences within some context. In doing so he accounts (without necessarily being aware of it) for a fact that was pointed out by Uhlenbeck (no date, p 102): that a native speaker will judge a sentence or word to be correct if he can "think up an actual situation in which such a construction or form would fit". And this obviously implies reference to both the linguist's preconceived ideas and the native speaker's knowledge of the world. Evidently, even the ostensibly "clean" structuralist conception of sign, which claims to operate without recourse to substantive knowledge, is unable to identify the constitutive differences in the "nature of things" with a purely objective procedure; instead, these differences have to be pointed out by a native speaker whose difference-finding mechanism is susceptible to all the factors established by cognitive psychology over the entire range from psychophysics to social perception. What structuralists have invoked to define a sign, namely, its distinctness from other signs, cannot be determined with any precision without recourse to some concrete application of the sign. There is no such thing as difference *per se,* there are only differences in particular situations, for particular speakers and hearers, and for particular purposes. By focusing on language-in-itself the structuralist conception has adopted a sort of point zero from which to begin, on the unfounded assumption that the many diverse functions and situations of language add up to zero. The structuralists believe that the native speaker knows his language also in abstraction of its concrete applications and that this is what enables him to use this *knowledge* when serving as informant.

We have started out with a discussion of the sign concept and now we have reached the point at which we must introduce the conceptual framework of this idea of *knowledge,* i. e., the concept of competence and its concomitant, the concept of performance. But before inquiring into these concepts and their far-reaching impact on psycholinguistics we shall have to devote a separate section of the book to the developments in psycholinguistics which preceded its confrontation with competence and performance.

Chapter 2

The Rise of Psycholinguistics

The resounding triumph of behaviorism in the 1930s and 1940s had directed the interests of investigators away from the problem of the psychological nature of language, its workings, and its diverse functions in the life of the individual as well as in human interactions. This neglect of language was only natural for the behaviorist bent upon describing and explaining behavior: the study of language *behavior* could account for just one aspect of language.

Both linguists and psychologists remained oblivious of the period when representatives of the two sciences – Wundt and Paul, or Steinthal and Dittrich – had been engaged in fruitful dialogues. It was not until 1970, when Blumenthal came out with his brilliant archeology of psycholinguistics, that modern psycholinguists were reminded of the historical background of their science.

What was characteristic in the relation of linguistics to psychology in that period was the way linguists of the Bloomfield school used to define meaning – the least important component of language; they defined it with distinct reference to contemporaneous psychology: meaning is the stimulus situation in which a word is uttered, and the response it calls forth in the hearer.

The connection with the S-R theories that prevailed in psychology in those days comes here very clearly into evidence. These theories appeared to offer ready solutions to two intimately related, if not identical, problems which troubled investigators interested in the psychology of language: the emergence of the sign and the acquisition of language. Both were interpreted in terms of instrumental or operant conditioning. In the early 1950s, two developments were noted within the rather language-indifferent behaviorist psychology: one was the appearance of mediation theories, the other the emergence of information theory. Both new trends combined to stimulate interest in language phenomena. Of more general significance was the fact that orthodox behaviorism had arrived at the point of diminishing returns.

Mediation theories postulated the intervention between the overt stimulus and the overt response of some sort of covert elements (for instance, emotional factors):

$$S- \widehat{(r__s)} -R$$

Not only did this approach relinquish strictly orthodox behaviorism; it facilitated the theoretical handling of a function essential for any psychology of language, namely, the formation of concepts and the use of generalized concepts (and words). This intervening element is for Osgood the key to the relation between sign and referent (see also Chap. 8).

Information theory applied the notions of probability and transitional probability to stimuli (signals) and response elements, and in this way confronted a problem of singular importance for structural linguistics: how to identify the basic units of linguistic processes. Furthermore, emphasis was placed on the serial and probabilistic aspect of verbal utterances. At the same time, information theory remained sufficiently aloof from the problem of meaning to avoid misgivings on the part of linguists or behaviorist psychologists. GA Miller's early work on language and communication (1951) revealed the impressive productivity of this approach.

From 1951 to 1953, a series of conferences sponsored by the Social Research Council were held in the United States at which a number of psychologists of neobehaviorist background discussed the relation of linguistics to psycholinguistics. Using the term *psycholinguistics,* they at once proposed a model to answer the question of what and who a psycholinguist was. Marking the beginning of modern psycholinguistics and subsequently dominating the field for many years, neither this model nor the terminology in which it was couched can deny provenance from the theory of communication.

Linguistics was said to be concerned with the structure of messages. We are confronted here with the interesting fact that even psychologists took recourse to the linguist's conception of *language-in-itself*. The linguists sought to study the message in isolated form, as if petrified at some point in the process of communication. The psycholinguists conceptualized the same message as a link in the sequence connecting the human transmitter (speaker) with the human receiver (hearer):

Transmitter – Message – Receiver

The model evidently stands in close affinity to S-R theory.

Much more weight must be attributed to the goals set in this framework for psycholinguistics, and the resultant attitude to linguistics. The psycholinguists were expected to concern themselves with the processes by which the message is generated in the speaker and with the processes the message evokes in the hearer. The initial stage of the sequence came to be termed *encoding,* and the terminating stage *decoding,* meaning the transposition into and out of a language code. In information-theoretic terms this meant that states of the message were to be brought into relation to states of the transmitter and states of the receiver.

The model and the way it was phrased implied that the message-in-itself would be described by linguistics, that is, in the theoretical language of the

11

linguist, meaning the linguist of the Bloomfield type. And indeed, Bloomfield's preoccupation with what were considered relevant units of language "fits" perfectly, for instance, the probabilistic orientation of the early psycholinguists. The psycholinguist is assigned the distinctly secondary role of anchoring the structures and processes brought to light by the linguist in the realities of the language user's mental functioning. Thus psycholinguistics was firmly placed in the position of an interdisciplinary science instructed by linguistics in the relevance of particular linguistic structures and by psychology in what were the relevant features of the encoding and decoding individual.

We must keep in mind this model, its behavioristic provenance, and the period of its emergence, if we wish to understand fully the developments which shaped the history of modern psycholinguistics in the 20-odd years of its existence. This model was struck by a bolt from the blue when Chomsky came out with his entirely novel linguistics as contained in generative grammar.

This novel form of linguistics exerted an uncanny influence upon psychologists right from the beginning. The many reasons for this phenomenon will be mentioned here only in passing.

For one thing, generative grammar was distinctly anti-behaviorist, at a time when it was becoming fashionable to reject behaviorism. Chomsky raised the issue as to what kind of rules the ideal language user would have to know in order to generate well-formed sentences. Now, the notion of knowledge had been banned from psychology by behaviorism. Having adopted conditioning as its basic learning paradigm, behavioristic psychology could offer only the process of generalization and transfer to account for all the creative aspects of behavior, including language behavior. Whatever appeared to be new could be explained only through reduction – in a rather obscure and vague fashion – to what had been registered before.

The knowledge of a rule system as posited by Chomsky for the realm of language was much along the line of thought followed by Lashley (1951) and subsequently by Miller et al. (1960), in their description of plans as the basic form of behavior organization. There ensued the dethronement of the stimulus as the master of behavior in favor of a built-in hierarchy of action schemata.

The concept of generation proposed by Chomsky as a basis for prospective reorientation had a somewhat hypnotic quality for psychologists, adding to the impact of generative grammar on psychology.

In the same way as well-formed sentences are "generated" by grammar, the inner mechanism of the language user generates grammatical utterances. Such a rash and fateful conclusion was drawn by psycholinguists from generative theory. In disregard of Chomsky's explicit warning (which must, in fairness, be noted) psycholinguists came to the conclusion that the psychological laws to be searched for in the generation and processing of sentences were identical with the laws developed for the structural analysis of well-formed sentences by grammar.

This identity assumption was reinforced and furthered by what became the third reason for the psychologist's fascination with generative grammar: Chomsky's distinction between competence and performance.

12

Chapter 3

Competence and Performance

At its inception, generative linguistics derived a great deal of inspiration from a penetrating experience such as occurs when people are seized by a powerful affect. This kind of elementary emotion was aroused when an inquisitive mind noticed a miracle so commonplace that one had tended to overlook it completely in everyday life: that any human being in command of a language, the native language, is capable of telling apart, on the basis of his intuition and without the benefit of any linguistic training, *well-formed* from ill-formed sentences and this even in the case of sentences he has never heard before – and yet is unable to substantiate his judgment. He will discover – in strict reliance on that ability – that a sentence like

THE SHOOTING OF THE HUNTERS WAS TERRIBLE

is (syntactically) ambiguous; and he will know that

JOHN HIT MARY

differs from

MARY WAS HIT BY JOHN

only in a rather superficial way (Active-Passive distinction).

What kind of capacity underlies these judgments[1]?

Chomsky answers: it is the speaker's intuitive and implicit knowledge of the rules of his language. And this is where the great design of generative grammar began, in conformity with the age-old idea of science as formulated by Descartes: any intuitive and at once mysterious faculty ought to be mirrored in the performance of an automaton in order to be elucidated and eventually cognized. The task is therefore to develop a formal theoretical model that would function, as Chomsky (1962) puts it, "without benefit of intuition", one that would generate

---

[1] Whenever for reasons of economy the terms *grammaticalness* or *well-formedness* are used further in this chapter the reader is asked to supplement tacitly the underlying ability for syntactic disambiguation and identification of syntactic equivalence.

all and only the well-formed sentences of a language. The native speaker's intuition-guided judgment as to the grammaticalness of a sentence would be replaced by an in principle intuition-free comparison of the sentence against the sentences generated by the model: a sentence is judged to be well-formed if it is found to be identical with some sentence generated by the model – without any help from intuition (cf. also Lyons 1968, p 156).

Up to this point we would be inclined to agree with Apel (1973, p 13) who claims that

> Chomsky has reintroduced into linguistics the subject of speaking and understanding, in contradistinction to classical structuralism.

However, there are two circumstances which induce us to dispute this view most emphatically.

1) The well-formedness as assessed by Chomsky's native speaker is of a purely syntactic type, as can be seen from the famous sentence COLORLESS GREEN IDEAS SLEEP FURIOUSLY coined by Chomsky as an example of well-formedness in contrast to the ill-formed chain of words SLEEP GREEN FURIOUSLY IDEAS COLORLESS. The issue will be elaborated upon at a later point.

2) The proposed formal theoretical model is meant to substitute a rational theory of the idealized speaker-hearer for the native speaker's intuition in order to capitalize on his performance. To quote Chomsky (1965, p 3):

> Linguistic theory is concerned primarily with an ideal speaker-listener, in a completely homogeneous speech community, who knows its language perfectly and is unaffected by such grammatically irrelevant conditions as memory limitations, distractions, shifts of attention and interest, and errors (random or characteristic) in applying his knowledge of the language in actual performance.

Here we come face to face with a conceptual distinction that has vitally affected the development of modern linguistics; this is the distinction between competence and performance. The knowledge that underlies the linguistic skills of the idealized speaker-hearer is referred to as *competence*. Consequently, competence is at the same time the totality of the information fed into the model of generative grammar. Competence is made up of the system of rules without which the effective generation of all and only the grammatical sentences of a language would not be possible.

Performance, on the other hand, comes at first into evidence only as a deficient mode of the realization of competence, whereby the deficient, imperfect, rule-violating performance is due solely to the weaknesses human flesh is heir to. The "subject of speaking and understanding" which Chomsky had allegedly reintroduced into linguistics has thus turned out to be an uncommitted automatic device without any resemblance to the language-experiencing and language-inspired human being.

Indeed, the notion of the ideal speaker-hearer's competence contains *two* idealizations by which we are led astray from the realities of language processes. For one thing, competence itself is an idealizing concept in that it is, by definition, distinct from reality as an abstraction from the latter; it may, at best, interact with reality. The other idealization is the "ideal" speaker-hearer. This is why

Schlesinger (1971a) discards the ideal speaker-hearer's competence as a pleonasm.

Such deliberations should not be dismissed as outright hairsplitting: their relevance comes into evidence as soon as we realize that they bear on the relation of linguistic theory to reality, and hence also the relation of linguistics to psycholinguistics. In the present chapter we deal at length with the problems that have beset the competence/performance conceptual dichotomy and their consequences for the distribution of research responsibilities between linguistics and psycholinguistics.

When "after a long structuralist period during which a virtual separation of linguistics and psychology was predominant" – to recall Levelt's (1972) excellent and concise survey – Chomsky assigned a new place to linguistics in close proximity to psychology, it meant a revision of the relation between linguistics and psychology. Linguistics was to "account for linguistic competence, or the linguistic intuition of the speaker", strictly speaking, the idealized speaker.

The notion of competence encompasses grammar (as the competence-specifying theory of language) as well as the speaker-hearer's intuitive knowledge of the rules of this grammar.

Accepting for the time being the foregoing definition of competence, an attentive student of generative grammar and of the psycholinguistic research inspired by it cannot fail to raise a number of questions. Is there any unitary linguistic competence of this sort? If so, does generative grammar investigate only such a competence? And what do psycholinguists stand to gain from abiding by the notion of competence as imported from linguists?

For the psychologist, the status of *competence* bears at first glance a certain analogy (Levelt, 1972, p 21) to that of *intelligence:* it appears to be a theoretical construct referring to a relatively autonomous factor that codetermines a large variety of human behaviors. But unlike *intelligence, competence* has a distinctly cognitive aura: competence is supposed to subsume the speaker's knowledge of a language. The first question to be asked at this point is therefore: What does *knowledge* mean? As has been pointed out by Ingram (1968, p 318),

> it turns out that "knowledge" does not imply action or behavior of any sort; neither the ability to act on the knowledge, since the actual use of language is in the domain of performance; nor the awareness of ability to formulate the grammatical rules. The knowledge is "tacit" or "implicit"; in fact, it must be understood as knowledge in an epistemological rather than in any psychological sense.

Chomsky himself, as well as many of his followers, tend to speak of *tacit knowledge,* and it might be worth our while to examine this theoretical construct. Let us do so by quoting Polanyi's argument regarding *Tacit Knowing* (1962, p 601):

> We perform a skill by relying on the coordination of elementary muscular acts, and we are aware of having got these right by accomplishing our skillful performance. We are aware of them *in terms of this performance* and *not* (or very incompletely) aware of them *in themselves* ... There are vast domains of knowledge ... that exemplify ... that we are generally unable to tell what particulars we are aware of when attending to a coherent entity which they constitute. Thus, there are two kinds of knowing which invariably

enter jointly into any act of knowing a comprehensive entity. There is (1) knowing a thing *by attending to it,* in the way we attend to an entity as a whole and (2) knowing a thing *by relying on our awareness of it for the purpose of attending to an entity to which it contributes.*

Polanyi's distinction between *focal* and *subsidiary* knowledge is of considerable relevance when it comes to analyzing the notion of knowledge inherent in Chomsky's competence concept. The historical reversal undertaken by generative linguistics consists precisely in turning the investigator's attention to something that, being perfectly dependable in the routine of linguistic processes, merely contributes to what is the higher-order and truly relevant activity, namely, to the ability to tell grammatical from ungrammatical constructions. Language communication may have a number of diverse goals, but there is one that is certainly not pursued: to generate grammatically well-formed sentences and no other sentences. In Polanyi's terminology, Chomsky's theory seeks to turn subsidiary knowledge into focal knowledge. Is this feasible at all, and what could be the consequences? Polanyi takes a very radical position:

> We know subsidiarily the particulars of a comprehensive whole when attending focally to the whole which they constitute; we know such particulars not in themselves but in terms of their contribution to the whole. To the extent to which things are known subsidiarily in terms of something else, they cannot be known at the same time in themselves. We may call the bearing which a particular has on the comprehensive entity to which it contributes its *meaning,* and can then say that when we focus our attention wholly on a particular, we *destroy its meaning* (*loc. cit.*).

Polanyi's harsh judgment can hardly be applied to linguistics in such extreme fashion; students of language do indeed focus their attention upon what is in fact subsidiary (i. e., grammaticalness) in relation to the overall act of language communication. (Nearly a hundred years ago a similar allegation was made against psychologists in the argument that it was impossible to focus consciously, through self-observation, upon processes in one's own consciousness.) Yet serious thought will have to be given to the problem of the extent to which the grammar resulting from this trend in linguistics might contribute to an elucidation of linguistic processes in which grammaticalness is but a subsidiary phenomenon.

Once again we have come upon arguments that raise doubts about the validity of the basic relationship between linguistic theory and linguistic realities as posited by Chomsky. The realities of linguistic communication cannot possibly be treated as a deficient manifestation of the linguist's grammar. The point is that the form of constitutive knowledge itself does not offer sufficient clues as to what dislocations in the theoretical framework of linguistic events ensue from centering linguistic theory upon the essentially subsidiary grammaticalness (which Chomsky identifies with syntactic perfection)[2].

---

[2] Uhlenbeck (no date, p 107) has pointed out that the theoretical linguist had always felt a strong temptation "to make language more manageable by reducing it to one of its aspects". But "the trouble with language is that it is such a complicated, many-sided phenomenon."

In any event, even at this stage one may legitimately say that, in contradiction to Chomsky's assertion, the competence/performance distinction does not run parallel to Saussure's *langue/parole* dichotomy. From all we know, at no stage of his work would have Chomsky subscribed to Saussure's (1959) view that "language is not an entity and exists only within speakers" (p 9, footnote).

Even so, the question remains unsolved *how much* idealization there is in the notion of competence. If we rephrase the issue into the question: Where is competence to be found, as tacit knowledge in every speaker, or as tacit knowledge in the idealized speaker? – no clear-cut reply can be obtained. The notion of linguistic theory (which refers to language in general rather than to any particular language) has been pushed by Chomsky (1965, p 25) very close to innate predisposition in the child:

> Note that we are again using the term *theory* . . . with a systematic ambiguity, to refer both to the child's innate predisposition to learn a language of a certain type and to the linguist's account of this.

Are we wrong in speaking of a blurring of the distinction between *knowing a theory* and *being described by a theory?* (Stich 1971).

Thus, grammar as theory of language appears to operate on several levels. Any native speaker will naturally have some "knowledge" of his language. Asked to judge the well-formedness of some sentences, he will tell us this or that about the output of the grammar he "knows", rather than about the grammar itself (cf. Harman 1967). By sidestepping with Chomsky from the real native speaker to the ideal native speaker we may succeed in purging the output of "such grammatically irrelevant conditions as memory limitations", etc., but how can the linguist abstract from "grammatically irrelevant" things when he is only in the process of making a grammar from the rest[3]?

The obscurities that burden Chomsky's uses of the competence concept have caused other authors to distinguish various kinds or levels of competence. Katz (1966) posits the *tacit knowledge of the ideal speaker* – which is the goal of grammatical description – as separate from the competence of the individual speaker. Regarding the latter as a psychological construct, rather then as a construct of linguistics or the philosophy of language, he identifies it with the child's disposition – an issue open to debate. Schlesinger (1971a) in his lucid treatise distinguishes *communal* from *individual competence*. This distinction enables him to make allowances for two important considerations. For one thing, he seeks to draw a dividing line between the knowledge shared by each member of a speech community and the knowledge of particular individuals. Second, his use of the restricting term *grammatical* is meant to make clear that this kind of competence represents but a fraction of the knowledge and intuition a speaker has to employ when using language.

---

[3] This might be the right place to point out that the generative linguist's idealization is not in the manner of the abstractions practiced in general psychology. Rather than abstracting from individual variations of particular speakers or utterances, linguists tend to disregard a substantial portion of what is common to all speakers, i. e., the human species.

This brings us to an important point in our argument. Schlesinger is perfectly right in asserting that a Chomskyan grammar cannot make up the entire competence of the language user. By providing Chomsky's competence with the label *grammatical,* Schlesinger makes it possible to supplement it with a number of broader, or additional, competences: semantic, pragmatic, communicative, or even universal competence, which naturally serves to undermine the competence/performance dichotomy. The matter shall be taken up at a later stage (Chap. 5). In doing so, Schlesinger cuts the ground from under the orthodox generativists' conception of grammar as a unitary and general competence and hence *the* theory of language.

Chomsky's otherwise fascinating design to employ grammar (that is, syntax) as the basis for a theory of language – where language is simply defined as coinciding with grammar – must be questioned both in the light of these and other *linguistic* arguments. Chomsky has coupled his conception of competence as *the* unitary capacity for language with definitive views on language acquisition. From his linguistic conception he draws specific conclusions as to the human biological endowment that underlies the child's acquisition of language. Here we are forced to make a detour into the realm of the emergence of language to be able to juxtapose competence and performance. In this particular excursion – and there will be several more occasions to take such a biology-oriented approach, though in relation to different questions – we are solely concerned with Chomsky's thesis that the human capacity for language is a unitary competence which is either wholly present or totally absent in a person.

We shall choose as our guide in this terrain what is probably the most penetrating criticism of Chomskyan linguistics published in recent years: Toulmin's paper *Brain and Language* (1971), which may well be acclaimed one day as the counterpart to Chomsky's famous review of Skinner's book.

The problem of language emergence or acquisition is a matter of great importance for Chomsky for metatheoretic reasons alone. The language acquisition device (LAD) with which every human is equipped at birth must be of a kind that would enable the child to extract from the jumble of speech sounds the data needed to build his linguistic conception – as a basis, according to generative linguists, for the language of the adult. There is every reason to agree with Chomsky, however, that LAD cannot be conceived as an unstructured, general learning ability. Rather, we have to assume

> that the general form of a system of knowledge is fixed in advance as a disposition of
> the mind, and the function of experience is to cause this general schematic structure to
> be realized and more fully differentiated (Chomsky 1965, pp 51–52).

Chomsky's LAD represents an interesting attempt to substantiate a rational theory of language by postulating a biological (or anthropological) "mechanism": and it is through this mechanism that man acquires the knowledge – called competence – which this theory of language sets out to describe. On the other hand, LAD serves to reduce the input, i. e., the error-burdened utterances (that are part of performance!) perceived by the child, to the formalized grammar of the language of which it is a sample (Chomsky 1962).

In an excellent analysis of the problem, Levelt (1975) points out that "this language-*in-vitro* approach was closely related to dominant opinions on the status of linguistic competence in the adult" (pp 13–14). Adding to this the generativist's customary disregard of everything that has to do with performance, or the actual use of language, we see clearly why these investigators were bound to attribute so much importance to innate structures and generative mechanisms as to be pushed to the point of extreme nativism. Their assumption is that LAD is molded by both formal and substantial properties of *language* (rather than some particular language) – which explains the emphasis placed on universals.

At the same time, the commitment to biology made by the generativists with their emphasis on biological–anthropologically determined universals, has not been met by Chomsky. While postulating built-in structures for LAD as a biological apparatus, Chomsky has refused to look to human onto- and phylogeny for clues as to the nature of these structures. The reason for this self-restraint is Chomsky's claim that the linguistic competence of the ideal speaker-hearer is identical with a unitary human language capacity that is either there or not. If a human is equipped with this unitary language capacity, he can handle the system in its entirety; it is inconceivable that he should possess, for instance, only the transformational component of grammar. Possible faults in the operation of the system will be ascribed, not to its incompleteness, but to shortcomings of performance. The competence/performance distinction not only endows infallibility to competence but – by definition – makes it also an all-or-nothing affair.

In contrast, if we were to assume with Toulmin (1971, p 372) that our theory of language ought to meet some biological criteria, we might account for the human command of language by interpreting the ability to develop, learn, and use language as a result, not so much of a single unitary capacity, as of a unique pattern of interrelated capacities (in the plural), all of whose components are present in the required constellation only in the case of human beings (p 373).

The thus intimated heterogeneity of language will later be considered in greater detail; for the time being we shall remain with the Chomsky–Toulmin controversy.

One of the reasons for the dispute is the fact that Chomsky's is a completely different and much narrower conception of what is to be accounted for in language: namely, in the final instance it is merely the intuition of the ideal language user as applied to the well-formedness of sentences. But should our biological orientation induce us to inquire into what people *do* with their language, and hence to deal with what we mean and what we understand through language, both the origins and antecedents of human speech must come in for consideration.

For Chomsky, the problem of how language has emerged is "a total mystery". Refusing to speculate on the subject he does not care to hide his bias, stating that Darwin's conception of the evolution of organisms was "one vast tautology". His considered view is that acquisition of even the barest rudiments of language is "quite beyond the capabilities of an otherwise intelligent ape" (1968, p 59). Whereupon he is set right by a chimp named Washoe ... (see Chap. 12).

19

To be sure, there are also biological reasons for an out-and-out refusal to accept any phylogenetic connection between animal and human communication. Inquiring into the ontogeny of speech in the framework of developmental psychology, Lenneberg (1969) underlines the danger inherent in the handpicking of more or less conspicuous homologies between animal and human communicative behavior. He is prepared to accept such homologies as biological evidence only if they pass the following two tests:

a) they must be applicable to traits that have a demonstrable genetic basis;

b) the traits to which they apply must not have a sporadical and seemingly random distribution over the entire animal kingdom.

There is no communicative behavior that would meet both criteria:

> The fact that some bird species ... can make noises that sound like words, that some insects use discrete signals when they communicate, or that recombination of signals has been observed to occur in communication systems of a dozen totally unrelated species are not signs of a common phylogeny or genetically based relationship to language ... The similarities between human language and animal communication all rest on superficial intuition (Lenneberg 1969, p 642).

Against the background of this skepticism, Lenneberg poses his radical conclusion: randomly selected forms of animal communication do not enable us to shed light on the prehistory of language; moreover, it is not possible to reconstruct the origins of language (1967, p 265). But in contrast to Chomsky, Lenneberg is inclined to believe that man's capacity for language represents a unique combination of abilities, and that these various abilities may have something in common with parallel animal abilities.

Once we have moderated the range of our inquiry and abandoned the project to establish an uninterrupted descendance sequence for human language, trying instead to gain insight into the functions and functioning of language by comparing infrahuman and human modes or aspects of communication, we stand a chance of profiting from the *working hypothesis* that language as an organon – to come back to Bühler's notion[4] – looks back upon a biogenesis (or a plurality of them) rather than being – as implied by Chomsky's position – the outcome of a singular genetic mutation.

Thus we might follow Toulmin (1971) in advancing two hypotheses. The first of these keeps apart the physiological prerequisites of language and language itself by postulating that the nonlinguistic prerequisites were developing gradually to a point where a sort of discovery was made that language (as a complete system) was feasible on this basis.

> Just as monkeys can *learn* to unwrap candies, and sea-lions can *learn* to balance large rubber balls on their noses, neither capacity having anything to do with the reasons why their evolutionary ancestors developed the fingers and noses they did – so men can learn to invent and use language (p 377).

---

[4] Konrad Lorenz has shown in several places that the biogenesis of such tools as language can be described with considerable insight in terms of ethology and anthropology.

20

Finding it implausible that a basis for the *complete* capacity for language might have arisen solely by gradual genetic modifications in the species' physiological endowment, without the appearance of various protolinguistic forms of behavior at intermediate stages of this development, Toulmin rejects the first hypothesis in favor of the second one. His other hypothesis

> interprets the language capacity as something which developed in the hominid precursors of modern man by the gradual accumulation of physiological *and* behavioral changes which were advantageous, in part for "protolinguistic" reasons, in part for nonlinguistic reasons. The physiological changes which were progressively selected in this way were associated, behaviorally, first with the emergence of a partial language function, and eventually with a full language function ... We can even *state* this view only if we assume that there can be such a thing as a "partial language function", i. e., if the language capacity is not an absolutely unitary thing, characterized by an all-or-nothing grasp of deep structure, but rather something which can be developed gradually, and bit by bit (p 378).

Toulmin's strongly biology-oriented hypothesis is based, in addition to the hitherto adduced arguments, on further evidence which can be mentioned here only briefly:

a) Neurologists have noted plenty of cases which inevitably suggest the selective impairment of certain components of the human language capacity.

b) The genesis of utterances, as investigated by Russian psychologists of language (see Chap. 10), can be more easily accommodated in a framework where the human language capacity is not visualized as suddenly appearing as an all-or-nothing faculty.

c) The language-learning child does not start with grasping the meaning of the sentence but rather with becoming aware of what the speaker means. Guided by the protolinguistic elements of the changing total situation, by facial expression, gestures, posture, and intonation, the child learns to analyze the utterances produced in this situation in such a way as to make those accompanying elements almost redundant in subsequent discourse.

We shall see at a later stage (Chap. 12) that our conception of linguistic events as "the continuation of action with other means" (Hörmann 1971a, p 268) can be developed into an analysis of how humans *mean* and *understand* only if the sequence of actions effected through the verbal medium is not conceived as the manifestation of a separate, unitary language capacity, totally disconnected from the other human abilities. A biological orientation should likewise prove helpful in our discussion of the status and functioning of semantic markers, enabling us to treat these features, not as purely intralinguistic anchoring points, but as characterizing the functioning of the entire mental apparatus (see Chap. 5).

Chomsky's refusal to take biological arguments into consideration in conceptualizing his theory of language deprives the psychologist of language of any chance to try to build the badly needed bridge which would span the gap between Chomsky's Cartesian position and Bühler's functionalist approach. Toulmin (1971, p 383) has offered an enticing description of the road that would take us over such a bridge:

... language – with all the characteristic forms of "deep grammar" – might be, not the expression of a unitary and specific "native capacity" (as detailed in form as, and even isomorphic with, the linguistic behavior which is its expression) but the behavioral end-product of a much more general "native capacity", which issues in behavior of the corresponding grammatical forms when put to work on objective external problems of the appropriate kind.

For the first time, in the quoted text, the speaker-hearer's situation and intention are acknowledged as essentially affecting the utterance, at least as much as does grammatical competence.

The thesis of "native capacities" might still be retained, in a sufficiently generalized form; but the grammatical regularities in the resultant linguistic behavior would have to be accounted for in functional terms (p 384).

Whereby a basis would be created for a concordance between the nativist conception of language, with Chomsky as its main exponent, and the functionalist view represented by such investigators as Bühler.

Chomsky's idea of competence as a unitary language capacity has driven us into the field of biology. Returning now to the competence vs performance issue, we find our confidence in this notion of unitariness badly shaken. And rightly so.

The notion of competence calls for the concept of performance as its complement. As the matter stands, linguists have done precious little to develop a theory of performance, or even to produce a useful delineation of the concept. Thus, quite naturally, the field was taken over by the far more empirically-minded psycholinguists; they, on the other hand, gave little thought to their relation to linguistics and the theory of competence developed by linguists. The Osgood–Sebeok model of 1952–1953 was vaguely viewed as a frame of reference, though it had been proposed for a school of linguistics that knew nothing of either the competence/performance dichotomy or the ideal native speaker.

The reluctance to notice, over a fairly long time, the vagueness of such an important dichotomy, or to appreciate the deeper implications of the problem, was obviously reinforced by Chomsky's terminology. Chomsky had been using the categories developed to analyze sentences in alternation: in a predominantly linguistic and a predominantly psychological sense. His application of the same terminology to both linguistic and cognitive analyses made it difficult to hold those two spheres apart. This has been pinpointed by Uhlenbeck (1967b, p 269). The various psychological concepts which swarmed in Chomsky's writings caused many a psycholinguist to hope tacitly (and many a linguist to fear secretly) that the apocalyptic prospect of linguistics being turned into "a branch of psychology" (Chomsky 1968) was rapidly approaching. Of greatest seductive power was undoubtedly *the concept of generation*.

The generative aspect of the new grammar could not fail to appeal to psychologists who in some other spheres (e. g., in perception) had learned that dynamic theories were superior to static ones. Although there could be no doubt that hearing and speaking were in many ways different processes, the notion of generation seemed to open up *one* prospect (if you adhered to a strictly psychological approach) for coming to grips with what was common and

22

psychologically relevant in those two processes. – Competence as a single unitary capacity for language generation: one cannot fail to notice the precariousness of this deduction.

Whereby psycholinguists fell victim to a misunderstanding which Blumenthal (1966) vainly tried to bring to our attention. The notion of generation, borrowed by linguists from mathematical logic, states the following: "The number 2 *generates* the set, or series, of numbers 2, 4, 8, 16, 32, ..." (Lyons 1968, p 156). Knowing the generative rule, we can tell if any particular number (say, 9) belongs to the set or not. It is in this sense that generative grammar offers a decision-making procedure which enables us to find out if the tested string of linguistic elements conforms to our grammar or not. Psycholinguists have tended, however, to understand the term *generation* in an entirely different way – as the production (or even the mechanism underlying the production) of language behavior. Small wonder that, being guilty of such an inadmissible identification, they lost sight of the problem of the competence/performance opposition and shut their eyes to the fact that

> what is considered to be evidence of competence is always evidence obtained from projections of actual performance (Uhlenbeck no date, p 103).

Performance was thus envisioned primarily as the output of a generating mechanism that produces language and causes us to understand language. At that stage the relation of competence to performance was being conceived in complete analogy to that between *langue* and *parole*.

Halting for a moment in our argumentation, we might discover here the same developmental pattern in the history of science as the one identified in our discussion of the concept of sign: a static, use-ignoring conception of language (as competence) is being supplemented by a suitably tailored theory of language use (performance); just as syntax was supplemented with a semantics and eventually a pragmatics, in the case of sign.

Thus in the framework of the history of science we observe the same relation between linguistics and psychology as postulated by Chomsky on science-theoretical grounds: "investigation of performance will proceed only so far as understanding of underlying competence permits" (1965, p 10).

There we have a clear-cut formulation of what Schlesinger (1971 a) later called the priority hypothesis; the same hypothesis was expounded in a singularly happy-go-lucky way by Weksel (1965), who asserted that the theory of competence "rules out what appear to be fruitless approaches in any account of performance." Schlesinger rejects this view on the general argument that such a claim has never been made at the borderline of any other two sciences; a psychologist working on a theory of creativity is not urged to wait until he is supplied by aesthetics with a (pre-eminent) theory of art. That psycholinguists were willing to put up with the priority hypothesis for so long can be accounted for only by their fascination with linguistics in a new key and by the availability of the Osgood–Sebeok model, which had been developed for a different type of linguistic theory, however. Chomsky's subsequent (1967) statement that a competence model *cannot* be regarded as a convenient basis for developing a performance model must be seen as a subtle contribution to the existing confusion. Chomsky adduces distinctly psychological arguments against his syntax–centered model (to be discussed later):

> ... in implying that the speaker selects the general properties of sentence structure before selecting lexical items (before deciding what he is going to talk about), such a proposal seems not only without justification but also entirely counter to whatever vague intuitions one may have about the processes that underlie production (1967, p 436).

At this point no one can any longer disregard the problems raised by the competence/performance opposition. The initial, perhaps implicitly acceptable, equation: performance = competence plus human frailties, modifiable into: performance = competence minus idealization, becomes suspect of circularity. In short, every empirically available utterance from a real speaker is burdened with the "errors" and "limitations" resulting from the human biological endowment and the fact that language performs certain functions in man's life.

It is against the background of this problem that we must examine the argumentation of the participants in the 1966 Edinburgh conference in matters of competence and performance; among them were many psycholinguists guided by the desire to prove the "psychological reality of generative grammar"[5].

Wales and Marshall (1966, p 30) tried to muffle the vagueness of the competence/performance distinction by stating:

> A theory of linguistic performance is ... a theory of how, given a certain linguistic competence, we actually put it to use – realize it, express it. It is also a theory of the limitations of the mechanisms which enable us to express our linguistic competence. It is not merely the theory of competence with the idealization removed, as has been suggested by Chomsky. For we want to be able to explain *normal* performance ...

In this formulation of the goals of a performance theory, performance seems to be conceived as competence plus the (error-producing) mechanisms of linguistic realizations. Should competence be thus a component of performance? The answer increases the confusion still further: "competence and performance can be usefully and adequately integrated in the explanation of linguistic behavior" (p 33).

Blumenthal has convincingly demonstrated the amazing tautology produced by Wales and Marshall: what is performance if not "linguistic behavior"? True enough, a little further on Wales and Marshall thought it dangerous that someone could view competence grammar as belonging to linguistics and hence might assume that "psychological performance explanation will be distinct from competence" (p 53). Thus the confusion reached its climax.

Fodor and Garrett (1966) take an even more "psychological" turn by recognizing that a performance theory cannot possibly comprise a linguistic theory per se

---

[5] Some findings of this research are quoted for illustration: a click sounded during the presentation of a sentence is shifted perceptually toward the clause boundary; complex transformations take more time than simple ones. For details, see Hörmann (1971a).

as its component and that a psychological theory of language or a theory of language use could at most contain an analogue of a performance theory:

> While there can be no serious doubt that a speaker who understands a sentence does so by recovering its structural description, it is by no means obvious that the processes by which he converts a wave form into a structural description are identical to (or isomorphic with) the operations by which a grammar converts on axiom string into a structural description (p 143).

Which is certainly correct; but is it equally certain that the structural description assigned by generative grammar to a sentence is identical with the "structural description" which determines our understanding of the sentence? Quite clearly, the two authors have not the slightest doubt about the pre-eminence of competence. This was indicated on another occasion by one of them (Fodor 1971, p 121) in vindication of his "weak psychological reality position", which claims that

> insofar as the grammar assigns the correct structural descriptions to sentences, it specifies the structures that the performance model must recognize and integrate. But ... the grammar is neutral concerning the character of the psychological operations involved in sentence processing.

The hidden dynamics of the competence-performance relationship was critically assessed by Thorne at the same conference (1966, p 9) in a brilliant paper:

> Because we can produce such comprehensive and precise statements of our knowledge of linguistic structure it becomes difficult for us not to think of the process of understanding utterances as involving the use of this knowledge. Even more dangerous, it becomes difficult not to think of it as actually involving the use of these statements.

As can be seen, the priority of competence has emerged victorious from this confrontation, and so psycholinguists could go on with their job of supplying the performance version for the competence model construed by linguists. The notion that performance is some manifestation of competence in the realm of linguistic reality has carried the day, albeit only half-heartedly. Could we say under the circumstances that a competence model might prove its validity by making useful predictions about a speaker's performance?

Here we come once again to the old theme of idealization, played now in a different key. The fact is that a theory – and generative grammar as a description of the ideal speaker's competence has always figured as a theory of language – is tested for its validity or goodness, and hence usefulness, usually by having its predictions confronted with actual events.

Unless he has done so before, at this point any partisan of generative grammar will pull the emergency brake and abandon the train of our argument with the objection that the validity criteria of a Cartesian theory à la Chomsky are in no way of the verification-of-predictions kind. Chomsky has indeed devoted a great deal of sophisticated theorizing to the problem of quality standards for grammars. He contrasts the descriptive adequacy of a grammar with its explanatory adequacy, whereby he perceives a categorical difference between description and explanation, rather than envisaging them as a sequence of conceptual stages that tend to reoccur in the history of science. (Is it not so that an explanation today becomes a mere description tomorrow, calling in turn for a more "advanced" explanation?) Chomsky has further discussed the dependency of various simplicity indices on particular prerequisites. In doing so he has invariably referred to formal validity criteria that could be used for cross-comparisons of different theories of competence.

It has been argued by generativists at a fairly early stage, and with good ground within the adopted definition of competence, that a competence theory could not be questioned, let alone invalidated, on the evidence of its output sentences being rejected, or nongenerated sentences found acceptable by a native speaker; the reason being that a competence theory is focused upon an ideal, not a real speaker. (We must resist here the diabolic temptation to define the ideal speaker as one who accepts all the sentences generated by the grammar and rejects all the other sentences...) In actual fact, however, it is inadmissible to define competence as totally independent of reality while declaring, at the same time, the priority of competence over performance! And this is precisely what the generativists, and psycholinguists in their wake, have done. The result is a bewildering situation: the area between the competence model and linguistic reality (rather: the realities of language use) has been declared the domain of a theory of performance, and since such a theory has never been available and most probably could never be constructed in the framework of the priority hypothesis, competence theory has been shielded effectively against the risk of a confrontation with the daily routine of language. In a way, it is an admirable feat to construct a protective shield out of the non-existent. And this feat is one of the sources of the discomfort we noted at the outset.

How emphatically the leading psycholinguists of the period defended the relevance and validity of the competence/performance distinction, notwithstanding the ever more clearly felt hazards, is apparent from the following comments by Bever et al. (1965, p 494):

> Since the theory of verbal performance is directly concerned with the behavior of speakers, it may often be subject to fairly direct experimental examination. The theory of competence, on the other hand, is concerned with the formulation of the linguistic information underlying verbal behavior. The speaker's competence is only reflected in his behavior via the kinds of performance variables mentioned above. The direct experimental verification ... is correspondingly difficult. This is not to say that the theory of competence is in any sense conventional or arbitrary. For, its support rests not only on occasional experimental confirmation but also on considerations of theoretical simplicity and power, fruitfulness, availability for integration with theories of performance variables, and so on.

Our first objection is that any direct experimental verification appears impossible for the reason that performance will principally intervene. Anyone prepared to accept judgments of well-formedness as *direct* evidence of a speaker's grammatical competence should be reminded that the unreliability of such judgments has been empirically demonstrated by Blumenthal (1966) and Levelt (1972). As far as "theoretical power" and "fruitfulness" goes, one might ask, to what end? Certainly not in order to predict empirically observable linguistic behavior ... When reading in Bever et al. (*loc. cit.*):

> it is obvious that the more a scientific theory concerns itself with the fundamental mechanisms underlying the observables, the less susceptible it is to direct experimental test

one wonders whether to read into this consolation or cynicism. Even from Chomsky's criteria for testing the quality of different generative grammars it can be seen that he admits the feasibility of a variety of competence theories. And even if all of them represent "idealizations", they may well vary in the degree of their approximation of the "linguistic reality" (no matter how imprecise the concept) they seek to idealize. But when it is claimed by competence theorists, performance theorists (though such do not exist) and psycholinguists that their inquiries, theorems, axioms, postulates, and findings do account for reality, one suspects that these investigators have different things in mind. Not all realities are equally suited to becoming the touchstone of a theory. In any event, a psycholinguist working on a theory intended to describe and predict the actual behavior and experiences of real people is genuinely interested in the question as to what kind of "reality" is being accounted for by the linguistic (competence) theory he is expected to incorporate into, or at least make allowances for in, his theory of performance. Linguistics is largely self-sufficient in outlining the object of its inquiry, and it is fully entitled to be so, as long as it is so for itself. Once such a theory of linguistic constructs is submitted to psycholinguistics for further processing and clarification of the performance issue, however, very serious thought must be given to the possible consequences of a situation in which competence and performance are founded on different notions of reality. Nobody less than Chomsky has been insisting on the need to preserve a close analogy between a theory of language and a theory of mind, even though he has set the priorities in a somewhat peculiar way. The next question we have to ask is, naturally, whether Chomsky's generative grammar is the one, from among the many possible grammars, that fits best the purposes of psycholinguistics.

We have thus raised a rather unusual question for linguistics: for whom are grammars written? The merit of an early formulation of the question goes to Halliday (1964), who argued that linguistic theories might differ in their usefulness for different "customers":

> Is there one single "best description" of a language, or are there various possible "best descriptions" according to the purpose in view? (p 11).

Whereupon Halliday takes up the competence–performance issue – discussed by us so far in a rather formal way – in very concrete terms:

> It is difficult to measure the relative demands made on a theory by requirements such as, on the one hand, that "the structural descriptions of a sentence must provide an account of all grammatical information in principle available to the native speaker", and, on the other hand, that the grammar should be of help to the student learning a foreign language or the pediatrician in his diagnosis and treatment of retarded speech (pp 13ff.).

Is it perhaps that the competence grammar, whose pivotal importance has never been disputed in linguistics, contains some rules or anything else that is superfluous for the real speaker in his daily practice? Or conversely, and more importantly: does it leave out anything that is indispensable for language use and for the theoretical interpretation of linguistic practice? These questions express the discomfort intimated at the outset and subsequently brought into relation with the neglect of the sign's uses.

One should not evade the issue by withdrawing into the thicket of the competence–performance dispute, as was done by Wales and Marshall (1966, p 183) in their polemic with Halliday:

> ... we fail to see how conflict could, in principle, arise between the criteria for adequate competence and performance models. As a competence theory describes the knowledge which the speaker [the term *ideal* is missing here! – H. H.] ... possesses and a performance theory describes the overt realization of (parts of) this *same* knowledge in particular situations and under specific conditions, how can the two ever conflict?

A rigorous distinction between language as such and language use is evidently one of the few stances shared by practically all linguists, whether of the generative or any other variety. In stressing the need for maintaining this distinction, Uhlenbeck (1967b, p 288) invokes a long list of forebears running from Humboldt via Saussure right into the present. But precisely because, as he states,

> linguists actually consider as their ultimate aim the study of Language with a capital L, in other words, language in general,

psychologists cannot help but wonder how it is possible to get to the roots of Language by studying language alone, that is, in oblivion of the fact that there is no language without humans and their exercise of language in meaning and understanding. It has been stressed over and over again that language is characterized by a kind of "transparency" in the sense that humans tend to grasp its substance "right through" its words and sentences. How can you inquire into that characteristic feature of language unless you look through it, taking notice of the language user and his world?

Idealizations and abstractions are the natural tools of any science that seeks to mark out, from among the wealth of evidence and speculation, its terrain for intensive cultivation. What the consequences of these procedures are is a problem spelled out in full in the overall confrontation of linguistics and psychology of language, much in the vein of the dispute between Halliday and Wales and Marshall. Invoking an ideal speaker-hearer in possession of linguistic competence, the generativist leaves aside everything that distinguishes the human speaker-hearer from an automatic sentence generator – in accord with the definition of competence. This is a perfectly legitimate manipulation. In Searle's view (1969, p 56):

> This method, one of constructing idealized models, is analogous to the sort of theory construction that goes on in most sciences, e. g., the construction of economic models, or accounts of the solar system which treats planets as points. Without abstraction and idealization there is no systematization.

Rightly so; but it is surely a matter of difference from what exactly, and for what purpose, we are abstracting. In a representation of the solar system – to pursue Searle's example – one should not necessarily treat the planets as points, thus abstracting from their masses, since this would make their mutual attraction unaccountable by this particular model.

The linguist's position is that in abstracting from the dynamics of language use and its determinants, he has omitted what is irrelevant for his competence model of language as object of inquiry of his science. Strictly speaking, he even defines his object of inquiry partly in terms of what the omitted element is irrelevant to[6].

Psychologists have hitherto rarely been worried about the possibility that, from their point of view, either too much or the wrong things were omitted. Should the goals of psycholinguistics consist as before in filling up the Osgood-Sebeok model, then there would be no need to worry at all. But if the psycholinguist feels more like a psychologist of language, he is bound to broaden the scope of his work and set himself goals that reach far beyond the 1952 model. In fact, this is inevitable as long as linguists working in this field restrict themselves to producing data on well-formedness, i. e., the syntactic acceptability of sentences. Generative competence theory was once wrongly described by Wales and Marshall (1966, p 29) as "a theory of linguistic knowledge which attempts to account for our 'intuitions' concerning the language . . .", which it is not, inasmuch as this particular competence theory deals merely (if at all) with our intuitions bearing on well-formedness, and these are by no means all the intuitions of the language user.

This kind of theory is too narrow to serve as a basis for constructing a theory of how humans employ and experience language, a theory of the human actions of meaning and understanding.

We have dwelt on the competence/performance opposition without giving closer consideration to what generative grammer construes as the substance of linguistic competence. This neglect will be made up for in the next chapter.

To sum up the contribution of generative grammar to, and the dangers issuing from it for, a psychology of language, we propose a quotation from Friedrich Schiller (1795) in which the German poet speaks of a mind very much like Chomsky's:

> a speculative spirit . . . tempted to fashion the actual according to the conceivable, and to exalt the subjective conditions of its imagination into laws constituting the existence of things . . . fell a victim to a vain subtlety . . . because (it) stood too high to see the individual . . . (Engl. transl. 1954, p 42).

---

[6] Uhlenbeck (no date, p 107): "the history of linguistics may be largely viewed as a sequence of different reduction theories . . .".

Chapter 4

Grammar: Syntax Plus a Poor Relative

In the preceding chapter we attempted to show how the concept of sign-in-itself, as an autonomous entity detached from its uses, reemerges in analogous fashion at what might be called the molar level, in the form of the concept of language-in-itself, a language totally isolated from its actual uses and functions; in specifying the structures of this language, the competence-describing generative grammar has developed a system of rules which ignores all communicative functions and all communicative intentions of language. This parallel and – for linguistics and the closely associated psycholinguistics – general development can be accounted for by two factors, one operating at the fore, the other at the rear.

At the fore we see the magnificent edifice of a strictly formal theory which functions with the inevitability of pure logic or mathematics, independently of the more or less brilliant intuitions of a genius and unmarred by the chance properties of the individual instance. The attempt to conceive language as a formal combinatorics of "pure" signs could not but result in the preponderance of syntax as the distinguishing mark of linguistics in the past few decades.

Older still, and prevalent also in structural linguistics of the Bloomfieldian kind, is the rear view: distaste for everything that smacks of *meaning*. Anyone can easily contract this endemic disease, widespread among outstanding linguists, when he sits down to pore over the matter set down on paper, in sublime as well as crude idiom, in the course of centuries of investigation into *meaning*. A systematization of the relationship between sign and referent has turned out to be a Sisyphean task. Small wonder that semantics, entrusted with this task, after initial friendly encouragement has been relegated to the position of a poor relative (Greimas 1971, p 2) of glorious syntax.

The structural linguist's key question, "Same or different?", by which he probes for structures, under the upward directed procedure of primary data integration, segmentation, and unit extraction, is sometimes framed as "Same or different in meaning?", for example in the identification of morphemes. But even then the linguist does not inquire into the meaning of the morpheme, word, or sentence; the question is part of a *yes/no* formalism by which to distinguish between various elements of language, the only conclusion about the difference being that it exists. The linguistic units isolated in this way serve as handy building blocks for constructing a theory which conceptualizes linguistic utterances as rule-governed strings of these elements and seeks to impose structure on the strings. The handiness and manageability of the elements is directly responsible for the domination of syntax in structural linguistics.

In pre-Chomskyan linguistics, semantics makes its last appearance in Bloomfield's definition of the meaning of a linguistic form as "the situation in which the speaker utters it and the response it calls forth in the hearer" (1933, p 139). Viewing the definition from a historical perspective, we are made aware of a memorable farewell scene: together with the last behavioristic definition there vanished in this realm the predilection for S-R formulations, those very ones extolled for their clarity by their proponents and scornfully discarded for their naivety and unsophistication by their learned opponents. What followed was a surge of interest in cognitive factors, albeit *cognitive* has here an artificial ring, referring to knowledge not necessarily furnished with consciousness.

Taking the decline of Bloomfieldian structuralism as a frame of reference, the turn of the tide had its source in the fact that meaning is simply unaccountable in purely behavioristic terms: a sentence may be comprehended even if it does not evoke any overt behavior. The last stronghold of Watson's offsprings, the notion of meaning as disposition and the parallel linguistic construction of displaced speech, falls apart as we ask what is meant by disposition and displacement.

Viewed from the vantage point of incipient generative linguistics, however, the turn of the tide did not come because of the feeling that *meaning* had to be conceived in other, more sophisticated, terms than those of behaviorism. Rather, it was caused by the desire to construct a strictly formal theory *without* resort to the concept of meaning. To start with, meaning was not to be accounted for at all. From this angle we do not see any shift toward cognitive factors, unless we are prepared to accept as such the reference to competence as knowledge.

Generative grammar was launched with a now famous sentence which has since resounded like a fanfare proclaiming the irrelevance of semantics:

COLORLESS GREEN IDEAS SLEEP FURIOUSLY.

How this string of words, in spite of its absurdity, makes up a sentence needs to be investigated. Generative linguistics derives its program from the juxtaposition of that string of words with another one:

SLEEP IDEAS GREEN FURIOUSLY COLORLESS,

and from the assertion that the first string was a sentence while the second was not. One goal of the new linguistics is to account for sentencehood by explaining what ensures the grammaticalness of a sentence. Another is to achieve this with the aid of a strictly formal theory.

In another version, the goal is formulated by Lakoff (1971a, p 267) as inquiring into "the regularities that govern which linear sequences of words and morphemes of a language are permissible and which sequences are not"; the imprecision of the formulation reflects the degree of preoccupation with the ideas of generative linguistics: *permissible* is understood as *syntactically permissible,* and nothing else. Chomsky (1957, p 17): "Grammar is autonomous and independent of meaning".

One is tempted to speculate at this point how modern linguistics might have developed if Chomsky had chosen to demonstrate, not the irrelevance of meaning for sentencehood, but the irrelevance of sentencehood for meaning. Had he juxtaposed the "sentence"

COLORLESS GREEN IDEAS SLEEP FURIOUSLY

with the non-sentence

I EATING PREFER MEAT ROAST,

we might have stood a chance of arriving at the thought-provoking realization that the latter verbal string is communicatively more meaningful than the former. Was it really quite so natural for generative linguists to try and account for syntactic well-formedness rather than for the communicative function of language?

The generativists' choice of sentencehood rather than meaning or communicative function upon which to focus their attention, was certainly due in some degree to the fact that philosophy, or logic, had supplied the convenient distinction between sentence and utterance, thus making its own contribution to the conception of language-in-itself which linguists had hoped to consolidate with their separation of competence from performance. By inquiring into sentences (as objects of philosophy) in place of people's utterances, investigators have succeeded in reversing an old conception of psychologism that had offered to derive the laws of logic from the laws of thinking. Whereas "the psychological conception, or rather misconception, of logic appears to be overcome after Frege and Husserl and because of their influence" (Patzig 1970, p 7), there is now more of a danger of a misinterpretation of language under a kind of "logicism".

Bar-Hillel (1954, p 235) once suggested that the goals of logicians and linguists were much the same ("attempting to construct language systems that stand in some correspondence to natural languages"), a view in which Chomsky joined after initial opposition[1]. A presupposition is made about the parallelness of artificial and natural languages, in the hope of discovering some evidence on the essentials of natural language by studying the grammar of an artificial one. The abyss between the language we make and the language we speak (Uhlenbeck) is blissfully ignored.

Well, the generativists embarked on this road, and the psycholinguists followed in their wake. With the exception of a few investigators, among whom Osgood should be named, psycholinguists turned their attention to problems of syntax rather than to problems of meaning and the actual uses of utterances. The reasons for this development can be traced in the history of psychology itself, besides those associated with the historically determined leading role of linguis-

---

[1] For detailed comments see Uhlenbeck (no date, pp 86 ff.).

tics, as outlined above. Such highly differentiated areas of psychology as perception and learning reveal a more formal than substantive orientation. Some psychological theories as diverse as Gestalt psychology and associationism owe much of their success to the tendency of attributing less theoretical relevance to *what*-differences than to *how*-differences. The predominantly content-oriented psychoanalysis on the other hand has shown too little theoretical sophistication and internal differentiation to pose as a model for the now methodologically highly advanced psychology.

We might add here the success scored by the generativists with their design of the sentence generation model. The theory of competence can be viewed as a kind of flowchart model[2] whose stations mediate in the process of sentence production and comprehension. At this point it becomes clear that the verbal string has a structure that is not identical with the articulation at the surface. This could not fail to appeal to psychologists who, like Lashley and subsequently Miller, Galanter, and Pribram, had rejected strictly behavioristic interpretations with the argument that behind the overt behavior there was a hierarchy of plans, and not only associations of stimulus and response.

The flowchart model of the generativists has undergone a number of modifications since Chomsky's *Syntactic Structures* (1957), but one thing has persisted practically without change: the notion that syntax was the basis and core of it all.

The model in *Syntactic Structures* comprised two components: a syntactic (i. e., grammatical, this identity being perfect at that time) and a phonological one. The syntactic component – the one of real interest to Chomsky – comprised two kinds of rules: phrase structure rules and, acting on their output, transformation rules. A sentence is "parsed" with phrase structure rules in a specifying rewrite procedure. The output of the phrase structure subcomponent is subsequently (this temporal distinction is an additional attraction for the psychologist) exposed to obligatory or optional transformations. The output of the transformation subcomponent becomes the input to the phonological component of the model, yielding the next output – articulation. Should it occur to us to ask: Does the model make allowances for the fact that words and sentences tend to have some meaning? – we can expect only one answer: No[3]. Meaning, i. e., semantics, is supposed to be handled by a separate "theory of the use of language," with which

---

[2] The comparison with a flowchart model applies only with certain reservations: competence theory operates in actual fact only with static structures and describes the processes between these structures only in such vague terms as *mapping*, or *representing*, and *interpreting*. The "stratificational conception" which underlies generative transformational grammar has been criticized in particular by Chafe (1971a, p 6) who dismisses the notion of bidirectionality across the structural levels of language and argues for a semantics-to-phonetics (one-way) directionality.

[3] This can be upheld even if we consider that the final stage of rewriting yields lexical entries like N → *boy, girl, man, freedom, cholera* . . . because the model does not specify how to select from class N – which contains all the nouns of the language – the one noun whose meaning occurs in the sentence under analysis. For Chomsky this is no shortcoming, since his theory is meant to account for well-formedness, and not for the content of what is being said.

the grammar described in the "theory of linguistic form" would be supplemented. Meaning was thus pushed down to a position in which performance has been subsequently accommodated. A pertinent comment on Chomsky's 1957 model was offered by Maclay (1971, p 169):

> The status of meaning with regard to formal description is much like that found in structuralist accounts. It is outside of linguistics proper and clearly secondary to the description of syntax.

Chomsky specified his own goal in the following way (1957, p 102):

> ... we should like the syntactic framework of the language that is isolated and exhibited by the grammar to be able to support semantic description.

Very clearly, syntax (possibly plus phonology) is here equated with grammar.

Perhaps even more influential in the realm of linguistics and psycholinguistics has been Chomsky's second model outlined in *Aspects of a Theory of Syntax* (1965) against the same Cartesian background that stands also behind the competence/performance distinction. Chomsky revised his model under the influence of Katz and Fodor's *The Structure of a Semantic Theory* (1963). This enormously influential paper made it both possible and necessary to introduce a separate semantic component into the model. Leaving Katz and Fodor's treatise for later consideration, we shall first discuss Chomsky's 1965 model.

A modification of prime importance for psycholinguists at the time was the clear-cut separation of deep structure (DS) and surface structure (SS).

The distinction between DS and SS was one of the most seminal developments in modern linguistics with far-reaching consequences also for psycholinguistics. The realization that two sentences of almost identical (surface) structure,

JOHN IS EAGER TO PLEASE,

and

JOHN IS EASY TO PLEASE,

differ radically in their deep structures – and that it would be the task of linguistics to account for this difference, and the task of psycholinguistics to explore its determinants and implications[4] – brought tremendous progress in that it paved the way for the formulation of new questions, as in the case of any genuine progress in scientific investigation, rather than yielding new answers to old questions. The structures and regularities observed in language behavior are now in need of a more searching explication and interpretation. At the same time, new epistemological problems arise: the narrowly conceived language behavior (i. e., the string of words uttered or perceived) is reduced to an epiphenomenon which can merely serve as a clue to what is of "real interest". This in itself may have reduced interest in performance.

In actual fact, the distinction between deep and surface structure was somehow

---

[4] For example, Blumenthal (1967) has shown that the effect of a word (from a sentence) offered as a prompt in a recall task varies with the position of the word in the deep structure, not in the surface structure, of the sentence.

implicit in the early model and could be found between the kernel string as output of the phrase structure subcomponent and the sentence generated by suitable transformations from the kernel. But psycholinguists more than anyone else were led to believe mistakenly that the kernel string was equivalent to the simple active declarative sentence. In his 1965 model Chomsky makes it clear that any sentence has both a surface and deep structure (SS and DS) and that its DS specifies the desired transformations. Thus, DS should specify the syntactic information needed to disambiguate, for instance, the sentence

THE SHOOTING OF THE HUNTERS WAS TERRIBLE.

The semantic component may begin to operate on DS as generated by the syntactic base component in order to produce a semantic interpretation of the sentence. DS is at the same time fed into the transformation subcomponent to obtain SS as the prospective input to the phonological component.

In this book we shall guard ourselves against the use of *interpretation* and *mapping of a syntactic structure onto a semantic representation* (or the other way round) – which terms are carelessly used by linguists – unless sounding an appropriate warning. In particular, the first mentioned term is one of the most effective cover terms ever invented in the history of modern science.

Before we start examining the functioning of this new semantic component, we would be well advised to see what this component is supposed to yield according to Chomsky, Katz, Fodor, and the other M.I.T. linguists.

Chomsky's first model represented an attempt at formalizing one particular intuitive ability of the ideal native speaker: the ability to distinguish well-formed sentences from ungrammatical verbal strings. (That the proper articulation is safeguarded by the phonological component is irrelevant in this place.) Katz and Fodor (1963, pp 172–173) conceded that

> Grammars answer the question: What does the speaker know about the phonologic and syntactic structure of his language that enables him to use and understand any of its sentences including those he has not previously heard? ... Semantics takes over the explanation of the speaker's ability to produce and understand new sentences at the point where grammar leaves off.

Thus, semantics is needed to secure the speaker's judgment on the well-formedness of sentences, and it is needed where "grammar leaves off". In effect, Katz and Fodor can make the point: "Synchronic linguistic description minus grammar equals semantics".

This parallelness in the goals of grammar and semantics is stressed in all accounts of the standard model. The ability of the competent speaker-hearer

> to provide interpretations for sentences is resolved into the abilities to provide *structural descriptions* and *semantic readings* for sentences. These areas of competence may be elaborated in analogous ways. In both cases, speakers of a language are able to provide judgments of well-formedness, ambiguity, and intersentential relationship. That is, on the one hand, grammatical competences include the abilities
> 1. to distinguish structurally well-formed utterances,
> 2. to note when and in what ways an utterance is susceptible to more than one structural interpretation,

35

3. to relate sentences to each other by virtue of their structural similarity or difference.

Semantic competences, on the other hand, include the abilities

1. to detect semantic anomaly,
2. to note when and in what ways an utterance may be semantically ambiguous,
3. to note paraphrase and synonymity among sentences (Garrett and Fodor 1968, p 452).

Let us turn a blind eye for the moment to the dubious use of the term *interpretation* and also to the enumeration of as many as six competences in place of one (a matter of critical importance, for, e. g., the aphasiologist), noting instead that in the present model the semantic component is assigned the role of a rescue squad expected to deal with all those things the principal actor, syntax, cannot cope with. What exactly is that?

Grammar tells us that

COLORLESS GREEN IDEAS SLEEP FURIOUSLY

is a well-formed sentence; but even many generativists have been saying this with their teeth on edge, out of sheer loyalty to the (1957) Chomsky model. Well, the new model with its semantic component has now decreed: this *is* a sentence, but a semantically anomalous one.

The 1957 model was likewise unable to accomodate semantic ambiguities such as THE BILL IS LARGE; the new semantic component does disambiguate these. Later on, we shall inquire into the question of how anomalies are identified as such and how disambiguation is accomplished.

The third newly proposed semantic competence enables us to pronounce that the following two syntactically non–reducible sentences:

TWO CHAIRS ARE IN THE ROOM

and

THERE ARE TWO THINGS IN THE ROOM AND EACH IS A CHAIR,

are in fact semantic paraphrases, being perhaps synonymous.

It is in the case of this "rewrite" competence that we are struck by something latent as well in the other two semantic competences: that the purpose of the entire procedure is not to establish the meaning of a sentence, but simply to identify similarities and differences in meaning – as postulated by structuralism[5].

Having dealt with the role of the semantic component in Chomsky's 1965 model, let us now readjust our viewfinder to inspect the component at short distance, examining its structure and the way it functions in the model. The above mentioned paper by Katz and Fodor (1963) will be used for this purpose.

The semantic component consists of two parts: the dictionary (lexicon) and projection rules.

---

[5] The fact that those two sentences are interpreted as being synonymous, or paraphrases of each other, goes to show the narrowness of the notion of meaning adopted by generative linguistics: meaning boils down to reference, that is, the naming of things. That the notions of synonymity and paraphrasing are themselves debatable has been wholly left out of consideration. Cf. Husserl (1970), Chafe (1970, 1971a), Coseriu (1973b), Ziff (1972), Uhlenbeck (no date).

The dictionary lists the lexical items, or – using a simpler though more ambiguous term – the words of a language.

Lexical item is an awkward term which reflects the linguists' embarrassment over the fact that they lack a useful or even a generally accepted definition of the term *word*. The same is also true of such concepts as lexeme, archilexeme, seme, sememe, . . ., from which the dictionary might be composed. All these concepts are so closely interrelated that they can be securely employed only by someone who is determined not to trespass the boundaries of a particular school.

The dictionary entry of a word contains:
1) the data needed to classify the word (e. g., *adjective*)
2) semantic markers
3) semantic distinguishers
4) selection restrictions, upon which the projection rules operate.

The data stored in the dictionary ensure the syntactic classification of any word, but also enable the semantic markers of the word to find their place in the deep structure sequence of elements generated by the (antecedent and dominant!) syntactic base component.

The semantic characterization of a word is accomplished – and this we owe to Katz and Fodor – in such a way that by the integration of the *word* meanings, under the syntactical guidance of deep structure, the meaning of the *sentence* emerges.

To ensure an adequate systematization of word senses and their interrelations, Katz and Fodor dissect the meaning of a word into minute semantic elements. These elements can be represented as dimensions of a matrix; each word (lexical item) has a place in the structure of the matrix, and this place determines its meaning. (The analogy to structuralist phonology is evident: in it, a phoneme is constituted by the oppositions on which it differs from other phonemes.)

The idea of a matrix as a rigid structure of elementary semantic dimensions implies that each word has its definitive meaning as designated by its place in the structure.

The semantic elements are further subdivided into two classes:
1) *semantic marker,* equivalent to a semantic dimension on which the given word is placed next to other words sharing the particular feature; e. g., *woman* and *dog* share the marker (Animate);
2) *semantic distinguisher* as the feature(s) by which the given word differs from all other lexical items.

Katz and Fodor (1963, p 186) illustrate their semantic structure on the example of the lexical item (word) *bachelor* (using a tree diagram of course!). In their diagram, reproduced here in Fig. 1, elements of the syntactic classification are without any brackets, semantic markers are in parentheses, and distinguishers in square brackets.

Our attention is immediately drawn to a problem that will keep recurring in subsequent discussions of semantic markers: what Katz and Fodor chose to designate *distinguisher* in their example could be readily accounted for as a configuration of various markers. For example, the second and fourth senses of

bachelor
|
noun
/   \
(Human)   (Animal)
/   \   \
(Male)   (Male)
/   \   \

| who has
never
married | young knight
serving under
the standard
of another
knight | who has the
first or lowest
academic
degree | young fur seal
without a mate
during the
breeding time |

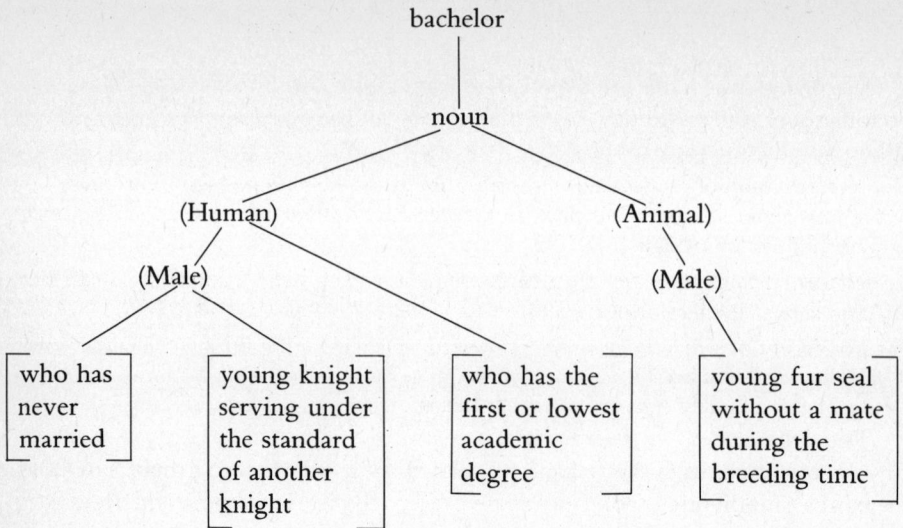

Fig. 1. Example of dictionary entry *(bachelor)* as construed by Katz and Fodor. (After Katz & Fodor, 1963, p. 186)

bachelor (*knight* and *seal*) could be entered under the common marker (Young). In more general terms, we inquire (as pointed out by Bolinger 1965) into the criteria by which to designate the number and hence the density of the markers in the dictionary. A possible answer, one that obviously cannot be accommodated in the framework of a competence grammar, has been suggested by Bierwisch (to be discussed below): in both kind and differentiation, the semantic markers correspond to the "resolution power" of the human perceptual apparatus designed to deal with the world at large, not only with language. It is as if *cognitive reality* were the ultimate criterion of *linguistic reality*.

Another point will be made in passing: in view of the weak hierarchical arrangement of Katz and Fodor's semantic markers, which derive from Scholastic logic and its vehicle *genus proximum* and *differentia specifica,* plenty of redundancy is revealed in the system with each upward step. By having (Male) in mind, one has implicitly opted for (Animate) and (Physical object). What kind of conception of the dictionary's mental functioning can accommodate this realization? (And there must be eventually some such conception if competence is going to retain its ascendancy over performance.)

Selection restrictions express necessary and sufficient conditions for the readings in which they occur to combine with other readings to form derived readings (Katz 1966, pp 159–160).

In the quoted example, all readings (distinguishers) entered under the marker (Human) are subject to a selection restriction which states that in these cases *bachelor* may apply only to human objects, just as the selection restriction imposed on the marker (Animal) rules out applications other than to animal objects.

This brings us to the other part of the semantic component of the Katz and Fodor model, the projection rules. Dictionary and projection rules go together. Whereas a dictionary provides

> a representation of the semantic characteristics of morphemes necessary to account for the facts about sentences and their interrelations that the grammar leaves unexplained (Katz and Fodor 1963, p 181),

projection rules control the uses of the data stored in the dictionary – albeit in a specific sense. Projection rules

> take account of semantic relations between morphemes and of the interaction between meaning and syntactic structure in determining the correct semantic interpretation for any of the infinitely many sentences which the grammar generates (Katz and Fodor 1963, p 183).

Thus, projection rules are meant to specify in a systematic manner how the meanings of individual words are to be integrated, but well within the restricted goals of the entire semantic component: to avoid semantic anomalies, to resolve semantic ambiguities, to identify paraphrases and synonyms. They fail to tell us anything about *how* a sentence is to be *understood,* or how, for instance, a noun and a corresponding adjective interact with each other, or how the meanings of the many modifiers in *dear good old granny* get integrated. These questions come under debate only with Osgood, Steinberg, Langendoen, Engelkamp, and others; they are discussed in Chap. 13.

Our preliminary conclusion is that Katz and Fodor's dictionary and projection rules, while offering information of some relevance on the outer framework of sentence comprehension (on anomalies, ambiguities, etc.), make no direct contribution to comprehension proper. Of course, Katz and Fodor are not to be blamed for this, the conveying and grasping of meaning being psychological acts, after all; but it would be legitimate to ask what kind of benefit might derive from the conceptualization of a dictionary (or lexicon) and a fraction of the rules needed to operate the system without showing interest in how this dictionary and the rules fit the "mechanisms" and functions of actual language use. We come face to face here with the antinomy to which linguistics has exposed itself by treating language in isolation of its uses, as language-in-itself: together with their dictionary, linguists were forced to postulate a thing as eminently psychological as a memory store, and together with their projection rules, a thing as eminently psychological as rules of operating the store, but in doing so they failed to make any reference to psychology. Indeed, this is where generativists and nongenerative linguists are remarkably unanimous, as can be seen from Uhlenbeck's (1967b, p 289) comment:

> The whole history of linguistics furnishes a long list of illustrations of the danger in letting ourselves be guided by nonlinguistic considerations; that is, by considerations which are foreign to the object of our study.

Should the language-using, language-experiencing, and language-inspired human indeed be "foreign to the object of our study?"

39

For the time being, the reader's attention is again directed to Katz and Fodor's semantic component. These authors developed their construct for the express purpose of supplementing Chomsky's generative grammar, and as such it was supposed to serve the same end as the latter: testing sentences for well-formedness. The usefulness of the semantic component should therefore come distinctly into evidence in cases where the syntactic base structure leaves room for it.

Such is the case with the many lexical items of multiple meaning (our specimen *bachelor* has got four). For each lexical element the appropriate meaning (reading) is selected with the aid of the projection rules in order to supply the correct meaning for each possible sentence structure. By this procedure we are able to disambiguate the sentence

THE BILL IS LARGE,

where one reading suggests the size of a bird's beak, the other the sum of a financial accounting. In case the sentence continues with ... BUT NEED NOT BE PAID, the selection restrictions sampled by the projection rules block the reading *beak* with reference to the selection restrictions of *paid*. In the sentence

THE SEAL IS ON THE LETTER

the selection restrictions geared to the various readings of *seal* should make the speaker-hearer choose the reading for sealing an envelope rather than for the marine animal.

Particularly noteworthy is the operation of projection rules in cases where success and failure are only one step apart and where the consequences of failure can be extremely far-reaching, as with semantic anomalies. There may be sentences like

THE PAINT WAS SILENT,

or even like our good old friend,

COLORLESS GREEN IDEAS SLEEP FURIOUSLY.

The semantic anomaly of these sentences results from the fact that they consist of word concatenations which, while conforming to the rules of syntax, violate the now familiar selection restrictions prescribed by the projection rules for the respective semantic markers. The *silent paint* is semantically abnormal because one of the semantic markers of *silent* is (Human), which cannot be accepted for *paint*.

At first sight this seems an admirably elegant solution of the problem of anomalies, with which linguists have been struggling so long. If it is true that selection restrictions as intrinsic components of the item-specifying dictionary entry "express necessary and sufficient conditions" for the presence or absence of a semantic anomaly, as claimed by Katz (1966, p 159), it follows that any concatenation of syntactically incompatible words that violates the respective projection rules results in an anomaly with linguistically determined (i. e., competence-conditioned) inevitability. In Chomsky's grammar, judgment on the (syntactic) well-formedness of a sentence issues from the operation of a rule system vested in the speaker-hearer's competence once and for all and which hence remains stable in all situations. In quite the same manner, the present model postulates the stability of the competence-vested matrix of semantic markers and projection rules: confronted with a rule-violating string of words the speaker-hearer sounds an alarm, upon which all efforts at understanding the word string are abandoned.

In reality, this is not the case, as the handling of metaphors shows. The matter will be examined in Chap. 7 (cf. also Hörmann 1973). At this point it is merely contended that once again, i. e., also in the case of the semantic component as a rescue operation on behalf of generative grammar, the constructs meant to effect a clear-cut separation of competence and performance have proved tenuous and the entire undertaking futile. That the distinction has to be abandoned altogether should become even more evident in the next chapter, where we discuss the lexicon, the status of its dimensions, and various conceptions of its functioning.

Chapter 5

The Lexicon and Its Dimensions

It was during our first encounter with the lexicon (or dictionary) as part of the semantic component in the 1965 generativist model that we became aware of the latter's essential trait: the claim that the meaning of a lexical item (or, using a less precise but simpler term: of a word) is equal to the aggregate of separately specified dimensions[1].

By the same token, the generativists followed the widely acclaimed example set by phonology, which considers speech sounds as made up of clusters of distinctive features; this construction has considerably reduced the number of categories required for an adequate description of a speech sound.

The same kind of reduction must be aimed at in a scientific treatment of the problem of meaning. To treat material scientifically means to try to impose order upon it. And to impose order means to select from among an abundance of properties those that repeat themselves and thus cease to be mere singularities.

Certain efforts to determine lexical meaning by resolving it into its components were made even before Katz and Fodor. In "pure" structuralism, for that matter, componential analysis as proposed, for example, by Lounsbury serves to extract from the arrangement

man	woman	child
rooster	hen	chicken
bull	cow	calf

the (vertically ordered) dimensions *Male, Female,* and *Childlike.*

---

[1] Strictly speaking, we ought to distinguish Chomsky's *feature* from the notion of *marker* as introduced by Katz and Fodor. A semantic feature is bivalent (e. g., Male + or −) and has no hierarchical arrangement; markers, on the other hand, are hierarchically ordered. But since we are not interested in comparing the relative merits of different linguistic theories, this distinction will be observed only when forced upon us by the problem under discussion. Nowhere is a strict differentiation between the terms *lexicon, dictionary,* and – most recently – *thesaurus* consistently upheld in linguistics.

In much the same way Katz (1967, p 129) believes he has grasped and revealed semantic markers:

> Consider the idea each of us thinks of as part of the meaning of the words *chair, stone, man, building, planet*, etc., but not part of the meaning of such words as *truth, together-ness, feeling, shadow, integer, departure*, etc. – the idea that we take to express what is common to the meaning of the words in the former group and that we use to conceptu-ally distinguish them from those in the latter. Roughly, we might characterize what is common to our individual ideas as the notion of a spatially and continuous material thing. The semantic marker (Physical Object) is introduced to designate that notion.

One might ask the structuralist of the Lounsbury type what made him choose these particular analogy sequences (man-woman-child; bull-cow-calf, . . .) if he had no idea of the semantic components beforehand, the same components he claims to have *derived* from these sequences. (It takes a worldling with a fair amount of knowledge of the world to omit the ox from such a sequence.) Katz, however, is immune to this question – now put in earnest – and so is his great predecessor Locke, who held an identical view: Ideas arise by a process of abstraction of what is common to a particular group of objects.

By using thrice the noun *idea* in the above passage, Katz not only reveals his affinity to Locke but also lays himself open to the suspicion that somebody had told him which words to line up in order to conjure up *the* common semantic marker or dimension; this "somebody" must no doubt have been the competent native speaker trained in the logical discrimination of *genus proximum* and *differentia specifica*. At this point, inquisitive questions come to mind like: Why should the word *devil* be missing in Katz's list of *chair, stone, man,* and *building* – from which he deduced the semantic marker (Physical Object)? He might have included the *devil* had he lived three hundred years earlier . . .

This kind of question shows that we are aware of a significant difference: far from being a discovery procedure, Katz's procedure is meant to justify subjec-tively the adoption of some particular semantic markers. Much as in factor analysis, the ostensibly intuitive choice of the base variables prejudges the com-mon factors obtained in the outcome.

The mention of factor analysis suggests a revealing analogy. Experts in factor analysis tend to assume today that, in place of psychological or kindred terms, it is perfectly possible to use numbers or letters to designate or identify the factors; in fact, some authors do so consistently. In psycholinguistics, Marshall (1970, p 191) has suggested in the same vein, though without reference to factor analy-sis, that

> the "names" of semantic markers are heuristically useful, but the *theory* would not be changed if they were all replaced by numbers.

Which goes to prove that neither the dimensions, nor markers, nor features are words (or lexemes, or sememes) in themselves, even if, *faute de mieux,* they are designated by words.

Here we come upon a whole string of problems. The word *male* may be construed as a feature complex made up of (Physical Object), (Animate),

43

(Human), (etc.); would it be possible to construe the *feature* (Male) as a complex of higher-order, lower-order, primitive, ... features in turn? What is it that distinguishes the word *male* from the lexicon dimension (Male)? Alternatively: Does *male* as a word figure only on the dimension (Male), or possibly also on those of (Physical Object), (Animate), etc.? And that question brings us back to the Katz–Fodor dictionary entries.

Is there a linguistic procedure by which we could conclusively determine the varieties (and hence the number) of the markers that specify a word? After thorough examination of the question, Macnamara (1971) gives a negative answer. He set out to draw semantic trees of the Katz–Fodor type for a number of words, and what he found was that any number of arbitrarily discriminated similarity dimensions can be proposed for structural segmentation of semantic space. He found it likewise impossible to satisfy the postulate that

> the relationship among semantic markers should remain constant from one word to the rest (Macnamara 1971, p 363).

There is evidently no master tree in the lexicon that would serve as a guideline for particular word trees: markers which are redundant in one branching tree need not be so in another. This in effect casts a shadow over the earlier mentioned aspect of economy which played so vital a role in the proposal for a dimensional lexicon.

At this point the vagueness of the lexicon conception reveals its psychological consequences: If the kind and number of word-specifying markers cannot be determined with any certainty, how can one hope to construe the meaning of the word used in a sentence as the sum total of its markers? Moreover, what is the relevance, in this context, of the psychological finding (cf. Perfetti 1972, p 248) that it depends on the particular situation which and how many markers of a word come into play? Anyone concerned with the definition of *whale* will have to think of many more markers than someone asked merely whether a whale is an animal. Much of what had lent support to the internal lexicon theory under the nice catchword *structure* has thus melted away.

Reverting to the Katz and Fodor model we might ask: Taking for granted that semantic markers provide an organizational frame for words (or lexemes, or sememes, ...), but are not words themselves, should we assume that at each node of the marker system there is an actual lexical item, i. e., a word? Are there, in addition to the innumerable words of a language that must find their place in the structure, some "possible" words that have not turned up yet in the vocabulary of the language? This kind of reasoning induced Chomsky (1965) to speak of "accidental" and "systematic lexical gaps". Taking a leap to the Sapir–Whorf hypothesis, we might ask: Should a matrix of semantic dimensions be available not only to the Eskimo's mind but also to our minds, enabling us to use different names for eighteen varieties of snow once we have learned the respective words?

Questions like this reveal two kinds of things:

1) Dimensions of the lexicon would make sense only in the framework of a theoretical conception of how these dimensions, and the lexicon as such, come

into operation and how they function; the Katz–Fodor construction lacks such a conception.

2) This breeds the suspicion that, if Marshall is right in asserting that the theory would not change if the "names" of the semantic dimensions were replaced by numbers, this is so because the dimensions have nothing to do with meaning at this stage and are merely meant to yield the material needed for a calculus whose results would be "semantically interpreted" at some future date – a promise we have come across before. Katz and Fodor have proposed the semantic component in order to reduce the indeterminacy gap between the formal and the substantive aspects of a sentence, which the mysterious act of interpretation is meant to fill in at an unspecified date, but they could hope to succeed in this undertaking only if the dimensions (or markers, or features) of their lexicon were construed without the limitations of the straitlaced concept of competence.

Looking at Katz and Fodor's conception from this vantage point, we can fully appreciate the statement:

> Semantic markers must ... be thought of as theoretical constructs introduced into semantic theory to designate language invariant but language linked components of a conceptual system that is part of the cognitive structure of the human mind (Katz 1967, p 129).

Though the system of markers is based on language, it is independent of any particular language, in that the lexicon is part of the human biological and anthropological endowment (*Homo sapiens = Homo loquens*).

We come here to a question of prime importance. To begin with, semantic markers are held to be language invariants, i. e., universals of language, or properties of human language in general, rather than of some particular language.

The problem of language universals highlights once more the precarious position of the Chomsky–Katz–Fodor linguistic theory and its concept of competence relative to biology and anthropology (mentioned before, in Chap. 3). Let us quote another of Chomsky's allusions to biology which lack any practical consequences:

> The very notion *lexical entry* presupposes some sort of fixed, universal vocabulary in terms of which these objects are characterized ... It is surely our ignorance of the relevant psychological and physiological facts that makes possible the widely held belief that there is little or no *a priori* structure to the system of "attainable concepts" (1965, p 160).

In their dictionary, Katz and Fodor make room for only one kind of structure: the logical kind in terms of *genus proximum* and *differentia specifica*. Here we come to the other reason why we believe the present stage in our argument to be so important. Postulating the universality of semantic markers, Katz and Fodor seem to fall back on the cognitive structure of the human mind; in doing so they ease a little, though in a tacit way, the constraints stemming from the notion of the ideal speaker–hearer's competence, a notion cut loose from any biologic properties of that structure (limitations of memory, limited processing capacity for sensory data, etc.). Envisaging the lexicon as a structured data store, one cannot possibly ignore the essential attributes of cognitive structure, and even less play them down as deficiencies of performance. Storing is possible precisely because of capacity, attention, intention, etc., and it is meaningless to refer to capacity without taking account of its limitations, or to speak of attention without accounting for its fluctuations, and the like.

Has the gulf between competence and performance been bridged by Katz and Fodor? Not in the least. In spite of their promising start they abide by the competent, but blindfolded, world-ignorant, and inert (ideal) speaker-hearer. In discussing the possible effect of world knowledge on what their theory holds to be anomalous sentences (e. g., "smiling meadow", which is perfectly acceptable for a *real* speaker-hearer as a metaphor!), Katz and Fodor (1963, p 179) maintain that a semantic theory accounting for such effects

> cannot in principle distinguish between the speaker's knowledge of his language and his knowledge of the world . . . And since there is no serious possibility of systematizing all the knowledge of the world that speakers store, and since a theory of the kind we have been discussing requires such a systematization, it is *ipso facto* not a serious model for semantics.

That the authors have opted to sacrifice the goals of their theory to preserve its elegance will be shown even more compellingly in our discussion of metaphor (Chap. 7, where the same passage is quoted once again).

The assumption that the status of semantic dimensions cannot be separated from the question about their origins and psychological functioning has been pursued far more tenaciously by Bierwisch (1967). After stressing that semantic dimensions or markers are "simply primitive formal elements", he immediately puts the question: "In what way, by what type of phenomena, are they motivated outside the structure of language in the narrower sense?" (p 2). With this one question Bierwisch has torn down the fence around language-as-such and language-in-itself, a fence that forced Katz to assume – in sterile fashion – that if we just look at any set of objects belonging to one class we are inspired at once by the idea embodied in the semantic marker of that class.

It is in the context of this problem that we can appreciate the magnitude of the advance made by Bierwisch over and beyond the Katz and Fodor position. Linguists commonly hold – he argues – that semantic properties are definable in terms of classes of objects and properties of the world. When learning a language we have to acquire precisely these object classes, properties, and relationships. According to this view (which Bierwisch himself refuses to accept)

> semantic markers happen to be universal only because different speech communities live in the same universe, and only to the extent that their cultural environment is alike (Bierwisch 1967, p 3).

Language universals are thus accounted for by the ubiquitous traits of the surrounding universe. A strictly functional attribute such as is contained in the fact that we are able to talk about things not directly given to the senses, causes Bierwisch to reject the view outlined above. The homogeneity of all languages and hence the presence of language universals cannot be founded on a homogeneity of the world; the only source can be the universality of the mental apparatus of the world-interacting human being. In effect, Bierwisch takes seriously a view on the origins of semantic markers which Katz and Fodor merely intimated without heeding its implications. He says:

> semantic markers in an adequate description of a natural language do not represent properties of the surrounding world in the broadest sense, but rather certain deep-seated, innate properties of the human organism and the perceptual apparatus, properties which determine the way in which the universe is conceived, adapted, and worked on (Bierwisch 1967, p 3).

With one stroke (which originates in Humboldt and, further back, in Kant) the curtain has been raised to disclose grand prospects before our eyes: linguistics starts to look for support in anthropology, and hence in psychology; the gulf between competence and performance, hitherto passable in only one direction, is thus closing, and mutual inspiration between linguistics and psychology becomes possible. The constructs needed to account for linguistic structures – in this case: semantic markers of different kinds and functions – can also be usefully applied to the description of other mental operations. And conversely, psychological evidence in the realm of perception, thinking, retention and recall, etc. can now benefit the linguist.

Invited by Bierwisch to consider semantic markers as "deep-seated, innate properties of the human organism and of the perceptual apparatus", we have not far to delve into psychology for the material by which to construct a bridge. It is clearly discernible in the edifice of Gestalt psychology: could the universally innate dimensions of the lexicon belong to what the psychology of perception and thinking called – vaguely and yet convincingly – gestalt properties? Should not (Animate) in semantic space be an equally "good" gestalt as is *vertical* in perceptual space? Bierwisch (1970, p 182) has no doubt something of this kind in mind when he says

> basic components of this type might be X GREATER [than] Y representing the general ability of comparison, ... X CHANGE TO P, X CAUSE P ...

A number of arguments speak for this. The ontogeny of the lexicon structure cannot conceivably start from a tabula rasa. The articulation of the external reality into figure and ground, or objects in general, is accomplished in such uniform fashion in otherwise very different individuals that their separate learning histories cannot be held responsible for this feat. Quine (1960) wrote of the skeptical linguist who set out to learn an unfamiliar language and got to hear something that could be taken to stand for *rabbit*. But how can he tell that it is not the word for *fur*, or *head*, or *animal*, or *rabbit-like shape*, or *brown*, or perhaps the *forefeet and the ground between them?* Evidently because both the linguist and his informant possess the same cognitive endowment needed to handle the external reality. At no point of development does the child form concepts or designations for, e. g., feet plus floor, or the spaces between tree boughs (cf. Macnamara 1972, p 3).

When in the course of order-imposing apprehension of reality anything is perceived as a figure against a ground, it is so (in any event at the level under discussion) because of the operation of "laws" which are part of the basic endowment of the human species. (The far-reaching implications of the figure–ground articulation are discussed at a later stage.) Associations cannot explain the fact that entirely different imprints on the retina, totally dissimilar tactile sensations, and wholly disparate acoustic impressions converge into the object *that dog Prince*. This convergence has its source in man's biological disposition to approach a world which consists of objects – objects the dimensions of which are determined by man's perceptual apparatus. "The human being arrives object-disposed to enter by the door of the moment" (von Allesch).

From this vantage point the semantic marker (Physical Object) is to be conceived, in its origins and effects, in quite another way than that suggested by Katz and Fodor with their list of *stone, building, planet, chair,* etc. A semantic marker does not spring up as an idea in the course of an abstracting inspection of a set of objects somehow belonging together. Rather, *stone, building, planet,* and *chair* are grouped together because one of the world-ordering categories with which we are endowed by biology is addressed by these objects in equal measure. Arnheim (1947, p 69) has described the process of perception in very similar terms:

> Perhaps perception consists in the application, to the stimulus material, of "perceptual categories", such as roundness, redness, smallness, symmetry, verticality, etc., which are evoked by the structure of the given configuration ... There is a fitting of perceptual characteristics to the structure suggested by the stimulus material rather than a reception of this material itself.

With this citation we are reminded of some arguments advanced earlier in a different context (Chap. 1). How closely interrelated perception and comprehension might be can be read from the question with which Arnheim supplements his speculation:

> Are these categories not the indispensable prerequisites which permit us to understand perceptually? (*loc. cit.*)

Very clearly, Arnheim anticipated a theory which twenty years later was popularized by Neisser and others under the term *analysis-by-synthesis*. The sensory or perceptual categories mentioned by Arnheim – in analogy to which we have tried to conceptualize the semantic categories of the lexicon – function in a manner offering certain clues as to how understanding proceeds:

> Our assumption is that the individual stimulus configuration [in analogy: the word as received by the ear – H. H.] enters the perceptual process only in that it evokes a specific pattern of general sensory categories, which *stands* for the stimulus [as the cluster of the respective semantic markers stands for the meaning of the word – H. H.] in a similar way in which in a scientific description a network of general concepts is offered as the equivalent of a phenomenon of reality ... If this theory be acceptable, the elementary processes of perception, far from being mere passive registration, would be creative acts of grasping structure ... Perceiving would represent individual cases through configurations of general categories (p 70).

Enriched by the notion of analysis-by-synthesis which runs parallel to that of isomorphism, Gestalt psychology seems to offer certain clues as to the nature of those "deep-seated, innate properties of the human organism and of the perceptual apparatus" which – in perception as well as language – "determine the way in which the universe is conceived, adapted, and worked on," to quote Bierwisch again. (Roundness), (Verticality), (Physical Object) and, presumably, (Animate) may safely be supplemented by (Cause/Effect), a relationship present also in the unanalyzed phenomenon about which we have learned from Michotte.

Undoubtedly one could successfully search for more evidence of these inborn assimilating procedures, particularly in ethological literature, but we would soon tire of it. We ought rather to ask at this point whether Bierwisch's nativist search design allows us to find enough structure to arrange a lexicon of the Katz-Fodor type – as initially aimed for. By upholding, with Bierwisch (1967, p 3), Postal's postulate that

> each of these primitives bears a fixed relation to the universe which is determined by the biological structure of the organism

and hence inherited (to add after Bierwisch), we can certainly link up with the findings of Gestalt psychology, but these findings are too meager and undifferentiated to yield anything resembling, in order of magnitude, the matrix required by the formal calculus of a theory of the Chomsky-Katz-Fodor type. Bierwisch has himself noticed the precarious situation resulting from the assumption of genetically determined structures. He makes it clear

> that the idea of innate basic elements of the semantic structure does not entail a biological determination of concepts or meanings in a given language, but only of their ultimate components. These components can be combined rather freely and differently in different languages (Bierwisch 1967, p 4).

The view that the human "perceptual apparatus" owes its differentiation (as evidenced also in language) to the recombination of a few genetically determined ultimate components seems to me untenable, in the same way that the (Berlin) Gestalt psychologists' confinement to the perception of "inborn" figures had been untenable. Gestalt psychology was eventually forced to accommodate the perception of figures acquired by learning (e. g., letters, digits, phonemes, faces) within its theoretical framework, hoping thus not to hear the cracking in the foundations of its edifice. In fact, it has never supplied us with an explanation of how the physiology-inspired isomorphism hypothesis – developed to account for the perception of "inborn" figures (circle, square, . . .) – could be extended to cover the perception of "acquired" figures.

An attempt at conceptualizing the structural traits of the lexicon in as language-like and hence as differentiated a fashion as was done by Katz and Fodor (for whom practically every word, except for proper names, could become a marker) cannot possibly be based on a complete genetic determination of the system. Being biologically disposed to cope with his environment (and thus capable of perceiving objects and distinguishing top from bottom and cause from effect), the human being deals in his use of language with a world that is much too complex to be grasped by the mere projection of various recombinations of a few inborn markers. The perceptual apparatus must acquire ever new structures by learning, among them new ordering and semantic dimensions at different levels of abstraction and complexity.

There is a further complication in sight. The ability to perceive things as similar and to group them accordingly does not necessarily lead to an identification of what is responsible for the similarity. Deese (1969, p 520) makes the point that

> as often as not the ability to perceive grouping does not lead to the correct identification of the underlying features which account for or justify the grouping.

Grouping and extraction of underlying attributes are not as intimately and inevitably interlocked as has been assumed by logicians ever since Locke. In Deese's words,

> there is not always the kind of relation between these operations that there should be. There is, in fact, some slippage.

The frequent overdetermination of linguistic processes makes it difficult to identify the underlying structures.

Here we find our craft drifting into open waters. Our original lead ("genetically determined") has faded away and our point of departure (Katz and Fodor's semantic theory) has been compromised by its uncompromising competence/performance dichotomy. Let us stop and think it over.

What we want is to gain insight into the structure of our internal lexicon and – by the same token – into the functioning of that lexicon in actual language use. Moreover, we may consider ourselves unconstrained by any boundaries as between competence and performance, or between linguistics and psychology, or even between syntax, semantics, and pragmatics (which remains to be shown).

Unconstrained, but at the same time unsupported, by the various solutions proposed by linguists to date, we are now ready to delve anew into the question of the lexicon, this time one step closer to actual language processes.

It has been noted before that Katz and Fodor's design for framing the meaning of words as the sum total of a limited number of semantic dimensions is not a novel idea in linguistics. As was pointed out by Marshall (1970, p 189),

> The notion that ... the lexical items of natural languages are represented as compositional functions of more "primitive" conceptual elements ... occur(s) ... under a wide variety of names: *sememes* in stratificational theory, *meaning components* in componential analysis, *minimal units of content* in the writings of Hjelmslev, *semantic markers* (or *features*) in transformational theory.

These semantic elements are in two ways more "primitive" than a word. Primitiveness was understood by Bierwisch as "genetically determined and hence preceding words". An alternative interpretation of primitiveness would be as "simpler and more limited in number" than are words, in the sense that the structural description of many words can be accomplished with a smaller number of elementary dimensions. This is a vital aspect: one such elementary dimension is shared by many words that are similar, or identical, in a particular respect. The notion of similarity on which our discussion now focuses coincides, on the one hand, with Katz and Fodor's procedure but on the other, gives access – by the technique used to assess similarity – to a broad range of psychological evidence including the first pregenerative developments in modern psycholinguistics as authored by Osgood and Carroll (which is not a mere coincidence of history!).

Similarity as embodiment of a connection, of some kind of belonging together, may be reversed into *connection as index of similarity*. And by this token we come now to the key concept of a psychology that laid the foundation for the modern era of this science over a hundred years ago: the concept of association.

In employing the concept one ought to bear the following distinction in mind: the term *association* refers both to the interconnection existing between two mental states and the resulting reciprocal calling into mind of these states (e. g., two words), *and* to the presumed cause of the interconnection, i. e., the mechanism or process of associating itself. Two such causes have been known since antiquity: temporal contiguity and similarity.

The most famous psycholinguistic instrument for the identification of dimensions in semantic space, Osgood's Semantic Differential (SD), falls back on all these aspects of the association concept. In view of the intricacy of its theoretical groundwork – itself an impressive feat of "enlightened neobehaviorism" – and the striking relevance of its output, no empirically-minded psychologist of language can any longer afford to heed the taboo under which Chomsky has put the entire complex of learning theory, behaviorism, S-R theory, and associationism; neither can we heed the protests of Fodor, Garrett, and others. The generative grammarians had set out to develop a formal theory accounting for the intuitions of the ideal speaker-hearer concerning the well-formedness of sentences, and their goal could not be served by a simple associationist-behavioristic theory. But the conclusion drawn therefrom by many linguists to dismiss as unreasonable every piece of evidence contributed by associationist-motivated theories of verbal behavior reveals its unreasonableness as soon as an attempt is made to break down the walls surrounding the concept of competence.

Osgood is well outside these walls. What was his idea? Whereas Katz and Fodor were in pursuit of structuring the lexicon of the competent language user (and hence describing the meaning of words) in a manner that would render the structure useful for developing a theory of the sentence (e. g., with a view to resolving ambiguities), Osgood was guided by the desire to describe words so as to ensure

1) that the description would satisfy specific criteria of objectivity

2) that the description would be usefully employed in developing a theory of verbal (and nonverbal) behavior

3) that the structure described in this way would be compatible with existing psychological theorems and theories.

As we shall see later, these three goals can be kept apart even when one wishes to form a general opinion on the success or failure of the Osgood design.

Osgood has published several accounts of his procedure and its theoretical framework. In what follows we shall refer mainly to Osgood (1968 and 1971a).

It might be useful to start with a specification of the three conceptual models integrated in the SD: a spatial model, a measurement model, and a behavioral model. In describing the origin of the SD we shall deal with the first two models, whereas the third model will enable us to discuss the theoretical framework (and substantiation) of Osgood's project.

Semantic space can be most readily conceptualized by invoking the familiar three-dimensional color space as an analogy. Its origin, or zero point, indicates colorlessness, i. e., the neutral grey: in the analogous semantic space the origin would represent meaninglessness. Any color elsewhere in the color space (any concept or word located elsewhere in semantic space) can be specified by the vector extending from the origin. The length of the vector represents the saturation of the color (the meaningfulness of the concept or word), and the direction of the vector represents luminosity (brightness) and hue; what it represents in semantic space can be first defined only in formal terms as the dimensions of semantic quality. In the case of the color space the dimensions have been empirically determined: the brightness dimension is physiologically based on the activation or deactivation of receptors of *all* types and the hue dimension is based on the differential activation of specific types of receptors. The dimensions of semantic space are initially undefined in both number and quality. They could be identified if there were a way to measure the length and direction of the vector extending to the respective concept (or word). This is where the measurement model comes in.

If a person is asked for the meaning of a word, she or he is apt to give a verbal reply, unless there is the possibility of an ostensive definition. We may obtain verbal replies that are amenable to interindividual comparison only if we present subjects with standard samples of replies.

Such standardized replies must be translatable into the semantic space model – states the next requirement. This can be achieved by using bipolar scales (big-little, beautiful-ugly, swift-slow); the midpoint of each scale indicates neutrality or "meaninglessness" on the respective dimension. Any midpoint corresponds to the origin of semantic space.

To start with, the experimenter is free to choose any number of any scales, but he should mind one criterion: that the distribution of these scales over semantic space be such as to reveal the hitherto unknown dimensionality of the space (for which only the origin is known in advance). Osgood argues like this: anyone who rates the word *sin* on the scale *good–bad* near the *bad* pole is apt to rate *sin* closer to *ugly* than to *beautiful,* and closer to *reprehensible* than to *desirable.* On discovering such interconnections between scales also for other concepts (e. g., *nurse* is rated likewise closer to *good, beautiful,* and *desirable*), we may interpret this as evidence of a certain affinity between the respective scales: in spite of the differences, the covarying scales have one semantic dimension in common.

By reversing this line of reasoning we can apply factor analysis to the intercorrelations of such ratings to obtain the minimum number of mutually independent dimensions needed to account mathematically for those intercorrelations.

In line with his reasoning, Osgood presents his subjects with a single concept (a word or phrase), like *sin, America,* or *I beg* you, with the instruction to rate it on a number of bipolar dimensions as if in response to the (tacit) question: is *sin* more beautiful or ugly? Not being interested in individual semantic spaces, the investigator sums up the ratings across subjects, factorizes the data, and arrives in this way at three dimensions of semantic space: Evaluation (E), Potency (P), and Activity (A).

What are these dimensions like?

Application of the factor-analytic measurement model provides a framework of under-lying dimensions which is common to both concept meanings and scale meanings and in terms of which both can be described in relation to each other. These underlying dimensions thus have the functional properties of semantic features (Osgood 1971a, p 14).

The author refers here to the same notion we were discussing in the first part of this chapter in connection with a conception of the lexicon proposed by linguists.

The term *semantic feature* as used by Osgood requires some elaboration; for the moment we only know how he arrived at these features. Osgood tries to explain what he means by his features by referring to the behavioral model. His "rep-resentational mediation theory" is neobehavioristic in so far as it calls in the principles of classic learning theory (primarily the concept of conditioning) in a precarious effort to explain how "connections" are formed that have no observ-able representation in behavior:

A stimulus pattern S which is not the same physical event as the thing signified Š will become a sign of that significate when it becomes conditioned to a mediation process, this process: (a) being some distinctive representation of the total behavior (R_T) pro-duced by the significate, and (b) serving to mediate overt behaviors (R_x) to the sign which are appropriate to ... the significate (*op. cit.*, p 11).

The same idea is presented in diagram form in Fig. 2.

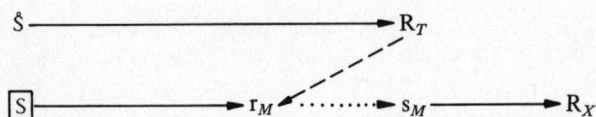

Fig. 2. Osgood's mediating response (for legend see quotation). (After Osgood, 1971a, p. 17)

There we have the sign concept of learning theory in merry jubilation: things that frequently go together (Š and S) get associated, so that S now evokes the reaction which previously was produced by Š, the significate, alone. Well, it is not quite as in Pavlov! The essential difference is that Osgood has inserted a covert link, another segment of the S–R connection, the mediation process r_M ... s_M. This hypothetical construct is accompanied by two postulates:

1) The mediation process is a covert response which acquires the character of a stimulus for subsequent behavioral responses.

In the adult human language user, ..., these mediating events have become purely cortical processes, processes whose neurological nature and locus will remain obscure for a very long time (*op. cit.*, p 13).

2) The mediation link $r_M \ldots s_M$ is made up of components:

A relatively small number of independent r_m components, by virtue of their combination in diverse simultaneous patterns, can serve to differentiate the meanings of a very large number of distinctive total r_M's, each related to its source behavior (R_T) uniquely[2] – but uniquely as a whole, not in terms of its unique components (*loc. cit.*).

In fact, the components of a particular r_{M_1}, that is, r_{m_1}, r_{m_2}, ..., when functioning in other combinations, may determine the character of r_{M_2}:
$$r_{M_2} = [r_{m_2}, r_{m_8}, r_{m_{12}}].$$
That is to say, r_M is resolvable into a "simultaneous cluster of distinctive features"; the number of the latter is smaller than the number of r_M.

By spanning the three models we realize that Osgood *identifies*:

a) the semantic factors or features of the measurement model with the affective components (the r_m's) of the representational mediation process, and

b) the points of the measurement space and semantic space representing the meaning of concepts with the global and the specific mediation processes (the r_M's) purportedly evoked by signs.

However unwillingly, we might accept this view of the genesis of the internal representation of signs (though neither temporal contiguity nor differential reinforcement can lend validity to the notion of conditioning as a vehicle of learning). But the idea that r_m is anchored in R_T, by which semantic differences are attributed to differences in behavior toward things, rather than to differences in the perception of things must evoke strong protest.

Osgood's position has indeed attracted a great deal of "metaphysical repugnance", as Osgood himself is prepared to admit, even though he had taken pains to point out that this anchoring is located somewhere in the history of the individual speaker and not in the genesis of the current linguistic event.

In any case, Osgood has in this respect some strange bedfellows, namely:

a) Marxist psycholinguistics from Vygotsky to Leontev, where genetically the emphasis is placed on the priority of activity

b) Piaget with his derivation of cognitive conceptualization from the sensorimotor behavior of the child[3].

In postulating this anchoring, Osgood has two goals in mind: (1) "to eliminate the circularity of defining semantic features in terms of perceptible distinctions", and (2) to be able to tell "what differences that are perceptibly discriminable ... come to make a difference in meaning" (Osgood 1971b, p 526).

The "anchoring in observable behavior" postulated by Osgood would greatly increase the value of his theory if it could be shown to exist. Short of this, the concept is burdened with a major weakness: Osgood withdraws by and large

---

[2] Earlier Osgood used to say that the mediation link consists of easily conditionable affective components of the total response R_T.

[3] One is tempted to speculate that Piaget's approach is called cognitive chiefly because his account of how cognition emerges is less precise than that of the behaviorist Osgood.

into some unspecified biographic past and seeks to account for the *process* of anchoring by means of a theoretical construct that fails to explain precisely the *persistence* of anchoring. The point is that conditioning is inseparably linked with extinction.

In one way or another, we cannot fail to notice the limitations of Osgood's theory which, on the one hand, is locked within the narrow S-R framework and, on the other, is not prepared to envision the possibility that the mediation link, instead of being a mere r_M-s_M aggregate, might be conceived of as a state of consciousness.

According to Osgood (1971a, p 15), the sign-related mediation process represents a "set of simultaneous responses in a number of different reaction systems". If we assume that the components of the mediation process (the r_m's) represent those aspects of the global behavior (R_T) toward an object ($\check{S}$) that have been differentially reinforced (this being the only way of their association with $\boxed{S}$),

> it follows that the most common and therefore shared components of the meanings of different signs will be derived from those reaction systems which are behaviorally significant, which make a difference in meaning. The affective reactions underlying E, P, and A have just such properties (Osgood 1971a, p 16).

Osgood's claim that with his mediation model, or in any case with the SD, he is able to explore the basic dimensions of semantic space, is open to the kind of test provided by empirical science for the purpose: the construct must prove its usefulness in explaining observable behavior. The most convincing test is for Osgood his large-scale cross-cultural project under which the semantic differential has been applied to twenty different speech communities at 25 points of the globe and the data were factorized, yielding everywhere the factors Evaluation, Potency, and Activity.

Hence, E, P, and A are those dimensions of meaning that have more ground than any other to be regarded as universals of language, although it remains open whether they can be viewed as innate in a strict sense, or whether we merely inherit the inevitability with which they develop in the course of culturally nonspecific learning processes.

Linguists who have followed our account of Osgood's theory up to this point, possibly with some reluctance, are apt to come up with the remark that the SD may have proved useful in the identification of dimensions of connotative (or affective) meaning. And since the other sciences are prone to allocate the sphere of emotions to psychology, it may be acknowledged that Osgood the psychologist has discovered something about connotative meaning; the true and really important meaning however is denotative meaning. But upon closer scrutiny we find that a clear-cut distinction between denotative and connotative meaning is extremely difficult to uphold, in the absence of an ostensive and at the same time complete reference. If we take words like *love, freedom, Jesus, animal, to weep,* and *tired* – where should we place the boundary between denotation and connotation?

The more difficult it is to find such a boundary, the more weight Osgood's investigation carries for linguistics as a whole. To exemplify this weight, let us contrast Osgood's semantic dimensions with those proposed by Katz and Fodor.

The latter authors postulate a theoretically unlimited number of possibly relevant semantic markers; by saying *possibly* we wish to stress that their relevance has been demonstrated so far only in the resolution of semantic ambiguities, the justification of paraphrases, and the avoidance of anomalies (where it does not work, as will be shown in due course). Katz and Fodor have devised their semantic markers for the description of words in such a way as to use the descriptions for developing a theory of the sentence. By contrast, Osgood employs a very precise discovery procedure – which does not rely on the "springing up" of the common denominator – to obtain a limited number of semantic features that enable him to describe words in such a way as to make this description compatible with a theory of behavior.

Osgood is able to link up his design with a general theory of behavior not only by providing an account of the emergence of his dimensions in terms of learning theory, but also by establishing a connection between affective word meaning and the role of affect in human behavior. He says:

> ... why E, P, and A? It has nothing to do with connotations of the term *connotation* which I used to call what the SD measures, but rather, I think, with the importance of emotion or feeling in human affairs.

He further points out

> the essential identity of ... E-P-A factors to the dimensions of feeling as described ... by Wundt ... and in studies of communication via facial expressions ... Consistent with my behavioristic theory of meaning, it is these pervasive affective features which dominate much of our behavior, including language behavior; we really are – Chomsky and the mentalists to the contrary – still animals at base ... What is important to us now, as it was way back in the age of Neanderthal Man, about the sign of a thing is: First, does it refer to something *good* or *bad* for me? ... Second, does it refer to something which is *strong* or *weak* with respect to me? ... And third, for behavioral purposes, does it refer to something which is *active* or *passive*? ... These "gut" reactions to things and their signs, by every criterion used by linguists, lexicographers, and philosophers, have the properties of semantic features ... (Osgood 1971a, pp 37–38).

Osgood is fully aware of the fact that the "metaphorical" usage of adjectival scale terms enforced by the SD (where the subject *must* decide whether *sin* is closer to *sweet* or to *sour*) causes the scales to rotate toward the E-P-A-dominated space, and that the amassment of scales tending to increase the E, P, and A loadings, serves to emphasize affective features at the expense of nonaffective, i. e., denotative features.

> This is why the SD does not provide a sufficient characterization of meaning. For example, both the pair *Nurse* and *Sincerity* and the pair *Hero* and *Success* have near identical E-P-A factor-scores, that is near identical affective meanings; yet I can say *she's a cute nurse* but I cannot say *she's a cute sincerity* ... But let me hasten to point out that any subset of semantic features must be equally insufficient; if I use only the familiar hierarchical features Concrete/Abstract, Animate/Inanimate, and Human/Non-Human, then all of the semantic ways in which humans differentiate humans ... will disappear, and *Wife* will have the same meaning as *Husband* ... and *Boy* will have the same meaning as *Man* (*op. cit.*, pp 38–39).

In this way Osgood himself singles out one of the most vexing problems that beset the use of the concepts *lexicon* and *semantic feature*. As we have seen with Katz and Fodor, and now with Osgood, semantic features function as designations of categories (comprising the words considered to be equivalent in the critical respect). In effect, all words with the feature (+ *Human*) have in that respect the same "rights and duties" in a sentence that is intended to be acceptable; all the words marked by E+ tend to evoke a positive, rather than a negative, reaction in the language user. Is this sufficient to understand the word? And conversely: is the feature-marked property indispensable to understand the word? On hearing "Look at those beautiful tulips", must I experience a sense of (− *Animate*) in order to understand the utterance?

Evidently, in the final analysis, the inquiry into the dimensions of semantic space cannot be an end in itself. The point is that the question of the number and quality of the dimensions can only be decided when it has become clear what aspects of language use are to be accounted for by the construct and what criteria have to be met in the process.

Rather than pursuing this line of thought let us revert to the point where we began our discussion of Osgood's semantic space. At that point we were concerned with two related issues: (1) are there universal dimensions of word meaning? and (2) do these universal dimensions extend also to nonverbal behavior? Once we agree with Osgood that a certain equivalence of two otherwise different words, such as *sin* and *nurse,* is due to the fact that the r_M's of these words share a particular r_m, we would like to know if the same equivalence might operate – as suggested by Osgood's theory – not only in the rather specific behavior of semantic differentiation but in other kinds of behavior, too.

The anticipation that extreme rankings on dimension E (Evaluation) would be accompanied by either approach or withdrawal reactions, and extreme rankings on dimension A (Activity) by the urge to either perform movements or not, etc., was voiced long ago by Carroll (1959), in his review of Osgood's earlier publication. In an empirical study of the issue, Solars (1960) found significantly shorter latencies for "compatible" reactions (pulling "pleasant" words closer and pushing "unpleasant" words away) than for "incompatible" ones. Ertel and his students have made a number of studies to establish a connection between Osgood's affective semantic dimensions and self-observations from which certain personality factors could be deduced. Thus, Ertel (1970, p 264) was able to report:

> Extravert subjects possess a strongly activity-positive, and further a potency- and valence-positive self-concept, neurotoid subjects a valence- and potency-negative, and rigid subjects an activity-negative self-concept with medium valence and potency.

This and other findings (Ertel 1967; Ertel and Prodöhl 1969; Ertel and Theophile 1966) have induced Ertel to interpret Osgood's affective semantic factors as symptoms of "deep-set" base factors (conceived in distinctly Gestalt-psychological terms) which we might designate as vectors of linguistic and nonlinguistic processes.

The conceptual line adopted by these authors is one of deepening the dimensions identified by Osgood – and here one ought to bear in mind the fact that in his earlier work Osgood had thought of his constructs merely as dimensions of connotation; only in recent years has he identified them with dimensions of the emotional sphere. The original purposes of Katz and Fodor's semantic markers and of Osgood's early semantic features were to serve the description of lexicon structure and, eventually, of language structure. In effect, the features specified primarily the attributes needed to identify the linguistic units admissible in particular places of the sentence (Katz-Fodor) or at particular moments in behavior (Osgood). Semantic features of this sort answer the question: "What is this?"

The course taken by Osgood in recent years, as well as the line followed by Ertel in extension of Osgood's ideas, is basically the same as the direction followed by, for instance, Bever, and also by the linguists Fillmore and Chafe. They all pursue a somewhat different question: "What does it do?" Their attention has shifted from the exclusively identifying attributes of linguistic units to the functional role of semantic (or cognitive, or conceptual, or relational) units.

Ertel's primary goal is to replace Osgood's associationist position, as revealed in his description of the semantic differential (*father* is more strongly associated with *square* than with *round*), by a relational approach. The judgmental object O *(father)* fits phenomenally better the relational object A *(square)* than the relational object B *(round)*. Exploring the quality of subjective experiences, Ertel has been able to identify some other types of relations, and has arrived at three: consonance, dominance, and connectedness. By consonance is meant a marked similarity or concordance between the rated object and the self. From this formal relation there emerges the (affective) general quality of Evaluation, as we know it from Osgood's SD. In similar fashion, from the relation of the self's dominance over the object there arises the (inverse) quality of Potency, and from the complexity of the interconnections, the state described in the SD as Excitation or Activity.

Ertel's approach is both important and interesting on a number of counts. For one thing, he is a modern exponent of the old tendency of Gestalt psychology to reduce differences in substance to differences in form. For another, we cannot fail to notice that he is responsible for a remarkable generalization of an idea (Osgood's) that was initially aimed at pinpointing the meaning of words:

> A characteristic trait of the theory is its general nature, which prevents us from pigeonholing it as a theory of thinking, of perception, of emotions, and so on. The theory enables us to construct hypotheses for diverse phenomenal observation spheres and for interphenomenal relationships (Ertel 1967, p 53).

Inspired by his theoretical position, Ertel himself has been able to predict and explain findings obtained in the study of sound symbolism, an area traditionally foreign to the mainstream of psychological theorizing. Perhaps the most impressive piece of evidence to the effect that both linguistic and nonlinguistic actions are pervaded with specific relational structures was furnished by Ertel in the account of an experiment conducted together with Bloemer (1975); this is described briefly below, even though it anticipates in many ways the further course of our argument.

The difference between affirmation and negation is, according to Ertel, that the former emphasizes consonance (as conceived in his theory) while in negation something like the separation of two dissonant cognitive entities takes place. Affirmation joins together, negation takes apart.

> If it is true that there are associative and dissociative *components* of action underlying the processes of linguistic affirmation and negation, then these should also be effective as components of appropriate *nonlinguistic* action (Ertel and Bloemer 1975, p 337).

To test his hypothesis, Ertel devised an experiment in which subjects were required to learn affirmative or negative sentences and at the same time were given the task of either putting together or separating plastic squares that had been cut in two. His subjects performed significantly better in the condition of consonance between the action components of the manual task and those of the sentences than in the other condition.

Ertel interprets this outcome "within a model of sentence use which emphasizes a general constructive component" (*op. cit.,* p 335). For the time being we shall content ourselves with the conclusion that, by his reduction of Osgood's affective dimensions to formal-relational ones, Ertel has succeeded in uncovering manifestly deep-seated structures of meaning that go far beyond the sphere of language. Put alongside all the hitherto discussed semantic structures, Ertel's construct comes presumably closest to Bierwisch's postulates. Reviewed here in a cursory fashion, these elementary cognitive impulses and tendencies are later discussed at several places (e. g., in Chap. 12), in a variety of contexts.

Let us switch again from those fundamental psychological structures back to those standing closer to language, and repeat the contention that attention has, in the classification of identifying attributes, shifted from "What is it?" to "What does it do?" of a more functionalist approach.

Admittedly, it is difficult to draw a strict dividing line between the problems underlying these two questions. The former is bound to dominate the more one concentrates on the description of a non-functionally conceived linguistic competence, in keeping with the primary theorems of generative grammar. With a more functional approach to language behavior and its embeddedness in the remaining behavior one will tend to emphasize the dynamic qualities of semantic factors – thus overcoming the division into semantics and pragmatics. As can be seen from this, a major recent development in linguistics and psycholinguistics is therefore the gradual rephrasing of the problem "Meaning of a lexical item as function of its location in a structure" into the problem "The function of a lexical item's meaning in relation to the structure and functions of linguistic processes". Semantics is the point where an ostensibly self-contained linguistics is forced to open up toward the world:

> Semantics is that facet of language *[langue]* wherein . . . language may not be envisaged by itself, for it is that facet by which one passes incessantly from language to the world and from the world to language (Mounin 1963, p 138).

As we now return for the third time to the description of lexicon structure, the reader is requested to keep in mind the question "What do the units of this structure do?" as a search design.

Osgood's Semantic Differential serves to describe similarity relations between the concept (word) as a lexicon entry and the dimensions of semantic space. How the semantic features responsible for these relations come into being is explained (by Osgood) with the aid of a learning theory.

Similarity, i. e., the belonging together of words (lexemes), was treated long before Osgood as an indicator of semantic segmentation in the vocabulary of a language, though without the help of a dimensionally structured lexicon. This approach was adopted by the field theorists in German linguistics in the 1920s and 1930s. The following citation characterizes their position (and also their diction):

> It is not that the word as sign is allocated to some existing, clearly delimited, singular conceptual entity; it is only when the word is available in the field that some entity begins to stand out clearly from the earlier available conceptual complex. We fling out a net of words over our hazy and global anticipations to trap them in articulated and delimited concepts. The formation of a concept with the aid of a word is a process by which segments are clarifyingly extracted from a totality ... Reality itself, that is, as given to us, is not independent of type and segmentation in the linguistic structures of symbols (Trier 1931, p 1–2).

What *wise* means can be clearly seen only by someone who knows also that *prudent, clever, intelligent,* ... are available in the vocabulary of his language[4].

What Trier was trying to accomplish with his construction was undoubtedly different from, and perhaps less than, what Katz and Fodor or Osgood were aiming at with theirs. These latter were seeking to reduce the sheer infinity of word meanings to elementary components that could be used in a sort of calculation; the "calculus" was effected by Katz and Fodor with their analysis of sentence meaning, and by Osgood with his analysis of verbal behavior.

The field theorists were not in the least interested in finding out how many (or rather, how few) elementary semantic dimensions the meaning of a word could be reduced to by comparing it with the meanings of other words; on the contrary, they set out to discover even the most subtle differences between words by such comparison.

Their conceptual framework was indeed totally different from the previously discussed one. The Chomsky-Katz-Fodor theory, and also Bierwisch and Osgood, start out by assuming that the substance represented in the vocabulary has some prearranged structure: whether a language-inherent structure of the Chomsky school, or a structure that tallies with the human "perceptual apparatus" (Bierwisch), or a structure of behavior as determined by the inborn laws of learning plus the individual's conditioning record.

In contrast, Trier's concept of field presupposes an "*a priori* undifferentiated

---

[4] Trier's concept of field contrasts sharply with Porzig's. Whereas Trier's concern was to identify a "content mosaic", Porzig (1934) sought to account for "essential meaning relations" between, say, predicate and object (*to fell* applies only to a tree), or between predicate and subject (*to bark* implies *dog* as subject). Thus Porzig was clearly preoccupied, not with any mosaic-like setting, but with dynamic relations as they are discernible in certain contemporary approaches of generative semantics.

substance of the content plane" (Lyons 1968, p 429), which obtains its structure only when the vocabulary of a particular language is imposed on it by what is in fact a process of segmentation.

These radically differing views on the question of linguistic universals prejudge the approach to what investigators from Sapir to Whorf have come to call the problem of linguistic relativity, or linguistic determinism. The fact that the Eskimo have eighteen designations for different varieties of snow would be explained by Trier as showing that their language serves to articulate an initially unstructured conceptual field into eighteen different concepts. Chomsky-Katz-Fodor would probably say that the Eskimo's matrix of the respective semantic dimensions is more densely set with lexical items (and hence displays fewer "accidental lexical gaps") than in the case of speakers of European languages. Bierwisch, in turn, short of assuming some deep-seated psychological differences between Europeans and Eskimos, would point out that the European is essentially capable of attaining the eighteen Eskimo designations for snow. Finally, Osgood might derive the extraordinary differentiation of the Eskimo language from the differentiation of the Eskimo's behavior in relation to snow.

By contrasting the opposing presuppositions of the field theorists (the designations of a language impose structure on an amorphous conceptual field) and the generativists ("behind" the lexical items there is a structure which is not completely isomorphic with them), we are made aware of the dangers involved in the injudicious use of such seemingly innocuous terms as *lexical gap*. The fact is that a lexical gap (and Chomsky distinguishes two kinds of gaps: accidental and systematic ones) can be identified only if it is assumed that "beneath" the gap there extends a continuous structure of the lexicon a certain segment of which remains empty. Before speaking of "lexical gaps" (and also of "attainable concepts") we should carefully check whether by any chance our conceptions of the structure of the lexicon do not stem from an analysis of our vocabulary, and whether we did not make the additional assumption that the structure exists even where there is no evidence for it . . .

The theory of semantic fields is certainly thought-provoking, but it firmly resists any attempt at making it more explicit. Geckeler (1971, p 177), himself a proponent of the conception, says ruefully:

> A major shortcoming of every engagement in world fields to date has been the lack of a method . . . In the absence of an articulate field method, the study of fields has proceeded chiefly on the basis of intuition.

In particular, it has not been possible to elaborate the concept of semantic fields so as to make it serve a sentence semantics or a theory that would bring word meaning in relation to characteristics of behavior. As argued by Baumgärtner (1966, p 169),

> a basic requirement would be not to terminate the inquiry once global meanings have been designated and examined, but to proceed with an analysis of meanings to their minutest components.

Under his own procedure, Baumgärtner merely submits semantic fields as conceived by Trier to componential analysis. His method heeds Katz and Fodor's postulates that the number of components be smaller than the number of meanings. And as practically each component (feature) can be ascribed to more than one lexeme (word), it is viewed as a contextual component, that is, one that can accomodate a plurality of words in one and the same context. *Horse, donkey,* and *mule* belong to the (language-inherent?) semantic class that could be designated *Ridable.* In the process of producing verb components it is realized that the major ones possess the structure and function of adverbial phrases. The components of verb lexemes are thus produced within deep syntax under the category of adverbs and only then elevated to semantic components under a secondary step (leading from object language to metalanguage).

This is an extremely laborious method, one that is open to the dangers posed by both accidental and systematic gaps of the respective vocabulary (perhaps I am unable to discriminate between two verbs only because no differentiating adverb occurs to me?). It is also at the mercy of the linguist's personal inventiveness or unimaginativeness.

Very similar difficulties seem to confront Coseriu (1967), who approaches the word field as a lexical paradigm that emerges from the "segmentation of a lexical content continuum into the various word units of the particular language" (p 294). He proceeds from the assumption that primitive lexical structures (similarly as systems in phonology) are analyzable into smallest discriminable features. But as soon as he is ready to admit that the constitutive features of a word field need not coincide with the features of the respective "thing" itself (cf. Geckeler, 1971, p 199), the identification of these distinctions is again at the mercy of the linguist's individual discriminative powers.

We can put our feet on more solid ground again by turning now to predominantly psychological studies of word fields. We might as well start with an emerging research line which is too young to have discovered its own significance for the theoretical framework of psycholinguistics – the study of *semantic excitation.* Meyer et al. (1974) and Schmidt (1976) describe an experimental paradigm under which subjects have to tell whether a tachistoscopically presented letter string is a word or not. On each trial, two letter strings are presented in brief succession. Shorter response latencies were obtained for words preceded by words from the same semantic field. The processing of the preceding (context) words seemed to lower the excitation threshold in the "neighboring" neural structures. This would mean that the semantic field has its neural equivalent in the form of an interconnected structure.

The theoretical significance of this research design lies also in the inducement it offers for a revival of the probabilistic approach to psycholinguistic problems of the kind dealt with by Miller (1951) in his interpretations of certain regularities of speech perception; the approach has been dropped, unfortunately, from the theoretical armory of psycholinguistics in the wake of the Chomsky-inspired passion for syntax. But the matter will not be pursued here further.

Whereas the study of semantic excitation aims at discovering correlates of the semantic field, the investigations by Szalay and his associates (published between 1970 and 1973) center upon the sociopsychological and ethnopsychological determinants of differences in the scope and structure of semantic fields. Szalay's starting point is not unlike Osgood's. The "subjective culture" he is after is conceived as a group-specific cognitive organization. A group develops a particular way of thinking because its members have acquired convergent "semantic reactions" (of the Osgood type). Szalay is interested in how these reactions interconnect, overlap, and how they come to form fields in the individual. His next step brings him into the realm of ethnopsychology: how do those fields differ from group to group in terms of their scope, composition, and delimitation? For a Christian Scientist (Szalay's example) the word *drug* will have close affinity with *hell,* for a drug addict with *heaven.*

As can be seen from that example, Szalay's concept of semantic field leans more heavily on psychology than on linguistics. Rather than contemplating the "lexical meaning" of words, Szalay visualizes them as Elementary Meaning Units (a term borrowed from Greenberg), i. e., as resolvable units of cognitive processes, each consisting of disparate components:

> an individual's meaning of *drug* includes elements of visual images (white pill), contexts of use (headache), brands (Bayer), affective reactions (bitter taste, dislike), and function (restoration of health). The saliency of imagery, cognitive elements, and evaluations varies (Szalay and Maday 1973, p 34).

Employing a multiple-association procedure, Szalay identifies the priorities established in different cultures for the respective domain: American students tend to group around the word *educated* concepts chiefly relating to knowledge and learning while (South) Korean students include the aspect of social and moral leadership. The semantic fields around the concept *educated* is obviously not identical in the two cultures. (The term *education,* by the way, shows much more concurrence.)

In contrast to Osgood, whose Semantic Differential serves to disclose primarily the universal, i. e., language- and culture-invariant structures of semantic space, Szalay seeks to demonstrate the existing differences between cultures, and also subcultures within one language [e. g., Szalay and Bryson's (1973) comparative study of American blacks and whites].

A strictly psycholinguistic investigation of semantic fields is that by Fillenbaum and Rapoport (1971). Unlike Szalay, who set out to discover the structuring and boundaries of such fields, these two authors start from what intuitively appears to them to be a semantic field (much like Trier and Baumgärtner).

Their study is theoretically less sophisticated but mathematically much more elaborate than Osgood's, and methodologically incomparably more precise and better controlled than Baumgärtner's. Theirs is a structuralist approach, as can be seen from the following definition:

> ...the meaning of a lexical item is a function of the meaning relations obtaining between that item and other items in the same domain (p VII).

Thus, meaning is interpreted as function of position held in a particular structure. Whereas the field theorist scans his memory in search of whatever adjectives or adverbs might occur to him as he inspects a particular semantic field composed of verbs, Fillenbaum and Rapoport use no further analytic specification when asking their subjects for similarities between test words, in keeping with the rational precept: words of similar meaning belong together, and what is grouped together in the lexicon is indicative of its structure.

In their attempt to reveal these structures, the two authors take advantage of the more moderate climate of the post-behaviorist era: they feel no need to bother their subjects with a procedure purporting to investigate associations as a form of behavior (as in the case of Osgood) and are free to put direct questions about similarities between lexical items. Having developed a number of quite sophisticated classification and scaling procedures, they apply them to the presumed domains (subdivisions) of the subjective lexicon (kinship terms, prepositions, verbs of judging, . . .). In the classification procedure proposed by Miller (1969, p 170) for the study of semantic problems for instance, the subject is given a number of words with the request to assign them to any number of groups, as they seem to belong together. To perform his task, the subject must

> ignore some of their distinguishing features. The fewer the features distinguishing two terms or the less important these features, the more likely that the terms will be assigned to the same group ... The issue then becomes one of trying "to discover which conceptual features have been ignored and, thus, by indirection, what the features are" (Fillenbaum and Rapoport 1971, p 187).

A very important point comes here to our attention, one that is only implied in Katz and Fodor's study and totally irrelevant in Osgood's: the features of a lexical item vary in importance, hence it is possible to identify a hierarchy of features. For Katz and Fodor and people like them a word is an "unstructured heap of features" (to repeat Weinreich's caustic remark). This finding is by no means contradicted by the fact that Katz and Fodor revel in displaying the meaning of a word in a tree diagram: despite appearances they treat all semantic markers as being of equal importance, and they present no valid arguments for any particular sequence in which their markers should be applied in generating a sentence. Osgood, on the other hand, states explicitly that his E-P-A features are not ordered hierarchically. Indeed, the relative importance of different features is a problem which cannot be separated from that of the number and order of features.

Going beyond "the study of dimensionality of semantic spaces", Fillenbaum and Rapoport (1971, p 4) have set themselves a more ambitious goal:

> employing graph and clustering techniques which make minimal assumptions about the data, we have attempted to extract additional structural properties.

Trying to exemplify Fillenbaum and Rapoport's analysis in the case of kinship terms, we are bound to introduce here two rival anthropological models, used by the two authors as an extralinguistic frame of reference.

Wallace and Atkins (1960) proposed a three-dimensional system: a sex dimension (with two levels: male and female), a generation dimension (two above ego, one above ego, ego, one below ego, two below ego), and a lineality dimension[5].

---

[5] "Lineals are persons who are ancestors or descendants of ego; colineals are non-lineals all of whose ancestors include, or are included in, all the ancestors of ego; ablineals are consanguineal relatives who are neither lineals nor colineals ..."

The rival model of Romney and D'Andrade (1964) has likewise sex as its first dimension, but its generation dimension provides for only three levels (ego, ego ± 1, ego ± 2); a third dimension, named "reciprocal" takes care of such distinctions as grandfather/grandson; there is further a contrast between direct and collateral terms.

The evidence produced by Fillenbaum and Rapoport with the aid of their diverse techniques speaks clearly in favor of the latter model. Whereas in the Wallace-Atkins model *grandfather* and *grandson* stand far apart, Fillenbaum and Rapoport's subjects tended to group them close together, and this fact finds a ready explanation in the reciprocal dimension.

The general psycholinguistic relevance of Fillenbaum and Rapoport's study rests, however, on what the data suggest in matters of the relative *importance* of the dimensions. For instance, it was found

> that terms differing only with regard to sex characteristically fall very close together, while collaterals are usually considerably displaced from the direct terms, etc. (p 82).

This finding cannot fail to arouse the attention of students of lexicology. Are we indeed justified in regarding the finding that father and mother, uncle and aunt, and son and daughter are described (pairwise) as very similar, as evidence that the sex dimension is attributed less weight than, say, the generation dimension (which distinguishes between son and grandson)? Is it legitimate to speak of "less weight" in general, or should we rather add the qualification: "weight in a particular decision"? In this study the scaling is performed on words as such, rather than words embedded in any message. Pursuing the matter: might not the sex dimension become important if the scaling was performed, not in terms of similarity in general, but similarity in respect of qualification for child care, or even similarity in respect of qualification for sexual relations?

Could it be that the sex of a person and the role of sex affiliation in a particular communication setting is represented by extralinguistic factors? Or is sex affiliation so deeply rooted in our language-based knowledge of the world that the words used for its designation need not reflect its weight? It might even be suspected that the sex dimension is so evident and so obviously important that it is simply disregarded by subjects asked to scale the similarity between two words.

Before questions of this kind are – however reluctantly – allowed to enter our deliberations one might reflect upon their possible consequences. What would the assignment of greater weight to one or another dimension imply for the conception of the lexicon? It would mean that in addition to naming the dimensions of a lexical item the investigator would have to determine their relevance profile. And this raises the next question: is a lexical item to be specified in terms of dimensions that remain fixed in one and the same hierarchy of relations as designated by their relevance profile irrespective of circumstances? As soon as we admit the possibility that the relative ranks of those dimensions might vary under the impact of external factors, both linguistic and nonlinguistic, the entire conception of the lexicon as a fixed store of items is in jeopardy. For Fillenbaum and Rapoport, whose aim it was "to determine how people 'reckon' in assessing relations among terms in a given domain" (p 235), the prospect of having to include the "value" of a dimension for a particular item as codetermined by many additional (lexical and nonlexical) factors, would mean an enormous complication of their calculations.

Another problem besetting the investigation of semantic field (or space) is described by Ullman (1962, p 249) as follows:

> The neatness with which words delimit each other and build up a kind of mosaic, without any gaps or overlaps, has been greatly exaggerated. This is true only of specialized and rigidly defined systems such as army ranks; in ordinary language, vagueness, synonymy, ambiguity and similar factors will produce a much less tidy picture.

Well, Fillenbaum and Rapoport (1971) have also employed their method to analyze such ill-defined fields; from our point of view their study has yielded particularly interesting results for the field of HAVE verbs.

The above authors entertain no illusions as to the methodological difficulties in their way.

> Just because a domain is ill-defined, it is impossible to exhaustively specify or identify all of its members, it is unclear how to sample from an extensive list of putative members, it is unclear what the effect may be of having a relative concentration of items (many quasi-synonymous and perhaps relatively infrequent) in some region of the conceptual space, or of omitting items that appear to be scattered widely over other regions of the space, and it is unclear where one domain merges or overlaps with some other domain (p 169).

Their analysis of HAVE verbs carried out with a number of techniques has yielded four subdivisions of the particular field. At the two ends of one axis (dimension?) there are: the DISPOSE OF cluster and the ACQUIRE cluster. The opposition of these two word groupings can be illustrated as follows: (1) presently having and being in the process of disposing of (e. g., sell, get rid of, give, offer, return, lend), (2) presently not having and being in the process of acquiring (e. g., receive, steal, take, find, buy, earn, accept, gain, get).

Another dimension is designated by an OWN or HAVE cluster toward one end and a NEED or LACK cluster toward the other (keep, hold, belong, save, own, as opposed to need, lack, want).

The authors are not entirely free from second thoughts about the validity of such an interpretation, at which point they review the results of other investigations of HAVE verbs, e. g., those by Bendix (1966) and Wexler (1970):

> what we seem to have obtained is a kind of meaning organization in which local, componential, or paradigmatic properties are embedded in an overall cluster structure (Fillenbaum and Rapoport 1971, pp 187–188).

The various words being located in concentric heaps rather than at two ends of an axis, how much validity is there in the conception of lexicon dimensions? Similar skepticism was voiced by Weinreich (1963, p 149) some time ago:

> Whereas in the highly patterned or "terminologized" domains of vocabulary, such as kinship and color, distinguishing components recur in numerous sets of signs, the bulk of the vocabulary is of course more loosely structured and is full of components unique to single pairs or small numbers of pairs, of synonyms.

On relinquishing the concept of lexicon dimensions, however, we find ourselves deprived of what seemed to be the most elementary model of how words are comprehended. Comprehension cannot any longer be conceived of as a complete cross-classification of all dimensions listing the given word.

What kind of conception could take the place of the idea of (equipotential) lexicon dimensions? Fillenbaum and Rapoport speculate that it could be a taxonomic structure of the lexicon marked by inclusion relations where, for example, *lend, grant, confer, impart* might be seen as varieties of giving, each being provided with some qualification (e. g., lend is to give with the qualification that the given thing should be returned in future). *Find, take, steal* have a common presupposition – ACQUIRE, but *find* is marked by the additional feature CHANCE, *take* by the feature ACTIVE – as contrasted with *receive,* and *steal* by the feature ILLEGITIMACY.

We have thus arrived at a crucial point in the course of our argument. We have come to conceive of the word-specifying features (or semantic components, or semantic markers) as being arranged hierarchically in that some of them dominate others. Exploring the logical and psychological implications of this formulation, we are reminded of the aforementioned notion of *presupposition,* which suggests that in this case a particular feature (RECEIVE) becomes the precondition for another (e. g., CHANCE). This relationship is logically irreversible, which distinguishes this type of ordering from the highly redundant hierarchy proposed by Katz and Fodor.

It is the natural task of a psychology of language to investigate how the various linguistic processes (understanding of words and sentences, production of descriptions, comparing of sentences, etc.) are affected by such anisotropic (direction-dependent) relationships between the features of a word[6].

Two things will be stressed at this point:

1) The specification of word meaning cannot consist of a mere sum of equipotential characteristics, since it has to account for a sort of word-inherent dynamic. By this token we approach a new problem: in what relation does the word dynamic stand to the dynamic of a sentence, of a communicative utterance, and to the dynamic of the speaker-hearer's experiential field?

2) Reverting for a moment to the clustering technique again, we should find it instructive to follow Fillenbaum and Rapoport's (1971, p 188) deliberations:

Suppose that ... differences with regard to some features, as say ACQUIRE versus DISPOSE OF, have much greater weight or importance than differences in other features. Then it follows that items differing in regard to the former features will be assigned to different clusters and that items with these features in common but differing in other features will fall close together, i. e., in the same cluster, and that paradigmatic, componential distinctions among these items, which might be revealed if one were dealing with limited subsets, may be masked.

Is it really true that the manifestation of, for instance, the CHANCE component in *lose* and *find* depends on the previous addressing of the ACQUIRE/DISPOSE

---

[6] Some attempts along these lines (Miller, Quillian) are discussed in the next chapter.

OF component pair? A positive answer would bring in jeopardy a basic assumption of all the constructions that employ the concept of lexicon or dictionary, namely the assumption that any word has just one meaning, irrespective of how this meaning might be involved in, or addressed to, the above-mentioned psychological processes. If this were so, we could not hope to grasp – along with Katz and Fodor – sentence meaning as a function of syntactic structure plus word meaning. Instead, we would have to proceed in reversed order: first we grasp the meaning of the utterance and only then can we get at the meaning of the words which make up the utterance.

Let us make it clear that by our attempt at "undermining" the concept of lexicon we hope to gain access to phenomena that are beyond our reach as long as we cling to the notion that the meaning of a word is fixed once and for all and remains uniformly effective under all circumstances. The approach which seems now to be in sight should enable us to explain how people understand such phrases as "smiling meadow," how they know what "kick the bucket" means, why they do not take the request "Would you mind opening the window?" to be a question, and the like.

The abandonment of a lexicon concept that views words as ready-made units which are marshalled from left to right at the command of syntax is a precondition for gaining an insight, by way of functional analysis of linguistic processes, into the intentional dynamic which pervades all acts of meaning and understanding as performed by goal-pursuing human beings.

Chapter 6
Functionalist Analyses of Semantic Dimensions

We are now at a point from which we may proceed along either of two paths: one is traced out by new applications of association techniques in the exploration of meaning – beyond the work of Osgood and Fillenbaum-Rapoport – and would lead us to Deese and Clark; the other pursues the notion of presupposition, with which the reader is already acquainted from the preceding chapter – and would bring us, in first place, to Miller.

Since we can only take one path at a time, and since the one leading to Miller enters the border zone of sentence semantics, discussed in subsequent chapters, we would be well advised to commence by taking a fresh look at word association techniques.

Osgood has proposed an associationist S-R theory to account for the ontogenesis of his representational mediation links: originating from the recurrence of particular S-R connections and S-S combinations in early childhood, our subsequent language facility enables us to judge *nurse* and *sincerity* as similar in meaning, both terms ranking very positively on E(valuation). Semantic similarity can be assessed by having subjects rate words on the Semantic Differential, Osgood's association technique.

For several decades word association techniques have been employed for testing S-R connections. Originally, investigators used to estimate the degree of association between a response word and a stimulus word in order to account for the particular sequence or reciprocal substitutability of words in a sentence, but they soon came to realize that their goal was too ambitious, or altogether misconceived. Though important findings were contributed by the attempts to interpret the word sequence in a sentence in terms of strength of associative habits between words (as epitomized in Miller's *Language and Communication*), this approach was found to have fundamental limitations which are subsumed under the heading "the creative nature of language."

Although they threw overboard their S-R orientation at Chomsky's instigation, the psycholinguists still had had enough undergraduate training in the word association technique to remember it when summoned to explore psychologically the semantic structure of language.

Once employed as an explanatory construct to account for co-occurrence of words, the concept of association now itself needs explanation. None the less, the word association technique has retained its validity as an instrument for disclosing structures in the lexicon.

Why does the stimulus *man* produce, in the association experiment, the response *woman* with very high probability, and why is the response *boy* much less probable? The answer: "Because *man* and *woman* are associated with each other," is today unacceptable, as a tautology. Both the co-occurrence of words in the association experiment and the entire process from the input of the stimulus word to the output of the response word are believed to go together and hence together call for explanation. This might be taken to mean that the rift has been overcome between the study of the lexicon as a component of competence and the investigation of the psychological processes involved in the use of the lexicon – which count as performance; there is no reason to marvel at this development, if one considers that both Deese and Clark, as the principal investigators in this area, are psychologists.

Long before Deese and Clark, i. e., in the early twentieth century, it was discovered that the responses offered to a stimulus word in the free association experiment, far from being random choices from the vocabulary, stand in a particular relationship to the stimulus. Thumb and Marbe (1901) found that, on the whole, adults give nouns in response to nouns, and adjectives in response to adjectives. Should the stimulus word perceived by the subject arouse some (memory? lexicon?) structure modelled on the categories of our school grammar? Kinship terms are mostly responded to with other kinship terms, vegetables with other vegetables: should our memory store, accessed by the stimulus word, comprise the same classes by which we have learned to structure the world? *Big* tends to evoke *small, beautiful ugly;* have we come here upon on area where the distinction between semantic and logical structure evaporates? A frequent response to *dog* is *animal,* but *animal* is rarely responded to with *dog.* Is the pathway from the subordinate to the superordinate concept in any way more distinctly traced, or simply shorter, than the path in the other direction?

These questions direct our attention to a different aspect of the issue, one of long standing in the psychology of thinking and language, i. e., the strict intermeshing of the problems pertaining to meaning and the lexicon with its associative structure, on the one hand, and the problems of *memory,* on the other.

Whereas in the framework of conventional associationism we would have to make an effort to show that *big* and *small* tended to go together in some unspecified past, the matter is now approached by Deese (1968, p 99) from quite a different angle:

> The fundamental analytic fact is not that A leads to B, but that the interrelations of A, B and other verbal elements related to both imply a structure, an organization which cannot be in any sense described by the elements which enter into the manifest sequence . . . . . . the important fact in the manifest organization of associations in not that *mother*

leads to *father, hot* to *cold,* and *sleep* to *dream,* not that these superficially similar pairs are contiguous or derived in any form from the law of contiguity, but that they in their *obvious* differences ... reflect different organizational processes at work.

By this approach Osgood has been clearly outdistanced, for his main concern, as it were, continues to be – notwithstanding the evolvement of his behaviorism into a neobehaviorism and finally a cryptobehaviorism – the chaining of stimulus and response in a manner where a bundle of semantic features is inserted as a sort of invisible mediating link (and his approach has proved remarkably successful!).

Earlier still, Deese was an associationist himself. He employed factor analysis to extract something like semantic dimensions from the data of his free association experiments (cf. Hörmann 1971 a, p 167), within an impressive project. Yet today Deese thinks that associations are "certainly not the cause of organization in recall" (1968, p 100); at best they are indices of a structure whose components interact (and may become manifest in behavior) along other as well as associative principles.

Whereas Osgood derives our capability to use language from the growth of all kinds of associations in the course of individual experience, both Deese and Clark consider the growth of associations as an epiphenomenon of our command of language.

How is it possible to explore this structure which forms the groundwork of language use? By means of a distinctive feature analysis as we know it from Katz and Fodor, and also, obviously, from phonology.

Deese's early methodological concept was to consider the overlap between responses to any two (or more) stimulus words rather than individual S-R connections. In the case of an extensive overlap, as for instance with the stimulus words *man* and *woman,* it is reasonable to assume that these words differ only in a few of their semantic markers (features).

Here we come again upon the now familiar pattern of drawing conclusions from the presence of *similarities.*

The features as conceived by Deese are binary: the gender dimension, for example, has the values Male and Female (or ± Male).

Now, what happens in a free association experiment? HH Clark (1970a) conceptualizes the underlying processes, in close analogy to ordinary communication, by identifying three stages:

1) The hearer must "understand" the stimulus word
2) He must "operate" on the meaning of the stimulus
3) He must produce a response.

If we now follow the example set by many linguists and psychologists in assuming that understanding a word implies an analysis of its relevent features, we might consider the stimulus word *man* as comprehended if it has been decomposed into +Noun, +Determiner, +Count, +Animate, +Human, +Adult, +Male.

In the next phase the subject has to act on the instruction, i. e., has to respond as quickly as possible with a word other than the stimulus. An immediate possibility would be to change the sign of the last feature, turning +Male into

– Male. In the third phase the subject searches for a lexical item that would fit the so established list of features; in doing so, he reverses the procedure followed in the first phase. In effect, he responds with *woman*.

Besides accounting for the predominance of antonyms in subjects' responses – a finding that has always baffled students of word associations – the *minimal contrast rule* proposed by Clark also serves to reveal an important thing about lexicon structure: the word-specifying semantic features are evidently not an "unstructured heap of features", as deduced by Weinreich (1971, p 321) from Katz and Fodor's design, but rather are arranged in a particular order. Their order can be read from the frequency distributions of the responses to the given stimulus word: being the second lowest, the feature +Adult is less frequently changed than the bottommost feature +Male. *Boy* is therefore a less frequent response to *man* than is *woman*.

Let us note in passing that this is a clear case where a study of performance contributes to a revision and specification of competence.

Taking a backward look at Osgood and at Fillenbaum and Rapoport, and a forward look at Miller's sorting experiment, we find that in all these studies the subjects are queried directly for some similarity between words. Under this procedure, the "owner" of the lexicon is required to act in a way rarely practiced in everyday language use. Deese and Clark, on the other hand, have based their arguments, not on such metalinguistic evidence, but on the investigation of real-life language behavior.

Clark has supplemented his minimal contrast rule (which leads from *man* to *woman*) with some other rules that make the frequency with which certain response modes occur in the word association test appear plausible. For instance, the frequent occurrence of generic names (superordinates) is accounted for by the *feature deletion rule* (*apple* leads to *fruit, dog* leads to *animal*); the *category preservation rule* sees to it that nouns are responded to with nouns, adjectives with adjectives, etc.

One of Clark's rules is the *marking rule:* if the stimulus word is marked, the response is often the unmarked form of the same word.

What is meant by marked and unmarked[1]? Linguists have long been familiar with the fact that with certain word pairs one word in the pair functions as the generic name for the pair, whereas the other word has a more restricted meaning within the class designated by the generic name. The distinction will be made clear by two examples: (1) dog/bitch: *dog* is the unmarked, generic name, while *bitch* refers to a dog marked in terms of sex; (2) big/small: the latter refers to a marked form of the concept signified by the former, unmarked word of the pair. The distinctive functions of marked and unmarked words in utterances come into evidence when one considers that the question "How good was the movie?" is perfectly sensible under all conditions, whereas the question "How bad was the movie?" presupposes that the movie was not good. That is to say, unmarked adjectives designate both one pole of a scale and the entire scale as such. In effect,

---

[1] Cf. Bierwisch (1967) on the subject.

an unmarked adjective has two meanings: a nominal meaning, as in the question "How good was the movie?", and a contrastive one (as in the statement "The movie was good" – in contrast to "The movie was bad").

Clark (much like Bierwisch 1967) conceives the distinction between the marked and unmarked form as the difference in the *number* of characteristic semantic features; *bad* carries all the features of *good* and the additional feature – Polar. The theory seems to account for the associationists' finding that the marked stimulus *better* evokes the unmarked response *good* more frequently than is the case in the opposite direction. Obviously, it is easier to omit an additional (marked) feature than to add a feature.

The marking rule is of limited validity, however: *man* produces more often the (marked) response *woman* than the other way around.

The various rules proposed by Clark function smoothly as long as we do not raise the question of which rule applies in what conditions. We then realize that all these rules represent an impressive construction of ad hoc explanations[2].

Quite naturally, Clark seeks to enhance the heuristic value of his rules – and hence also of his feature theory – by demonstrating their applicability in areas other than that of the free association experiment. He has undertaken two attemps along these lines. Together with Eve Clark, he studied marked and unmarked adjectives (their order of appearance) in children of different ages. One of the questions pursued in this study was whether children acquire the unmarked adjective *big* before or after the marked form *wee* (small).

The other area in which Clark seeks to bolster his conception of the lexicon as a hierarchy of partially marked features is that of research on memory. In a series of studies he attempted to grapple with phenomena hitherto interpreted in entirely different terms. It is worth our while to examine Clark's two pursuits, since they represent fairly advanced *psychological* contributions to the elucidation of the lexicon concept.

Turning to the ontogenesis of features, we are confronted at the outset with two striking observations:

1) Three- and four-year-olds show a better comprehension of the unmarked adjective in a pair than of the marked one

2) The same children employ the comparatives *more* and *less* synonymously in the sense of *more*.

Clark (1970b) invokes his feature theory to account for the two findings. The unmarked adjective, he argues, is used by the child only in its nominal function, to start with: *long* refers initially only to the *dimension* of length, not to one (positive) pole. *More* and *less* are likewise used at first in a nominal (i. e., non-comparative) sense. And since the nominal concept is usually employed also in reference to the positive pole of the dimension, the child considers both *more* and

---

[2] Moran et al. (1964) have demonstrated idiosyncratic preferences for, e. g., the rule responsible for contrastive responses, thus interpeting the domination of one rule over another as an individual characteristic. Their approach has not been pursued in the psychology of language, which remains largely indifferent to individual differences.

less as equivalents of *a quantity of.*

> If a child first understands both *taller* and *shorter* as meaning *having tallness,* he should err more often on *shorter* than on *taller* (p 273).

Besides their broader applicability, there is also a perceptual factor conducive to the use of the positive pole (unmarked) terms:

> the best example of something with length is something with much length, because that is the example which best distinguishes length as a dimension to be attended to from other dimensions (p 274).

Not only is the foregoing reminiscent of Bierwisch's ideas about the basic properties of our perceptual apparatus, but it also reveals that Clark has abandoned the claim that his arguments derive from orthodox competence theory; indeed, he suddenly turns to psychology for evidence in support of his conception of the lexicon.

Eve Clark (1973a, 1973b) proposes, accordingly, a general theory of early language acquisition: at first, the child attaches only some feature(s) of meaning to the word representing some object, and these basic features (primitives?) are of a perceptual nature: e. g., *four-legged, big, runs,* for the word *dog.*

These ideas come very close to the basic categories of comprehension in Gestalt psychology, as also to the basic categories of action proposed by Piaget, on the one hand, and by Fillmore, Chafe, and Schlesinger, on the other (to be discussed in Chap. 12). In the course of language acquisition, the basic features are supplemented with other features, by which the word's meaning is specified with increasing precision, parallel to a reduction of the initial overgeneralization of meaning which characterizes the child's early lexicon. In the feature structure of, for instance, *before* and *after,* there appear such additional features as *time, simultaneous, earlier,* etc.

Practically nothing can be said, however, about the origin of these linguistic rather than perceptual features. Does Eve Clark, too, fall back on the mysterious process of "abstraction of critical attributes," the same one invoked by Locke and by Katz and Fodor, in order to explain

> how people identify the commonalities among things in order to group together a set of things, resulting in a concept (Nelson 1974, p 273)?

A further weakness of this theoretical construction lies in the supposition that the child knows how to extract linguistic (i. e., lexicon-ruled) features straight from his or her perceptual experience. (More detailed views on the issue are discussed in Chap. 12.)

The notion of features inevitably suggests that the processes of concept formation and acquisition of meaning are effected via an *aggregation of features.* Such an implication is probably unavoidable inasmuch as features are conceived – by Katz and Fodor as well as by the Clarks – as the identifying, "referential" attributes of a word. The totality of features constitute a cross-reference system that serves to identify a word by gradually restricting the categories under which it might fall. A word is thought to be understood through a successive "calling to mind" of its various features, much as in the Twenty Questions game where the player may eventually discover the target object by reviewing its features (physical object, animate, animal, etc.). In Chap. 13 we shall discuss designs which begin with a similar word-identification procedure only to conclude that the features of a word, rather than adding up to a sum total, reveal eminently dynamic interrelations.

Clark's other attempt to support his feature conception of the lexicon with psychological evidence consisted of a memory research project built up around two seemingly incompatible findings, one originating from the syntax-centered era of psycholinguistics, the other from a more "semantically oriented" trend.

In a recall test, Mehler (1963) presented passive sentences *(John was given a book by Mary)* to his subjects, who tended to recall the sentences in active form *(Mary gave a book to John)*. In keeping with the then dominant theory, the investigator interpreted his finding as showing that the kernel string and the (passive) transformation are separately stored in memory and hence may be separately forgotten.

For this and similar findings Fillenbaum (1966) has offered the first, albeit tentative semantic interpretation. He argues that among recall errors, there are many more meaning-preserving than meaning-changing errors. For example, the sentence *The seaman is not dead* tends to be recalled as *The seaman is alive*. In his recall task the subject relies, claims Fillenbaum, on the semantic information he has preserved in memory, and this is independent of the syntactic form in which it was presented.

Taking these two studies as a point of departure, HH Clark and E Clark (1968) try to show that the notion of semantic information, used by Fillenbaum in a global sense, can be specified as being comprised of features, or markings, that may be separately forgotten. This claim is substantiated in the following experiment.

In a recall test, the experimenter read out sentences all composed of a main and a subordinate clause, in which each of the clauses referred to temporally disparate events. For example:

HE TOOTED THE HORN BEFORE HE SWIPED THE CABBAGES;
AFTER HE TOOTED THE HORN HE SWIPED THE CABBAGES;
BEFORE HE SWIPED THE CABBAGES HE TOOTED THE HORN, etc.

In interpreting their results, the Clarks assumed that three kinds of semantic differentiations were stored by the subjects: (a) the temporal sequence of events, (b) the sequence in which they were mentioned, (c) the main clause-subordinate clause relationship of the events. A further assumption was that the sequence of events mentioned may be marked (whenever the first-mentioned event was temporally the second event), and that the main clause-subordinate clause relationship is marked whenever the subordinate clause comes first. Under these conditions, the Clarks' results dovetail neatly with the claim that it is a property of the lexicon to have markings stored separately and hence forgotten separately.

If we consider that the Clarks' construct offers *semantic* differentiations, and that a syntax-centered interpretation (as proposed by Mehler) is inadequate to account for these data, the feature theory advanced by Clark emerges as a successful elaboration of Fillenbaum's general and rather loose idea of semantic information.

A further step closer to psychology has been made by Flores d'Arcais (1973a) who found that the comparison of two objects or events (e. g., a sentence and corresponding picture) takes less time when an unmarked word is used in the sentence. Flores d'Arcais concluded that

> the internal coding is more likely to be in terms of the polarity which corresponds to the unmarked adjective. The reason would be that we probably encode such properties according to some general principles of perceptual organization (p 10).

Thus Flores d'Arcais invokes perceptual, rather than linguistic, regularities, of the kind mentioned by von Allesch and Arnheim (see Chap. 1). The linguistic fact of a certain asymmetry between marked and unmarked words, which psycholinguists adduced to account for some behavioral data, is attributed by Flores d'Arcais to some more basic cognitive principles that underlie the entire human perceptual system.

Whereas Clark tended to rely on a linguistically defined notion of marking, Flores d'Arcais puts more emphasis on the cognitive basis of this linguistic concept.

Finally, Ertel (1974a) found that the kind of asymmetry of polar adjectives which Clark sought to explain with the aid of the linguistic notion of marking applies also to artificial words, i. e., verbal units that have no entries whatever in our mental lexicon. Quite naturally, he does not speak of a linguistic (marking-controlled) imbalance but rather of a conceptual anisotropy:

> Whenever ... an individual has to opt for one out of a number of components of an entity to represent that entity, he chooses the one of greater affective dynamics. The affectively more dynamic, phenomenally more important, more relevant, and more powerful component of the entity is the more conspicuous and more available one ... (p 288).

The notion of perceptual relevance ("the best example of something with length is something with much length") broached in Clark's developmental considerations and elaborated by Flores d'Archais is taken even more seriously by Ertel. In addition, Ertel draws our attention to a new, enormously important factor: the ego-centered dynamics of language processes, a topic to be discussed at length in Chap. 13.

Clark's feature mechanics does not leave room for anything of the sort; in fact, it has proved ineffective in a number of investigations. Carpenter (1974), for example, was able to demonstrate the effect of the marking factor in some, but not other, tasks. Brewer and Lichtenstein (1974) ran experiments which

> strongly confirmed the memory-for-meaning theory and contradicted the marked-feature theory whenever these two theories made opposing predictions (p 180).

Has Clark not overstretched his claim, originally developed to account for the data of word association experiments, when amplifying it into a comprehensive theory of behavior? In the free association task the subject modifies some minor aspects of the feature list of the stimulus word to produce *woman* in response to *man, alive* in response to *dead,* and so on. Can the same mechanism be held responsible for the processes occurring in a recall task? It has been rightly argued (Barclay et al. 1974) that, on the grounds of Clark's feature theory, in case of forgetting anything, subjects would recall the exact opposite of the word they had originally read or heard: *woman* instead of *man, alive* instead of *dead, small* instead of *big.*

Thus we are confronted squarely by the fact that a feature theory alone cannot yield an adequate account of the diverse processes observed in language use: association is not the same process as retention, verification is not the same as understanding.

These diverse techniques are not equivalent as instruments to explore one and the same structure of memory and lexicon. There is some elegance in a model that conceptualizes language as having *one* structure with different applications (association, comparison, recall), but we should not be seduced by its elegance to accept a reification of the concept of structure. Rather, let us be warned by the unhappy case of the concept of sign as an entity that has some meaning and *may* also have some uses.

Once we have conceived of structure as inextricably bound up with the processes involved in its realization, we are compelled to make a certain differentiation; the matter will be discussed at a later stage under the heading *levels of understanding.* At this point, let us merely note that a similar view was voiced by Posner and Warren (1972, p 34), who – on examining the conventional word association and sorting procedures – commented that in the free association experiment, for instance, "in some cases (the subject's) response comes effortlessly, in other cases only after a conscious search", and thereupon suggested that two rather different processes were at work within the same experimental paradigm. The notion of levels of analysis is likewise supported by the evidence marshalled by Van Lancker (1975) – discussed at the end of the present chapter. For the time being, we shall return to Clark's theory.

It is not enough to deplore the fact that HH Clark has clearly overestimated the explanatory power of his theory; the inadequacy of his approach should be analyzed for its sources, in the hope that it might yield suggestions as to the next steps in our investigation. Bearing this in mind we now return to the area in which Clark's feature theory appears to have been most successful: the associative processes.

The responses obtained in the word association experiment are fundamentally of two kinds: paradigmatic (man – woman, old – young, dog – animal) and syntagmatic (man – big, treee – green, sing – beautiful). In paradigmatic associations both stimulus and response belong to the same syntactic category, in syntagmatic ones they belong to different syntactic categories.

For syntagmatic associations, which tend to dominate in children, Clark offers the following account: Among the word-specifying features there are some which codetermine the word's potential context, i. e., the sentence in which the word might occur; Clark calls them *selectional features*[3]. The word *young* can and may modify only the nouns of a particular category. The finding that the stimulus *young* elicits *boy, girl,* and *child* in response is accounted for by Clark with his selectional feature realization rule:

> Take the features specified by a selectional feature adding as many features as necessary for a surface realization; in addition, restrict yourself to the "significant" part of the selectional feature, the portion specifying a lexical word (1970a, p 281).

This precept postulates the insertion, between the onset of the process, i. e., the extraction of some feature(s) from the stimulus word, and the availability of the response, of a specific number of features in a specific sequence, namely, "as many as necessary for a surface realization".

Can we really reach the surface, and hence the producibility of a lexical item, only by starting from the last item of a complete list of features? And what does "complete" mean? Is it not that this conception of the lexicon takes something for granted which is not self-evident? The feature deletion rule proposed by Clark may operate only on condition that the production of a lexical item can be initiated at *different* levels of the feature hierarchy. You may say either *Jonathan,* or (leaving out one feature) *apple,* or (leaving out another or more features) *fruit.* Up to this point, a word could be produced, in principle, by starting from any place of lexical structure, provided that the place was not a lexical "gap"[4].

Now Clark assumes that the lexical realization of a feature list is determined by the length or completeness of that list. In this way he tries to bypass a hitherto disregarded but serious difficulty involved in his feature deletion rule (and also his feature addition rule). If the feature list used for the specification of a word to be uttered can be of any length, then the uttering of the word cannot be accounted for by the activation of *the* feature list that fits the word, unless allowance is made for an additional mechanism by which the speaker would decide whether the intended lexical item could be specified with a list of x features or only with a list of $x + n$ features.

A feature list by itself qualifies neither as a word generator in language production nor as a generator of language understanding; such a generator would be much too rigid to accomplish the postulated automatic aggregation of and decomposition in features. This can be seen from word association data. There is need for (at least) one more factor that would determine for how long (over how many features) the process of analysis should run. In the further course of our argument we shall try to meet the postulate by introducing the concept of sense constancy (Chap. 7); that is to say, reaching comprehension of an utterance will be conceptualized as the factor terminating the analysis of the utterance.

---

[3] This is an interesting variation on Katz and Fodor. Whereas the latter authors attach their selection restrictions to words as entities, rather than conceiving them as features, Clark includes them among features.

[4] In his eminently readable paper *How Shall a Thing Be Called,* Brown (1958a) analyzed the motivations behind adult preferences for one rather than another name of an object (animal, dog, boxer, our Prince).

There is a further snag in Clark's feature theory that may help in clarifying our argument. Clark failed to account for the effects of both verbal and nonverbal contexts on, say, associative behavior. A seminal approach to the problem has been proposed by M. G. Johnson.

A former student of Deese, Johnson (1970) maintains that any cognitive act (linguistic, perceptual, etc.) can be broken down into what he calls Elementary Cognitive Characteristics (ECC). To some extent, his elementary units correspond to semantic markers or features, except that they are of a cognitive, not linguistic, nature. The vector of the currently activated ECCs represents the content of consciousness. Nouns are specified by numerous, adjectives by few ECCs. When several adjectives are joined as a stimulus in a word association test, their effective ECCs combine to produce a response with lower uncertainty (in terms of information theory) than in the case of the responses to each adjective separately. When several nouns are joined into a single stimulus, however, their ECCs do not add up in that simple manner; rather, each ECC comes into action with differential saliency, resulting in the following associative principle: the response is determined primarily by those ECCs that are present in more than one of the nouns. For example, none of the words *river, milk,* and *story* is likely to produce the response *flow* when presented separately, whereas the noun triad *river – milk – story* leads to *flow* with considerable certainty. The same process is held responsible for the fact that responses to adjective-noun compounds are of higher uncertainty than responses to the noun alone.

Thus the ECCs of different stimulus words interact in different ways, depending on circumstances. In some cases they simply add up, in others, converging ECCs strengthen each other, in still other cases diverging ECCs get attenuated.

What can we gain from these findings for our line of argument? First of all the following: the elementary cognitive characteristics (or semantic features) of a word should not be conceived of as forming a bundle where each piece has the same valence and the sum is independent of the arrangement of the components. Furthermore, the influence of a particular ECC or feature upon language processes evidently depends – even in the relatively isolated word association experiment – not only on the other features of the word but also on the features brought in by context. To quote MG Johnson (1970, p 291):

> The results also show that constraint is imposed by context, but that the constraint is on the size of the sets of elementary characteristics which underlie verbal units and not on the overt verbal units themselves. This in turn provides an explanation for the fact that the consequences of context on meaning (i. e., the specification of meaning) are not necessarily the same as the consequences on free associations.

This view breaks new ground. Context must be seen, not as additional data to be processed, but as a factor that determines the kind, number, and composition of elementary characteristics from among the potentially made available by the word, characteristics relevant for the processing of the given utterance. Thus we have gone beyond Clark's model which leaves words as stimulus and response units essentially intact. By this token, we have succeeded in untying the bundle of features regarded by linguists and many psycholinguists as representing a word.

By way of an interesting cross-reference, let us mention Uhlenbeck's argument against the generativist emphasis on the creative nature of the sentence. What is new in an utterance we hear for the first time, he claims, is connected with the word, rather than with the sentence itself. A new sentence is new not because it offers a new combination of well-known and immutable components (words); rather, it is the words in the sentence that are new in certain respects, in so far as besides the familiar constancy, a word reveals "at the same time a certain mobility" (no date, p 81). This mobility is connected with the fact that the word-constituting elementary characteristics tend to shift in their relative importance under the influence of both linguistic and nonlinguistic factors.

The inability to conceptualize a satisfactory relationship between the word's mobility and its constancy has prevented both linguists and psychologists from developing a theory of the internal lexicon that would answer the needs of psychologists of language.

With the mention of the importance of individual features relative to context we have moved closer to a long series of memory studies. In his multi-component theory of memory traces Bower (1967) claims that in order to understand a word we have to encode it on a number of diverse aspects, or attributes, or conceptual dimensions. (These attributes or dimensions are the exact counterparts of the markers or features or elementary characteristics with which we are now familiar; the term *encode* means simply "construe as X for storing purposes.") What these dimensions are like can be seen, for example, from a method described by Wickens (1970) by the term "release from proactive inhibition": In a learning task where three words of a particular class (sharing at least one feature) are given in succession, if these are followed by words of another class, then the first word of the new class is immune to the retroactive inhibition that has built up around the words of the first class. Release from proactive inhibition suggests that the new word has been construed and encoded for feature(s) other than those of the preceding words; the proactive inhibition of the second and third word of the first group shows, on the other hand, that the dimensions of features for which those words were coded are weakened in their capacity as memory aids precisely because they had been used for coding the first word[5].

The variations in impact of the particular features, or semantic dimensions, under the influence of diverse factors, reveal an aspect of language processes with far-reaching implications. These can only be fathomed once we have fully explored the dynamic forces obtaining between communicating partners and within the verbal utterance itself.

At the present stage we arrive at the following conclusion: In view of the fact

---

[5] The validity of this method in determining the memory-relevant coding dimensions is also revealed in the following facts: in a learning task where the first three words are located near the positive E pole of the semantic differential, a fourth word taken from the negative pole of the same dimension is recalled much better than a word taken from the positive pole. A linguistically striking finding from the same area is that the grammatical class of the words to be learned does not affect coding: in this case our memory does not attend to grammatical class.

that words can no longer be conceived as fixed bundles of elementary components, and since these components apparently modify the weight with which they affect the meaning of words and language behavior in general, any feature theory (or marker or dimension theory) is bound to lose much of its persuasiveness.

The attraction of such theories resided in their proposal to conceive of language processes (whether in free association tests, or verification tasks, or problems involving thinking – Clark 1969a, 1969b; Clark and Card 1969; Clark and Chase 1972) in terms of an automatic interaction of semantic elements. Clark's theory is a specific theory of memory in that it seeks to explain differences in reproduction or recall by claiming that the stored units are subject to some modifications (e. g., may lose their +Polar marking) during the storing and/or retrieving phases. As it is, the theory is based on a tacit – and by now untenable – assumption: that at the beginning of the storing (encoding) phase all the units to be stored are intact. In other words, the claim was that linguistic material is understood and stored irrespective of context and intention, and that only what has been understood can be entered into the store. If we are right in questionning this assumption, that is, if it is not true that every linguistic input is automatically decomposed into its components, the theory can aspire to validity only in those rare cases when absolutely all features are simultaneously handled by our cognitive apparatus.

From our analysis it becomes increasingly clear that the "processing of verbal utterances" is a tune that can be played in a variety of keys.

Most of the material reviewed in the preceding section is pervaded by a tenet that appears to be built into the research program of contemporary psycholinguistics. Roughly speaking, the tenet is that the (internal) lexicon as explored by linguists is directly related to what the psychologist considers to be memory.

There is nothing suprising in this identification. The linguist's lexicon is a store of word (morpheme, sememe, lexeme, semanteme) meanings which have to be stored somewhere if they are to be available to the speaker-hearer. Memory as conceived by the psychologist, on the other hand, is precisely such a store of those (not always consciously) available things.

As long as the grammar construed by the linguist deals with the same language as that studied by the psychologist of memory, the step from "lexicon" to "memory" is not great. But linguists have tended to conceptualize their lexicon as if it had nothing in common with human memory and as if no evidence were available on the functions of recall and forgetting. We need not marvel at this, bearing in mind the fact that the feats and blunders of our memory were disposed of by Chomsky by way of a wastepaper basket labeled "performance", where we find all the things the linguist can dispense with.

Clark's and Deese's research has shown that attributes of the lexicon as inspired by linguists (such as the notion of feature) can be usefully applied in the psychological study of language processes; at the same time it has become clear that the psychologist's attempts at utilizing these concepts inevitably raise specific demands in relation to the lexicon conception.

The functioning of the memory store can be traced in Clark's feature theory chiefly in the deletion of features and the change of polarity in associative and recall processes. In the present section we shall examine the functioning of memory more strictly from the vantage point of the psychology of language.

Clark has proposed his "rules for handling of features" in order to account for certain results of word association tests and for the findings of recall experiments with adjectives, comparatives, and the like. All these rules are meant to elucidate what is ordinarily inaccessible to our awareness, i. e., processes by which the feature structure of the lexicon leads to the uttering of a word. As pointed out in the foregoing section, these processes cannot occur in a purely automatic fashion, in that a word is produced only when the appropriate feature list is available in its full length. Well, what hope is there to lighten the darkness lying between the feature structure and the word?

One such possibility lies in examining a familiar phenomenon: bringing to mind a partially forgotten name. For example, what do you call that well-known navigational instrument used in measuring angular distances, such as the altitude of the sun . . .?

It might be in order to point out the difference between the procedure we now propose to discuss and Clark's analysis of the word association test. In the association experiment, the investigator is interested in the prompted transposition of a stimulus into a response; lasting a fraction of a second, this process takes place at a level to which our awareness has no access. Clark (and others) have tried to explain it in a rather behavioristic fashion: clues as to the black box process can be obtained by comparing R against S. The response *woman* to the stimulus *man* indicates that something has occurred in the black box, and according to Clark it is a reversal of the sign of the lowest feature.

Proceeding now – in the footsteps of William James, Wilhelm Witte, and Roger Brown – to examine the processes underlying our own recollections, we embark upon a profoundly unbehavioristic concern. We want to make scientific capital out of the fact that it is possible sometimes to peep into our black box, provided things do not move too fast there. May we, by looking at our own process of recalling a word or name, learn something about the nature of the material held in memory (say, about the constituent features of our recollections) or about the manner in which our memory operates with this material in the process of recall?

The phenomenon we have in mind was once described by James (1890, p 251) in superb fashion:

> Suppose we try to recall a forgotten name. The state of our consciousness is peculiar. There is a gap therein; but no mere gap. It is a gap that is intensely active. A sort of wraith of the name is in it, beckoning us in a given direction, making us at moments tingle with the sense of our closeness and then letting us sink back without the longed-for term. If wrong names are proposed to us, this singularly active gap acts immediately as to negate it. They do not fit into its mould. And the gap of one word does not feel like the gap of another, all empty of content as both might seem necessarily to be when described as gaps.

Brown and McNeill (1966) made an empirical study of the tip-of-the-tongue phenomenon. They define the tip-of-the-tongue (TOT) state as "failure to recall a word of which one has knowledge" (p 325). Fifty-six subjects were read definitions of uncommon English words without hearing the words themselves (e. g., apse, nepotism, sampan) and were then questioned for their experiences when searching for the suggested words. In this way the authors obtained a wealth of data that allowed them to go beyond the observations made earlier by Wenzl (1937) or Witte (1959a, 1959b).

Brown and McNeill's findings can be summarized as follows:

> When complete recall of a word has not occurred but is felt to be imminent there is likely to be accurate generic recall. Generic recall of the *abstract form* variety is evidenced by the subject's knowledge of the number of syllables in the target and the location of the primary stress. Generic recall of the *partial* variety is evidenced by the subject's knowledge of letters in the target word. ... The accuracy of generic recall is greater when the subject is near the target (complete recall is imminent) than when the subject is far from the target. A person experiencing generic recall is able to judge the relative similarity to the target of words that occur to him and these judgments are based on the features of words that figure in partial and abstract form recall (1966, p 333).

Brown and McNeill also interpret their results in terms of features. From the definition of the target word ("a navigational instrument used in measuring angular distances, especially the altitude of sun, moon, and stars at sea"), the subject extracts semantic features such as *navigation, instrument,* and *having to do with geometry.* These features form a search design with which to scan one's lexical memory. In doing so, the subject produces semantically similar words *(astrolabe, compass, divider, protractor)* as kinds of memory props.

The feature combination used during the first phase of retrieval, besides yielding similar words, makes some additional information available in the process. The information is contained in the features that specifiy similar words: recalling the term *astrolabe,* the subject obtains access to information from which it becomes evident that this is not the right word. In their account, Brown and McNeill propose the following model: In our lexical memory, words are entered on something like keysort cards punched for their respective features. Starting out on a search, the subject uses the features extracted from the term's definition (navigation, instrument, having to do with geometry) to turn up a number of word cards. The words entered on these cards usually are found to have additional features that do not fit the definition of the target word.

This alone does not explain the nature of the tormenting TOT state, where the subject is on the verge of retrieving the critical word and has not yet succeeded in doing so. To account for this phenomenon, Brown and McNeill had to go beyond the feature concept. Pursuing their punched card metaphor, they say that the first retrieval must also include a card with the target word entered on it. Why then does the subject not read the target word right away? Because the entry there is ... incomplete. For *sextant,* "the card might, for instance, have the following information about the word: two syllables, initial *s,* final *t.*" In other words, the entry is only partly legible.

Here we come upon a completely new – and certainly an indispensable – aspect in handling the feature concept. In the work reviewed in the preceding sections, the features of any word were conceptualized as uniformly accessible units. The presence of these features would invariably lead to the retrieval of the word. Now it is proposed that in addition to the feature list specifying the word there is the question of "reading" the entry.

Even if the entry is only partly legible, the subject "will know that he knows the word" (p 334). And this is where the second phase of retrieval begins. According to Brown and McNeill, the subject is now guided by similarity in sound (SS), rather than similarity in meaning (SM). During this phase, he may produce words like *secant,* or – leaving out one of the relevant features – *sexton*.

Putting aside for a moment the implications of this theoretical interpretation, we take note once again of the seminal character of the feature concept: once the subject has retrieved a number of words similar in sound to the target word, he is often in a position to rank-order these SS words correctly in terms of their similarity to the target word. Brown and McNeill offer the following account:

> If the incomplete entry for *sextant* (the partly legible word on the retrieved card) includes three features of the word, then the SS words having only one or two of these features (e. g., *sexton*) should be jugded less similar to the target than SS words having all three of them (e. g., *secant*) (p 334).

First of all, why should the subject undertake another retrieval (now guided by sound clues) if he has already come upon the right card? Whatever the number of phonetic features additionally heeded in this process, the subject cannot get hold of anything better than the right card. It is through awareness of the various sound-similar words that the entry on the critical card gains legibility during the second retrieval!

> We must still explain how it happens that the faintly entered and at first illegible middle letters are made accessible in recall ... Perhaps it works something like this. ... Whenever an SS word (such as *secant*) includes middle letters that are matched in the faintly entered section of the target then those faintly entered letters become accessible. The match brings out the missing parts the way heat brings out anything written in lemon juice. In other words, when *secant* is retrevied the target entry grows from *Sex tan*T to SE*x t*ANT (p 335). [Italics used to mark the still missing letters.]

Such a construct cannot be accommodated into any theory that conceptualizes the word-specifying features as an aggregate of attributes that are indispensable to comply with the logical definition of the word. The *activation of features* necessary to make the word fully legible becomes a problem in its own right. In the present case such an activation is achieved by the retrieval of sound-similar words, leading to some sort of analysis-by-synthesis, or hypothesis testing ("is the fourth letter a *t*?"). Could other factors contribute to feature activation? Would it be easier for the subject to retrieve *sextant* as the target if he were shown the instrument, say, during the second phase? Or if he were allowed to operate it?

These questions raise the suspicion that the characteristics of recall enumerated by Brown and McNeill are also at work in the process of understanding a word, The grasping of a word seems to involve an active matching of patterns, a kind of projection of the possible interpretations upon the word, interpretations to which the word may "respond" or not. We discussed the process when dealing with the similarities between perception and understanding. Grasping the meaning of a word implies acitvely bringing schemata to bear upon the word under analysis; this process of projection and active responding (not passive resonance!) evokes an echo if the projected schema "fits".

Brown and McNeill's interpretation has set up a link with an age-old finding of memory research: recognition is easier to accomplish than free recall. The point is that the "echo" may sound – or the pattern may be found to match – even in the case of incomplete identity.

> It is ... *possible* to recognize words when one has not stored the complete letter sequence. The evidence is that we do not store the complete sequence if we do not have to. ... An incomplete entry will serve for recognition, but if words are to be produced or recalled, they must be stored in full (p 335).

In their brilliant study of a familiar everyday experience Brown and McNeill have treated features (both semantic and formal-phonetic) as cues for searching the lexicon. These cues may lead to a retrieval of the right "punch card" on which the entry can be read once it has become sufficiently legible.

If we conceive the meaning of a word as represented by the features listed on the pertinent card, how should we conceptualize the process of understanding the word? Obviously, the TOT-experiencing hearer (subject) need not employ *all* the word-specifying features in scanning his memory for the target. There is correspondingly no need to assume that in word understanding *all* the word-specifying (card-entered) features must be activated, or called to mind.

From this assumption ensues with compelling force the following theoretical postulate: since the understanding of a word does not necessarily involve the availability of *all* the meaning-constitutive features of the word, any theory of language understanding must provide for a mechanism (or "device") that would decide on each occasion *when* to discontinue the scanning of the relevant features. In the further course of our argument we shall refer to that mechanism as *sense constancy*.

Having utilized Brown and McNeill's study for gaining insight into the process of understanding, we may also profit from a look at Brown's earlier study concerned with the act of meaning. In *How Shall a Thing Be Called?* Brown (1958a) argues that one and the same thing or perceptual event can be referred to in different ways:

"there is an animal"
"there is a quadruped"
"there is a dog"
"there is a boxer"
"there is Prince"

Each successive designation calls for the application of a greater number of features. In other words, the speaker-hearer decides – in one way or another – how many features should come into play in the process of meaning or understanding. Brown quite emphatically points to the pragmatic aspect of the process: in our distinctions we are guided by what appears important to us at a particular moment.

This of course means that we must be in a position to make the necessary decisions. Very clearly, the word-specifying features (whether in their totality or in part) do not provide a sufficient basis for the decision of how a word is to be understood (in hearing or in speaking) in the particular circumstances. Between the complete lexical specification and the intended or realized effect of a word extend some degrees of freedom. The feature concept will be of questionable explanatory value so long as this gap has not been closed. A variety of factors are further discussed that could act to close the gap: language-inherent, intention-bound, situational, and personality-specific.

There is another way in which Brown and McNeill's *generic recall* is seminal for our line of thought. When starting his search for the target word, the subject tends to become aware of what are the practically "nonverbalizable" features of the object in question. Wenzl (1937) points out that at this stage we are often aware merely of the general tone of the word's phonetic form (sombre, gay, mellow, etc.). Witte (1959a, p 516) draws a parallel to the actualization of a perception: "At first there emerges but a tentative quality: we sense, for instance, the word as being soft, lush, heavy ...".

Imagine also the case of a subject who, searching for *sextant,* might say: "I can see the thing clearly, it has a quadrant attached to it, but I don't know what to call it". We are bound to realize that word-specifying features need not be exlusively of a linguistic nature[6]. What kind of lexicon could contain such nonverbal entries?

Features of this kind are certainly not a novelty in psychology: they have been known for a long time as *images*. A broad prospect is laid open by this concept.

For James (1890, p 265), "the static meaning, when the word is concrete ... consists of sensory images awakened". This position gave rise to a dispute which deeply affected the development of psychology in the first half of this century (cf., e. g., Hebb 1960; Paivio 1969; Kessel 1972). In this place we are solely interested in the current status of the question. Let us look at it from the vantage point we have reached in our discussion.

That a one-to-one correspondence between word and image (as claimed, for instance, by Titchener) does not exist has been established beyond the shadow of a doubt. It is likewise certain that imagery looms large in language learning and search processes of the kind reported above. Working initially within the theoretical framework of associationism, Paivio used to view images as "stimulus pegs from which associates can be hung and retrieved by means of mediating images" (1970, p 388). Hence the image holds here a comparable place to Osgood's s_M-r_M mediating link. The origin of images was described by Paivio in familiar associationist terms:

---

[6] It will be recalled that different kinds of elementary meaning units are likewise invoked by Szalay (see concluding part of Chap. 5) in his attempt to characterize the psychological meaning of words.

Images are regarded as symbolic processes which are linked developmentally to associative experiences involving concrete objects and events. In relation to language, they could be regarded as conditioned sensations for which appropriate words function as conditioned stimuli (1969, p 243).

A little later Paivio came to view imagery and verbal processes as two alternative coding systems: concrete words or sentences are codel and stored in both the imaginal and the verbal system, abstract words or sentences only in the verbal system (possibly with the aid of verbal "features"?). Whatever the case, we are left guessing whether the image of a word (or of the corresponding object) is an integral whole or whether it is separable into components. It would certainly serve our argument if we could operate conceptually with image components, in other words, if some of the word-specifying features turned out to be of the imaginal kind.

The first tentative evidence for the productivity of this construct was offered by MG Johnson (1970) in his study of compound associations (which we bear in mind on account of the term *elementary cognitive characteristic* – ECC). Employing, for instance, three nouns as a compound stimulus, Johnson made an interesting observation.

Most of the subjects spontaneously reported seeing images as they read the noun triads. This suggests ... [that] there may be a very close relation between ECC's and perceptual experience (1970, p 291).

Being now familiar with the idea that humans cognize the world more by projection than by "pure" perception, we are perhaps less impressed by Johnson's finding than we might otherwise have been. But we certainly take it to be an indication that new entities of cognition may emerge in the course of processing meaningful elements which represent the external world in our minds.

In the free association experiment, the subject is under pressure of time. Should imaginal features become particularly effective in associative processes at early stages of grasping the meaning of a stimulus word?

Replicating Brown and McNeill's TOT state experiment, May and Clayton (1973) amplified it by instructing their subjects to draw the target while having it on the tip of their tongues. When these drawings were ranked by competent judges in terms of similarity to the target object it was found that those produced by subjects unable both to recall the name and to imagine the object were significantly inferior to those drawn by subjects whose TOT state involved a visualization of the target. Now, the drawings of the latter subjects did not differ from those to whom the target word had occurred at once! It seems obvious that activation of visual information may precede recollection of the verbal designation.

This warrants the view that imaginal features, while forming a separate class of features, interact with other kinds of features in the language processes of meaning and understanding. One of their specific properties might be their activation in early stages of the process of understanding.

If we consider that Wenzl and Witte also found imaginal elements that resisted verbalization in early stages of the actualization of recollections, we cannot fail to ask the question as to possible connections with *inner speech,* which Soviet psychologists of language conceptualize as the first stage in the actualization of the sentence to be uttered. As we know, inner speech is likewise dominated by dynamic images of a prelinguistic character. Zhinkin postulated for this stage an *inner speech code,* a code consisting of "images and schemes" (outlines), also called "subject's depicting code" (AA Leontev, 1972, p 6). These images, by the way, are not exclusively of a visual type, many of them being motoric (articulation); later, the matter will be given more attention, notably in connection with the research of AN Sokolov, in Chap. 10.

At this stage, it will be enough to conclude that, in trying to develop a theory of meaning based on the feature concept, the psychologist would have to envisage the internal lexicon of the language user as also comprising nonlinguistic features. The border area between nonlinguistic, paralinguistic, and prelinguistic processes is surveyed in some detail in Chap. 11.

With our reference to "early activation" we have struck a note that will resound with increasing force as we continue our argument. Its most immediate implication is that any psychological theory of the acts of meaning and understanding must allow for the fact that the activation of language-relevant features proceeds at different levels and in stages. In this manner we are once again confronted with a notion that will henceforth claim a fair portion of our attention, the notion of *levels* at which linguistic material is organized in the mind. In fact, two different notions of level are involved, and these have to be held apart, even though they are interconnected in various ways. In one sense the term refers to *structural tiers in our internal lexicon,* or, more broadly, in any model of (lexical) memory; in its other sense it refers to the various *stages of language processing* as presupposed by the acts of meaning and understanding. It is not until we know more about meaning and understanding as *processes* that we can discuss levels of processing in any detail. For the time being we shall continue to deal with the material on which these processes operate.

The notion of a structural hierarchy in the lexicon (or memory store) was already implicit in Katz and Fodor's (1963) conception as we know it from Chaps. 4 and 5. These authors chose to display their semantic markers in the form of tree diagrams. The fact that (Animate) is entered above (Human), however, is apparently lacking in any psychological significance. In their study of the subjective lexicon Fillenbaum and Rapoport (1971) assert that some features precede other features in that, on examining the meaning of *to find,* we discover the feature ACQUIRE as a basic presupposition, complemented with the feature ACCIDENTAL as a specification of this particular manner of acquiring. The hierarchical organization of features in levels is a distinctive mark of Clark's theory: his account of associative behavior etc. stands or falls on the postulate that the word-specifying features are processed (by, e. g., a reversal of the sign) in a rule-determined order.

A hierarchical arrangement of stores for particular units of memory (or aspects of meaning) is likewise suggested by a number of studies which have more in common with the tradition of the psychology of thinking and memory than with psycholinguistics. Since they bear directly on our argument, these studies will be discussed at considerable length.

Quillian (1969) set out to devise a computer-based system for the storing of semantic (or lexical) information. In his memory (or lexicon) model, words are represented by nodes made up of configurations of pointers to other words and their various properties. Such a configuration comprises the meaning of the given word[7].

If the meaning of the word *canary,* for instance, is to be stored as "yellow bird that can sing", there is a pointer in Quillian's model linking *canary* with *bird* as the next highest (superset) designation. Two other pointers extend to what Quillian calls properties (features): *Is yellow* and *Can sing,* and these are entered next to *canary.* What is characteristic of the model is that only the highest word has the relevant properties listed, but not the next lowest words. For instance, properties shared by all birds, such as *Has feathers* and *Can fly,* are stored only next to *bird* and are not repeated for *robin, canary, eagle,* etc. The fact that a canary can fly is registered in the memory model by the pointer linking *canary* with *bird,* where the information *Can fly* is stored.

This "space-saving" model enables us to make some testable predictions. Should the subject be asked to decide whether the sentence "A canary can sing" is true or false, he has only to become aware of the properties stored with *canary.* If the same is to be done for the sentence "A canary can fly", the subject has to follow the pointer from the node for *canary* to the next highest node of the superset category *bird,* where *Can fly* is stored. The latter process is bound to take more time than the former. This prediction was verified in a study by Collins and Quillian (1969), who found longer verification times for "A robin is an animal" than for "A robin is a bird"; a greater number of nodes have to be run through in the first case than in the second.

Quillian's model introduces us to the class of network models that have become quite popular in psychology in recent years. It would be difficult not to notice their affinity to the much older semantic fields, discussed in Chap. 5, but it is equally clear that network models yield predictions of much greater precision in matters of the storing and retrieval of lexical material.

The relations obtaining between any two nodes (words) in a network can be approached from two different angles: one is that of the (semantic) distance between any two nodes – to which Collins and Quillian addressed themselves – the other is that of the quality of the relation between a word and its superordinate (e. g., from *canary* to *bird*) and between the word and its properties. Though it would be too early to go into the quality type relations, we might mention the work by Rumelhart et al. (1972), where the predicative relation between a word

---

[7] It might be useful to recall that the idea of a word's meaning as made up of the word's associations with other words is a conception of long standing in the psychology of language. It should suffice to mention the work of Noble, Osgood, and Deese. (Cf. Hörmann 1971a, pp 138–147.)

and its superset concept is termed an "isa" (*is a* . . .) relation, and the other one, a "has" relation[8].

In most network models, as in Katz and Fodor's conception of the lexicon and in many works since Locke, the organization of memory and the lexicon is conceptualized as closely reflecting the "logical structure of the mind"[9]. The principle of *genus proximum* and *differentia specifica* is still very much in evidence: an eagle is a bird, a bird is an animal, and an animal is an animate thing . . . And yet the real relations between concepts need not follow this pattern. For instance, in a true/false verification experiment, a response to the sentence "A lion is a mammal" was found to take longer than to the sentence "A lion is an animal", which seems to point to a greater semantic distance between lion and mammal than between lion and animal.

Should one want to interpret this finding psychologically, by claiming that *animal* was entered on a sort of intermediate level between the particular mammals (lion, horse, donkey, mouse) and their superset concept *mammal,* the sentence "All animals are mammals" would have to be judged true by subjects in view of the inevitability with which logical hierarchy defines the truth value of such propositions; the predicative pointer extending to the next highest level cannot be mistaken! In an alternative interpretation, we might assume that *animal* is entered twice at two different levels: between *lion* and *mammal* (as suggested by the empirical finding) and again on top of mammal (as postulated by logic). Then we would need a decision-making procedure to determine if the term *animal* used in the particular sentence is located on one or the other level.

There is still another snag that makes trouble for all linguistic lexicon models as well as the psychological network and set theoretic models of memory. All these models follow the injunctions of logic[10] in assuming that the superordinate, or the category-defining feature, applies to *all* subsumed words in equal measure. For Katz and Fodor, (Animate) applies to *bachelor* as much as to *snail*, and to *lion*, and to *animal*. Indeed, this feature has been entered precisely in order to establish an equivalence of all the words that belong to the class Animate. The selection restrictions attached to the feature extend to the entire category without any exception.

Can we really assume that the language-using, purposefully acting human being operates with such feature-delimited and internally undifferentiated

---

[8] This restriction to "isa" and "has" relations shows once again the overriding influence of logic. As pointed out by Macnamara (1971), there are conceivably many other relations in a lexicon: "greater than", "father of", "cause of", "implied by", . . . This of course reminds us of Bierwisch and his claim that such semantic dimensions reflect some deep-seated properties of the human perceptual apparatus.

[9] The same can be said of the somewhat kindred set theoretic models (e. g., Schaeffer and Wallace 1970), where semantic distance between two concepts is represented by the overlapping part of the two concept-specifying sets of features. For these and some other issues discussed below see Rips et al. (1973).

[10] One is reminded here of Chafe's admonition that the close association of linguistics and logic has not always been to the advantage of the former . . .

classes? Are really all things which belong in the same drawer ("birds") equivalent?

The assumption seems unwarranted in the light of our discussion of the concept of semantic field alone, though field theory could not provide us with clear-cut findings that would bear on the hierarchical relations between a generic concept and the individual elements of the subsumed semantic field. Definite indications of a psychologically relevant inner structure of logical classes and categories ensue from Deese's early factor-analytic studies of word association data. Henley (1969), an associate of Deese's, employed a number of techniques to establish which aspects within the category *animal* were psychologically responsible for the internal structuring of the category. She found these aspects to be inconsistent with either the logical or the zoological systems:

> The general picture ... for the Ss of this study is one in which animals are preponderantly mammals, and in which mammals fit into a few fairly well-described categories. These categories are (1) small wild animals, (2) herbivores, including farm animals, (3) primates, and (4) other carnivores ... The elephant belongs to a separate class. The important dimensions in classifying these animals are those of size and ferocity (p 183).

Thus we are made aware of two counts on which the existing conceptions of the lexicon and category-bound models of memory are in need of revision:

1) The structure of the vocabulary stored in our memory does not coincide with logical structure. The age-old philosophical distinction between analytic and synthetic truth is called into question insofar as we are unable to identify the basis upon which analytic judgments are made.

2) The various kinds or instances of beings subsumed under the category *animal* differ in their "animalness": some are more typical animals than others. This challenges the notion of class or category which implies by definition that all members of the given class are equal as such.

The point made under (2) wes elaborated by Rosch (1973) in her study of the internal structure of perceptual and semantic categories. She begins by criticizing the view – prevailing both in linguistics and in concept formation research – which treats semantic categories as bundles of discrete features that clearly differentiate the category from all others and which approaches these categories as though they were composed of undifferentiated, equivalent instances. Rosch further asserts

> that there are categories in perceptual domains such as color and form which are not arbitrary. Neither a "concept-formation model" of category formation in terms of learning the "correct" (defined either by an experimenter or a culture) combination of discrete attributes nor an "abstraction-process model" of category formation in terms of abstraction of the central tendency of an (experimentally or culturally determined) arbitrary grouping of distributions of attributes is adequate to account for the nature and development of categories in these perceptual domains. The following alternative account ... is proposed: there are colors and forms which are more perceptually salient than other stimuli in their domains. A working hypothesis is that salient colors are those areas of the color space previously found to be most exemplary of basic color names in many different languages (...) and that salient forms are the "good forms" of Gestalt psychology ... (pp 113–114).

In a series of experiments with perceptual categories (colors, forms) and semantic categories (fruit, sport, bird, toy, etc.) Rosch was able to show that a generic concept such as redness, or squareness, is conceived, not as an internally unstructured class, but as an area with a focus containing the most typical representatives of the category (focal examples) and a periphery of diminishing "examplariness". Among fruits, for instance, she found some to be more representative of fruits than others: apple is a more typical fruit than fig or olive. In the same vein, football is a more typical sport than archery and weightlifting, murder is a more typical crime than embezzling and blackmail, and cancer and malaria are more typical diseases than rheumatism and a cold.

Psychologists and linguists alike must admit the possibility that, by learning (though not of the associative kind), centers of gravity develop in memory to form points of reference for our perception of, and interaction with, the world around us. The meaning of *fruit* as much as the meaning of *crime* is specified not by an enumeration of the properties that are common to *all* varieties of fruit, or all varieties of crime, but by centering around and focusing upon the typical example.

The immediate question that arises is of course about the factors responsible for focusing upon a particular point in a developing conceptual or semantic field. What makes murder appear a more "exemplary" crime than embezzling, and what makes an eagle a more typical bird than a duck? Frequency of occurrence does not explain this.

Quite similar views, although supplemented with the feature concept, are held by Smith et al. (1974). Heeding Wittgenstein's suggestion that a precise delimitation of concepts is often impossible (see Chap. 9), the authors contend that the word-specifying semantic features can be distributed over a continuum

> along which some features will be more defining or essential aspects of a word's meaning, while others will be more accidental or characteristic features (p 216).

Like Rosch, they made their subjects rate the typicality of various instances of the category *bird* (sparrow, robin, chicken). These typicality ratings were found to rise with the number of word-specifying features the given instance shared with the superordinate. Lower typicality values were recorded for words with congruence only in the defining features (e. g., *chicken*).

Different typicality ratings are paralleled by characteristic linguistic constructions, as described by Lakoff (1972). In a sentence comprising both a category name and a word designating an instance of that category, we are bound to build in appropriate "hedges" for low typicality words, to make the sentence acceptable. In the case of a high-typicality word like *eagle* we may safely say "An eagle is a true bird", but for words of lower typicality we feel the need to insert hedges like "Technically speaking, a chicken is a bird". When the subject of the sentence shares some characteristic, but no defining features with the predicate noun, we need a hedge (or, more appropriately, a crutch) like this: "Loosely speaking, . . ." or "If you like, a bat is a bird".

As in the previous case, we are vexed by the question as to what factors are responsible for a particular placement of a word-specifying feature along the dimension extending from *defining* to *characteristic*. It has been suggested by Wett-ler (1970) that the pattern of relations between concepts depends less on their hierarchical arrangement than on the functional and situational relationships be-tween concepts and between concepts and actions.

The question is essentially the same as when we asked ourselves how it is that *long* represents both the positive pole and the entire dimension of length. Together with Clark and Ertel we noticed the determining influence of experi-ence: the best example of something with length is something with much length. The present case is very similar: a typical disease is a grave sickness, and a typical crime is a particularly striking crime. This goes to show once again that perceiv-ing and understanding involve the development of schemata or plans, and it is in the nature of a schema to be well formed and *prägnant*. The matter will be treated at length in Chap. 12, devoted to language acquisition.

The structures of the lexicon – on the evidence reviewed so far – do not necessarily follow the orthodox logic of the concept of superset and of *genus proximum* and *differentia specifica*. Such a logical arrangement would be necessary for the operation with features conceived as additive properties of otherwise internally undifferentiated categories. It has been shown on numerous occasions (e. g., Bock 1976) that the range of features scanned by the subject varies with intention or task, the various features being of differential importance for word or sentence understanding, for memorization, for recall, etc.

At an earlier stage in our discussion we encountered a view that contradicts the orthodox notion of features as immutable and equally effective units. In their study of the subjective lexicon (reviewed in the latter part of Chap. 5) Fillenbaum and Rapoport contend that some features function as prerequisites for activation of other features, which reflects cognitive, rather than logical, implications be-tween features. Relations between concepts founded on knowledge of the world rather than on logical deducibility are likewise emphasized by Smith, Shoben, and Rips in the above reported study.

Turning our attention now squarely to the notion of presupposition we wish to recall Fillenbaum and Rapoport's suggestion that the various word-specifying features might stand in a presupposition-specification relationship.

We pursue the matter on the basis of the evidence and ideas offered by GA Mil-ler (1968, 1971). This work provides a connection with a development in linguis-tics that has taken place since Chomsky's second (1965) model: In one respect, Miller's study falls into the large group of projects which seek to elaborate the principles of cognitive functioning as language universals; in another respect, however, it can be located well within the Katz-Fodor tradition on account of its approach using semantic markers (features) as the relevant factors of sentence generation; furthermore, Miller employs classification procedures of the type we have become familiar with.

Much in accord with Katz and Fodor, Miller asserts that it is not enough

to provide characterizations of the meanings of individual lexical items. The definitions must be formulated in such a way that interpretations can be constructed, according to rule, for combinations of words that can occur in grammatical constructions. In order for any cognitive analysis of verbal concepts to have linguistic relevance, it must be compatible with this goal of linguistic semantics (1968, p 21).

Miller is no longer interested in proving "the psychological reality of grammer"; instead, he is concerned with the "linguistic relevance of cognitive analyses". We shall soon realize, however, that in his "cognitive analyses" he continues to draw heavily on linguistic concepts: evidently, the priority thesis (so named by Schlesinger) is very resistant to extinction.

All hitherto reviewed psycholinguistic and linguistic attemps at coming to grips with semantic features or markers employ, in one way or another, the notion of similarity. Miller now comes to consider the important question: When trying to assess similarity by, e. g., substitutability, what is the subject supposed to uphold while substituting: grammaticalness, truth, plausibility . . .? By this token Miller has tacitly resorted to a functionalist approach: verbal utterances – and similarities between them – may only be assessed if allowances are made for their functions. Under this novel view Miller reduces the native speaker – previously held to be able to refer his judgments to langugage-in-itself, that is, to language cut off from its uses and its purposes – to realistic proportions.

Accordingly, in his own experiment, Miller (1971, originally published 1967) adopts the following procedure: He selects arbitrarily 48 nouns to cover a broad range of concepts, half of them being names of objects, the other half being names of nonobjects (concepts). These nouns are entered on cards, one per card. Written on each card is further

a dictionary definition of the particular sense of the word that was intended and a simple sentence using the word in that sense (1971, p 576).

This seemingly minor innovation in customary classification procedures cannot be overestimated. Miller conceptualizes the semantic markers of a word in such a manner as to involve them in the dynamics of sentence construction. To achieve this, he puts the critical word into a sentence; strictly speaking, he presents it in two contexts: in the definition and in the sentence. In doing so, he does not deem it necessary to comment on his novel design, but we would assume that he feels the need for providing his subject, who is to make a judgment on the sentence-constituting features of the given word, with a sentence in which the word is used. We have thus travelled some distance from the syntax-centered model of generative grammar in which sentence constitution was solely a matter of syntax and word meaning solely a matter of semantic interpretation. For Miller, the meaning of a word has come to depend on the broader meaning of the sentence.

Fifty subjects (judges) were asked to classify 48 cards, sorting them into as many piles as they wished, on the basis of similarity of meaning. In keeping with the logic of a subsequent cluster analysis, words judged to be similar by a large number of subjects are thought to possess more features in common than those so judged by fewer subjects.

In addition to the two (dichotomous) categories built into the set of test words by the experimenter (object and nonobject), the study revealed five more specific categories: living and nonliving (objects), social, personal, and quantitative concepts (nonobjects). By way of illustration: 49 of the 50 subjects grouped *cook* and *doctor* together, 44 also included *umpire* in this group, 42 admitted *mother,* and 37 also *knight* to the same group.

Miller frames this empirical finding into a psychological and at the same time linguistically relevant interpretation by gearing it to his keynote question: What are well-formed sentences uttered for? His answer is: to predicate. The essence of verbal utterance is predication, which is based on a specific relationship between subject and predicate.

Thereby Miller has joined in with a development in linguistics that will repeatedly demand our attention in these pages. At the same time he has come to consider the eminently psychological question as to what the intention of the speaker is. By inquiring into the speaker's intention we conceive the utterance as a continuation of whatever action (verbal or nonverbal) has preceded it. An utterance supplements or modifies the speaker's (pre-)suppositions that induced him to make the utterance: on the basis of these suppositions a predication is now made.

This interaction of a persisting basis with the resultant predication founded on it is a pivotal feature of any acting by means of language, a feature whose importance cannot be overrated. By whatever we say, assert, allege, relate, allude to, divulge, exclaim, interject, or ask – we make reference to our own and the hearer's content of consciousness and thus provide for the indispensable continuity of things. It is in this sense that language must be seen as a "continuation of action with other means" (Hörmann 1971a, p 268).

The very same pivotal feature of language has come to be recognized by Miller as underlying our internal lexicon: "our lexical memory must be organized to facilitate predications" (1968, p 20). Consequently, it is in the word itself that Miller locates the distinction between presupposition and assertion, as a basis for the act of predication – which constitutes for him the foundation of the lexicon. Presuppositions are those features that are shared by the given word with other, similar words[11].

The most adequate paraphrase of presupposition as conceived by Miller might be the following: by using a particular word in an utterance, the speaker presupposes the hierarchically higher features and asserts only the lowest feature (or the distinguisher). To quote Miller (1968, p 25):

> ... an adult speaker of English must have his lexical information stored in such a manner that he can distinguish the presupposition from the assertion of any common noun. Since the presupposition of one noun may include the assertion of some more abstract noun, this requirement imposes considerable structure on the subjective lexicon.

Let us illustrate this with an example. *Knight* is defined as "a man who has been raised to honorary military rank". The utterance "Is Leslie a knight?", while

---

[11] Also the generative semanticists (e. g., Fillmore) show a tendency to anchor the presupposition in the word, and hence in the lexicon, not in the utterance. But Fillmore considers the lexicon as organized in terms of predicate-argument structures rather than in terms of feature dimensions.

inquiring whether the assertion "is a knight" applies to Leslie, implies the correctness of the presupposition that Leslie is a man.

Are Miller's cluster analysis data amenable to such an interpretation? Do the card-sorting subjects actually rely on the presuppositions and assertions of the test words as contained (or implied) in the definitions and sentences? Let us inspect one of the clusters from Miller's study.

COOK, DOCTOR and UMPIRE are nearly always grouped together; they are joined by MOTHER and KNIGHT with somewhat lower frequency. Miller offers this interpretation:

> MOTHER – a *woman* who has borne a child.
> COOK – a *person* who prepares food by using heat.
> DOCTOR – a *person* who is licensed to treat diseases.
> UMPIRE – a *person* who rules on the plays of a game.
> KNIGHT – a *man* who has been raised to honorary military rank.
> Since COOK, DOCTOR, and UMPIRE all presuppose *person,* they can be combined on that basis simply by ignoring these assertions that distinguish them. Since a MOTHER is a *woman* and a WOMAN is a *person,* and since KNIGHT is a *man* and a MAN is a *person,* MOTHER and KNIGHT presuppose all that COOK, DOCTOR, and UMPIRE presuppose, plus a little more. Some judges might not be willing to ignore those additional presuppositions, and so the number putting MOTHER and KNIGHT with the *person* cluster would be correspondingly smaller. This pattern is confirmed by the results (p 49).

Miller's theorizing seems to be borne out by the analyzed group of data: the features in terms of which the subjective lexicon is structured do make allowance for the fact that words (or their features) perform some functions in the utterance as a behavioral act in which both speaker and hearer participate.

It might be worthwhile to recall that in Katz and Fodor's semantic theory, words (or their features) perform certain functions in the sentence, making it semantically unambigous, semantically normal, and paraphrasable.

Miller's (and our) satisfaction at having developed a dynamic principle of lexicon organization with some practical uses did not survive the following objection. On theoretical grounds Steinberg (1971, p 494) asserts that Miller's classification method can yield valid results only if all subjects (judges) are guided by the same criteria in their similarity judgments (which imply yes-no responses)[12].

After a scrutiny of his data, Miller himself concluded that this was not so: "It is obvious that other considerations influenced many of the judges' decisions" (p 51). Learning that *jack* and *wheel* were grouped together on account of what Miller calls "mutual entailment", and *yacht* and *skate* "because both imply recrea-

---

[12] Steinberg's objection does not apply to, e. g., Fillenbaum and Rapoport's multidimensional scaling, which admits of the possibility that *son* and *daughter* are rated as more similar than *daughter* and *father;* in effect, it enables the extraction of several features in parallel – which Miller's method does not.

tional activities", we realize that in some cases the judges did go by those "presuppositions", but in other cases they did not. Did they consider some other, psychologically inscrutable presuppositions as criteria of their sorting? Should there be alternative presupposition-assertion relationships? Or should the subjects have ignored all presuppositions on account of having stored the words in alternative ways (their lexicon lacking the respective presupposition entries), or else, because they failed to make use of their presupposition markers under the influence of the guiding sentences? Or is it that words have altogether no fixed, cross-situationally stable markers, and that their features merely respond to the situation in which the word is understood?

Questions like these are heresy. As we know, the lexicon and its structures were devised on the tacit assumption that, as in grammar, all the postulated processes of generation and interpretation were obligatory. No allowance whatever had been made in any of the linguistic theories, and in any of the psychological systems discussed so far, for the language user's option (whether conscious or not) to make use of his lexicon in this way or another, or not to make use of it at all. It will have to be recognized that language is exempt from iron rules of use, that it is always in the control of the language user who may choose to handle it this way or that. The linguists' old conception of language as an autonomous entity, fully accountable within that entity, seems to be losing all grounds. To be able to use language evidently means, not least, being able to do it both one way *and* another. This aspect of indeterminacy in language will come into focus as we draw closer to the end of the book, since it underlies our conception of understanding.

There are also purely linguistic reasons for postulating indeterminacy in language. Wunderlich (1970b) is one of those linguists who would like to know if the lexical entry *whale* should be labelled *mammal*, or *fish*, or left without either of the two markers. (This is the linguistic counterpart of Henley's psychological analysis – see earlier in this chapter.) Depending on what we decide, the sentence

A WHALE IS A FISH

is either analytic, or contradictory, or synthetic.

> Our conclusion is that there are a number of semantic markings which may neither be fixed permanently nor non-entered in the lexicon of the speaker. They may be admitted only as depending on some particular dialogue situations or communicative functions, or else as depending on the personal record and learning history of the speaker (Wunderlich 1970, p 154).

If the question of what can be entered in the lexicon is essentially unresolvable, then the lexicon's heuristic utility is cast into doubt. Incidentally, Wunderlich is likewise guilty of heresy when asserting that it depends on the situation and the communicative functions as to what the speaker-hearer might include in his lexicon for the particular occasion. True enough, communication should not be viewed as the net effect of the meanings of the words employed in the process. Instead, the meaning of these words follows from the particular communication. This thesis will be a recurrent theme in our further discussion. But now

97

we want to resume our argument with Miller by raising another awkward question.

From Mandler's (1967) research we know that in any such sorting and recall tasks, category size and category number are mutually related in a particular manner: a subject who might group the instances into too many narrow categories will be forced to adopt some superordinate concepts, just as a subject who has adopted too few broad categories will be forced to subdivide them into smaller ones. Type and number of categories formed depend on load imposed by the task, differentiation of the material, availability of superordinate concepts, and the like.

Miller's subjects were free to choose any number of categories when classifying their 48 words, as we know. Would they have arranged the words according to quite different features had they been confronted with 480 rather than 48 items? Would they have used different semantic dimensions in analyzing *mother* if they had had to compare it, not with *cook, umpire,* and *knight,* but with *grandmother* and the names of three aunts? Do the features identified by Miller *always* apply to the words in question?

These as well as the preceding questions cannot be answered for the time being, but their cardinal importance is beyond dispute. Their consequences can be seen from the following analysis.

Miller had chosen his 48 words so as to be able to use them both as nouns and as verbs, and he tried the latter in another study – which yielded different results. Miller (1971) explains:

> the verb senses of these words were defined and illustrated on the cards that the judges were asked to classify. When they are thought of as verbs, of course, the object/concept distinction that is so obvious for these words in their noun usages is no longer relevant; the object marker would not be expected to appear in the results of the verb classifications, and in truth it did not. The results of the verb study are not presented here, however, because I do not yet understand them. The object marker did not appear, but neither did anything else that I could recognize (p 577).

This clustering technique has thus miscarried as far as detecting the evidently different ways in which words are entered in the lexicon. It may be a valid tool for the exploration of one type of entry, but it also gives rise to further questions:

a) Are there any other kinds of lexicon entries?

b) Are there different kinds of entries for any one word?

c) What factors cause one or another type of entry to apply in a particular case?

Once again we have a feeling that the conception of a lexicon structured in terms of semantic markers or features is badly in need of revision. If it is true that a word (or a group of words) can be specified by different *types* of features, and if the activation of a particular variety of features does not automatically ensue from the occurrence of the respective word, then the lexicon must allow for the effect of factors and strategies responsible for the activation, in the particular circumstances, of some but not other features.

A further important implication is that the lexicon, conceived as a store of instructions for utilization of words, loses its theoretical relevance if there is no guarantee that such instructions can be effective at the word level. Speculating on the possible reasons for the failure of his verb classification experiment, Miller himself conjectures:

perhaps verbs signify rather special formulae – complex functions into which particular nouns can be substituted as arguments (1971, p 577).

This question is explored in depth by generative semantics (discussed in Chap. 8), which tends to conceptualize a verb as being linked with "its" nouns (e. g., the subject and object of a sentence) in a predicate-argument structure.

Miller's reference to *formulae* reveals one more important aspect of the issue: a formula is not a mere instruction on how to proceed, it is a general instruction in the sense that it is more general than whatever is actually done under the guidance of this instruction. Up to this point Miller has tried to account for the more general nature of "his" presuppositions by employing, in their definitions, fewer features than in the case of the assertions. In order to achieve this, he assumed – as pointed out by Steinberg – that his "natural" hierarchy of features, ranging from the most general (object) to distinguishers, obtains for every condition and every subject.

In another of his experiments Miller (1972) moves even closer to psychology (and farther away from linguistics). He now confronts the problem that language, on the one hand, is used to characterize and store our experience, and that, on the other, "the symbols of language must themselves be stored in memory" (p 335). Thus the distinction between lexicon and memory fades away and Miller adopts the notion of *lexical memory* as a store of prelinguistic, conceptual representations whose particular form determines the verbalized version of our recall.

It stands to reason that this only served to shift the problem to a different level of analysis: the construct of mental lexicon was originally introduced to account for the "translation from concept to word and vice versa". When saying that the information stored in lexical memory is retrieved and expressed "in many alternative linguistic forms" (p 335), Miller realizes that he will need, besides a theory of lexical memory, also a theory of "linguistic expression" of lexical memory content. In any case, he is aware of the following:

A bridge from the structure inherent in the lexicon to the psychological processes inherent in verbal thought must span a larger gap than one might at first suppose. A description of what a person knows tells us very little about the uses he can or will make of that knowledge (p 337).

Having got into trouble when trying to conceive how the semantic components of words (markers) could be arranged in a hierarchy, Miller now construes them, not as the components of word meaning, but as components of the concepts which underlie words. This escape route is available to him only because he does not care to define his notion of concept with any precision. Analyzing word meaning, he simply distinguishes between two parts:

one part having to do with extralinguistic things and events to which a word can refer, and the other being the semantic relations of the word to other words and phrases in the language (p 336).

After underlining that those two parts of a word's meaning go close together in actual language use, he proceeds to investigate the second of the two.

For his sorting experiment Miller (1972) selects – from a list of 217 motion verbs (go, ride, swim, walk, etc.) – subsets each comprising from 10 to 20 motion verbs; in his selection he employs a number of variable criteria.

He seems to adhere to the assumption (which has been shown to be questionable) that with the sorting technique the psychologist "hits" precisely the essence of what is involved in the processes of forming and understanding sentences; in other words, that his classification method serves to pin down the subject's *knowledge* of the structures prevailing in the semantic field of motion verbs, rather than the specific *uses* the subject makes of this knowledge in the experiment. However, he is aware of this limitation when saying:

> the present analysis does not even tell us anything about mental processes whereby basic lexical information of this kind could be used to produce or comprehend intelligible, grammatical utterances (p 367).

Despite Miller's investigation we are lacking in a theory of lexicon use, and this is all the more distressing as Miller's lexicon has become more removed from language. What is it like now?

The semantic field of the motion verbs centers around the concept of moving from one position to another (change of location). While there is no English word that would exactly describe this concept (*to travel* being the closest approximation, according to Miller), each of the various motion verbs has some additional, differentiating component(s). Miller identifies the following semantic components of the English motion verbs: motion, reflexive-objective, causative, permissive, propellent, directional, medium, instrumental, inchoative, change-of-motion, deictic, and velocity.

Thus, the designation "directional–downward–reflexive" would apply for instance to:

HE DESCENDED THE STAIRS
HE DROPPED
HE FELL

The designation "directional–downward–objective" would include:

HE LOWERED THE BATON
HE DEPRESSED THE PEDAL
HE DROPPED THE BOOK
HE FELLED THE TREE

Another example: the group *walks – strolls – tiptoes – runs – sprints – jogs – trots* reveals the component *travel* on *land by foot* but at the same time does not show the (expected) component *velocity of motion*.

This analysis enables Miller to propose elaborate paraphrases of many verbs of motion. For example, the componential paraphrase of

HE JUMPS THE FENCE

is given as *He applies force with his legs to make himself begin traveling through the air over the fence*. The "translation" of *to jump a fence* into such an awkward paraphrase is justified, in Miller's and many other psycholinguists' view, because the terms in the paraphrase (to apply force, to begin, to travel . . .) correspond more closely to underlying concepts than does *to jump*.

A similar attempt, more comprehensive and theoretically more sophisticated, was made by Schank (1972), who investigated dependencies among concepts implied by an utterance in order to develop "a theory of natural language understanding". There is at least one conceptualization behind each sentence; its basic unit is the concept. There are three elementary types of concepts: nominals, actions, and modifiers. Nominals are the entities that can be thought of without bringing them in relation to other concepts; they are image-producers. An action is what a nominal does or can do. A modifier is a concept that becomes meaningful only in association with a nominal and an action; if specifies an attribute. These concepts may enter into relations of diverse kinds; most relations involve a governor and a dependent.

Schank's ideas show certain affinities to those of the generative semanticists, but he does not submit his theory to empirical verification – thus depriving us of the opportunity to discuss it in greater detail.

With their attempts to locate the possible dynamic relations a word may enter into in the concept, Miller and Schank succeed in surmounting to some extent the disparity between syntax and semantics and, in any case, the much less venerable distinction between syntactic base structure and interpretive semantics. Miller in his new constructions has shifted some of the dynamics inherent in the sentence (to be accounted for, in the orthodox models, by syntax) to the lexicon entries. The trouble is, however, that the instructions for the language user who wishes to convey some meaning or tries to make sense of an utterance are only *in some cases* entered with the lexical item (word); in many other cases they are contained in much more complex and comprehensive "formulae" (comprising both verbal and nonverbal elements) of which we cannot tell as yet whether they are entered in some kind of formula lexicon or in a syntax more content relevant than any one known so far.

Let us have as our concluding example Chafe's (1970) brilliant analysis of idioms, where it is pointed out that the meaning of, for example,

GEORGE IS ON THE WAGON

can*not* be derived from an analysis of the words and its features. What is in fact meant by the idiom (i. e., abstinence from alcoholic drinks) can be discovered in entirely different ways; should we possess a sentence lexicon for that purpose? Are we to believe Feltkamp (1971) who maintains that the grammar of a speaker-hearer comprises two lexicons without a strict separation: an atomic lexicon of the kind proposed in systematic linguistics, and a molecular lexicon for storing the larger units (sentences, predicate phrases, and the like)? Or should we shrink back from accepting this suggestion for fear of reducing the lexicon concept to absurdity?

A brighter prospect opens up with Van Lancker's (1975) neurolinguistic study.

From her survey of the relevant material and her own experiments there emerges the following picture.

The ability to produce constructive, propositional utterances is usually impaired in aphasic disorders associated with lesions in Broca's speech area in the left hemisphere. At the same time, such stereotyped speech elements as expletives, digits, figures of speech, and conventional phrases are retained. The latter linguistic units are apparently produced in other ways (and possibly other areas of the brain) than "cognitive" or propositional utterances. Van Lancker (1975, p 6) argues:

> There is a functionally significant dimension describing language use called a *propositional-automatic* dimension . . . Propositional speech is made up of newly-created, original, novel utterances. Automatic speech includes conventional and overlearned expressions, idioms, swearing, emotional language, and other modes . . .

Deduced from a wealth of empirical data, Van Lancker's dimension of language use is a concept of considerable heuristic utility. Such a construct is, however, incompatible with a lexicon of the conventional type, which cannot accomodate the contention that the various components of practically every utterance occupy *different* places on the propositional-automatic dimension. In order to produce or understand any utterance, the speaker-hearer must be able to move freely along the dimension, and we would have to imagine him consulting, in quick alternation, here the word lexicon, there the figure of speech lexicon, elsewhere the idiom lexicon, and over there the proverb lexicon . . .

The importance of stereotype in language was recognized already by Jespersen. Lyons (1968, p 177–178), on the other hand, seems to have a pat solution at hand for dealing with "ready-made" utterances. He says:

> they might be classified as (grammatically unstructured) sentences, since they bear the same intonation contour as sentences generated by the grammar . . . they are to be accounted for simply by listing them in the dictionary with an indication of the situation in which they are used and their meaning.

The matter is not quite so simple: glossing over the fact that a "grammatically unstructured sentence" is difficult to imagine if the sentence is defined as a comprehensive grammatical structure, we would like to know how the proposed dictionary (lexicon) would decide between *not* analyzing *George is on the wagon,* in the case that George is in fact a teetotaler, and analyzing the very same utterance in the case that George has got on a wagon? Should it be that, in order to understand what is being said, the hearer must already have an inkling of what the speaker means?

The lexicon in its conventional version leaves no room for a fundamental aspect of Van Lancker's conception: that everyday language is replete with stereotyped expressions, idiomatic figures of speech, phrases, and schemata to an extent that defies linguistic orthodoxy, and that a large portion of our utterances are less based on grammar than simply reproduced from memory in convenient chunks. Nobody less than Bolinger (1976) has told us: "Speakers do at least as much remembering as they do putting together" (quoted after Van Lancker 1975, p 174).

Language use as a feat of memory, rather than as incessant rule-governed creativity, is a conception that does not fit into the foundation of the generativists' competence grammar, where grammar is defined as being independent of memory with its various capacity constraints and inconsistencies.

It might be useful to cast a final glance at the idea of the lexicon as developed by the generativists. The lexicon was conceptualized in defiance of what is going on in the process of actual language use. But you don't construct a hammer and think *afterward* what hammering is.

The lexicon has been treated by the generativists as a sack where syntax could stow away semantics short of dumping it altogether. With all the trouble caused by the distinction, one wonders how much sense there is in proposing two separate sets of instructions – syntax and semantics – for the language user. Because the really important problem is to pick out from amongst all the goings-on in the sentence those threads that make for its comprehension.

Chapter 7

The Concept of Sense Constancy

Does it make sense to maintain two separate sets of instructions, one called syntax, the other semantics? This question, raised at the end of our discussion of the lexicon, brings us back to Katz, Fodor, and all the others who postulated the dichotomy. Using the term *grammar* in its narrowest sense, Katz and Fodor (1963, p 172–173) state:

> Grammars answer the question: What does the speaker know about the phonological and syntactic structure of his language that enables him to use and understand any of its sentences . . .? Semantics takes over the explanation of the speaker's ability to produce and understand new sentences at the point where grammar leaves off.

In the course of our argument we found the semantic component – subdivided into lexicon and projection rules, and meant to supplement syntax – to be wholly ineffective as a construct with which to account for the "use", "production", and "understanding" of sentences in real life, and hence in dynamic, communicative settings. The lexicon as a store of linguistic "spare parts" does not dovetail, in the practice of communication, with syntax conceived as the place-assigning system.

This disappointing conclusion was drawn from our discussion of the concept of lexicon in the preceding chapters; the matter may be regarded as closed for the time being. We shall therefore make a fresh approach: taking Katz and Fodor again as a point of departure we propose to examine, from a *psychological* perspective, the language phenomena these authors sought to account for with their *linguistic* theory.

As we know, Katz and Fodor introduced their semantic component "at the point where [the syntax-centered] grammar leaves off", that is, proves ineffective. The ineffectiveness of syntax was glaringly revealed in its failure to resolve semantic ambiguities (THE BILL WAS LARGE), identify paraphrases (TWO CHAIRS ARE IN THE ROOM – THERE ARE AT LEAST TWO THINGS IN THE ROOM AND EACH IS A CHAIR), and to prevent semantic anomalies (THE PAINT WAS SILENT).

With their semantic theory, Katz and Fodor maintain that the combined application of (syntactic) competence and the information contained in semantic markers and projection rules suffices, say, to prevent the production or understanding of a semantically anomalous sentence. The case of semantic anomaly will now be used to show that this claim is unwarranted, and by examining the reasons for the failure we may hope to strengthen our own argument.

A sentence is semantically anomalous if it is composed – in keeping with the mandatory rules of syntax – of words (morphemes, lexemes, . . .) with mutually incompatible semantic markers. THE PAINT IS SILENT is semantically anomalous because *silent* carries, among others, the marker Animate and because *paint* does not satisfy this condition. Anyone who may wish to speak of a *liquid ax* will produce a semantic anomaly because one of the markers of *ax* is Solid, which is incompatible with the markers of *liquid*. The selection restrictions which prohibit such compounds express necessary and sufficient conditions for the selected readings to become compatible.

From the contention that these selection restrictions (which are part of the meaning-specifying lexicon entry) express "necessary and sufficient conditions" for the presence or absence of a semantic anomaly, it follows that such an anomaly must inevitably arise – because automatically ensuing from the speaker-hearer's competence – whenever incompatible words, or markers, are strung together in violation of the rule. Selection restrictions belong to the class of semantic markers, and markers are automatically consulted in the generation, and hence production and understanding of sentences – provided competence *is* the basis of performance.

In parallel with Chomsky's grammar, where judgments on the well-formedness of sentences ensue from a system of rules that is part of the speaker-hearer's competence and as such invariant across situations, Katz and Fodor construe their semantic markers, which represent the meaning of a word in the lexicon, as invariant across situations to the same extent as are for them the ways of handling this matrix in the process of speaking and understanding. Equipped with the Katz-Fodor lexicon, the competent speaker-hearer cannot respond to a prohibited word string otherwise than by sounding the alarm signal "Semantic anomaly!" and abandoning further attempts at understanding the defective sentence.

Opposing this view, I argued (Hörmann 1973) that the juxtaposition of two not entirely commensurable semantic matrices, far from sounding an alarm, might prove illuminating for the speaker-hearer. The fact is that it may depend on a number of factors – some of them going beyond the sentence or even beyond language, being nevertheless bound up with language – whether this kind of constellation is perceived by the speaker-hearer as semantically anomalous or not.

Take these two examples:

An inventor is demonstrating his innovative technique of tree felling. Ejected under high pressure from his device, a jet of water pierces the tree trunk in a matter of seconds. The liquid ax turns out to be less noisy and more economical than all hitherto known devices.

The body of a murdered man was found behind a freshly whitewashed wall. Although the site was scrupulously searched, the police did not find any clues pointing to the murderer. The paint was silent.

By providing an adequate context, we are able to resolve almost every semantic anomaly. Deliberating on the functions of context, Olson (1970, p 260) suggests that

> such anomalies are less a function of incompatible semantic components than of the limits of experience or imagination ... Imagination would here be construed as the ability to intellectually rearrange our perceptual experience ...

Speaking of "intellectual rearrangement" Olson undoubtedly refers to the language user's freedom of wielding his tool, a freedom that defies the automatism of syntactic rules and the automatism of selection restrictions[1]. So much for the moment; we shall leave an analysis of the processes that result in an anomaly-avoiding intellectual rearrangement of our experience until later.

The decision as to whether or not any two semantic matrices are mutually compatible is arrived at not by some matrix-inherent and hence automatically applied, invariable criteria, but by the speaker-hearer who is in a certain situation, who has knowledge and specific expectations of this situation, and who tends to understand the utterances heard even if they contain unusual word configurations. He may follow this tendency as long as his experience and imagination permit. The criterion of what is acceptable, or normal, is thus shifted from language-in-itself to language as used by the human for his own purposes.

Here we anticipate an objection on the grounds that Katz and Fodor did themselves recognize the possibility of resolving anomalies (and also ambiguities) by taking account of the context ("setting") of the utterance. They do indeed touch upon the issue of the context's selection function, arguing that once such a function is elaborated for ambiguities it might be possible to do the same for anomalies. But they very soon conclude:

> Since a complete theory of setting selection must represent as part of the setting of an utterance any and every feature of the world which speakers need in order to determine the preferred reading of that utterance ... such a theory cannot in principle distinguish between the speaker's knowledge of his language and his knowledge of the world ... Since there is no serious possibility of systematizing all the knowledge of the world that speakers share, and since a theory of the kind we have been discussing requires such a systematization, it is *ipso facto* not a serious model for semantics (Katz and Fodor 1963, p 179).

This argumentation deserves to be examined closely for it shows the deplorable consequences for semantics of clinging to the competence/performance dichotomy, a construct with which even syntax has had considerable difficulties. There can be no doubt that any semantic theory that would recognize the true

---

[1] Taking advantage of an argument used by Uhlenbeck, we discover an interesting connection with the notion of competence. According to Uhlenbeck, a native speaker queried by linguists would judge a sentence as well-formed if he could "think up an actual situation in which such a construction or form would fit" (Uhlenbeck no date, p 102). Accordingly, the acceptability of Colorless green ideas sleep furiously is less of an argument for the essential separability of syntax (as present in the mind of the competent native speaker) from semantics, than a measure of the vividness of the native speaker's imagination. In any event, Uhlenbeck's argument presupposes the kind of freedom of the language user in using his instrument that we have been talking about.

role of situational factors in meaning would have to build in components and/or rules accounting for the speaker's knowledge of the setting in which a sentence is uttered. But since a systematization of *all* the knowledge in question is both indispensable – as Katz and Fodor assert – and impossible, these semantic theorists restrict their theory to facts and factors contained in the speaker-hearer's linguistic competence. The history of science provides few cases where the authors of a theory – as pointed out in Chap. 5 – would have shown that much determination in seeking to preserve the elegance of their theory at the expense of its goals.

One would have thought that the goal of semantic theory, and indeed of any theory, is to make predictions, in this case predictions as to what the (competent) speaker-hearer would assess as semantically anomalous. Such predictions, it seems to us, are inconceivable unless we make allowances for extralinguistic factors as contained in the wider context (setting) of the utterance.

We are reminded here of a point made earlier in our discussion of competence and performance: that, by all appearances, this semantic theory is devised for a kind of language that does not exist in real life. Language does not occur in a vacuum hermetically sealed off from the rest of the world. Those who construe language as the object of linguistic inquiry in terms of a Chomsky-Katz-Fodor type competence visualize the competent, ideal speaker-hearer as a blindfolded monad – which view is mistaken even if this ideal person is delivered (by act of Chomsky) from the frailties and imperfections of the real speaker-hearer.

Thus, a "semantic anomaly" is usually anomalous only in an asituational, competence-based language laboriously pieced together by the linguist, a "language" far removed from language as we use it in our lives. Should we care to consult our knowledge of the world, however – against the advice of Katz and Fodor – we might find the sentence *Man is a wolf* anything but anomalous since, as pointed out by Abraham (1973, p 9),

> our experience of this world warrants the attribution of (Bloodthirsty), (Ferocious), and (Rapacious) as *definiens* to the *definiendum* "man".

The implausibility of drawing a strict dividing line between linguistic and, shall we say, behavioral determinants, and the resulting difficulties in founding a grammar, inclusive of a complementary semantics, solely on linguistic substance, caused Bever (1972, p 411) to assert that

> currently available grammars unavoidably take into account facts contributed by behavioral processes, as well as facts contributed by ideal linguistic structure ... I explicitly assume, along with Chomsky and others, that there is an "actual linguistic structure". My doubts concern the extent to which current generative grammars describe that structure alone, free of facts introduced by behavioral properties of manifesting intuitions.

As can be seen, Bever holds somewhat different views than we do: he is skeptical about the claim that current grammars restrict themselves to linguistic structure; we, to the contrary, are inclined to trust the generativists when they claim to account solely for linguistic structure. Whatever the case, it is indisputable that linguistic structure alone does not get us far enough.

Among other things, it does not get us far enough in an attempt to account for semantic anomalies. As asserted before, the juxtaposition of two seemingly incompatible semantic matrices in a sentence need not result in a semantic anomaly by which the understanding of the sentence is obstructed; it may even provide the language user with an illuminating insight and thus foster understanding.

It is now time to pursue this line of reasoning, which should lead us beyond mere criticism of Katz and Fodor's semantic theory into a more constructive discussion of the various determinants of language use.

It must be seen as a lasting merit of the generativists that throughout their work they have taken care to treat the sentence as a focal phenomenon and the principal goal of scientific analysis in linguistics, and further, that they conceived the sentence as a dynamic structure ("dynamic" to the extent that it presupposes the realization of certain postulates), rather than as a collection of disparate and contrastingly classified words. The structure of the (uttered) sentence has its psychological counterpart in the process of understanding on the part of the hearer; the nature of this correspondence need not concern us at this juncture. One thing stands out as indisputable: understanding the meaning of a sentence cannot be identified with understanding the meaning of the individual words in the sentence. But if for linguistic reasons no well-formed sentence results, say, because there is a semantic anomaly, according to current models of generative linguistics the process of adequate structuring would not be accomplished – and therefore the act of understanding this utterance would not reach its goal.

However, when we hear, in a suitable context, THE PAINT WAS SILENT, or about a smiling meadow, we do understand, we do accept these sentences as perfectly sensible utterances. It may well be that the relevant dynamic structure does not emerge as smoothly as in the case of conventional word configurations, but it is precisely this fumbling for structure that forces the language user to enlist additional information in an effort to understand the peculiar utterance.

The linguistic construction that causes us to pause and grope for additional information in search of a new view, and which on many occasions induces us to pursue the process of understanding to unusual depths, is known under the familiar term *metaphor*.

The metaphor *smiling meadow* is, on the grounds of Katz and Fodor's theory, precisely such a prohibited configuration of incompatible markers: *to smile* entails the selection restriction that it may refer only to humans, while meadow is (Human-). As rightly pointed out by Abraham, "metaphors arise without restrictions through violations of the compatibility of lexemes in syntactic combination" (1973, p 6). The same author contends

that it is the coincidence of contradiction and a somehow legitimate claim to meaningfulness which warrants the predication "is metaphoric" ... (p 8).

Leisi (1953) has the same in mind when he says that any metaphor, though "wrong" in terms of semantic congruence, turns out to be correct at a higher level, so to speak.

How should we understand the development from *wrong* to *correct* or *right*? Or the coincidence of contradiction and claim to meaningfulness? Why is it that on encountering a metaphor we do not resign ourselves to the finding "it's a semantic anomaly"?

These questions induce the psychologist of language to follow an interesting train of thought. In order to account for the fact that in search of an illuminating clue, a fitting situational determinant, or a suitable context, the language user starts to ransack his internal lexicon and keeps doing it until he has established the meaningfulness of the utterance, or even attained – at a higher level – an understanding in depth, the psychologist must construe some motivating force behind these operations. Employing a striking metaphor, Abraham says that the craving for meaningfulness acts as a kind of pull. Such a pull presupposes a suitable control: the language user is in need of what Feltkamp (1971, p 234) calls a "steering device" enabling him to handle his internal grammar. Following the tradition of functionalist psychology, we propose to identify the goal-oriented pull (comprising driving force and steering device) as the striving for *sense constancy*.

Before we can delve into the concept of sense constancy it will be necessary to discuss a certain property of all the models hitherto proposed by generative linguistics.

The generation of a sentence is represented in these models by a flow chart in which the speaker-hearer's competence-based knowledge is entered and made effective at certain points of the process. There are differences between the first Chomsky model, the Chomsky-Katz-Fodor-Postal model, and the models of the generative semanticists (discussed in the next chapter) as to the places where, and hence the order in which, the various elements of competence are entered; but the models all agree in one fundamental respect: they state that a "correct" (grammatical, well-formed, semantically normal, . . .) sentence will be generated if and only if all the stations of the flow chart are activated in the prescribed order.

The same essential property must be likewise present in the performance model if the (linguistic) theory of competence is to have any prescriptive power for a theory of performance, and hence the linguistic model any explanatory value for language as used in real life. Irrespective of the differences in their professed goals, all the models in question state, for instance, that a (heard) sentence can be OK'ed only after passing through the prescribed stations. Should it get stuck anywhere in the "generating mechanism" (say, because – as in the case of a semantic anomaly – two syntactically interlocked words are found to be semantically incompatible), the sentence is refused the stamp of approval in either production or understanding.

As argued in the preceding section, the realities of everyday language use run counter to these theoretical predictions: semantically anomalous sentences tend to be understood none the less, being perceived as perfectly "correct", "grammatical", and "normal". Indeed, many metaphors result in particularly insightful understanding.

How might the model maker cope with this? He might try to save his flow chart model by adding some more competences that would account (in a hitherto unexplored way!) for the production or understanding of a metaphoric and hence "anomalous" sentence. The simplest way to do this would be to postulate the operation, above linguistic competence and its lexicon, of supplementary competences that would prevent nonsense from occurring, even if it were prescribed by linguistic competence. These supplementary competences would be vested primarily in some additional lexicon where, for example, the verb *to smile* would not come under the selection restriction 'referring–only–to–humans', so that the *smiling meadow* need not be branded as an anomaly. Aside from the difficulties involved in the construction of lexicons enabling words to function literally on some, and not fully literally on other, occasions, such supplementary competences would have to be provided with the power to distinguish between different situations, in order to ensure that the proper lexicon as well as the proper "grain" of linguistic analysis be chosen for the particular situation. On examining the various "communicative" or even "universal" competences proposed by some for this purpose, one wonders if these authors have ever realized what the problem really is. A brief illustration of our point is in order.

The notion of *communicative competence* provides for an additional stage beyond syntax and semantics, a stage ensuring that the constructs of syntax and semantics are applied in adequate correspondence to the situation. This stage is more or less identical with the concept of *pragmatics,* the idea being that the sign (or, in this case, the sentence) can be fruitfully discussed only if suitable allowances are made for its actual uses.

Wunderlich (1968, p 19), for instance, postulates the incorporation into the model of

> the speakers' and hearers' ability to make themselves intelligible or to understand utterances in (idealized) situations of discourse.

He identifies this ability with "pragmatic" or "communicative competence". In keeping with linguistic tradition, the emphasis is put on the idealized character of the discourse situation, particularly in the work of Habermas (1971). And indeed, there is no other option as long as one clings to the notion of competence. By the same token, both Wunderlich and Habermas are trapped in a *regressus ad infinitum:* postulating some new competence, they are bound to introduce a further metacompetence to decide whether the new competence should be activated in the given case or not. (For example, should the metaphor competence be "turned on" or not?) Wunderlich (1968, p 20) is prepared to admit that

> ... nothing short of such a meta–competence can account for the fact that ... there are variations ... in the speakers' competences ... and, finally, that language systems are subject to alterations.

Habermas (1971, p 106) seeks to escape the *regressus* by simply postulating a "universal pragmatics"

> since communication, involving shared knowledge of objects, presupposes parallel meta-communication, i. e., shared knowledge at an intersubjective level concerning the particular pragmatic meaning of the communication[2].

---

[2] Habermas's view that "any speaking presupposes an actual initial agreement on what it involves to

What is significant for this approach is that it construes communication as a process running in parallel on several "levels", whereby mutual understanding concerning objects is assured by the partners' shared agreement as to the pragmatic sense of the communication. (This is where Habermas falls back on ideas voiced by his opponent Luhmann, 1971, whose views are discussed below.) Quite apart from the fact that the notion of universal pragmatics, or communicative competence, is not a particularly efficient tool of analysis, any approach of this sort is bound to run aground because of its reliance on the conceptual distinction between competence and performance; the language-immanent character of competence implied by the distinction makes this construct totally immune to the realities that shape, and indeed give rise to, the process of communication. Wunderlich and Habermas are compelled to take recourse to idealized or standardized situations, being unable to specify in what way such a standardization or idealization can be effected in the absence of a language user whose performance is the primary factor.

Quite a different approach to the concept of communicative competence was taken by SJ Schmidt (1973) in his attempt to develop a theory of text. The reversal from a sentence-centered generative grammar to a text linguistics, which is gaining ground in some places at present, is largely motivated by the obvious inadequacy and incompleteness of a model concerned solely with sentence-linguistic components. Communicative competence is defined by Schmidt (1973, p 106) in terms of

the factors that make language communication possible in the first place: knowledge of a natural language (its lexicon, its grammar) and knowledge of the rules ensuring the success of the process of communication.

Consequently, linguistic competence (knowledge of the lexicon and of the grammar of a language) is turned into a component of communicative competence; the other component is made up of the knowledge of the rules ensuring the success of (presumably nonlinguistic, or prelinguistic, or protolinguistic) acts of communication. And since the notion of communicative competence implies the concept of communicative performance as a corollary, we are bound to inquire about the relationship between communicative competence and communicative performance, and between communicative performance and linguistic performance. There is evidently no escaping from the prison of pure idealization – abhoring everything that smacks of actual language use – as long as one indulges in the dialectics of the competence/performance dichotomy. The postulation of ever new competences does not bring us any closer to a solution of the problem.

An attempt to assign the language user's faculty of distinguishing between anomaly and metaphor to performance, on the other hand, could succeed only if we decided to ignore all that has been decreed so far about the competence/performance dichotomy.

---

communicate by language" (1971, p 111) is among the many points questioned by Bar-Hillel (1973) in his trenchant critique of Habermas's hermeneutic philosophy of language. It would seem, however, that on this one point Habermas is perfectly right, though for reasons other than those he adduces.

There seems to be sufficient ground now to call into doubt the basic generative model of language production and comprehension as outlined a few pages back. The inadequacy of this model has come into evidence on a number of occasions in the course of our argument. For instance, it has proved impossible to construe lexicon entries in their interaction with syntactic rules in a way that would guarantee that a "correct" sentence is produced or comprehended automatically, that is, without the intervention of an agency from outside the grammatical model. Furthermore:

a) Clark is found to be lacking an agency that would determine when a particular feature list would be long enough to enable verbalization;

b) Brown and McNeill are lacking a construct that would explain why in the tip-of-the-tongue state the search for the word in question is discontinued prematurely in some cases;

c) Miller is lacking an agency that would decide what kind of lexicon (one ordered in terms of presuppositions or any other) should be used for dealing with a particular word;

d) Wunderlich (1970a, p 15) is lacking a construct that would explain why the sentence EITHER YOU GO OR YOU DON'T ist not necessarily understood as a veritable tautology, but possibly as an invitation to make up one's mind, or as an indication of the speaker's vacillation;

e) We all feel the need for an agency or "mechanism" that could be held responsible for the fact that COULD YOU OPEN THE WINDOW? is perceived (in spite of the Q-transformation and the question mark) as a request or as an inducement to action.

If we now transform our findings into postulates to be satisfied by a model of sentence production and comprehension that would meet both the linguist's and the psychologist's requirements, we are bound to recognize as untenable the assumption that there is a definite place in the flow chart model (i. e., following the application of a predetermined series of criteria) where the processing of a sentence could be regarded as being completed, i. e., where it is judged to be "correct", "well-formed", "comprehensible", "meaningful", etc. – or not. Rather, we have to assume that whenever the processing of a sentence has not yielded such an OK state at the "prescribed" point (or in the "prescribed" time?) in the flow chart model, the processing procedures can be modified to include new determinants (different criteria of OK'ing) in the processing.

This alone calls for a fundamental revision of the hitherto proposed models, in which the correctness, comprehensibility, normality, etc. of a processed sentence functions as the dependent variable – dependent on the satisfaction of a predetermined number of criteria. Under the proposed conception, the model would have to be provided in advance with a certain (formally defined) end state as a standard against which to check the outcome of any processing. The processing of a sentence would not be completed until a satisfactory concordance had been established between the predetermined state (standard) and the outcome of the actual processing. Unlike the old models, where the complete sequence of processing stages was rigidly specified by the model, the processing in the new model might follow a number of alternative routes and might involve the use of alternative stores of knowledge. The analysis of a sentence is discontinued as soon as the desired concordance between outcome and standard has been achieved.

Now, what kind of end state do we have in mind in terms of which a sentence is constructed or analyzed? This state is the *meaningfulness* of the sentence.

Whereas in the models proposed so far the meaningfulness results from an analysis of the sentence, the present model treats meaningfulness as a predetermined criterion which has to be satisfied by an analysis of the sentence. That is to say, a sentence is processed until it is felt to make sense.

Suppose the sentence THE PAINT WAS SILENT has been analyzed according to the Katz-Fodor model; the verdict is: "This is an incompatible co-occurrence of lexemes". But rather than discontinuing the processing, the *real* speaker-hearer is apt to proceed with the analysis precisely *because* the sentence does not as yet make sense. Additional determinants are entered, new information – possibly derived from context and/or the environment – is called in, and another "lexicon" proposing alternative readings is searched. It may prove necessary to revise the tacit presuppositions of the initial analysis; otherwise, attempts may be made to reexamine the syntactic segmentation of the text in search of an alternative interpretation.

The meaningful comprehension of a sentence is thus viewed in our terms less as a dependent variable of the process of analysis than as an independent one: *the process of analysis is guided and codetermined by the speaker-hearer's desire to make sense of the sentence.* The analysis is bound to result in the actual concretization, in this particular case, of a globally predetermined schema.

The meaningful interpretation of a perceived sentence is thus approached from two sides: a general and a more particular-concrete one. Something of this sort was hinted at by Oldfield (1966, p 21) when he wrote:

> The existence, in practice, of a rather fuzzy margin between "understanding" and "not understanding" an utterance suggests that a number of functional levels are involved in the process, and that, while within certain limits it might be possible to describe each of these separately, they are likely to modify each other's working.

The finding that a semantically anomalous sentence might "turn out to be correct at some higher level" (Leisi 1962) and might be understood eventually (e. g., as metaphor) demands from the psychologist an explanation of *why* exactly the analysis is continued at a different level, *how* this level is reached, and *what* the processing there is like.

The task might appear less formidable once it is realized that the "mechanism" or "agency" in question is by no means reserved for some isolated cases of language use, but rather that it serves to determine language processes in general; in fact, we are confronted here with a principle that is at work also in other spheres of psychology.

Take for instance the case where, in an experiment in visual perception, the subject expects some stimulus and yet none whatever is offered. Nevertheless, he or she reports seeing some hazy, fluffy, or fuzzy shapes (e. g., Kolligs 1942). Very clearly, perception is not a passive process; on the contrary, it tends to press for "reactions". Von Allesch (1942, p 33) used to speak of the tendency to rein-force, delineate, and hold constant such labile and vague impressions, and also to turn them into concrete objects. There is a *Generaldetermination* tending to formulate all impressions – wherever that is possible – according to some "general principle of validity".

The same determinant comes into focus as we move one step further, to the perception of actual stimuli. Human perception tends to ignore random fluctuations in brightness when performing its object-constituting mission. These mechanisms are known under the terms brightness constancy and color constancy. The distortions of an image falling on the retina that are caused by eye movements or by the motion of the observed object or the observer himself, are compensated for by a mechanism known as shape constancy or object constancy. In effect, a table retains its rectangular top as we move around it even though none of its corners receives a rectangular projection on the retina. A visitor who appraoches us and stretches out his hand does not appear to double his size in the process: thanks to the mechanisms of size constancy our brain brings into operation the proper computation program which integrates the diverse data obtained, according to circumstances, from depth perception, binocular disparity, our memory, retinal image size, etc. Although perceived size is determined by these diverse data, it does not ensue directly from the sum total of the individual data. We owe it to the mechanism of size constancy that each datum is assigned a particular weight in the overall computation; in doing so this mechanism is guided by what we might call a preconceived idea as to the formal criteria to be satisfied by the product of the computation. The outcome must be such as to enable the individual to "handle" the perceived size with the aid of both inborn and acquired action schemata.

Such a preconceived idea comes into evidence also in the many investigations devoted to attribution as inspired by F. Heider (1944). Even as we watch moving dots or geometric figures we tend to attribute to them some motive and discover causal relationships in their interactions; Michotte (1963) was able to demonstrate that the perception of causality has its origin in our organism.

It is against this background that the term *sense constancy* is proposed for the domain of language phenomena. In much the same way as the human being is "fixed" and "tuned" to perceive, whenever possible, objects – objects that have some meaning to him! – he is ready to impart meaning to specimens of language under the inspiration of his intrinsically human urge to action. Sense constancy is the purest manifestation of that "effort after meaning" which Bartlett (1932) considered a fundamental property of any cognitive activity.

Rather than laboriously joining together the meaning of an utterance – for instance, by consecutively interpreting sign after sign with the aid of a particular code – we have the "intention to meaning" at our disposal right from the beginning, long before it could emerge from a painstaking semiotic analysis. The philosophical and psychological tradition which we approach in this manner can be identified at once: it leads from Brentano to Meinong and Husserl[3].

---

[3] It has to be stressed that our reference to Husserl does not imply agreement with his view on, for

A fundamental notion is here the *intentionality of consciousness,* i. e., the directional (rather than purely associative) relation of my own act to an object which thus takes on meaning as the recipient of that act. What we are faced with in our environment are not things-in-themselves but things-for-ourselves; it is the latter "for" that turns the world from chaos into things and events that have meaning for us. In biology, similar ideas have been voiced above all by Uexküll (1926).

The *intentional act* by which the self-conscious mind establishes a relationship with the world around it is in our view (which is of course not Husserl's) very similar to the core or "impulse program" of the act that constitutes for Bridgman (1959), and – in somewhat different form – for the later Wittgenstein, the rudiments of meaning, a principle beyond which there is no sensible inquiry. In the case of language it is an intentional act carried out in a relationship encompassing two human beings, the speaker and the hearer.

And as the intentional act forms the basis for the mutual understanding of human beings in a meaningful world, the Latin root of the term *intendere* suggests a temporal relationship between the self as it is here and now and the not-here and not-now, a relationship that is basic to the concept of sign. Bühler views the awareness of the self here and now as the *origo* of the communicative act. As the term *origo* itself suggests, origin is given to something, and this something is the intention. *Origo* and intention constitute the communicative space, says Wunderlich (1972, p 81). The center of the communicative space is my unitary self-consciousness.

Here we come to a point at which psychological and philosophical considerations converge. The problem now is how this unitary self-consciousness has emerged to become a steering device for the self. Is it merely a residue of the personal experience accumulating in the brain? This view is contradicted by an essential characteristic of self-consciousness, namely its lasting unitariness. (As has been shown by Sperry, 1969, the unitary character of self-consciousness is preserved even when, due to a bisection of the brain, man is split behaviorally into a left half and a right half.) Should the unitary and sovereign self-consciousness be an epiphenomenon of the individual's actions? The counter-argument is as follows: standing at the top of a hierarchy, man's ordered and ordering self-consciousness cannot be fully accounted for by the operation of the lower echelons of the hierarchy. A compelling argument was set forth by Polanyi (1966, pp 44–45) with the claim that

> the hierarchic structure of the higher forms of life necessitates the assumption of further processes of emergence. If each higher level is to control the boundary conditions left open by the operations of the next lower level [as suggested by our postulate that the decision whether to switch to "anomaly" or "metaphor" is made at some higher level – H. H.], this implies that these boundary conditions are in fact left open by the operations going on at the lower level. In other words, no level can gain control over its own

---

example, the entity of ideal objects (senses) – see also Schaff (1962, p 233 ff.). Our concern is less with the logical content of an assertion than with the psychological act of asserting; the latter is for Husserl but a "transient experience" (1970, p 285) while for us it is the essential principle.

boundary conditions and hence cannot bring into existence a higher level, the operations of which would consist in controlling these boundary conditions.

From the logical structure of the hierarchy thus outlined, it follows, argues Polanyi, that a higher level cannot be fully accounted for by the processes manifest at the lower levels: the boundary conditions that set a limit on the operation of the particular processes obtain independently of the latter. This goes to show that our query as to how self-consciousness acquires its unitary character is due to a misconception. Self-consciousness is in control precisely because it is an integral entity capable of integrating all incoming data. As such, it constitutes the "primary reality" (Eccles 1970) for which the realities of the physical world (and in the case of language, also the realities of World 3 – cf. Popper and Eccles 1977) are a necessary precondition, but which is not reducible to those realities. Being in a sense "more" and "older" than the current linguistic input, the mind (which is identified here with self-consciousness) is in a position to extract the relevant information from that input. Though currently modified by such input, self-consciousness is certainly not constituted by it.

The self-conscious mind being both the starting and the terminal point of the act of comprehension, the human being presupposes the events and developments in the surrounding world to be, in principle, intelligible to him, rather than random and arbitrary. Any human being who acts (and speaking is a kind of action) means something; any human being who perceives (and hearing speech is a kind of perception) understands something. That is to say, the human being grasps in and right through the physical medium some meaning which goes beyond that medium and which establishes a relation with that significant unitary structure which already exists in the hearer.

But even if this anticipated meaningful relationship fails to be established in the particular case, i.e., if the listener does not understand what the speaker means, he has to assume that, in principle, the situation does make sense and is, therefore, comprehensible. Otherwise the human being would not be able to lead his life and to pursue his goals. Blatant violations of the intelligibility and meaningfulness of developments around us result in total incapacitation, which we sometimes try to shake off by bursting into laughter[4].

Late at night Mr. A sees Mr. B crawling on the pavement near a street-lamp, evidently searching for something on the ground. The following dialogue develops:
A: What d'you think you're doing there?
B: I'm looking for my wallet.
A: Well, where did you have it last?
B: I remember dropping it on a lawn half a mile away.
A: Look, you can't expect somebody to have brought it here!
B: Not exactly, but I'm looking for it here because the street-lamp is giving enough light.

We take refuge in a humorous interpretation, for otherwise we could not tolerate the unintelligibility of B's behavior. This behavior is anomalous at a level beyond the semantic plane. B's behavior is unreasonable because "looking for a lost

---

[4] On the following cf. also Forguson (1968) and Hörmann (1973).

thing" is intelligible only if the looking takes place where the lost thing can be found. He who has lost something and is looking for it, or speaks of losing and finding, acts reasonably only if he can identify the logical and psychological interdependence of the actions involved (and, secondarily, of the words involved) and their interrelations with the web of developments in the world. An action – as much as a sentence – makes sense only if it is brought into relation to a system of connections, but at the same time it points beyond these demarcations. (A somewhat similar view is held by Luhmann 1971, p 40.)

Forguson (1968) has some interesting things to say about intelligibility of behavior:

> When someone's behavior is normally (at a glance) intelligible to me as the performance by him of such-and-such action, my understanding is grounded on certain *presumptions*.

Here we come again upon the notion of presumption, or presupposition, which tends to be gaining in weight in present-day linguistics. In the case of GA Miller (see our discussion toward the end of Chap. 6), a presupposition functioned as the tacit assumption of certain features that go into the definition of a *word*. In the quotation above, Forguson refers to states of the world which underlie any *use* of language.

Among these presumptions we find the assumption that a speaker is guided by some intentions, goals, motives, beliefs, etc. We may ascribe the speaker such intention etc., quite unwittingly, but our presuppositions will always build up into a meaningful whole. As argued by Forguson (1968, p 94),

> my understanding of anyone's behavior in this manner is dependent upon my general ability to ascribe these beliefs to him meaningfully: my ability to "place" his behavior as the performance of certain actions. For, if I could not ascribe these beliefs to him, I could not identify his behavior as his performance of an action.

In order to identify as such an action – an act of language use included – we must be able to fall back on a web of presumptions. These presumptions may be available in a tacit way, no doubt (cf. Chap. 3). We become aware of the process only when the perceived event does not fit into the structure of sense. Anyone who has watched a game of baseball (or, say, soccer) without knowing its rules will realize what unintelligible actions are. He will likewise know why the ignorant observer persists in his attempts to make sense of the observed actions (and utterances): "human nature abhors a semantic vacuum" (Schlesinger 1971 c, p 68).

How does this web of presumptions concerning the goals, motives, and beliefs of our fellow creatures come into being? Judging by our present knowledge of these processes, it is not solely a product of our experience. Much as the dimensions of perception are vested in the perceiving subject, and the personality traits of another person are largely anchored in the trait repertoire of the judge, so is a "naive theory of human actions" a component of man's biological endowment; and it is through the projections of such a theory that we interpret the behavior of other people – a point brought home by Laucken (1974).

That specimens of language must be studied within the frame of all these supralinguistic presumptions, beliefs, etc. has become clear as we were discussing the concept of presupposition. In the psychology of language, the closest approach has been proposed by Olson (1970, p 264), when he says that words

> designate, signal, or specify an intended referent relative to the set of alternatives from which it must be differentiated. . . . Thus, the meaning of an utterance is dependent on the context of alternatives.

Leaving a closer analysis of Olson's approach for later (Chap. 13), we must note here that he is concerned with the relation of the "intended referent" to the other possible referents. Our concern is, however, with a much stronger hierarchic structure: meaning is something more than simply an elimination of uncertainty as to reference. We grasp the meaning of an utterance by fitting a vague "something" into a broad horizon of contingencies that is activated in our consciousness. As argued by Oller (1972, p 48),

> meaning in even the simplest of sentences involves relations with settings. Linguistic structure does not exist apart from the knowledge of the world which the speaker-listener communicates about. Neither meaning nor syntax exist in a vacuum; nor do the two of them together exist independent of situational settings.

The distinction between a meaningful and sence-imparting general setting, or background, and the singularity addressed by the particular utterance should not be confused with the relationship between sign and code. In the case of both sign and code, and indeed generally in using the concept of information, emphasis is placed on the process of choice by which one sign from among many available ones is addressed. Upon the completion of the choice, the quality of the remaining, non-chosen signs is irrelevant. In terms of information theory, the chosen and the nonchosen alternatives do not differ in their level of reality. The matter is otherwise in the case of sense. Sense makes up a *general* setting, which persists as a wide horizon or backdrop. Only parts of it can be concretized into "instances" in comprehension.

Consequently, it is wrong to assume that an oft-repeated message does not make sense any more. By construing language as mere information transmission, the investigator foregoes the hope of understanding the lover who never tires of repeating his avowals of love. That repetition does not deprive a message of its meaning is obvious to anyone who considers the utterance to be an "instancing" within an enduring scaffolding of sense: from the wide horizon of what could be meant, a particular segment is concretized to enter consciousness. Or, alternatively speaking, we understand the particular instance by formulating it verbally; the words open the particular instance to what is general and so they *make* sense.

Our two men from under the street-lamp have demonstrated to us how an action makes sense (in this case, does not make sense). The example has served to outline a "figure of thought" which may now be elaborated with the aid of a strictly linguistic example: IT'S RAINING, BUT I DON'T BELIEVE IT (Forguson 1968).

Why is this sentence felt to be "outrageous" (Forguson)? GE Moore (1947, p 78, orig 1912) offers an answer with his distinction between

> what a man *means* by a given assertion and what he *expresses* by it. Whenever we make

any assertion whatever ... we are always *expressing* one or other of two things – namely, either that we *think* the thing in question to be so or that we *know* it to be so.

The intolerable character of that sentence is due *also* to its internal incompatibility, though it is not a mutual incompatibility of its elements but the *psychological* incompatibility of its content and the fact of its being uttered. The latter fact is only implied in the sentence, but this is enough to destroy the fragile structure of sense, against the background of which we judge the truth or falsity, well-formedness or anomaly, and happiness, or unhappiness of an utterance[5].

At this point it would be well to consider the juncture at which we have arrived in our discussion.

The various theories of competence have been concerned with the production and understanding of sentences-in-themselves and have ceded the actual uses of these sentences, together with all accompanying errors, to the theory of performance. For different reasons, some philosophers (e. g., Bar-Hillel) have drawn a dividing line between the sentence (as a linguistic structure which need not be uttered) and the utterance. We find that we cannot talk about sentences-in-themselves, that a separation of the sentence from its utterance is as untenable as a separation of sign and its uses. Sentences can be said to "reckon with their being spoken as well as interpreted against a background of extralingual data" (to quote Uhlenbeck no date, p 148). In the next chapter we shall deal with a major contribution to the solution of this problem, a contribution which stems, characteristically, from neither linguistics nor psychology, but from philosophy.

Before we proceed, let us shed some more light on the environs of the concept of sense constancy as proposed in these pages. When stating that sense constancy safeguards the understanding of a sentence, what exactly do we mean by *understanding?*

Without trying to come to grips, in the next few pages, with a problem to which most of this book is devoted, we would like to make it quite clear that in any investigation of language and grammar it is simply inadmissible to ignore the problems of the process of "semantic interpretation' as linguists have done so often. By turning a deaf ear to the issue, both linguists and psycholinguists have found themselves led up the garden path.

The crux of the problem was perhaps most clearly articulated by Deese (1969, pp 515–516), who starts by asking: "what happens when we understand something? How is a failure to understand different from understanding?" His immediate answer is: "certain linguistic segments ... can be interpreted by the use of other linguistic segments", by which he means paraphrasing.

> The basic fact of paraphrase is that one individual can take a segment of language uttered by another individual and restate it in such a way that the hearer is pleased to accept the restatement as equivalent to the original.

---

[5] In much the same way Wunderlich (1970b, p 162) declares as ungrammatical the sentence OTTOKAR KNOWS THE MOON TO BE SQUARE, except for the case that the utterance comes from, e. g., a half-wit, that is, a "less competent" speaker. Thus, grammaticality is judged in terms of the world (and not only the language) of the speaker.

Thus, interpretation presupposes understanding. The latter is a psychological concept, whereas the notion of paraphrasing interpretation is used (also) by linguists. With his statement, Deese has reversed the causal and temporal relationship between the two phenomena as compared with what is asserted by linguistic theory. The linguist conceives of interpretation as a step leading from the perceived linguistic structure to the mental state of understanding (to be explored by introspection). For Deese, understanding is a state of our consciousness which indicates our readiness and ability to produce a paraphrase (or a reply, or a suitable action):

> Understanding is the inward sign of the potential for reacting appropriately to what we see or hear ... The important point, however, is that understanding leads to no particular behavior.

A similar – perhaps even more precise – account of understanding was given by Wittgenstein (1953, § 531):

> We speak of understanding a sentence in the sense in which it can be replaced by another which says the same; but also in the sense in which it cannot be replaced by any other.

This does not say anything about *how* understanding (as the outcome of a process) is accomplished, i. e., through what kind of mechanisms. Some aspects of what goes on (and what does not go on) in understanding were explored in the preceding chapters. Right now we have to consider how understanding is related to "making sense" as discussed above.

The events of the world around us and the behavior of other people are presumed to make sense and to be intelligible. The state of making sense is of a latent or potential kind: it awaits realization by the language user. In actual communication the speaker, by uttering a sentence, seeks to induce the hearer to perform a particular realization in a particular place: the speaker *means* something. The hearer, having achieved an "introspectively discovered inward sense" (Deese), realizes that it is now up to him to show that he has discovered the sense meant by the speaker. He may show this in different ways: by paraphrasing the utterance, by performing an action, or even by silence. In any case, understanding does not imply any particular behavior or disposition to behavior[6].

To understand an utterance means therefore to process it successfully, that is, to relate the incoming information to the general "horizon of sense", the relevant general setting of contingencies in a manner that corresponds to the speaker's intended meaning.

How successfully an utterance has been processed by the hearer can be authoritatively established only by the speaker, after an evaluation of the hearer's response. On hearing a paraphrase of his own utterance offered by the hearer, the speaker may conclude: "Yes, this is what I meant". In this case, understanding coincides with what was meant.

But there are cases when the speaker has been misunderstood, so that he says:

---

[6] An implication of this kind was suggested by behaviorist psychology and behaviorist linguistics whenever they could not avoid the problem of meaning.

"No, this is not what I meant." What has actually happened in such a case? On the hearer's part there is an inward feeling of understanding, nonetheless. A misunderstanding has developed because the hearer, while establishing a relation between the utterance and the surrounding horizon of sense, has "located" this relation wrongly, not in the place intended by the speaker.

An excellent illustration of the process was offered by Lashley back in 1951; the investigator was talking of rapid writing and thereupon read the following sentence to his audience: "Rapid righting with his uninjured hand saved from loss the contents of the capsized canoe".

On hearing "capsized" the listener experiences something that is of immense interest to us: he realizes that he has up to here misunderstood the sentence, i. e., that he has been trying to make sense of it by relating it to the wrong setting. What is actually meant is not rapid writing but righting a canoe. Until this critical moment, the sentence was perfectly meaningful, though not in the sense intended by the speaker.

Pursuing the same argument, Ziff (1972, p 715) offers the sentence

I WATCHED HER DUCK WHEN THEY WERE THROWING ROTTEN EGGS; IT SWAM OUT TO THE MIDDLE OF THE LAKE

to demonstrate the need for his proposed cohesion factor, which is linked to a belief system. An utterance is understood only when it has been inserted into the context of what the speaker has in mind, and this can be achieved on condition that the hearer's system of views on the events in the world is essentially the same as the speaker's.

We cannot fail to notice the kind of correspondence that exists between understanding and intended meaning; we can further see that the two need not be symmetrical.

This is also the point where we can establish the relationship between *making sense* and *being understood*. An utterance makes sense if the hearer finds it possible to construe it as a realization of the structures that are responsible for the intelligibility of human behavior and events in the world. An utterance has been understood when it can be ascertained (by paraphrase, some action, or the like) that the hearer's realization coincides with that intended by the speaker.

It follows that understanding must be seen as a form of making sense that is marked by additional criteria. It also follows that Being Understood and Making Sense are the two poles of a dimension along which extends a continuum of intermediate states – which reminds us of Oldfield's view quoted earlier in this chapter. This dimension is of importance for any theory of communicative processes. Upon which point along the dimension the hearer's apperception of the particular utterance falls is a matter to be assessed primarily by the speaker, who is free to apply any criteria of understanding he may wish to choose. Still, the fact that an utterance will be placed anywhere along this dimension is due to sense constancy.

Having returned full circle to the mechanism of sense constancy, we find it to be responsible for the fact that a "click of understanding" (R Brown) can be heard also when understanding in the sense of a speaker-hearer consensus has not been achieved. Thus, sense constancy yields invariably an "introspectively discovered inward sense", to use Deese's term. But unlike Deese, we believe that this inward sense can be labeled "understanding" only if the speaker recognizes it as such. On the other hand, since the hearer has to act on his meaningful perception of the utterance, and since he can do this only in an intelligible world, he must be able to develop the sense of understanding by himself, prior to a confirmation from the speaker. What is held constant by the mechanism of sense constancy is therefore not the hearer's understanding of an utterance as attested to by the speaker, but the fact that the utterance does make sense for the hearer, as signalized by the feeling of understanding accompanying this state. But the meaning retrieved in this way need not coincide with what was meant by the speaker.

How does sense constancy operate? We might have a look at what Abraham (1973) has to say on this matter; he is one of those few linguists who have produced similar ideas. As mentioned earlier in the present chapter, in our discussion of metaphor, Abraham has developed the notion "pull of expected meaningfulness" (*Sog der Erwartung der Sinnvollheit,* p 9).He also says:

> The search for an interpretation of a co-occurrence of incompatible lexemes is tantamount to a search for a context (for an alternative world to the one proposed before) that would make the co-occurring lexemes compatible (p 14).

This search for the acceptable terminates when the utterance can be related to a particular world in a manner that makes sense. Thus it is our subjective view of the world, rather than any linguistic competence, that settles the question of an utterance's acceptability.

Surely the claim can no longer be made that the compatibility of lexemes is dictated by the lexicon and the rules for its operation, as was postulated by Katz and Fodor.

The case of an initially nonmeaningful and hence unacceptable utterance that is brought into relation to some alternative world, so that it now is meaningful – as happens with a metaphor – illustrates one of the functions of sense constancy.

By speaking of some alternative world we do not wish to suggest that a dramatic shift takes place in each such case. The sentence HE BENT HIS HANDKERCHIEF becomes immediately meaningful in a world with starched handkerchiefs (Fillmore, 1968b, p 390). Oller (1972, pp 47–48) has shown that the sentence THE THEORY OF RELATIVITY IS BLUE is apt to be shifted until a setting is ascertained in which the book entitled *Relativity Theory* is found to have a blue binding:

> Until such a setting is inferred, sentences like (this one) do not make sense. They leave us groping. . . . the inferred setting . . . is crucial to our understanding. A theory which treats meaning as independent of settings cannot explain them.

The postulated inspection of many alternative segments and paths of the sentence processing model comes into evidence with even greater force in Chafe's (1970) investigation of idioms (to which we referred when arguing for the concept of sense constancy). If the sentence

GEORGE IS ON THE WAGON

is understandable as an entity (meaning "George is no longer drinking alcoholic liquors"), it need not be submitted to a piecemeal analysis. There is absolutely no need, say, to activate the features of *wagon* and then to delete them on the strength of a supplementary "idiom competence". It depends on the particular meaningful setting to which the hearer may relate the sentence (this being an activity on the hearer's part!) whether the syntactic and/or semantic analysis is continued or not. The sentence

POOR LOUIS HAS KICKED THE BUCKET

is about Louis's death, but the hearer will know this only if he does *not* use his word or morpheme lexicon, i. e., if he does not approach *bucket* and *has kicked* as separate units. This in turn implies a certain freedom of decision for the language user. The choice of one rather than any other meaningful setting must be made before deciding for or against a detailed analysis of sentence components.

To proceed with proper linguistic analysis, the language user must first make certain decisions concerning the linguistic aspects of the utterance on supralinguistic grounds. Stretching the point a little, we might say that we can understand language only when we understand more than language.

It is fairly common today to speak of levels of understanding. A semantic anomaly on one level functions as a metaphor on another. But the matter is not settled by identifying the various levels of language processing. What is needed to explain the thing is a mechanism which causes the language user to shift his consciousness from one level to another. (The now hotly debated problem of levels of language processing will be discussed in Chap. 15.)

By invoking the examples provided by Lashley and Ziff, we were able to show that the mechanism of sense constancy can be held responsible for "molar" shifts of the overall meaningful setting of an utterance. But the same mechanism is found to operate at a "molecular" level, in that it shifts the meaning of individual words in an attempt to establish the meaningfulness of an utterance. Before we conclude this chapter, let us conduct a thought experiment which could bring to our attention a case of shift in meaning in the service of sense constancy.

There is a type of sentence that has always been considered as easily comprehensible and posing no problems for analysis: it is the analytic sentence, so called by philosophers.

A CIRCLE IS ROUND
A BACHELOR IS AN UNMARRIED MAN
ALL PEOPLE ARE ANIMATE

Precisely because of their simplicity, such sentences are particularly sensitive to negation: in view of an incompatibility of subject and predicate the (negated) sentence becomes meaningless – or it serves as an illustration for the effect of sense constancy! Take for instance the last of the three specimen sentences and watch your thinking as you read its negated form:

NOT ALL PEOPLE ARE ANIMATE

At once we switch to a different sense of *animate* (and perhaps also of people) in an attempt to preserve the meaningfulness of the (negated) sentence: animate now signifies not the biological property of the species but a particular trait of human beings, namely, vivacity. And indeed, this trait is not present in all people, as stated in the sentence.

Thus the meaningfulness of the sentence is guaranteed in that its negation is compensated for by the replacement of one sense of the word *animate* with another. This is an excellent example of sense constancy in operation.

A final comment will be in order. By proposing the concept of sense constancy as a mechanism of language comprehension which works on the hearer's discernment of understanding (or "discovered inward sense"), we take an immensely more cognitive approach to language than any of the generativists could claim to have made. Chomsky has always insisted that his theory is a cognitive theory, and rightly so: the rules and the lexicon are vested in the speaker-hearer's cognition. How this knowledge relates to consciousness need not be specified in the theory; the competent speaker "knows" the rules of grammar, just as he "knows" how to ride a bicycle.

The conception proposed here deals, in addition to rules that are "known", with conscious understanding as a major determinant of language processes.

In this way the acts of meaning and understanding have been granted the central status they deserve in linguistics and even more so in a psychology of language. In generative theory, they have been consistently denied such a status.

In subsequent chapters, we will deal extensively with the utterance – and all that accompanies it – as action. Before we can do this, however, we shall have to examine plenty of material from other areas: generative semantics, philosophy of language, and Russian psychology of language with its inquiry into the microgenesis of the utterance. These are the topics of the next three chapters.

Chapter 8

Generative Semantics

In the preceding chapters we examined some of the psychologically relevant implications and consequences of the Chomsky-Katz-Fodor model, which centers upon syntax and is secondarily supplemented with an (interpretive) semantic component. In our analysis we followed the intrinsic consequences of the model. The concept of semantic markers as the structure-inducing elements of the lexicon has proved useful in a number of ways. Eventually, however, it has become abundantly clear that semantic markers should not be conceptualized as static categorial attributes, by which *each* word is defined *exhaustively* and *invariably* as belonging to a particular category. We have noted how easy it is to fall prey to the very same error that was made in semiology, by inquiring first into the nature of a marker and only then investigating its actual functioning. We have come to realize that it is essential to start by learning a lot more about how "semantic markers" are manipulated by the language user.

In adopting Katz and Fodor's theory as a point of departure, we have had to cope, throughout our discussion of the lexicon concept, with two important consequences:

1) The lexicon becomes effective, in the generation of acceptable sentences, at a circumscribed place: deep structure as generated by the base component of the syntax-centered model is only subsequently interpreted semantically. In other words, deep structure itself is semantically undetermined at first – which is a very unfortunate assumption if the linguistic competence model responsible for generating acceptable sentences is to be treated as a basis for a psychological performance model that would account for how language is meaningfully produced and understood in the process of communication.

2) The lexicon as discussed heretofore has been of the words-as-entries kind. (Our occasional use of the term *lexical item* was merely meant to make it clear that we are aware of the linguistic difficulties inherent in the word concept.)

These assumptions of our discussion eventually turned out to be untenable as we tried to include the goal-directed character of communicative processes in the explanation of real-life language processes.

In our attempt at explaining language processes, we found it necessary to go beyond purely linguistic factors by resorting to extralinguistic phenomena, while broadening the scope of the processes subject to and worthy of theoretical interpretation. Sense constancy as discussed in the preceding chapter might be designated most aptly as an anthropological determinant of linguistic processes in so far as these constitute sequences of interaction between human beings.

Freed from the self-imposed constraints of the orthodox model of generative grammar, we now turn to a more recent trend in linguistics, which unquestionably has stronger anthropological leanings than any of its predecessors. Language is no longer treated as a thing in itself, and some allowances are made for the fact that language is used by human beings.

A kind of metamorphosis is taking place in linguistics, possibly also as a result of the sense of discomfort noted at the beginning of this volume. Uhlenbeck (no date, pp 133–134) records:

a) an increasing interest in semantics

b) an increasingly sober appraisal of the role of syntax

c) growing recognition of the fact that the sentence is not the only framework for the description of linguistic facts

and hence a withdrawal from extreme theoretical positions, and at the same time also a profound pessimism in view of the now clearly discernible complexities of language.

The leading "school" within this new trend, known as generative semantics, is identifiable as such only by its rejection of one of the dogmas preached by the Chomsky-Katz-Fodor linguistics: the sharp distinction between syntactic base and semantic interpretation.

The generative semanticists do not approach meaning as something that makes its appearance only when an otherwise completed deep structure is dotted with the colors of the lexicon. Rather, meaning acquires "status as an integral part of linguistics", as McCawley has put it. The structures of meaning are just as primary as are the syntactic structures.

Both the concept of deep structure and that of lexicon are thus called into question. In their revision of generative grammar, the generative semanticists move within the confines of these concepts and their interrelations.

The generative semanticists started out from a question that was formulated by Lakoff (1971a, p 267) in the following way:

What are the regularities that govern which linear sequences of words and morphemes of a language are permissible and which sequences are not?

The characteristic incompleteness of this statement of goals lies in what we have pointed out before: that *permissible* is used in a particular sense of the term, namely, "syntactically permissible". Indeed, this is the only way in which COLORLESS GREEN IDEAS SLEEP FURIOUSLY can be declared permissible. The stunning success of Chomsky's theory has greatly delayed the realization that Lakoff's question cannot be handled independently of another:

What are the regularities by which the surface forms of utterances are paired with their meanings? (Lakoff, *loc. cit.*)

Katz and Fodor became aware of the fact that a grammar composed of syntax and phonology alone does not suffice to describe competence as the speaker-hearer's knowledge of his language. But what they have supplied with their model, as a supplement to Chomsky's base component, is not the mysterious "semantic interpretation" itself – which would be of interest to any language user – but "yet another algorithmic operation defining structures" (Seuren 1972, p 245). With their model, Katz and Fodor could make only a minor contribution to the major task of explaining how language functions in the process of human communication.

The question of how syntax and semantics are mutually related and how their relationships can be accomodated in a generative model continues to be discussed by linguists in the same terminology in which Chomsky's grand ideas of generative grammar were originally couched: deep structure, transformation, surface structure. This is a time when

> the question comes into sharp focus in what manner the syntactic relations between sentences and parts thereof are represented, and whether the representation system as comprised by Chomsky's deep structure may or must provide a link between syntax and semantics. This question ... obviously cannot be resolved independently of a lucid picture of the role and structure of semantics. A major responsibility in the realm of semantics would be to scrutinize the logicians' contributions and to compare them with the results of linguistic semantics as contributed specifically in association with lexicology (Schnelle 1970, pp 12–13).

On surveying the relevant work by Fillmore, Lakoff, McCawley, and others, Schnelle recognized the far-reaching consequences of any such new approach – consequences of particular interest to the psychologist of language:

> There is an urgent need for a thorough discussion of the question to what extent it is admissible to abstract in semantics at large from the ordinarily strong dependence of language on context, or else, how much such an abstraction would benefit linguistics and its goals. This is also a point at which a new discussion of the goals and bounds of linguistics ought to begin (*loc. cit.*).

The various developments unleashed in linguistics by the discomfort over the Chomsky-Katz-Fodor model since 1967 or 1968 can only be termed "a grandiose turmoil". Numerous formalisms have been proposed to uphold one's own and undermine others' positions. Pursuing the disputes waged by Chomsky, Lakoff, and Seuren from 1971 to 1972, for instance, one learns that Chomsky (1971) referred to his position as the "standard theory", whereas Lakoff (1971a) asserted in the same volume that it was not at all clear whether Chomsky had ever seriously held such a position ...

Some of this jumble is certainly due to the fact that the imprecision of numerous terms within the system comes into evidence as soon as major departures from or specifications inside the Chomskyan system are attempted. This applies in particular to the key notion of deep structure.

One would like to know, for instance,

in which form deep structure is supposed to exist: whether it is a preterminal, or terminal string, or a bracketed sentence, or something else (letting alone the problem of what it consists of from the point of view of content, about which practically nothing reliable can be found yet) ... Deep structure is the most important category ... and lack of clarity concerning it is disappointing ... The transformational generative grammar in whole has not yet achieved a more precise notion of this most interesting category (and it is not by chance, for this category is immediately connected with semantics).

The aforegoing was written, characteristically, by a Russian: V Raskin (1972, p 91). But Chomsky (1971, p 191) himself is prepared to recognize as "quite natural" that the relationship of semantic representation to syntactic structure had come under criticism: "No area of linquistic theory is more veiled in obscurity and confusion".

Fillenbaum (1971, p 253), in his account of an essentially intralinguistic discussion, stresses those aspects that are of immediate relevance to psycholinguists:

There have been changes in Chomsky's views since then: for example, surface structure now is regarded as relevant, in some cases at least, to semantic interpretation (Chomsky, 1971). And it is no secret, even to psychologists, that various linguists (see, e.g., McCawley 1968b) have argued that "deep" structure of the sort postulated by Chomsky is just not deep enough, that indeed there is no warrant for assuming an autonomous level of deep structure, that semantics must be generative, not simply interpretive, that semantic and syntactic representations are essentially of the same formal nature, and that (a somewhat enriched) symbolic logic constitutes the most appropriate general framework for the representation of meaning.

While it is not clear for the moment what the meaning of the new development for psycholinguistics is, one thing seems certain:

To the extent that psycholinguistic work is based on some linguistic formation, it may be embarrassing or likely much worse, to find that linguists have now rejected that formulation, making very difficult indeed the interpretation of any results (*op. cit.,* p 254).

Thus Fillenbaum announces the end of an era in psycholinguistics, a period in which, starting with the Osgood-Sebeok-Carroll model and inspired by GA Miller's early investigations, the new science strove to explore the relationships between structures of the message and states of the transmitter (speaker) and receiver (hearer). The era during which psycholinguistics received theoretical guidance from linguistics as the science describing message structures has come to an end, because the linguists had overstated and drawn out in time their exclusive preoccupation with syntax as the core and crux of grammar.

The present state of generative linguistics was termed a grandiose turmoil a couple of pages back. The impression of grandeur is probably due to the harbinger flashes that can be seen projecting from the billowing clouds. Let us inspect the area illuminated by these flashes.

Trying to assess the "psychological relevance" of generative semantics as an innovative trend in linguistics, we immediately come to realize that it would be wrong to overestimate the scale of what some might be tempted to regard as a linguistic revolution. Maclay (1971, p 178) commented in his excellent overview:

The battle between Chomsky and his critics is being fought according to rules which Chomsky himself developed and is essentially a sectarian war among scholars who share a common understanding as to the general goals of linguistic analysis.

The innovative element lies in the claim that syntax and semantics must go together. Nonetheless, the representatives of the new trend, and in any case the generative semanticists in a narrower sence, cling to the notions of *generative* (regarded by Lakoff 1971a, p 232, as synonymous with "complete and precise", as it were) and *competence*. This alone forebodes that there may be difficulties again when trying to account for the fact that language has a function to perform in relation to human beings.

Why is it not possible to draw a sharp dividing line between syntax and semantics? Because the output of the base component, at the lowest level of the model, as comprised by the relations obtaining among the elements of a sentence, is not independent of the meaning of these elements and their (syntactic) relations. If it is true that the basic elements (or concepts) have always a particular tendency, that is, are vectors that show a particular direction, then their combination in the sentence need not and cannot be completely defined by meaning-indifferent syntactic rules.

Analogously, the co-occurrence of seemingly incompatible lexemes (to use Abraham's designation of semantic anomaly and metaphor) has been freed from the stigma of the impermissible, deviant, and abnormal. As cogently argued by McCawley (1971, p 219), a person who utters

MY TOOTHBRUSH IS ALIVE AND IS TRYING TO KILL ME

"should be referred to a psychiatric clinic, not to a remedial English course."

The generative semanticists have definitely parted with Chomsky by taking the following step: Just as it is essentially impossible to draw a sharp dividing line between syntax and semantics, it is likewise impracticable to postulate syntactic deep structure as a separate level in the model. At the same time, the distinction between surface structure and some lower-level structures is upheld – as a lasting contribution of generative linguistics – and so is the rather general concept of lexicon, though there is no agreement as to the lexicon's content and the place (or a plurality of places?) at which it comes into operation in the generation of utterances.

Once a clear-cut separation of semantics and syntax has been declared impossible, nothing can be done to save the old model of autonomous syntax supplemented with an interpretive semantics. Consequently, Seuren (1972, p 257) is fully entitled to suggest the term *semantic syntax* in place of *generative semantics,* since

both the syntactic and the semantic properties of the same objects, sentences, can be adequately predicted by one single set of rules, the syntax.

Obviously, the syntax meant by Seuren is not identical with Chomsky's syntax, as it has swallowed semantics in the meantime.

In making the next step in our analysis, we ought to bear in mind that many terms known from orthodox generative grammar are used by the semanticists in a different sense.

There is one more important tendency in generative semantics to be noted at this point. Syntax and semantics resist a clear-cut separation, and their functions have been taken over by a construct variously called *semantic syntax, semantax,* or even *abstract syntax.* In their attempts to describe linguistic meaning as contained in this framework, McCawley (1968a) and other authors have resorted to the apparatus of symbolic logic, thereby strengthening a rather unfortunate tendency characterized by Chafe (1971a, p 11) in the following words:

> Linguistics – in the area of semantics more seriously than elsewhere – has been and continues to be impeded by ideas carried over from philosophy.

One such idea claims that the truth value of sentences could serve to determine if a sentence is a paraphrase of another sentence. And since both

BERTRAND RUSSELL DIED

and

BERTRAND RUSSELL KICKED THE BUCKET

are true only in the case that Bertrand Russell has really died, the two sentences are taken to paraphrase each other, i. e., have the same meaning. In the same way, generations of linguists used to consider *Morning Star* as a synonym of *Evening Star* on the evidence that the two words referred to the same heavenly body[1].

The tendency to investigate linguistic processes with the aid of a totally unsuited conceptual apparatus borrowed from logic or philosophy, and to ignore the functions of language, is very common in generative semantics. We will try to steer clear of it during our excursion into this terrain.

The hitherto discussed models of semantic analysis of utterances are based on the principle that the meaning of an utterance derives – in one fashion or another – from the meaning of the words and the relations between the words in the utterance. The generative semanticists are likewise preoccupied with the question of what the speaker-hearer's knowledge of the vocabulary must be like in order to make him produce and understand sentences or utterances. Designating the knowledge of this vocabulary by the term *lexicon,* we are again faced with the question: What is contained in such a lexicon?

Katz and Fodor tried to answer this question by grouping the words of a lexicon under particular categories (Animate, Liquid, etc.). The features according to which the words are assigned to the respective categories are subject to a formal "calculus", which in practice involves addition or logical conjunction.

In his critique of this approach, originally published in 1966, Weinreich (1971, p 321) argued that for Katz and Fodor (KF),

> ... the meaning of a complex expression (such as a phrase or a sentence) is an unstructured heap of features – just like the meaning of a single word. The projection rules as formulated in KF *destroy the semantic structure* and reduce the words of a sentence to a heap.

---

[1] It is only now that logicians themselves are prepared to notice the dependence of truth conditions on the human condition (cf. Patzig 1970).

In effect, an analysis of the sentences:

CATS CHASE MICE

MICE CHASE CATS

would yield identical semantic interpretations, because it could not account for the dynamic of the underlying events. While originating in the meaning of the respective words, this dynamic is not given in their features. Attempts to distinguish the chasing agent from the chased object on syntactic grounds (i. e., by marking them as subject and object, respectively) have led to immense difficulties, as in the case of the passive voice.

Weinreich's critical appraisal of Katz and Fodor's theory culminates in the postulate of conceptualizing a *semantic* structure in which the relations demanded and admitted by a word (or semantic unit, to be precise) are specified in their directionality[2]. What is needed is – in Bierwisch's (1971, p 411) words – "additional machinery for the combination of semantic features"; such machinery is made available by revising the concept of feature: features become predicate constants in terms of predicate calculus.

This is where Fillmore comes in. His contribution to linguistics might be introduced under the heading "The Agent hit the Patient with an Instrument." Trying to place him in the field of forces extending between interpretative and generative semantics, we realize once again the confusion prevailing in this domain. In his own words, Fillmore (1968a, p 3) says that the view of syntax's being central is an assumption "taken for granted by workers in the generative grammar tradition". But then he goes on to propose what is in fact a *semantic* base par excellence. So Maclay as well as Lakoff count him among the generative semanticists. Fillmore himself (1972) declares his allegiance to "interpretive semantics", but hastens to add that for him the operations of interpretation imply something else than for Chomsky, as his "lexicon" contains different things.

The two key concepts of Fillmore's (1968b, p 373) position are *predicate* and *argument:*

A predicate is a term which identifies some property of an object or some relation between two or more objects. The objects concerning which a predicate asserts something are the arguments of that predicate.

The sentence HARRY HITS MARY, which exemplifies a two-place predicate, can be written on the pattern $P_{a,b}$ as Hit $_{Harry, Mary}$[3].

By this token, vectors have been envisioned as functioning as elements of semantic structure. The units of language are construed as possessing intrinsic

---

[2] A certain foretaste of this kind of directionality has been offered with the discussion of markedness and its psychological consequences (see the first part of Chap. 6).

[3] What exactly is specified by this notation and what is not – a question of crucial importance to us – is not answered by Fillmore with satisfactory precision. In his view, this particular record represents "the claim that in the act of hitting Harry is the one who did it and Mary is the one who felt it." Regrettably, he adds in the same breath: "Viewed as an abstract relation, of course, it is irrelevant which role in a hitting situation is assigned to the left element, which to the right " (1968b, p 374). This is where we disagree: from the viewpoint of the recipient of the message Chase $_{cats, mice}$ it certainly matters whether the mice are chased by the cats or the cats by the mice.

tendencies, rather than deriving some tendencies solely from the syntactic, and hence heteronomous, structure. The relation between predicate and argument(s) is conceived by Fillmore – a matter of prime importance – in an immensely more substantive, or shall we say psychological, manner than in the case of the formal relation "subject of" or "object of". He obviously cannot do without typifying these relations, or else nothing of general validity could be stated about them.

> I believe that human languages are constrained in such a way that the relations between arguments and predicates fall into a small number of types. In particular, I believe that these role types can be identified with certain quite elementary judgments about the things that go on around us: judgments about who does something, who experiences something, who benefits from something, where something happens, what it is that changes, what it is that moves, where it starts out, and where it ends up. Since judgments like these are very much like the kinds of things grammarians have associated for centuries with the uses of grammatical "cases", I have been referring to these rules as case relationships, or simply cases (p 382).

The predicate (verb) that underlies the given sentence is linked with the respective arguments by definite case relationships. Fillmore adduces the following allegory to illustrate his point:

> Suppose that we view the idea expressed by a simple sentence as analogous to a scene in a play, and suppose that we think of speakers of a language as dramatists working within a theatrical tradition that limits itself to a fixed number of role types, with the further constraint that at most one character in a given role type may appear in any given scene (p 383).

Any scene may have (at most) one prince, one villain, one hag, and one clown. The villain appearing in one scene need not be identical with that in another, of course. The variety of role types appearing in any one scene will depend on the circumstances.

Closing the theatrical episode, we may now turn to linguistics again. In the sentence

THE MAN SPLIT THE ROCK WITH A WEDGE

the verb *split* is a three-argument predicate whose first argument *(man)* takes the case of *Agent,* the second argument *(rock)* the case of *Patient,* and the third argument *wedge* the case of *Instrument.*

In the sentence

THE WEDGE SPLIT THE ROCK

the verb *split* is a two-argument predicate with *wedge* taking the case of Instrument (first argument) and *rock* the case of Patient (second argument).

Whereas in Chomsky's theorizing, case is a secondary aspect of surface structure, Fillmore places it in deep structure. The "grammatical subject", on the other hand, is assigned to surface structure; in the two instances above, the grammatical subject is in one instance the Agent and in the other it is the Instrument. The syntactic role of a sentence component ensues secondarily from the speaker's choice to employ these rather than any other options offered by the verb. He may abstain from mentioning the agent of the rock-splitting by turning *wedge* into the grammatical subject without affecting its deep structure role as Instrument. Should the roles of Agent and Patient be filled *(The man split the rock)* and should the need arise to assert something about the Instrument, there remains the option of introducing *wedge* with the preposition *with*. This time *with* signals the case role Performed by *wedge* in the sentence. (Please note that *with* does *not always* signal this particular role: in the sentence I WENT FOR A WALK WITH PETER, this preposition does not signal that Peter is the Instrument.) The problem of the surface realization of arguments imPlied herein will be elaborated in another place.

What Fillmore is aiming at with his conceptualization is "understanding the proPositional core of simple sentences" (1968b, p 393). His goal is by no means identical with that of orthodox generative grammar, which has been to discover what is responsible for well-formedness. A proposition is what a speaker does in relation to a hearer in order to achieve something. In contrast, well-formedness – which is not really deliberately aimed at by any speaker – bears an autistic stamp. The semantic analysis of actually uttered sentences, argues Fillmore, must explore the ways and means by which to account for the speaker's and the hearer's participation in the speech act. With his construct of case in analogy to role-playing as observed in human actions, Fillmore has succeeded in narrowing the gulf between competence and performance. It is in this sense that verbs have for Fillmore a beginning and an end between which some process takes place. This process occurs in the sentence, and the sentence itself – let us add – realizes some action. Words are assigned different roles in this game, in accordance with their semantic content.

Many a generativist may take the foregoing interpretation as stretching Fillmore's ideas a bit. Even if this were so, our action would be justified by the hope of establishing a connection to an almost extinct tradition in linguistics and the psychology of language.

As a matter of fact, *case* was a core concept in Wundt's psychology of language. Wundt used to distinguish between cases of external and cases of internal determination (*Dativ, Lokativ, Ablativ,* and *Instrumentalis*). Designating *Wohin* (direction), *Wo* (location), *Woher* (source), and *Womit* (instrument), these case relationships are closely reminiscent of Fillmore's. Showing intense interest in the evolution of language(s), Wundt envisaged the four internally determined cases just mentioned as having evolved from the externally determined ones: *Nominativ, Genitiv, Akkusativ* (called grammatical-logical). Whether we accept the evolutionary tenet or not, if any kind of evolution has ever taken place, it must have run over the stretch which extends in Fillmore's model between deep structure and surface structure. That is to say, if we wish to compare Fillmore's with Wundt's approach, we are bound to project Wundt's cases as distributed over the two levels to the deep level where they function in Fillmore. What we find in the process was much earlier described by Bühler (1934) – certainly not a follower of Wundt's[4] – in a section of his *Sprachtheorie* entitled "The Indo-European Case

---

[4] But: "Wundt's well-reasoned and perceptive theory of case ... has ... advanced the relevant

System as an Instance of a Field Tool". Bühler notices, in the case of Indo-European to start with, a kind of emphasis on action: not only are acting subjects the starting point of the operation but they also reemerge as partners to the action. To quote Bühler (1934, p 239):

> When juxtaposing two sentences such as PAUL LOOKS AFTER HIS SICK FATHER and PAUL DRINKS WATER, we notice a certain difference through our linguistic intuition as it is today ... What is happening between Paul and his father is (by our habits of thought) an action occurring between two human partners; we may imagine their roles reversed, as when father looks after a sick Paul for a change. What happens between Paul and water is (by our habits of thought) an action too; but we could scarcely think of water to drink Paul for a change, unless we agreed to be led astray by a metaphorical use of language.

Bühler identifies the action pattern as the basic and dominant schema of Indo-European languages and postulates an origin for its coordinates. In the surface structure of English such an origin is clearly discernible in the N-V-N pattern. Exceeding this restriction to surface structure, Bühler (1934) concludes

> that there is profound wisdom in the conjecture that the places preceding and following the verb are precisely the most convenient and economical way of signifying the basic connotations of the verb (p 243).

Very clearly, for Bühler the verb stands right in the center. Taking the sentence CAIUS NECAT LEONEM (Caius kills the lion) as an example, he inquires:

> Why does the verb induce the questions Who and Whom? Because it gives expression to a particular world conception in the most rudimentary sense of the word, a conception that comprehends and represents states of the world in terms of (animal and) human behavior (p 249)[5].

A verb that implies the conceptual pattern of an action "connotes" two empty places where, according to Bühler, we may insert the nominative and accusative or dative as "tokens of a particular symbol field", thereby describing that field. In Fillmore's theory these tokens become argument places.

For the moment we need not concern ourselves with the fact that Bühler has also described some other sentence patterns. What we have learned about his functionalist approach so far seems to disclose two seminal tendencies in his theorizing: in general, it is his openness to biological and anthropological trains of thought (it might be useful to recall here Toulmin's critique of Chomsky), and, in particular, it is his *grounding of semantic categories in a psychology of acting* (which happens to meet Bierwisch's postulate that the structures of the lexicon ought to correspond to those of our mental apparatus).

Turning from Bühler to Fillmore again, we come upon Tesnière (1959) with his dependence grammar, which similarly assigns the verb a central position. Under this conception, the verb has zero, one, two, ... valences which govern

---

problems to an extent that no one intent upon making further progress dare overlook Wundt's contribution (*op. cit.,* p 236).

[5] Bühler's circumspection prevents him from overplaying the tune of "inner experience", however. He says: "No, this interpretation in terms of a psychology of experiencing is not a *conditio sine qua non;* the situation can be made plain also within the behaviorist conceptual framework" (p 250).

zero, one, two, ... actants. In like manner, Brinkmann (1962) refers to "the verb's ability to demand further places in the sentence" as valence, and to the places that have openings for further relationships as "co-players".

All the same, it would do no good to ignore a major difference between Wundt's, Bühler's and others' emphasis on case and Fillmore's approach to case. Those early conceptions of case as a pivot notion of semantic relationships in the sentence could not but refer to case as we used to know the term from our school grammar, describing nothing but surface structure at that time. In contrast, Fillmore was able to take advantage of the distinction between surface and deep structure introduced and widely popularized by Chomsky in the meantime[6]. Fillmore construes his cases as structuring the propositional core, this core being the deep-structure counterpart of the surface-structure sentence; hence, these cases need not be identical with the cases of school grammar.

Case theory identifies the structures in a sentence as "meaningful", i. e., directional structures of processes. Following Bühler, we are led to discover in these processes an elementary schema of human activity in general. At this point, the choice of the next step in our analysis depends on how much significance we ascribe to the shift of emphasis from the previously unchallenged reign of syntax to a recognition of the central position of semantics.

Should we wish to pass on at once to psychological issues, we might pose the question of whether the role of the verb (as predicate) in sentence processing is as crucial as claimed by case theory. It is in this context that a study of speech perception by Hörmann et al. (1975) deserves to be mentioned. The investigators had subjects listen to, and immediately reproduce, tape-recorded sentences made partly unintelligible by white noise. On the one hand, the verb was found to be the least intelligible among the various grammatical classes presented for perception. On the other, a correctly perceived verb improved the intelligibility of the respective subject and object to a significantly higher degree than did a correctly perceived subject or object in relation to the verb in question. Contrary to Chomsky's view ("there is no alternative to selecting Verbs in terms of Nouns"), the predicate-verb clearly holds a key position in the perception of the sentence.

Before we make further inroads into psychology (where, among others', Engelkamp's work is to be discussed), there is still much to be said about generative semantics. Reverting to Fillmore's initial question, we may now project it upon the verb by asking: What are the verb's characteristic lexicon entries? (Alternatively: What does a speaker "know" when using a particular verb?) On the understanding that the lexicon entries of conventional generative grammar represent what we prefer to call the speaker-hearer's knowledge (of language), we intend to use this question once more – and for the last time – as a point of departure into a discussion where we examine not the action contained in a sentence (as hitherto) but rather the sentence within an action. Our contention is

---

[6] Parenthetically speaking, Chomsky is by no means willing to grant the verb a dominant position in the sentence: "There is no alternative to selecting Verbs in terms of Nouns ..., rather than conversely" (1965, p 115). Fortunately, there *is* one. More on this subject can be found in Engelkamp (1973).

that the speaker-hearer of a sentence must have some knowledge of the things that are only intimated in that sentence. Whereas our argument so far has served to challenge the separation of syntax and semantics, the discussion which follows is meant to contest the restricted preoccupation with the sentence, thereby making an opening toward a text linguistics on the one hand and an action-oriented psychology of language on the other.

By applying the constructs of predicate logic to sentences (or parts thereof), Fillmore has demonstrated how to identify the propositional character of such sentence or phrase structures. In McCawley's (1971) argument there is a minor but quite significant place where we are told in what respect an utterance as described in terms of predicate logic still differs from a "genuine", i. e., real-life utterance. The realization that formal logic is unable to represent some aspects of the sentence that are essential for its comprehension calls to mind the chasm gaping between competence and performance, a chasm in which many a psycholinguist has come to grief.

The point is that "symbolic logic has largely been used as a device for representing the content of propositions of mathematics". Saying this, McCawley (1971, p 223) draws our attention to

> an important way in which the sentences of natural languages differ from mathematical propositions. In mathematics, one enumerates certain objects which he will talk about, defines other objects in terms of these objects, and confines himself to a discussion of objects which have been either explicitly postulated or explicitly defined and which thus have been assigned explicit names; these names are in effect proper names. However, one does not begin a conversation by giving a list of postulates and definitions. One simply starts talking about whatever he intends to talk about, and the bulk of the things which he talks about will be things for which either there is no proper name (. . .) or the speaker does not know any proper name (. . .). Moreover, people often talk about things which either do not exist or they have identifeid incorrectly.

The underlying structure of the sentence

1) THE MAN KILLED THE WOMAN

can be brought to light, according to such authors as Fillmore, by postulating a certain event y of killing in which the man x_1 participated as Agent and the woman x_2 participated as Patient, with the provision that y took place prior to the speech act (Past tense). Working with the apparatus of symbolic logic,

> one might propose that the semantic representation of (1) is obtained simply by conjoining all these assertions . . .:
> 2) $\text{kill}_y (x_1, x_2) \land \text{Past} (y) \land \text{Man} (x_1) \land \text{Woman} (x_2)$[7] (loc. cit.).

That certain things are missing in this kind of representation becomes clear on examining the following sentence:

3) I DENY THAT THE MAN KILLED THE WOMAN.

Now, (3) does not deny (2), since the denial of a conjunction involves the assertion that at least one of the conjuncts is false.

---

[7] Such "conjoining of all assertions" underlies every single research project in this sphere, starting with Katz and Fodor and not excluding Engelkamp.

However, in (3) the speaker is not asserting that one of the four terms of (2) is false but is asserting specifically that the first term is false and assuming the other three terms to be true: it would not be correct to say (3) when one means that x_1 did in fact kill x_2 but that x_2 is not a man *(loc. cit.)*.

Yes, but from what can we deduce this? We are offered no clues for any such deduction; it is somehow being *assumed* that y is the central term of the sentence. The terms x_1 and x_2 evidently are in a subordinate position in relation to y, and symbolic logic as we know it to date has failed to grasp this relationship of super- and subordination. It lacks the tools to represent the fact that sentence (1) is uttered in respect to y (the killing) and that the denial is consequently addressed to y. This entails that for an adequate analysis of a sentence it is indispensable to know the function of the utterance as intended by the speaker. Bearing in mind what we have said in the preceding chapter, we might drive this to the point of stating: *You have to know what the speaker means in order to understand what he says.* The presuppositions underlying an utterance are prerequisites of its integral analysis.

In the language of psychology this means that anyone saying "I deny that the man killed the woman" or any other such sentence, does not start *ab ovo* but continues something that has been in progress for some time. He uses an existing foundation to build upon, and he presumes the hearer to share this foundation with him.

We might take another approach to the issue in order to thrash out the all-important concept of *presupposition*. This time we would be guided by no one less than Chomsky himself. Chomsky (1971) proposes a seemingly insignificant modification of his "standard theory": surface structure is believed also to contribute to semantic interpretation, the idea being to account thereby for the information that is conveyed by intonation. Chomsky feels the need for this revision since, even under his restricted goal-setting, which is to account for well-formedness, he recognizes the importance of focus and presupposition.

Focus and presupposition are clearly interrelated, no doubt. Focus refers, roughly speaking, to that part of the utterance which conveys the genuinely new information, in addition to what the hearer knows already. Presupposition is the opposite: it refers to what the speaker presumes to be in the mind of the hearer; the exact status of presupposition is discussed further below.

The interrelation between focus and presupposition will be illustrated with the following example of an imaginary question which one soccer fan addresses to another: "DID BAYERN MUNICH PLAY AGAINST REAL MADRID?" The four possible presuppositions are:

    a) that Bayern Munich has played against some other team

    b) that some team has played against Real Madrid

    c) that Bayern Munich has done something, or merely

    d) that something has happened to which reference is made in this question. What exactly it is, follows from the focus as indicated by intonation. Should the stress be put on the first word *(has)*, the underlying presupposition would be that this kind of meeting is likely to take place. An appropriate reply would be: "No, it was raining too hard", whereas "No, Górnik Zabrze has played against Real Madrid" is based on a presupposition that does not correspound to the focus indicated in the question.

At first glance one might agree with Chomsky that the modification is a minor one: why should the semantic interpretation of a sentence not be affected by taking account of intonation (which counts as an element of surface structure)? But upon closer scrutiny we discover the fallacy of this conclusion.

To embarrass the linguist we only have to raise the simple question as to where in the model of *linguistic* competence we ought to insert the knowledge needed by the speaker-hearer for handling both presupposition and focus. It is the speaker-hearer's knowledge of the actual or prospective activities of the soccer team Bayern Munich, and hence the knowledge of the world of the individual language user, that determines the adequacy of this and no other utterance with its intonation. A complete description of a sentence evidently requires designations, which go not only beyond the sentence itself (as pointed out in our discussion of pronouns) but possibly beyond language itself – certainly in the sense that the speaker-hearer does not give them a linguistic expression. Designations of this kind belong to that knowledge of the world which Katz and Fodor are compelled to leave out of their considerations as evading a complete systematization (see quotation in the first section of Chap. 7).

In pursuing our discussion of generative semantics into its ultimate consequences, we are led to a vista which orthodox generativists have either refused to notice for decades, or the landscape behind which they have described as irrelevant, dangerous, or tabu. The vista leads us to the *communicative function* of language.

We may now examine the ways in which linguistics (or rather: some linguists) has tried to evade the implications of the "simple question" posed two paragraphs back. McCawley (1968a, p 257) considers two sentences:

4) MY NEIGHBOR HURT HIMSELF
5) MY NEIGHBOR HURT HERSELF

in the following words:

> The description of such sentences raises the question of whether the choice between himself/herself/itself is made on the basis of linguistic properties of the antecedent noun phrase or on the basis of one's knowledge about the intended referent of that noun phrase.

Obviously, the latter kind of knowledge cannot be counted as part of linguistic competence.

McCawley seeks to evade the linguistic problem by distinguishing between presupposition and meaning: the information in sentence (5) that the neighbor is female is labelled a presupposition and excluded from the meaning of that sentence, because

> one would not utter such a sentence in order to convey the information that the neighbor is a female but only the information that that individual has suffered an injury *(loc. cit.)*.

But this only takes McCawley from the frying pan into the fire: by identifying meaning in this case with the message that is intended to reach the hearer, McCawley can no longer ignore the speaker's intention, and hence extralinguistic facts. If ist is true that it depends on the speaker what he builds into the presupposition and what he puts as information into the utterance, then there can be no sensible discussion of adequacy in sentence construction without reference to the speaker's intentions. This point will be pursued in due course, but first let us comment on the proposed distinction between meaning and presupposition.

To distinguish *meaning* from *presupposition* is a highly debatable measure, especially when one considers that meaning used to be identified not so long ago with what the speaker-hearer has to know about a lexical item in order to use it correctly in a sentence. Fillmore (1969), who makes a similar distinction by juxtaposing presupposition and proper meaning, is vainly trying to grapple with the same problem: in one place he defines presupposition as the "happiness conditions for the use of the lexical item" (p 109). A little later he exemplifies the matter with the sentece

6) PLEASE OPEN THE DOOR

which

can be used as a command only if the hearer is in a position to know what door has been mentioned and only if that door is not, at (that time), open (p 120).

Presupposition is here the knowledge of a particular door that is closed. But on the next page we read again:

The presupposition about the closed state of the door is a property of the verb *open* (p 121).

So we are left guessing: does presupposition pertain to the lexical item or to the sentence?

Miller conceives of presupposition and assertion as being somehow contained in the word (see latter part of Chap. 6), McCawley locates presupposition in the sentence, and Fillmore leaves us unhappy with three alternatives: does "happiness" apply to the lexical item, to the sentence, or to the speaker uttering the sentence? Searle (as will be shown in the next chapter) envisions presupposition-like contingencies as the mental states of the speaker; Chafe (1971 b) proposes to represent presuppositions as contextual features ...

Deploring the lack of a useful definition of presupposition, Katz (1973a, 1973b) complains angrily over the great confusion caused by the tendency to label each newly discovered property of the sentence "presupposition". Nonetheless, Katz takes it for granted that presuppositions are nothing but properties of the sentence. Well, is he actually right?

Perhaps we ought to raise the more general question: Do presuppositions belong to grammar? According to Chomsky, they are part of grammar, and in order to document his contention, Chomsky supplements the lexicon with an additional dimension, that of intonation. But the fact is that focus and presupposition go beyond the sentence, while the goal of generative grammar is to account for the well-formedness of *sentences*.

Lakoff (1971 b) maintans that any discussion of well–formedness has to include presuppositions about "the nature of the world". The *type* of inclusions, he says, depends on linguistic competence, whereas the actual judgments about well–formedness relative to extralinguistic knowledge are vested in performance. According to Lakoff, a grammar ought to generate not only descriptions of sentences but also pairs (P, S) which consist of the presupposition P relative to which S is grammatical. While welcoming Lakoff's attempt to bring the notion of grammaticality closer to that of the intelligibility of the world, we still miss the necessary psychological treatment of presupposition. The matter will be taken up further below.

Perhaps the clearest exposition of the issue has again been offered by Chafe (1971 b). Chafe compares the following sentences:

7 a) YESTERDAY I MET A MAN WHO CROSSED THE ATLANTIC IN A ROWBOAT
7 b) YESTERDAY I MET THE MAN WHO CROSSED THE ATLANTIC IN A ROWBOAT

Obviously, (7 b) would be used only if it could be assumed that the hearer has heard of the Atlantic crossing. As a linguist, Chafe now wants to know which linguistic element this information is plugged into: "Atlantic" (= crossed by a man in a rowboat), or "rowboat" (= used by a man for crossing the Atlantic), or some preceding sentence of the kind "A man crossed the Atlantic in a rowboat"? Chafe ventures the answer:

> I have the impression that such knowledge is not tied to particular sentences, but that it is instead capable of being plugged into a variety of semantic structures of particular sentences, of which (7 b) is but one of many possible examples (p 66).

Semantic structure as conceived by Chafe is, once again, not limited to language: semantic structures are discernible in language as well as in the cognitive world of the language user; in fact, they seem to us only partially verbalizable in the processes of meaning and of understanding.

The problem of what might be recognized as presupposition is squarely faced by Chafe when he says that, whereas the linguist is asking

> what kind of knowledge allows us to treat *man* in (7 b) as definite, we ask instead what the definiteness of *man* in that sentence tells us about underlying knowledge – what it "presupposes" about such knowledge. We don't ask how knowledge influences what we say, but instead how what we say provides clues to what is known (p 68).

There we have a radical shift: language-in-itself is based on language-in-its-function-for-the-self.

From the discussion of presuppositions it transpires once again that it is inadmissible to separate meaning from language use. Here we can sense Wittgenstein looming in the background; we shall have an opportunity to inspect his views in the next chapter.

Basing ourselves on Fillmore's specimen sentence, we will now make another approach to the problem by bringing the notion of *world view* into play.

8) THAT HARRY IS STILL LIVING WITH HIS MOTHER PROVES THAT HE IS A BAD MAR-RIAGE RISK

Fillmore (1969, p 121) comments:

It is apparent that if I were to say (8) about somebody who is an orphan, nobody would say that I was speaking falsely, only that I was speaking inappropriately. If *prove* has a THAT-clause subject and a THAT-clause object, we say that the truth of the first THAT-clause is *presupposed,* and that the verb is used to assert a causal or logical connection between the two clauses and thus (when used affirmatively) to imply the truth of the second clause.

Is it not that by this "not false, but inappropriate" we are pushed back, perhaps as far as Chomsky's furiously sleeping colorless green ideas, which may well be not so much false as inappropriate? Both *false* and *inappropriate* signify a violation of norms, and any such violation gives rise to a sense of discomfort. Clearly, two different kinds of norms are violated by Chomsky's and by Fillmore's specimen sentences. However, it is to be recognized that the zero level at which such norms begin to operate is tied up with our individual striving to make sense of the world around us and of the messages originating from this world. The logically perfectly acceptable sentence

9) DRYADS ARE NOT ALLOWED TO MATRICULATE AT HAMBURG UNIVERSITY

is baffling because it involves two incompatible presuppositions:
   a) Dryads exist only in mythology,
   b) anyone qualifying for matriculation must exist in reality.
But suppose we modify sentence (9) into

10) I DREAMT THAT DRYADS WERE NOT ALLOWED TO MATRICULATE AT HAMBURG UNIVERSITY.

On realizing that now our misgivings are much less acute we are prompted to revert to an argument used in the preceding chapter: *I dreamt* refers the sentence to an unreal world in which the two otherwise incompatible presuppositions do not come so much into conflict. The world of dreaming allows for a certain loosening of the network of presuppositions that serve to make the world intelligible and meaningful. Sense constancy can be more easily achieved if we can sidestep into the world of dreams.

Elaborating this with respect to the problem of presupposition, we would say: presuppositions serve to anchor the utterance in the world of the speaker and hearer. It is in terms of *this* world, rather than any linguistics-immanent or language-inherent world, that we judge the appropriateness of what is conveyed by the utterance.

There is a further aspect of Fillmore's attempt to distinguish between presupposition and meaning which moves us in the right direction. When sentence (6) is negated:

11) PLEASE DON'T OPEN THE DOOR,

its "presuppositional conditions" remain the same: the speaker must likewise be in a position to assume that the hearer knows what door is meant and knows that the door is closed. The modification is, according to Fillmore, in the meaning of the sentence – but what does he now mean by *meaning?* Fillmore employs the term in a sense never encountered in the hitherto discussed linguistics. This time meaning emerges as the purpose or goal of the utterance! Fillmore (1969, p 121):

> If the presuppositional conditions . . . are satisfied can a sentence be appropriately used for asking a question, issuing a command, making an apology . . . or making an assertion.

Evidently, Fillmore is likewise willing to recognize the pragmatic aspect of the sentence. Thus presuppositions refer neither to lexical items nor to sentences, but to the communicative function of the utterance. Among linguists, the most articulate formulation along these lines was offered by SJ Schmidt (1973, p 93):

> speakers make or hold presuppositions that are meant to apply to sentences or texts . . ., i. e., presupposition is a concept at the level of communication, not at the level of grammar.

What this implies, among other things, is that prior to any attempt at describing the grammar contained in any one utterance, we ought to explore what the speaker means by this utterance and what the hearer understands by it. Putting it differently: the meaning of an utterance may not be separated from the function it performs in the speech act between speaker and hearer.

The procedure of grammar construction under which the linguist has a native speaker revise his soliloquies loses validity as soon as the grammar obtained in this way is represented as a theory of language. With the latter goal in mind, the linguist (or psychologist) must watch at least two native speakers involved in a social interaction comprising some elements of discourse. Discussing the crisis in psychology more than half a century ago, Bühler (1927, p 38) insisted that "it is in society, not in the individual, where we have to look for the origins of semantics".

The emergence of meaning from the social acts of meaning something and of understanding something has its philosophical aspects too, and these are discussed in the next chapter.

At this point we have to examine one more contribution of a semantically oriented linguist whose ideas can benefit the psychologist of language. Alongside Fillmore's contribution, Chafe's work must be seen as one of the most important conceptions offered by linguists in recent times.

Chafe (1970) gives three reasons why the Chomsky-inspired generative grammar appears to him unsatisfactory:

1) a moral one: he notes the arrogance with which these ideas are propounded, especially when one considers that

> the complexities of the universe, linguistic and otherwise, are so vast that one cannot help but be awed and humbled by them, and (. . .) arrogance in a linguist betrays at least a lack of perspective on the problems which confront him (p 2);

2) an aesthetic one: the semantic component of the Chomsky-Katz-Fodor model "is left hanging on the side" (p 65); thus it cannot possibly account for the actual role of semantics;

3) a pragmatic one: the model is far removed from any theory of performance and thus unable to account for language use.

Chafe contrasts this model with his own, wherein he proceeds from the assumption that language is a mode of converting meanings into sounds. This conversion, he asserts, is unidirectional: though the individual may act either as speaker or as hearer, the actual linguistic process will always run from meaning to sound, not the reverse. Chafe (1970, p 59) supports his contention with the following argument:

> The speaker creates a semantic structure and converts it into sound. The hearer does not create a phonetic structure and convert it into meaning. Normally the hearer assumes that the sound which he hears has a meaning underlying it, already produced by the speaker. Presumably, the hearer retrieves that meaning by applying the phonological, symbolization, and postsemantic processes of his language in reverse, but he applies them to something which has already been produced by these processes during their original application ... The hearer's role is a matter of recovering what the speaker began with, a second-hand role at best.

Is that not too much? (Incidentally, Olson asserts the opposite: that nearly everything is redundant from the speaker's point of view ...) The question is not whether the speaker or the hearer is the principal actor in the process. Instead, Chafe's analysis offers this important clue: in ordinary discourse, the hearer takes it for granted that there is meaning in what he hears. This is precisely what was asserted earlier in these pages (Chap. 7); more arguments in support of the thesis are given further on.

Language conceived as a means by which meanings are converted into sounds: in accord with this idea, Chafe develops his model from and around *semantic structure*. The units of this structure are cognitive concepts[9]. The latter need not correspond to words; Chafe might readily subscribe to the "psychologistic" treatment of the issue as proposed in these pages. Indeed, he refuses to fall back on the notion of image and argues that speakers of perhaps every language

> have in their minds a piece of knowledge which can be called the concept *dog*. This piece of knowledge is not an image of a particular dog on a particular occasion, but rather an underlying unity of which images of dogs are only particular and accidental manifestations (1970, p 75).

Naturally, Chafe is well aware of the difficulties involved in a precise description of semantic concepts. These difficulties, as we know, were the source of the élan with which Bloomfield's structuralism and Chomsky's "syntacticism" degraded semantics to the subordinate position of a "poor relative". For Chafe, these are not insurmountable difficulties: "If concepts have their locus within our minds, that is the place to look for them" (1970, p 76).

Chafe evidently lends support to a cognitive psychology of language – or even a psychology of consciousness – which, in our view, constitutes the most promising approach to language as used by people. The fact that in view of their

---

[9] We came across a similar approach to the problem, though in a different context, when reviewing the work by Schank (1972) and Miller (1972), in the latter part of Chap. 6.

complexity these semantic concepts are far more difficult to study than the sounds of language, for instance, cannot excuse our default in this respect.

By postulating that a semantic concept is manifested "in a focus and a gradual, perhaps irregular fading away from that focus", Chafe (1970, p 79) clearly opposes Katz and Fodor's view of concepts as classes within the dictionary (lexicon) which together provide a more or less complete coverage of the cognizable world, each class resisting any further differentiation. (Here we might recall Rosch's findings as reported in Chap. 6.)

Semantic units never occur in isolation; they invariably are embedded in more or less complex configurations. The resulting semantic structure encloses the most subtle distinctions in meaning. Whereas for orthodox generativists the phrases

A BACHELOR
UNMARRIED ADULT HUMAN BEING
A MAN WHO WAS NEVER MARRIED
HUMAN BEING WHO IS ADULT, MALE, AND HAS NEVER HAD A WIFE

represent one and the same deep structure with four different surface realizations (paraphrases), Chafe identifies in them four different (albeit similar) semantic structures.

This should suffice as an account of Chafe's concept of semantic structure. An aspect of his views that is of particular relevance in this context is the idea that the utterance is composed of semantic units, and hence of conscious, intentional concepts. The psychologist of language might derive even more inspiration, however, from Chafe's conception of what goes on in the underlying semantic structure of an utterance in the process of language use. The semantic structure of an utterance is transformed, via different postsemantic processes and through a number of intermediate stages, into a surface structure. In the sentence IT IS RAINING the word *rain* is fairly directly related to the cognitive concept of water falling from the sky; the symbolization involved is of a fairly direct kind. The word *it,* on the other hand, lacks such a direct relationship to semantic structure; a relationship is established only by a postsemantic process. In contrast, when an approaching train is announced with the words IT IS COMING, there is a direct relationship between *it* and the train.

One of the steps leading from semantic to surface structure is linearization, by which semantic structures (e. g., *cat* for the furry animal and *-s* for plural) are sequentially ordered on one dimension *(cats).*

Examining idioms, Chafe succeeds in showing that in the case of HENRY IS DRAGGING HIS FEET it is indispensable to transform a unitary semantic structure *(procrastinate, delay, temporize)* by postsemantic processes into a postsemantic configuration before converting it into sound. Hence there is a discrepancy between many semantic units (concepts) and their literalizations: both *feet* and *dragging* lack in our example any direct representation at the level of semantic structure.

Chafe's theory is the only one in modern linguistics that meets a requirement derived from Van Lancker's (1975) arguments as reviewed at the end of Chap. 6:

sematic
structure

    postsemantic process

↓
intermediate
postsemantic
structure

↓ ⋯ ↓

    further phonological processes
    and intermediate structures

surface
structure

    phonological process

↓
underlying
phonological
structure

    symbolization

↓
intermediate
phonological
structure

↓ ⋯ ↓

    further postsemantic processes
    and intermediate structures

phonetic
structure

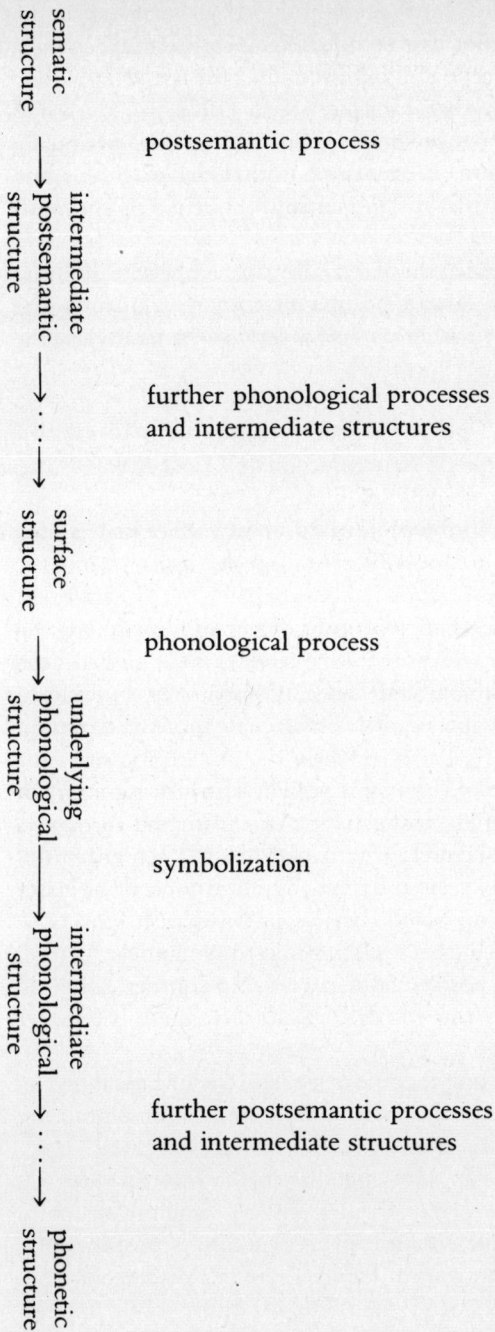

Fig. 3. Chafe's model of language processes. (After Chafe, 1970, p. 56, © 1970 by The University of Chicago Press)

145

the various postsemantic processes serve to bring into operation the many kinds of automatic speech (prefabricated in varying degree) which make up a fair portion of our language output. There are highly differentiated semantic configurations which, after being subjected to a variety of postsemantic processes, eventually may receive one and the same surface realization; there are, on the other hand, relatively simple semantic configurations that thave to be transformed into fairly differentiated and "novel" postsemantic configurations before they can be converted into sound.

The requirement to determine the degree of literalization for practically each component of the utterance, which has to be met in conveying meaning or grasping it in discourse, is one of the basic reasons for proposing the concept of sense constancy.

There is no need to enlarge here on the other stages and the processes mediating between them as proposed by Chafe; these processes are chiefly responsible for converting phonological into phonetic structure. Chafe's final model is presented in Fig. 3.

There are many places further on in the present volume where Chafe's ideas are revisited. For example, linearization and literalization are brought into our discussion of the Russian psychology of language (Chap. 10). But of paramount importance for us will be Chafe's fundamental idea: the acts of conveying and grasping meaning both extend over a number of stages and qualitatively different processes, each of them advancing the respective act (in varying degree) along the path leading from meaning to sound. This idea will dominate the final chapter of this book.

The foregoing discussion of ideas proffered by linguists of a semantic orientation (and hence called semanticists) has yielded a number of important suggestions, not the least one being the conception of meaningful speaking and understanding as arising from inherently directional acts of enormous complexity. This kind of "genesis of meaning" naturally has its philosophical aspects, to which we may now turn.

Chapter 9

Philosophy of Language as Aide and Ally

In the foregoing chapters we tried to picture the acts of meaning and understanding as concretizations of the language user's intentions; the latter were found to be anchored in a network of presuppositions, expectations, presumptions, and elements of knowledge.

The thus intimated implication of intention, context, and action in the discussion of how "meaning" might be most pertinently conceptualized and accounted for was originally proposed neither by the generativists, nor their docile followers, the psycholinguists, but by philosophers. Whereas it would be unfair to say that generative linguistics entered its semantophile phase without taking notice of what philosophers had earlier or contemporaneously said on the subject of meaning, it would be equally mistaken to claim that the ideas expounded by Moore, Ryle, Austin, Wittgenstein, and Searle left a distinct impression on the conceptual framework of the generativists. Evidently, linguists were loath to aggravate the thorny problem of appending a semantic component to their generative model of language by going into the question of how to construe the "semantic relation" between sign and referent. The time-honored view that meaning is identical with the (word-)sign's reference to the pertinent object is implicit in the entire discussion on the lexicon (or dictionary), as much as in the psychologists' debates on coding and decoding. This relation of reference between sign and referent stands unchallenged under the protective shield of competence, where it actually belongs.

A psychology of language that rejects the bisection of the world into competence and performance, however, cannot ignore the philosophical inquiry into the relationship between *word, object,* and *intended meaning.*

These relationships have become a central topic in present-day philosophy. In elaboration of what might be seen as a sweeping generalization, let us point out that whereas in earlier periods philosophers were mostly preoccupied with the question "How is it that we know what we know?", at present their attention seems to be focused on the problem "How is it that we can speak about what we know[1]?"

The general trend of philosophical inquiry is evidently toward a critical appraisal of methodology. Ever since Descartes – if not earlier – the aim of methodological criticism has been to improve the validity and reliability of philosophical statements. Noting with amazement the continuing imperfection of their statements, philosophers today are prone to put the blame on the linguistic obscurities of these formulations. Hence their preoccupation with questions such as "What does it actually mean to state that X means this or that?", "What is really meant by the statement that a word is synonymous with another word, or that a sentence is a paraphrase of another sentence?", and "What do we actually mean when saying that a sentence is analytic, i. e., true in terms of its meaning?"

In effect, the language of philosophical inquiry becomes itself the object of inquiry, the presumption being that the persistence of many problems in philosophy is due less to their inherent unsolvability than to the fact that even philosophers have succumbed to the bewitchment of language. Indeed, Wittgenstein (1953, § 109) describes philosophy as "a battle against the bewitchment of our intelligence by means of language."

In the face of this challenge you may either proceed like

a projecting reformer (Russel, Quine, Goodman), who sits down in an armchair to determine how we should speak clearly in the light of reason (Hampshire 1967, p 242),

or you may base yourself on language as used by people, i. e., on ordinary language.

The ordinary-language philosophy discussed in the following pages has grown from just this motive. Our survey is neither complete nor veridical; instead, it is meant as an account of the personal impressions formed by a psychologist of language on reading the relevant material. In selecting this material the author was guided by his own ideas; the presentation of the material is expected to make these ideas more intelligible.

The most enlightening among these philosophers seem to be the later Wittgenstein and Austin, along with the latter's follower Searle.

Wittgenstein's later philosophy (from *Philosophical Investigations* and the *Brown and Blue Books*) is expressed predominantly in negative form. Wittgenstein is a genius of "that can't be so", and this alone makes him a congenial soul for the psychologist of today. Roughly speaking, he is very critical of the uncritical semantics that was once described as "the myth of a museum in which the exhibits are meanings and the words are labels" (Quine 1971, p 142). The fact that *meaning* can be employed as a noun may be responsible for the irresistible tendency to treat the meaning of a word or sentence as an object or thing in itself. Not only does this add to the world of things and to the world of words a world of meanings; it also suggests that any word or sentence has a single meaning, a specific meaning that can be labeled with the pertinent word as soon as we know it – which is a suggestion of disastrous consequences.

---

[1] On this and what follows, consult especially von Savigny (1969).

As in the fairy tale: you *have* a thing if you only know what to call it. Thus, according to the theory which Wittgenstein refuses to accept, to know the meaning of a word implies identification of Y as it appears in the equation "X has the meaning Y". Wittgenstein (1953) starts his argument with a concise formulation of this idea:

> Every word has a meaning. This meaning is correlated with the word. It is the object for which the word stands (p 2).

This is where Wittgenstein begins his objections. There is no denying that in our attempt to juxtapose Wittgenstein's views with those he critically reviews we run into difficulties due less to the author's manner of writing than to his manner of communication[2].

Wittgenstein resists the temptation to append another term to the list of the meanings of *meaning* known to philosophy and linguistics (denotation, designation, reference, opinion, sense, connotation, etc.) and proposes a different formulation of the problem. Instead of asking "What is the meaning of a word?" and thus falling into the trap of reification, he raises the question: "How can we account for the meaning of a word?" That is to say, his starting point is the act of communication in which the term *meaning* is supposed to function, in contrast to the many other approaches which start with determining *meaning* and then (perhaps, later on, eventually . . .) treat of its functioning in communication as an eventuality.

As a kind of example, Wittgenstein (1953) tries to understand what a game is:

> Consider for example the proceedings that we call "games". I mean board-games, card-games, ball-games, Olympic games, and so on. What is common to them all? – Don't say "There *must* be something common, or they would not be called 'games'" – but *look and see* whether there is anything common to all. – For if you look at them you will not see something that is common to *all,* but similarities, relationships, . . . Now pass to card-games; here you find many correspondences with the first group, but many common features drop out . . . – Are they all 'amusing'? Compare chess with noughts and crosses. Or is there always winning and losing, or competition between players? Think of patience. . . . And the result of this examination is: we see a complicated network of similarities overlapping and criss-crossing . . . (§ 66) . . . And this is how we do use the word "game". For how is the concept of game bounded? What still counts as a game and what no longer does? Can you give the boundary? No. You can *draw* one; for none has so far been drawn. (But that never troubled you before when you used the word "game".) (§ 68)

Before resuming this rather philosophical argument, let us spell out the direct implications of the foregoing for linguistics. Wittgenstein clearly rejects the idea of a lexicon structured in terms of classes or categories that are defined by their

---

[2] Von Savigny (1969, p 15) comments: "The *Philosophical Investigations* make the impression of a file in disorder; the book is incomprehensible, not because of its language, which is lucid and plain, but because of the desultory argumentation, and also because in many cases Wittgenstein fails to state his findings." The bewildered reader may find solace in the fact that even Bertrand Russell had to talk to Wittgenstein for three days before he could write a three-sentence assessment of the latter's philosophy (as we read in Russell's *Autobiography* 1968).

boundaries. Anyone holding his view has dissociated himself from a linguistic theory whose supreme goal is to account for the correctness of utterances by positing a system of rules which consists essentially in lining up those logical classes. And since it is difficult to tell the difference between a game and a non-game, one would be well advised not to center his linguistic theory upon the procedure of distinguishing between correct and incorrect uses of *game*. "That never troubled you before when you used the word 'game'."

Reverting now to Wittgenstein's argument, we find him deliberating on how we might explain to someone what a game is:

> One gives examples and intends them to be taken in a particular way. – I do not, however, mean by this that he is supposed to see in those examples that common thing which I – for some reason – was unable to express; but that he is now to *employ* those examples in a particular way (§ 71).

There we have a notion of paramount importance: in order to account for the meaning of a term, you need not point out what is common to the examples at hand – as claimed by the ancient paradigm with which philosophers and psychologists tried to explain the formation of concepts – from Locke to Katz and Fodor. The sought-for meaning does not automatically spring from what may be common to the quoted examples: instead, it requires an *intention* on the part of the speaker to make the hearer aware of some particular sense implicated by the examples. Moreover, it is indispensable that the hearer join in this intention by completing the thus initiated act of communication. Understanding involves an awareness of sense precisely where and how it was intended by the speaker. In order to comprehend the speaker's explanation (of what a game is), the hearer must already have an inkling of what the speaker might have in mind. It is not by accident that Wittgenstein speaks of intending in the foregoing quotation: he does so in direct reference to the intentional appeal which pervades the acts of meaning and understanding.

What exactly do we know once we have grasped the meaning of a word? This knowledge is not "somehow equivalent to an unformulated definition" (§ 75). What we know is how the word might be used.

> For a large class of cases – though not for all – in which we employ the word "meaning" it can be defined thus: the meaning of a word is its use in the language (§ 43).

This definition does not tell us enough, however. But our attention is thus drawn to the fact that linguists have invariably taken it for granted that a word can be used only if and because its meaning is known. Wittgenstein asserts the opposite: we know a word's meaning only if and because we know how to use it. If we were to revert once again to the unfortunate competence/performance dichotomy, we would now acknowledge the preeminence of performance over competence. Endowed with intentional content, the acts of meaning something and of understanding what is meant must be seen as a language-effected "continuation of action with other means" (cf. Hörmann 1971a, p 268).

Wittgenstein's advice "Don't ask for the meaning, ask for the use", reveals that we are on familiar ground again:

a) it is not that a sign carries some meaning and *can* be eventually used

b) any attempt at exploring the contingencies of language must make allowances for language's functions.

A word of caution will be in order as we now resume Wittgenstein's train of thought. Despite appearances, he does not advocate a reduction of semantics to pragmatics (as generally thought); in fact, he distinctly opposes the notion of meaning as something that either may or may *not* be used, a notion that often stands behind the triad syntactics-semantics-pragmatics.

Neither does Wittgenstein support a simplistic theory of meaning of the instrumentalist kind (e. g., for Skinner, a *mand* is a demand because it is complied with). Wittgenstein only succeeds in explaining what the meaning of words, sentences, and utterances is by bringing into focus "the whole, consisting of language and the actions into which it is woven" (§ 7). This whole he has chosen to call the *language game*.

All sorts of language games can be imagined:

a) Giving orders and obeying them

b) Reporting an event

c) Forming and testing a hypothesis

d) Making up a story

e) Guessing riddles

f) Playing and discussing chess

g) Asking, thanking, cursing, greeting, praying, etc.

"And to imagine a language means to imagine a form of life" (§ 19).

The relationship between a word and a language game as construed by Wittgenstein is of a distinctly structuralist kind – even though the author does not employ the term himself. This is demonstrated by his example of the king in chess:

> When one shows someone the king in chess and says: "This is the king", this does not tell him the use of this piece – unless he already knows the rules of the game up to this last point: the shape of the king. . . . The shape of the chessman corresponds here to the sound shape of a word. One can also imagine someone's having learnt the game without ever learning or formulating rules. . . . He too might be given the explanation "This is the king", – if, for instance, he were being shown chessmen of a shape he was not used to. This explanation again only tells him the use of the piece because, as we might say, the place for it was already prepared. . . . And in this case it is so . . . because in another sense he is already master of the game. Consider this further case: I am explaining chess to someone; and I begin by pointing to a chessman and saying: "This is the king; it can move like this, . . . and so on." – In this case we shall say: the words "This is the king" . . . are a definition only if the learner already 'knows what a piece in a game is'. That is, if he has already played other games, or has watched other people playing 'and understood' – *and similar things* (§ 31).

Thus, when you inquire about the designation of an object or about the meaning of a word, you are bound to know something about it. We are faced here by an analogy to the relationship described in the chapter on sense constancy: the relationship between a general setting or horizon of making sense and the particular realization of meaningfulness accompanied by a sense of "having understood". The case also illustrates the interloocking of (word-) "meaning", sentence, knowledge, and intention in a meshwork of interdependencies and mutual trade-off as controlled by the process of sense constancy.

Evidently, an ostensive definition – the protoparadigm of nearly every philosopher concerned with the emergence of language – does not do the job. To learn a language game, you have to

> know or guess what the person giving the explanation is pointing to. That is, whether for example to the shape of the object, or to its color, or to its number, and so on (§ 33).

This kind of knowledge cannot be conveyed by an ostensive definition, of course ("Point to a piece of paper. – And now point to its shape – now to its color – now to its number"). A vague idea of what the speaker might have in mind must already exist in the hearer before the acquisition (or rather: the differentiation) of a language game can begin.

Such "presentiment" of what the speaker might have in mind can emerge only if speaker and hearer share a particular mode of life in at least a general outline[3].

The statement by Frege that a word carries meaning only in the context of a sentence (quoted by Wittgenstein with approval) should obviously not be taken to mean that a word without sentence context is a semantic zero. But instead of inquiring into the properties of a word, we ought to examine the role it plays in a particular language game. "The question 'What is a word really?' is analogous to 'What is a piece in chess?'" (§ 108). That is to say, by analyzing the properties of the word we cannot expect to make any progress.

Exploring the particular uses of a word we must resist the temptation

> to think that if anyone utters a sentence and *means* or *understands* it he is operating a calculus according to definite rules (§ 81).

The use of a word is not everywhere bounded by rules; a rule pointing in some direction suffices if it meets its purpose in normal conditions. (This denial of automatic computation in the acts of conveying and grasping meaning is most intimately associated with the processes described by Garfinkel as occurring prior to the emergence of coding – see Chap. 11.)

Accordingly, the extent to which a language game is governed by rules seems to depend also on the particular function of the game. Here we have another illustration of the agency which determines for how long and to what depth an utterance has to be analyzed – a question discussed in the preceding chapters. It would be wrong to assume that an imprecise explanation is quite useless.

> The fundamental fact here is that we lay down rules, a technique, for a game, and that then when we follow the rules, things do not turn out as we had assumed. That we are therefore as it were entangled in our own rules. This entanglement in our rules is what we want to understand (i. e., get a clear view of). It throws light on our concept of *meaning* something (§ 125).

---

[3] "Suppose you came as an explorer into an unknown country with a language quite strange to you. In what circumstances would you say that the people there gave orders, understood them, obeyed them, rebelled against them, and so on? The common behavior of mankind is the system of reference by means of which we interpret an unknown language" (Wittgenstein 1953, § 206).

The persistent tension between a generally meaningful rule and the particular "instancing" of the general enables us to grasp – in understanding – what is intended by the speaker. The discrepancy between what generally makes sense and what is understood, the disaccord between rule and reality, is for Wittgenstein a source of cognizance. "It is in language that an expectation and its fulfillment make contact" (§ 441).

As has been pointed out before, Wittgenstein's account of a word's meaning bears a structuralist mark. A word conveys some meaning because it can be assigned a particular role in the interplay of knowledge, actions, and lexical elements. Indeed, are we entitled to inquire into what a word is before it has assumed a particular role in a particular language game? Can we act on "hearing" the word alone? "'It is as if we could grasp the whole use of the word in a flash'" (§ 191)[4].

But how is it that the potential uses are already contained in the act of grasping itself? This follows from the rule inventory of the language game and from what "to follow a rule" implies. A rule is not a rigid prescription, one person may follow it in one way, another person in a different way. "To follow a rule" is a practice.

> One does not feel that one has always got to wait upon the nod (the whisper) of the rule. On the contrary, we are not on tenterhooks about what it will tell us next, but it always tells us the same, and we do what it tells us ... (§ 223). The word "agreement" and the word "rule" are *related* to one another, they are cousins. If I teach anyone the use of the one word, he learns the use of the other with it (§ 224).

Thus, communication by language involves agreement in judgements, but "that is not agreement in opinions but in form of life" (§ 241). And forms of life – we might say – are "what has to be accepted, the given" (p 226)[5].

The problems stretching between *meaning* and *use* were treated in much the same way by Ajdukiewicz[6] (1934) long before Wittgenstein's *Philosophical Investigations*. Ajdukiewicz's central concept is that of sense, defined in the following way: "The sense carried by the expressions of a language determines in some way the rules of their uses" (p 106).

Ajdukiewicz's account of the procedure by which it can be established if someone uses a sentence in the same sense as we do or not surpasses Wittgenstein's in precision. The procedure itself is of paramount importance for the psychologist because it brings us close to the process of understanding:

---

[4] "– But have you a model for this? No. It is just that this expression suggests itself to us. As the result of the crossing of different pictures" (§ 191). "You have no model of this superlative fact, but you are seduced into using a super-expression. (It might he called a philosophical superlative.)" (§ 192).

[5] This interlacement of language and form of life bears an interesting analogy: Whereas in the philosophy of ordinary language both situation and intention serve to determine the meaning of utterances, in sociolinguistics the occurrence of particular types of utterances serves as a clue to identify the sociological status and intention of the speakers (cf. Ervin-Tripp 1972). Should understanding an utterance and knowing the speaker combine into one balanced, constant-sum system?

[6] I am indebted to Professor J. Pelc of Warsaw University for this reference to Ajdukiewicz.

We try to find for this sentence a particularly salient type of experiences, a type in whose nature it is that experiences of this type warrant a determined acknowledgement of the sentence. If we then find the person to reject the sentence in spite of becoming aware of an experience of this type, we conclude that the sentence has been associated with a different sense than in our case (p 107).

Thus there is a connection between the sense associated with the expressions of a language and the way this language is used:

The connection between, e. g., the sentence "It hurts" and the sense attributed to it in the particular language can be established only by someone who, becoming aware of the experience of pain, is ready to acknowledge the sentence (p 110).

We are confronted here with an eminently psychological aspect: This readiness to acknowledge an utterance reveals the agreement, not in opinions but in form of life, mentioned by Wittgenstein. Deese's (1969, p 516) interpretation of understanding as "the inward sign of the potential for reacting appropriately to what we see or hear" is related to this "readiness to accept": consonance in forms of life between speaker and hearer comes into evidence, under the control of language, in the particular place "meant" by the speaker with his utterance.

If we accept Wittgenstein's and Ajdukiewicz's view that language is invariably a component of the form of life, then each language (e. g., English) can be conceptualized as comprising within itself a plurality of languages which differ from each other in their *Sinngebung*. Pursuing this idea one step further, we might postulate that any utterance should comprise a number of different "languages" or language games in parallel (i. e., intentionally, historically[7], sociologically, ... different languages). Such a heterogeneity is indispensable for the hearer to have at his disposal an adequate supply of rule-sidestepping decoding procedures; this notion, which links up with Garfinkel's work, is elaborated in Chap. 11.

One is tempted to employ in what follows the concept of sense as proposed by Ajdukiewicz, in view of its close association with the rules of language use:

As to the question whether one should say that sense is determined by the rules of language or rather that the rules are determined by sense, I observe that there is mutual determination. That is to say: if the sense of an utterance is such and such, then such and such rules apply to the utterance, but also conversely, if such and such rules apply to the utterance, then its sense is such and such (1935, p 166).

But *sense* is a term which many authors in this domain omit altogether, or which is used in quite a different "sense" by some others; in accepting it, we would merely pretend that there exists order in matters of terminology.

Summing up: A language game (as Wittgenstein calls it, and as Ajdukiewicz seems to refer to, without using the term) is always an element of some form of life, i. e., is always a "complete system of human communication".

By thus adopting the form of the communicative act as a point of departure, we are able to eliminate the difficulties encountered by the concept of language as a system of signs, namely, the necessity to bridge the gulf between the sign and

---

[7] The presence of historically different layers in an utterance has been pointed out by, e. g., Mathesius (1964) and Uhlenbeck (cf. Uhlenbeck no date, p 129).

its uses[8]. But, as if in return, we are faced by another difficulty: having read Wittgenstein, one feels fascinated and forsaken at the same time. At first, there is no way in sight that would lead from the language games to the solution of concrete linguistic or psycholinguistic problems. Even though it might be legitimately claimed that by his overwhelming and yet desultory argumentation Wittgenstein has convincingly demonstrated that the problem of meaning can be tackled only by giving consideration to the uses of language, there is unquestionably a need for a typology of what can be *done* with words. Such a typology might emerge from testing the many different utterances (or sentences uttered by different speakers for different hearers in different situations) for what they have in common. In other words, we are interested in a typology of what is done by a person who utters a particular sentence.

This is precisely the goal of the speech act theory as initially proposed by Austin (1957, 1962) and subsequently elaborated by Alston (1964) and Searle (1962, 1968, 1969).

Here we ought to mention a fact that bears on our arguments and gives rise to a certain difficulty to be discussed in due course: the speech act theorists tend to base their deliberations on what they call *explicitly performative verbs*. He who utters the words "I promise to give you the money tomorrow" does not only produce a sentence; he also performs the speech act of promising by uttering the sentence.

> The action he is performing is related by means of the rules of the language he uses to the very fact that he utters the words mentioned. I promise, and I am committed to my promise by the fact that I produce, in a given social, psychological and physical context the sounds corresponding to "I promise" (Apostel 1972, pp 208–209).

But we would be well advised to proceed in a more methodical manner. Let us start with Austin, who is likewise aware of the dangers arising from a philosopher's abandonment to language. He too is interested in the question "What does he do who says this or that?" In his paper *A Plea for Excuses* (1957), for instance, he explores the many ways in which language enables us to modify the statement "He did this or that" so as to either enhance or reduce the impact and the implications of the utterance: by the use of adverbs such as *deliberately, intentionally, on purpose, by mistake,* etc., each utterance is assigned a particular place in a system characterized by the wording of the utterance itself as well as the speaker's intention and the effect on the hearer[9]. What does a person do when saying "He did it on purpose"? He performs the speech act of accusation. What does a person do when saying "He did it by mistake"? He seeks to justify the other with his utterance.

---

[8] Cf. on this issue SJ Schmidt (1973, pp 45f.), who proposes the term *communicative action game* for what Wittgenstein has called language game; the new term is meant to emphasize the relation between linguistic and nonlinguistic factors "whose interplay safeguards the 'ontological' reference, or social relevance, of speech acts."

[9] Here we discover an interesting and hitherto ignored conceptual link between speech act theory and word field theory.

Someone who is telling us "It's raining", may be advising us thereby to take an umbrella along on a walk. Or else, he might be giving an explanation for the glistening pavement. Alternatively, he might want to dissuade us from going out.

It is likewise part of the performed speech act that the hearer might fetch his umbrella, or might have his curiosity about the glistening pavement satisfied, or might decide to stay in.

Thus, a speech act is a comprehensive phenomenon, "the only actual phenomenon which, in the last resort, we are engaged in elucidating" (Austin 1962, p 147).

The speech act is for the philosopher of language the basic unit of analysis.

After closer scrutiny of the above described events we are persuaded by Austin to identify three aspects:

1) The uttering of the words "It's raining" is called by him a locutionary act
2) The concomitant advise (explanation, warning) is called an illocutionary act
3) The thus effected behavior of the hearer is called a perlocutionary act.

Austin's segmentation makes us realize that the concept of speech act with its three aspects (or subaspects) is a remarkably heterogeneous and vague construct. What is in fact the common element in locution, illocution, and perlocution, and what does *act* mean? In a critical review of the issue, Cerf (no date, p 361) maintains that Austin arrived at his concept of act by the following reasoning sequence: "to speak or to say something – to issue an utterance – to do something – to perform an action – to perform an act."

While action could scarcely be applied to locution, illocution, and perlocution alike, "to perform an act" is vague enough to subsume all three aspects, at least in a superficial treatment[10].

When it comes to the practical application of the notion of speech act, the three acts comprised by the term are not readily separable; moreover, there are many cases where the notion can be legitimately applied only to either the locutionary aspect, *or* the illocutionary aspect, *or* the perlocutionary aspect.

Discarding this distinction, Searle (1969) approaches speech acts in a manner that may at first sight appeal to the psychologist of language. His point of departure is the hypothesis (which we also know from Wittgenstein) that "speaking a language is engaging in a rule-governed form of behavior" (p 16). Further on, Searle argues:

> The unit of linguistic communication is not, as has generally been supposed, the symbol, word or sentence, or even the token of the symbol, word or sentence, but rather the production or issuance of the symbol or word or sentence in the performance of the speech act (p 16).

The author speaks plainly against operations with isolated tokens, i. e., signs detached from these operations. Next, Searle argues that

---

[10] The speculation that Austin may have opted for *act* in reference to Brentano's philosophy of acts would be totally misleading. As has been pointed out by Campbell (1973, p 288), "intentionality is entirely excluded from illocutions" in Austin's work. From this point of view, Austin's is a distinctly unpsychological approach.

the production or issuance of a sentence token under certain conditions is a speech act, and speech acts (. . .) are the basic or minimal units of linguistic communication. A way to come to see this point is to ask oneself, what is the difference between regarding an object as an instance of linguistic communication and not so regarding it? One crucial difference is this. When I take a noise or a mark on a piece of paper to be an instance of linguistic communication, as a message, one of the things I must assume is that the noise or mark was produced by a being or beings more or less like myself and produced with certain kinds of intentions. If I regard the noise or mark as a natural phenomenon . . ., I exclude it from the class of linguistic communication (p 16).

Thus, a theory of language is also for Searle part of a theory of action, in view of the fact that speaking is a rule-governed form of behavior. At the same time, the author refutes an objection that might be raised by, say, a partisan of the competence/performance dichotomy, namely the claim that his approach can serve only to explore the intersection of the respective domains of a theory of language and of a theory of action, whereas the two domains might be studied separately. Searle's argument is that although speaking, as a rule-governed form of behavior, does display certain formal properties that can be investigated in isolation, this "would be as if baseball were studied only as a formal system of rules and not as a game" (p. 17).

With his arguments Searle makes us aware of the fact that his definition of speaking a language as "a rule-governed form of behavior", while correct by itself, does not really satisfy us. Not every "rule-governed form of behavior" may qualify as part of a theory of action in the way speaking a language does. For example, piano playing is generally regarded as a rule-governed form of behavior (meaning the rendering of a particular piece of music by a pianist), but this cannot be taken to mean that a theory of piano playing is part of a theory of actions on a par with a theory of language. Searle seems to overlook the fact that speaking a language is a peculiar form of rule-governed behavior into which other forms of behavior can be translated and in which other forms of behavior find a reflection. Piano playing is a rule-governed form of behavior that does not meet these requirements. A theory of language is part of a theory of action also because – as has been stressed before on several occasions – speaking is the continuation of actions by alternative means.

In his analysis of speech acts, Searle proceeds similarly as Austin. He compares the following sentences:

(1) SAM SMOKES HABITUALLY.
(2) DOES SAM SMOKE HABITUALLY?
(3) SAM, SMOKE HABITUALLY!
(4) WOULD THAT SAM SMOKED HABITUALLY.

In uttering (1) a speaker makes an assertion, in (2) he asks a question, in (3) he gives an order, and in (4) he expresses a wish or desire (in an archaic form).

And in the performance of each of these four different acts the speaker performs certain other acts which are common to all four: in uttering any of these the speaker *refers to* or mentions or designates a certain object Sam, and he predicates the expression "smokes habitually" (or one of its inflections) of the object referred to. Thus we shall say that in the utterance of all four the reference and predication are the same . . . (p. 23).

Complete speech acts, such as asserting, commanding, questioning, etc., are called by Searle illocutionary acts, whereas referring and predicating are denoted as "performing a propositional act"; the two are distinct from the utterance act (uttering words, morphemes, sentences).

> I am not saying, of course, that these are separate things that speakers do, as it happens, simultaneously, as one might smoke, read and scratch one's head simultaneously . . . (p. 24).

Besides these three acts Searle adopts also Austin's notion of perlocutionary act to denote the effect produced by an illocutionary act on the hearer (e. g., persuading, scaring, enlightening).

> Illocutionary and propositional acts consist characteristically in uttering words in sentences in certain contexts, under certain conditions and with certain intentions . . . Propositional acts cannot occur alone; that is, one cannot *just* refer and predicate without making an assertion or asking a question or performing some other illocutionary act (pp 24–25).

According to Searle, one and the same proposition is contained in all four specimen sentences (1–4), but only in (1) the proposition is asserted.

As we step back to gain a broader perspective upon Searle's ideas, we discover in them both acceptable elements and objectionable ones. The emphasis on context, conditions, and intentions is most gratifying, but does the formulation "uttering words in sentences in certain contexts, under certain conditions and with certain intentions" characterize both illocutionary and propositional acts in equal measure? Would not the theory gain in clarity if we used the term *illocutionary act* to denote propositional acts "anchored" or posited or orientated by context, conditions, and intentions?

Searle's use of the term *propositional act* is equally disconcerting: can it really be claimed that the *same* kind of propositional act is performed in sentences (1–4) while in sentence (1) – and only there – the proposition is also asserted? How should an unasserted proposition be construed psychologically?

Two things come to our attention at this juncture. Firstly, we notice a striving to employ the rather vague notion of act as a common denominator for accommodating proposition, illocution, and even perlocution within one and the same genus. Secondly, we seem to discern the influence of something reminiscent of the concept of transformation; otherwise we could not account for the claim that there was no difference in reference and predication between sentences (1–4). Do (1) SAM SMOKES HABITUALLY and (2) DOES SAM SMOKE HABITUALLY? really *predicate* the same thing? One is tempted to say à la Wittgenstein: You may say that an assertion and a question predicate the same thing, and if you say so, they will. But do they do it if you do not say so?

For the psychologist, in any case, it is by no means certain that "a proposition is to be sharply distinguished from an assertion or statement of it" (p 29).

By voicing skepticism as to the legitimacy of construing the propositional act as the common element of different illocutionary acts, we arrive again at the problem of the interrelations between meaning and speech act. And here we find our initial misgivings reinforced:

> The speech act or acts performed in the utterance of a sentence are in general a function of the meaning of the sentence (p 18).

How disappointing! From all we have read in (and into) Searle so far, we would have expected the exact opposite: the meaning of a sentence might be construed as a function of the speech act performed with the utterance. What Searle is telling us now implies that the speech act is for him secondary compared to the meaning of the sentence (which need not be embedded in an illocutionary act). How can this be brought in line with his earlier quoted view that speech acts are the basic units of linguistic communication (p 16)? While maintaining that "it is always in principle possible for the speaker to say exactly what he means", Searle does not draw the necessary distinction with sufficient consistency when stating that

> it is possible for every speech act . . . to be uniquely determined by a given sentence (or set of sentences), given the assumptions that the speaker is speaking literally and that the context is appropriate (p 18).

But are literalness and appropriate context not by any chance constituents of a speech act?

Searle evidently confuses "uniquely determined" with "adequately described"; the latter formulation would not call into question the primacy of speech act over sentence.

The thesis that a speech act is determined by the sentence uttered in it holds only for explicitly performative verbs. In all other cases any speech act can be *described* by one or more sentences that are not identical with the sentence uttered in the speech act itself. Searle tries to evade this sore spot by adding immediately that

> a study of the meaning of sentences is not in principle distinct from a study of speech acts. Properly construed, they are the same study. Since every meaningful sentence in virtue of its meaning can be used to perform a particular speech act (or range of speech acts), and since every possible speech act can in principle be given an exact formulation in a sentence or sentences (assuming an appropriate context of utterance), the study of the meanings of sentences and the study of speech acts are not two independent studies but one study from two different points of view (p 18).

This is rather unsatisfactory: the claim that any sentence has its meaning and "in virtue of its meaning can be used to perform a particular speech act" brings us back again to the compromised view of the sign that has its meaning and derives its subsequent uses from this meaning. Obviously, we have hoped in vain that an analysis of the speech act would tell us anything of value about the meaning of the sentence with which the speech act can be performed. As we now yield to the urge to ask: what is the use of the speech act if the same can be learned from a study of sentence meaning existing independently of any speech act? – Searle withdraws elegantly to a position which is difficult to contest: these are not two theories, but two complementary research strategies (pp 18–19).

So we are left with the following problem: What is the difference between a syntactically correct and (at first sight) semantically "unobtrusive", isolated word string of the following kind:

5) SHE WASN'T CARRYING IT

and the same word string as uttered by a speaker engaged in a conversation with a hearer who knows what *she* and *it* and the entire sentence refers to?

Suppose you find such a sentence on a snip of paper: on reading it you identify it as a sentence, all right, but you are left guessing as to what it means, although you know what each word means and also know the syntactic relations between the words of the sentence. Here we touch upon a discussion of long standing – extending from Frege (1879) to Singer (1973) – over the course of which many attempts have been made to contrast ever new concepts and pairs of concepts in an effort to catch the subtle distinction between the mental state of the reader and that of the actual partner in communication: meaning, sense, reference, judgment, ect. Endless manipulations of these concepts in total disregard of psychological evidence have produced quite arbitrary results. For instance, meaning can be easily described as context-dependent, but what does *context-dependent* mean in psychological terms? How would a hearer distinguish decontextualized meaning from contextualized meaning? And please do not say that meaning in context should not be called meaning but sense!

We are left in no doubt as to one point, however: the shift from the isolated sentence on a slip of paper to the uttering of the same sentence in a communicative act corresponds to what occurs in the hearer as he shifts from something general to something particular. Recalling here our arguments on the subject of sense constancy, we wish to point out that there is always some overall scaffolding of sense available in the hearer and that the particular utterance is meant to "hook up" with a particular spot within this scaffolding, and to "concretize" this spot, if it is to be understood.

We may now proceed further by examining Searle's (1969) analysis of the speech act of promising, to find out what Searle has discovered about the meaning of *promising:*

> Given that a speaker S utters a sentence T in the presence of a hearer H, then, in the literal utterance of T, S sincerely and nondefectively promises that p to H if and only if the following conditions ... obtain (p 57).

Among the conditions which constitute the speech act of promising discussed by Searle are the following:

a) In expressing that p, A predicates a future act A of S

b) H would prefer S's doing A to his not doing A

c) It is not obvious to both S and H that S will do A in the normal course of events

d) S intends to do A

e) S intends that the utterance of T will place him under an obligation to do A.

By submitting his (all together nine) conditions of the speech act of promising, Searle has embarked on an eminently psychological undertaking (which statement should not offend Searle the philosopher): he seeks to describe the mental state of someone who, for instance, utters the sentence:

6) I PROMISE TO GIVE YOU THE MONEY TOMORROW.

And we find in his descriptions exactly what we wanted to have included in such an account: evidence concerning the speaker's expectations as implied in his actions, evidence concerning the speaker's views of the hearer's opinions, wishes, and intentions, and evidence concerning the speaker's intentions. We are offered information on the presuppositions[11] underlying the utterance, on the expectations aroused by it, and on the behaviors considered adequate in case of promise-fulfillment and in case of promise-nonfulfillment. The "language game of promising" thus emerges from the twilight of the overall meaningfulness of the utterance as an intricate structure of interdependent mental states and linguistic facts.

Once again, this time as a result of Searle's inquiry, we come to grips with the language-determining effect of the language user's knowledge of the world.

No matter how much the psychologist may be pleased with Searle's theory, the linguist is bound to worry about the problem raised in the same vein: Should the speaker of (6) have no intention of paying the money, thus violating one of the above listed conditions, what *kind* of rule is infringed? Is it a linguistic rule governing the use of the *word* "promise"? Or is it a behavioral regularity, that is, is the case one of violating the grammaticalness of the entire action (which presupposes an integration of the verbal and the nonverbal action sequence)? Or is it a case of flouting a moral rule[12]?

The question lies well within the range of problems extensively dealt with in these pages. In the light of the new evidence we might now formulate the question thus: Which knowledge is more basic, the knowledge which safeguards the performance of a speech act, or the knowledge pertaining to the meaning of the sentence in question? In other words, is our performance of the speech act of promising contingent upon our ability to "psychologize" in this way the meaning of the word *promise*, or is our knowledge of the meaning of *promise* contingent upon our familiarity with this word as the verbal label for a certain mental constellation?

The answer to this question will vary with the kind of language game to which it applies. The developmental psychologist studying language acquisition might find it most profitable to adopt the speech act as a point of departure; the psychologist investigating the processes of reading might want to start with the word calling into the reader's awareness the content and structure of the respective speech act. We have thus traveled full fircle back to Searle's two research strategies.

But the problem does not end here. Consider a sentence such as:

7) I DON'T PROMISE TO PAY YOU THE MONEY TOMORROW.

Even though *promise* does occur in the sentence, there can be no doubt that a speech act of promising is *not* being performed (cf. Hare 1970).

Searle makes a solution even more difficult by stating:

---

[11] Whereas the analysis of presuppositions as proposed by, e. g., Fillmore reveals what is presupposed by the subject of the verb, Searle tries to establish the mental states and intentions that must be present in the speaker. The fact that both instances can be discussed under the heading "analysis of presuppositions" suggests once more that it is unwise to draw a sharp distinction between sentence and utterance, as Bar-Hillel does.

[12] Cf. Holborow (1972).

> Any analysis of the meaning of a word (or morpheme) can be consistent with the fact that the same word (or morpheme) can mean the same thing in all the grammatically different kinds of sentences in which it can occur (p 137).

Thus, the word *promise* is believed to mean the same thing in sentence (6) and sentence (7). In (6) it is involved in performing the speech act of promising, but what kind of relationship does obtain between "I don't promise to . . ." and the speech act performed by the issuance of this sentence?

Here we might feel an urge to fall back again on some vague transformation concept. Hare (1970, p 14) argues:

> Not only have we shown (. . .) that there are some expressions whose meaning has to be explained in terms of speech acts. We have also shown that when it has been so explained, the explanation can be extended to cover the meaning of utterances in which the speech act in question is not performed, provided that the utterance is generated by a transformation, whose form we understand, of the original speech act.

The linguist may feel gratified by such recourse to a familiar formalism. The psychologist of language might be prepared to follow him in the case of performative verbs (the favorite paradigm of the speech act philosophers): since the performative usage of these words (promise, deny, assert, question, greet, ask, etc.) is the primary one, it may be feasible to derive from it the interrogative, negative, and other usages of the same words.

But is there an "indicator of the illocutionary role" (to use Searle's term) that would tell us that

8) COULD YOU OPEN THE WINDOW?

is uttered as a request, not a question? There is no other way than falling back on the intention of the speaker which the hearer is bound to identify in order to understand the sentence, the two being partners to this particular transaction. Searle does take note of this problem, but he fails to make the indispensable step beyond the verbal realm.

There are cases where the meaning of an utterance can be accounted for by having recourse to the perlocutionary act (the "effect of the utterance"). Bloomfield may have been right in one respect, after all, namely, when including in his behavioristic definition of *meaning* "the response it calls forth in the hearer": the meaning of an utterance is codetermined by the knowledge of what is ordinarily acceptable as a consequence of that utterance, even if the actual consequence cannot be assigned to the set of acceptable ones.

We are faced here with a case where an essentially behavioristic position converges with the views held by Ajdukiewicz and with Deese's ideas, provided that the notion of acceptability is not restricted to behavior, but encompasses cognitive and experiential acceptability as well.

At the same time, this acceptability is codetermined by the context of the world in which the particular language game occurs. If I say my wife had seen a unicorn in our garden, either she or I will be sent to a psychiatrist, as illustrated by Thurber (1974). But if I say the gnome had seen a unicorn in the garden, I am thought to be telling a fairy tale – and everything is in order. Thus we are back in a familiar place, i. e., with the driving forces behind sense constancy and Wittgenstein's self-stabilizing language game[13].

The procedure of cross-referencing between speech act and sentence poses increasing difficulties for a student of meaning and understanding as he moves beyond the realm of dynamic (and especially performative) words. The controversy escalates to an incalculable magnitude with attempts to inquire into such questions as whether or not the meaning of *good* derives from the speech act of commending, *true* from the speech act of endorsing, etc. Strawson (1949) says *yes,* Hare (1952) says *yes,* Searle (1969) says *no,* and Hare (1970) maintains he has said something different while believing Searle to have said *yes* and *no* . . .

Let this suffice. What has emerged from this review of speech act philosophy for the further course of our argument is not a pat solution by which to determine the one meaning of every kind of word or sentence or utterance. At the same time, we would not agree with Frye (1973, p 294), who says:

> The confusion of various pairs or triples of the notions of an utterance, an uttering, the meaning of a sentence, what a speaker says, what a speaker means by what he says, what a speaker intends to do in uttering an utterance, and understanding or grasping each of these, has put much of the contemporary literature and discussion on speech acts in a cloudy atmosphere of unnecessary muddles.

It is certainly wrong to speak of "unnecessary" muddles. You can always engage in neat mental exercises with concepts, provided these are treated as integral entities. It is the great merit of Wittgenstein and the speech act philosophers that they have always defined, redefined, and applied their concepts with the express purpose of providing an account of how language is used in real life. They might have bypassed the obstacles and obscurities encountered on their way by keeping their concepts "pure" in the indicated manner, but only at the cost of whatever relevance their inquiries might have had for the elucidation of real-life language processes.

The benefits that ensue from the present discussion of speech act philosophy for the further course of our argument consist not of individual concepts or entire subsystems of concepts, but rather of specific insights, attitudes, suggestions, and cautions.

The notion of speech act itself gives prominence to the ubiquitous intermeshing of speaking and doing. This point was made by Apostel (1972, p 220) in the following way:

> . . . it is not possible to separate the active and the symbolizing component of human nature because they are both factually (the perlocutionary forces) and institutionally (the illocutionary forces) tied up with each other. Moreover the institutional link becomes itself a factual force and a factual force becomes an institutional force.

This intermeshing is particularly evident in one class of words or expressions, the so-called performatives[14], where a direct link exists between the "lexical" mean-

---

[13] The question to what extent Bühler's *organon* model might prove useful in elucidating the little explored relations between sentence, utterance, understanding, and effect, deserves to be studied in depth.

[14] By their very issuance, performative verbs perform the actions they denote: I promise, I request, I welcome, etc.

ing of a word and the act performed by the uttering of the word. The utterance itself transforms the "kinetic force" of the meaning into an illocutionary force.

The conversion of one form of energy or force into another appears to be one of the most important facts revealed by speech act philosophy. It has been made clear that the acts of meaning and understanding are founded on the act of uttering itself, not just on knowing the rules which underlie the construction of the utterance. The rudiments of this view are also discernible in Fillmore's generative semantics: sentences are thought to contain a propositional core, and a proposition cannot be construed in isolation from the act of uttering. The Latin verb *proponere* denotes, as it were, an action performed by a speaker in relation to a hearer (or himself).

The hearer's awareness that it is a human being who utters the sentence endows the perceived sentence with the weight and dynamic impact that give it the necessary "transparency": only sentences experienced in this way become "transparent", that is, reveal the meaning intended by the speaker.

So we come again to a question that ought to have lain at the roots of linguistic theory and which certainly lies at the roots of the psychology of language: *why does a speaker utter anything?* The offhand answer readily supplied by sign theorists and information theorists, "to convey some information to the hearer", must be seen by now as totally inadequate. Information transmission is one of many possible purposes. The great diversity of language games explored by Wittgenstein, Ajdukiewicz, Searle, and others, leaves no doubt that utterances have a number of quite different purposes. Would it be possible to bring them to a common denominator in terms of their functions?

The speaker seeks to effect some modification in the hearer. To do this, he issues certain instructions. It is hoped that a change will occur in the hearer's knowledge, behavior, attitudes, expectations, affects, and above all in the content of his consciousness. A modification in the hearer's consciousness is desirable from the speaker's point of view because it would increase the probability of the hearer's accepting the implications advocated by the speaker[15].

Whereas it is a pivotal feature of any utterance, the speaker's intention to effect a modification should not be considered in isolation; rather, it has to be viewed against the wide horizon of the modifications which the speaker expects to take place, even without the particular utterance reaching the hearer. Accordingly, there are speech acts uttered with the intention that the hearer should not do anything and should not change in any way, but these can be intelligible and make sense only if a certain change is expected to occur in the course of events, that is, irrespective of the speech act. For example, Juliet's entreating Romeo not to go is intelligible only because she and all the readers of Shakespeare's play expect Romeo to go.

---

[15] Grice (1957) also defines meaning as the intention of producing an effect in the hearer, but this effect is brought about by the hearer's recognizing the speaker's intention of evoking the effect. This is psychologically certainly too complex. In most cases we understand what the speaker means without realizing that he means us to understand what he means.

The speaker seeks to effect some modification in the hearer's mind. At this point we come very close to what SJ Schmidt (1973, p 56) presents under the heading "instruction semantics":

A lexeme can be construed epistemologically as a rule (in a broad sense of the term) or instruction serving to produce a particular linguistic and/or nonlinguistic "behavior", or as a direction for a linguistic and/or nonlinguistic action, to be anticipated by virtue of its being well-established in the given speech community through analogous learning processes and customary recurrence. A semantics thus founded shall be called instruction semantics.

The connection between what happens in the course of the utterance and the form in which the same things exist prior to the speech act (i. e., Searle's plain meaning) becomes increasingly obscure as we move farther away from the realm of performative expressions (which do not constitute a sharply delineated class). In the case of adjectives, for instance, it becomes necessary to construe hypothetical acts (for *good,* the act of commending) before any such transposition from meaning to a modification–intending action can be shown to occur. We witness here a shift of what might be construed as the major determinant of the communication act. In performative utterances, this determinant is vested in the very fact that the words uttered convey the speaker's intention. In the remaining cases this determinant is transposed from the uttered word to the acting speaker, or to the situation. This aspect does not escape Searle's (1968, p 413) attention. But we cannot possibly concur with him as he brushes the problem aside with this gesture:

There is still left a distinction between the literal meaning of a sentence and the intended force of its utterance (. . .) but that is only a special case of the distinction between literal meaning and intended meaning, between what the sentence means and what the speaker means in its utterance, and it has no special relevance to the general theory of illocutionary forces, because intended illocutionary force is only one of the aspects (sense and reference are others) in which intended speaker meaning may go beyond literal sentence meaning.

What Searle considers to be irrelevant for a theory of illocutionary forces seems to us of paramount importance, this being the distinction between what the sentence means and what the speaker means. One wonders what discoveries Searle might make if he were prevented from employing the same verb (*to mean*) in reference to both speaker and utterance. He might reach the following conclusion: The difference between what a sentence signifies and what a speaker has in mind is analogous to the relation between means and end.

Such a realization opens up a new perspective upon the problems of language acquisition (which is explored in Chap. 12 in the context of Macnamara's arguments). The same realization calls seriously into question the mapping concept, which underlies both the notion of coding and the idea of mapping of deep structure onto surface structure and similar constructs of generative linguistics.

Now back to speech acts. There is evidently a need for distinguishing between completed speech acts and those that are brought to consciousness (in and by an utterance) as being possible: the latter were once called by Searle (1962, p 425)

165

speech acts in the offing. They may be considered as representing a kind of third modality, next to completed speech acts and words and sentences, which embody kinetic energy.

There are a number of ways in which a speech act may be kept in the offing: by the speaker's extralinguistically communicated intention, by a situation-conditioned dynamic, and also by the syntactic form of the utterance (example: the conditional).

Upon closer scrutiny, we find the "plain" sentence (as long as it is not embedded in an utterance), the speech act in the offing, and the completed speech act to differ on a significant dimension. Very clearly, this dimension has something to do with the dynamic which enables us – in the phenomenon of linguistic transparency – to identify and grasp, right through the sounds, words, and rules of the utterance, the intended meaning of the sentence.

The dynamic we have in mind is that of intention; as such, it is closely related to the impulsiveness which according to William James characterizes an idea or thought.

Taking note of something, understanding, or cognizing something implies some kind of movement toward the cognized thing. An interpretation of this phenomenon was offered by F Heider (1930, p 388):

> ... cognition [das Erkennen] invariably approaches the real in an opposite direction from the course taken by natural origination: it moves gropingly from effect to cause, from what is last to what was first.

The same idea, derived by Heider from Brentano and perhaps also Lipps, became a key concept of Brunswik's intentional psychology. In his approach, which he chose to call "a psychology (viewed) *from* the object" (of perception), Brunswik set out to study the *Tiefenstaffelung,* or arrangement in depth, of intentional processes. As a student of Karl Bühler, Brunswik (1934) conceived of "consciously intending an object" as "wishing to acquire or cognize it, or else, having it in mind" (p 18). A characteristic feature of the study in depth of his intentional psychology was the distinction

> between object and mediation in the depth arrangement of intentionally attainable objects. That which is intentionally "before" the intended object is used as mediator, but is lost in its mediating role, is neglected in consciousness, is lacking a covariant representation (p 230).

We are reminded here of what Polanyi (see the beginning of Chap. 3) had to say about the distinction between focal and subsidiary knowledge: by attending to one thing, we exclude the other things from our awareness. In language communication, the hearer's focus of intention is situated "beyond" the perceived sentence. Arguing in the same vein, Brunswik says that

> the intentional center of gravity is shifted "behind" the surface of things; you perceive ... the mood of a fellow creature "right through" his flushed skin ..., without being fully aware of the redness of his cheeks (p 230).

Brunswik's argument thus centers around what "philosophers and psychologists have noticed and recognized as essential since ancient times": the dynamics in the relations of subject and world. Being an analogue of the "pull of meaningfulness" discussed in connection with the concept of sense constancy (a pull which in the case of a metaphor compels us to penetrate the superficial anomaly in search of meaning), this dynamics causes us to understand the meaning of an utterance as intended by the speaker, right through the speech act. The fact that the dynamic of language communication follows a certain direction, is due, for one thing, to the framework of the particular language game in which speaker and hearer are engaged, and, for the other, to a variety of safeguards ranging from the probability structure of linguistic and extralinguistic processes to the norms of style and syntax.

The understanding of meaning right through the sentence comes into evidence particularly in cases where sentence form and meaning clearly diverge. We are referring here to what Clark and Lucy (1975) called "conversationally conveyed meaning". The question-like utterance "Could you open the window?" is to be understood as a request. How can we account for it? How is it that requests can be conveyed in the form of questions, and questions in the form of imperatives ("Tell me how far it is to Cambridge").

Clark and Lucy (1975, p 66) try to account for this by proposing the following model:

> The listener goes about comprehending the intended meaning of an utterance by (1) constructing a literal interpretation for the utterance, (2) checking its plausibility against the context, and (3), if there is conflict, bringing to bear certain rules of conversation in order to deduce a conveyed interpretation.

Thus the model stands or falls on the feasibility of a clear distinction between "literal" and "conveyed" meaning and also the availability of an agency that would be able to decide on the plausibility of the interpretation. The latter could be easily accomplished with the aid of the proposed construct of sense constancy. Evidence of the former is supplied by Clark with an experiment which shows that it takes longer to construct a conveyed than a literal meaning: as postulated by the model, the hearer establishes first the literal and only then the "conversationally conveyed" meaning.

There is however a strong argument against Clark's claim that literal meaning is identified prior to conveyed meaning: such an utterance can be misunderstood in one of two ways. The hearer may fail to perceive the "uptake of the illocutionary force" (Austin) and respond to the literal meaning of the phrase by saying: "Yes, if I pull very hard." The other kind of misunderstanding might consist in taking up the illocutionary force without grasping the literal meaning of the request, and this would be reflected in the response: "What do you want me to do?" In the latter case, the hearer would be aware of some sort of request being uttered, but would be looking in vain for the content of the request.

The dual kind of possible misunderstanding discloses the essence of the relationship between the speech act and the sentence (by uttering which the speech act is performed). Having discovered that a speech act may be understood by a hearer who has not understood the sentence, can we still assume that a speech act is performed by the utterance of the particular sentence? Moreover: who or what has been misunderstood in the first case, and who or what in the second case? Once again we come to grips with the problem that the hearer ought to be construed as understanding the *speaker* (and the latter's intention) rather than understanding the uttered *sentence*. As we have seen, the speaker's intention may be grasped by the hearer in a generalized manner while the wording of the sentence may escape the hearer altogether.

The most general problem raised in this way might be phrased thus: What does the speaker mean when uttering a particular sentence? In other words: *How does the utterance relate to what is conveyed by it?*

Ziff (1972) has made it clear that in order to grasp what is meant by an utterance, it does not suffice to be familiar with the particular language spoken. The meaning conveyed by implication, for instance, may be constituted by practically everything that does not coincide with the "literal" meaning of the utterance. Gründer (1975) has drawn our attention to the great variety of cognition-steering devices as represented by exegesis, taxonomy (as an exegetic procedure), simile, allegory, and the like. This is an impressive hierarchy of cognitive devices for seeing through the external surface of utterances. In the process, we move – in Polanyi's terminology – from a mere "from awareness" (of words, etc.) to a "from-at knowledge"[16] of the text. Polanyi (1968, p 1311) also shows how a semantic relation is established:

> The higher (level) comprehends the workings of the lower and thus forms the meaning of the lower. And as we ascend a hierarchy of boundaries, we reach to even higher levels of meaning.

This is where we gain one more insight: Before speaker and hearer can hope to reach common understanding on a specific point, they must share a broader understanding as to the kind of language game in which they wish to engage for the subsequent exchange of specific acts of conveying meaning and of understanding. The banality "communication is preceded by metacommunication", does not advance us any further. Instead, we ought to consider that there must be some constraints on the freedom of meaning and of understanding if these two kinds of cognitive acts are to perform their communicative function properly. These constraints are of diverse kinds and of different origin.

In an attempt to illustrate this diversity, Bühler (1934) invokes Plato who said, in *Cratylus,*

> you had to go to the weaver to learn about the principles of weaving and to the carpenter who has built the weaving loom to learn about the "principles" of the organon *weaving loom*. The proper analogue of the instruction at the carpenter is the study of intersubjectively regulated linguistic conventions. Certainly, as everything else we inherit from our ancestors, "language" too has to be received and restored to life in the speaker's monadic realm. However, *receiving* and *creating* (it) *yourself* (excerpting and positing) are two things; whereas positing is marked by the Husserlian freedom of

---

[16] "When we look at words without understanding them we are focusing our attention on them, whereas, when we read the words, ... we are looking *from* them *at their meaning;* the reader of a text has a from-at knowledge of the words' meaning, while he has only a from-awareness of the words he is reading" (Polanyi 1968, p 1311).

meaning-imparting acts, excerpting has its bounds, as a limit on that freedom and in correlation to it (pp 68–69).

What Bühler has to say with respect to Husserl applies also to the proponents of an extreme speech act philosophy: the assertion "any meaning can be expressed by anything" is described by Bühler as a maxim, which, "once elevated to a principle, would be the surest means to impair any linguistic communication" (p 231).

The interaction of intentional act (as a sort of prime mover) and specifying qualification deserves to be explored in greater detail. Says Bühler:

> To employ linguistic structures in intersubjective communication, . . . to employ them as all other members of the speech community do, is one thing; another is to give them the precise meaning prescribed by language structure from case to case, and, moreover, to endow them with a uniquely modified meaning here and there. These being two different things, you may not, as is attempted in the *Logical Investigations* (Husserl's chef d'oeuvre), contrive the entirety of a theory of meaning in terms of acts (pp 68–69).

Those who seek to pose the speech act at the inception of linguistic theory must be willing to say something also about the subsequent stages of the processes initiated in that act, as a coincidence of meaning and illocutionary force. He who emphasizes the notion that the rules of language acquisition are learned by the child "not as isolated rules for the construction of expressions, but together with the typical actions and with the role relationships of (the child's) primary environment" (Wunderlich 1970a, p 13), should give due attention to the history of the emancipation of language from environmental constraints – which function as props on some, and as fetters on other occasions.

> There has been an act of emancipation in the employment of human linguistic signs that might count among the most decisive in the evolution of human language . . . Though we are unable to reconstruct it historically, we may designate it systematically as emancipation from situational supports, to the extent this is feasible and has become possible; it is the progression from essentially empractical speaking to largely synsemantically autonomous (self-sufficient) products of language (Bühler, pp 366–367).

This emancipation of language from the situation is an extremely long process. Bühler illustrates its duration by contrasting the linguistic productions of two streetcar passengers, one of whom may simply say "straight ahead" – empractically buttressed by situational clues – while the other has to take recourse to syntax and lexicon to communicate the news, "The Pope is dead". But in order to traverse this long path, we have to begin – enlisting the aid of such philosophers as Wittgenstein, Ajdukiewicz, and Searle – with speech acts as originating from the common actions of speaker and hearer.

Prior to our present discussion of the emergence of the speech act from the course of the interpersonal action at what might be called the molar level, we looked at this idea on a different level. Let us recall that Fillmore likewise construes the "propositional core" of a sentence as the speaker's action upon the hearer, undertaken with a specific goal in mind (and thereby he seeks to give credit to sentence dynamics with his notion of case). In a similar manner,

McCawley's presuppositions seem to reemerge, albeit in modified form, in Searle's conditions for a performance of the speech act of promising.

In the next chapter we resume the problem of speech acts on a further level, the third one, which could be called molecular, as we explore the microgenesis *(Aktualgenese)* of particular utterances in particular cases. It stands to reason that the language game to be pursued for this purpose ought to be of a physiological type; the necessary tool is partially available in the evidence supplied by Russian psychology of language.

Chapter 10

Russian Psychology of Language

Russian psycholinguistics has never been a true psycholinguistics. This is what it has come to be called in English – in translation of the Russian term *psikholingvistika* – but in reality it has been a psychology of language from its very inception. The point is that Russian "psycholinguists" have never seen their goal in the demonstration of the "psychological reality" of primarily linguistic concepts, theories, or models. Their science has developed from psychology, not so much from social psychology, however, as from a psychology with a biologic-physiologic-genetic outlook. AA Leontev (1972, p 2), a leading Soviet psycholinguist – or psychologist of language, as we would prefer to call him – has brought this home in the following words:

> It is quite indicative that the Soviet Union was almost the only country in which psycholinguistics though quite developed did not succumb to the Generative Grammar epidemic ... The explanation is to be found in the specific scientific tradition which Soviet Psycholinguistics from its very origination has been based on ... Unlike American Psycholinguistics which is consistently antipsychological, theories prevalent in Soviet Psycholinguistics in the 20–50ies were not in the least alien to the analysis of man's speech activity, on the contrary, they were aimed at closing with psychology.

The scientific tradition mentioned by Leontev comprises two interrelated research orientations: one inquires into the relation between thought and speech, seeking to illuminate the problem by developmental analyses of language acquisition, the other inquires into the biological or physiological – chiefly neurophysiological – mechanisms which underlie and govern the actual uses of language, and does so by electrophysiological and pathological investigations.

The commonality of the two research trends derives, in the first place, from their Pavlovian orientation and even more from their common base.

The base we have in mind is LS Vygotsky (1896–1934)[1], whose prime interest

---

[1] Leontev's proud reference to the continuing tradition of Soviet psycholinguistics ever since the 1920s (in the quotation above) gives no credit to the fact that for political reasons Vygotsky's work encountered "nearly thirty years of official disregard and lack of interest" (Průcha 1972a, p 42).

was in the interrelation of thought and speech, an issue on which psychologists continue to be of two minds even today: whether it is a crucial or a spurious problem, or one and the other at the same time. Vygotsky's aim was to examine it from both a phylo- and ontogenetic angle.

In his phylogenetic investigation, Vygotsky (1962) drew chiefly on the ape studies of Köhler and Yerkes; he summarized his conclusions in the following way:

> 1. Thought and speech have different genetic roots. 2. The two functions develop along different lines and independently of each other. 3. There is no clear-cut and constant correlation between them (p 41).

The ontogenetic study of humans does likewise reveal some preintellectual roots of language: crying, babbling, and even the child's first words have nothing to do with the development of thinking, argues Vygotsky, being related instead to emotional development and socialization. Thus the roots of the subsequently emerging thought-speech complex can be traced to the first year of life, or the time when the two functioned in separation.

> But the most important discovery is that at a certain moment at about the age of two the curves of development of thought and speech, till then separate, meet and join to initiate a new form of behavior (p 43).

Thought becomes verbal, and language becomes intellectual. For a layman in psychology, Vygotsky's claim that thought and language are separable may sound perfectly plausible. Fodor (1972) has criticized the Russian psychologist for narrowly defining thought and language (as problem solving and as speech), for overlooking the other forms and purposes of thinking, and for ignoring the fact that language is more than speech (after all, Fodor is a follower of Chomsky).

Be that as it may: Vygotsky's lasting contribution consisted in his successful merging of a functionalist approach with the concept of stages. He was able to identify stages not only in the evolution and acquisition of language but also in the generation of an utterance. (The elegance with which the more broadly oriented developmental psychologists keep negotiating between phylogeny of language, ontogeny of language, and the microgenesis of an utterance contributes to the attractiveness but also to the dangers of their approach.) The way Vygotsky argues his theoretical position, chiefly in a polemic with the views held by Piaget at the time, deserves to be recounted here briefly because it serves to illuminate speech and language in a manner which benefits the psychology of language in general and is instructive even today.

Studying so-called egocentric speech, Piaget concluded that up to the age of 7 or 8 the child tends to speak for and to himself or herself. Such speech has barely a communicative function, being essentially monologue speech, i. e., egocentric speech. The child's speech is egocentric because such is the thinking of the child up to this age. For example, a child at play (building block structures) may keep silent during this activity as long as things go smoothly. The child is apt to speak on encountering any difficulty, but this speech is meant for himself.

Piaget invests language with the communicative function at a relatively late age, in contradistinction to the views held by, say, Bühler and Wittgenstein. For Vygotsky (1962),

> egocentric speech is a phenomenon of the transition from interpsychic to intrapsychic functioning, i. e., from the social, collective activity of the child to his more individualized activity – a pattern of development common to all the higher psychological functions. Speech for oneself originates through differentiation from speech for others. Since the main course of the child's development is one of gradual individualization, this tendency is reflected in the function and structure of his speech (p 133).

The "external" speech to which the playing child resorts in case of difficulties is "the turning of thought into words, its materialization and objectification" (p 131). By speaking to himself, the child mobilizes the potential that has built up during his life. In the medium of language (and by this medium) the child chooses the most adequate from among several alternative kinds of action.

Representing an incipient stage in a developmental sequence leading to inner speech (or completely internalized speech, to be exact), egocentric speech is still fully vocalized and not abbreviated. In the course of development, speech is progressively abbreviated, turning into "inward thought". That is to say, the sentence is contracted by omitting the subject and the associated words, whereas the predicate and its complements are retained. This "tendency toward predication" (p 139) established by Vygotsky plays a crucial role in contemporary linguistic, linguistic-philosophical, and linguistic-psychological conceptions, where it lacks however the typically Vygotskyan overtones (that concentration upon predication is an outcome of developmental processes) and merely means that predication is the core of the utterance.

The subject of the sentence may be omitted, argues Vygotsky, because it is directly given by the situation. The more clues are offered by the situation, the less complete may be the verbal message. Vygotsky illustrates his point by analyzing a scene described by Dostoyevski in *Anna Karenina*. He is led to the conclusion that just as in oral language in the case of shared knowledge an utterance may be reduced to a minimum, so in inner speech a similar progressive reduction takes place. "Inner speech is speech almost without words" (p 145).

We conclude our account of Vygotsky's theory of language and, returning from the year 1934 to the present day, take cognizance of three tasks that suggest themselves at this point.

1) We have to take note of how AN Leontev and Luria retrospectively provide Vygotsky's views with a solid Marxist theoretical foundation, simply because such is the basis of contemporary Soviet psychology of language.

2) We must examine the argumentation by which Vygotsky's stages of language development have been elaborated into stages of the generation of the utterance, for this is where I seem to recognize the most potent contribution of Soviet psycholinguistics to the psychology of language in general.

3) We must consider the arguments brought forward by some critics of Vygotsky's work (notably Fodor 1972), as far as issues of relevance for a psychology of language are concerned.

In his functionalist-genetic theory, Vygotsky bases himself squarely on a fundamental conception which he introduces by quoting Karl Bühler:

> It used to be said that speech was the beginning of hominization *(Menschwerden);* maybe so, but before speech there is the thinking involved in the use of tools, i. e., comprehension of mechanical connections, and devising of mechanical means to mechanical ends, or, to put it more briefly still, before speech appears action becomes subjectively meaningful – in other words, consciously purposeful (Vygotsky 1962, p 42).

We ought to realize, before resuming our argument, that this particular issue is of the greatest importance in quite a few, otherwise disparate, theoretical systems: for Köhler it characterizes the nature of intelligence before the bifurcation into human and animal intelligence; for Bloomfield it marks the point at which the linguistic event comes into being, between a stimulating practical event and the thus evoked speech event; for Skinner it boils down to verbal behavior which differs from other forms of behavior in that it is reinforced by the agency of other humans, as postulated by learning theory. Also, this is where AN Leontev and Luria start with their argument in the introduction to the Russian (1956) edition of Vygotsky's *Thought and Language:*

> It is precisely by the use of tools and other implements, precisely on account of this intermediate relation to the conditions of existence, that human mental activity differs fundamentally from the mental activity of animals ... The first and foremost among the socially generated means is language, and language – as Marx put it – is the "real consciousness" of man (p 7).

In keeping with Vygotsky's ideas, the two authors conceptualize the convergence of thought and language as being elevated to a paradigm in the word. In its two functions: as generalization and as means of communication, the word is one. To quote Leontev and Luria (1956):

> With its meaning, the word mediates in the process of direct, sensory reflection of the world: what the person sees is not merely something rectangular, white, covered with lines; ... rather, he sees a sheet of paper ... This is so because he has at his disposal prior objective experience acquired in the course of his practical, objective activity; also, it is so because this objective experience has been verbally incorporated in the respective meaning – "paper". He who does not know the meaning of *paper* ... actually sees only something white, oblong, etc. However, when he perceives paper, he perceives this real paper and not the meaning "paper"; meaning as such ordinarily does not enter consciousness: while refracting and generalizing the visible, meaning itself stays invisible (p 12).

If we manage to subdue our complaint that we cannot make out what this "process of direct, sensory reflection of the world" is, wherein "the word mediates with its meaning", we stand a chance of pinpointing two important things (brought to our attention already on previous occasions):

1) One is that we are thus reminded of what might be called the projective character of language

2) The other is that a word is thus assigned the role of a mediator between the general and the real particular, a view to which we have taken exception, especially in the context of speech act theory.

On the latter point, let us examine one more statement by Leontev and Luria:

Never is the meaning of a word totally absorbed by its reference to one particular thing; rather, it is tantamount to the generalization it serves to pin down ... (p 12).

Although the logic of this formulation is suspect on account of its circularity ("meaning is tantamount to the generalization pinned down by that meaning"), we would rather ignore this flaw and try to glean from it the familiar problem: to what extent is the general present in the particular and in what manner does the former determine the latter? The same problem was raised by Plato with his concept of idea and by Aristotle with those of *eidos* and *entelechy*. As shown in Chap. 8, the matter is of crucial importance for our notion of sense constancy.

Back in 1942, von Allesch examined the problem in a concise study, far removed from Soviet psychology and also from linguistics, and yet quite close to language. Having quoted it once before, we may only profit from having another look at it. Von Allesch makes an effort to trace the general in what is a particular process: the general principles of nest making in the nest made by this particular bird, or, what is general in this particular perception of a given person. It is in this context that he speaks of

the process prescribed only in general outline ..., the capacity for and the drive toward the symbol, the grasping of meanings through the meaning-carrying substrate (1942, p 29).

Leontev and Luria's concept of meaning as a reflection of reality *and* as a generalization of the particular thing comprised by that meaning could scarcely be reduced to a common denominator without running into trouble over the notion of reality: should the generalized be that reality? In a sense, the question can be answered in the affirmative. But is it actually a process of generalization, i. e., of making general, or is the (already existing) general merely put in relation to the particular in the process of language use? The notion of generalization places too much emphasis on only one, the upward, direction. The relating of the particular to the general in the process of speaking is by no means a one-way traffic. There is surely no reason to dread the metaphor that words are like doors by which we pass from the general to the particular and from the particular to the general. This is how the world becomes intelligible to us: we know how to utilize the general embedded in our common language and our common conduct.

Concluding this excursion into the realm of words, we may now return to Leontev and Luria's basic argument:

Generalization and communication are two intimately interrelated processes. ... Thus, it is precisely in the process of communication that one ought to search for the concrete conditions in which meaning develops (p 18). ... the child begins by entering into practical relations with the world, i. e., by acting in this world. "In the beginning was the deed" (p 20).

Clearly, Vygotsky and his adherents view action or activity as a fundamental trait of language processes. Leaving aside Bühler's functionalist theory of language and also Wittgenstein, this trait of Soviet psychology seems to have its "western" analogue in the conceptions proposed by the sign-code-information theorists.

But whereas the Russian view can be described as functionalist, the western one would have to be called metric.

How much these two views differ can be seen from the following formulations by AA Leontev (1969c):

> The concept of sign in general (and that of linguistic sign in particular) is thoroughly alien to linguistics and was imported from outside (p 43).

What, then, is linguistics?

> The object of linguistics is not the totality of isolated speech acts but rather the system of speech actions, speech activity (p 27).

But the theory of this activity is a (functionalist) psychology.

Also the other "manifestation" of Vygotsky's theoretical contribution – besides his strictly developmental ideas – is pervaded by the same functionalist approach. What we have in mind is his analysis of the microgenesis *(Aktualgenese)* of the utterance. As we now turn to the sequence of events leading from thought to speech, we again find a succession of different "languages", much as in the development from child to adult. This model of differential stages and languages deserves to be examined in some detail.

The emergence of an utterance is

> a process of gradual mediation of a communicative intention first by inner speech (by inner word) then by the meaning of outer words and finally in outer words themselves (AA Leontev 1972, p 3).

In a first attempt to characterize inner speech, Leontev lists the three features elaborated by Vygotsky:

1) the compressed, reduced form of its components
2) its predicative character
3) the high degree of situational and contextual conditioning.

It would be wrong to assume that a thought is prepared well in advance, waiting to be verbalized. Quoting a lesser known work by Vygotsky, Leontev (1972, p 4) writes:

> thought is not something ready to be expressed. Thought is working, it performs a definite function. This thought-work is a process of transition from being aware of the task[2] and building up its meaning to the unfolding of the thought proper.

The development that follows this incipient stage is marked by three interrelated and yet discriminable processes (Leontev 1969a, pp 11f.):

1) Inner speaking ("outer speech for oneself")
2) Inner speech,
3) inner programming of speech.

Inner speech has been perhaps most aptly delineated by AN Sokolov's research on "speech–motor afferentation and the problem of brain mechanisms of thought" (1967). Rejecting Penfield's view that the motor areas of the cortex have only executive functions, Sokolov maintains

---

[2] Here we come again upon the narrow conception of thought criticized by Fodor (see the beginning of this chapter).

that the motor link of the speech chain is not only an executive mechanism, but is at the same time a mechanism of the formation of the verbal code by means of reverse (kinesthetic) afferentation of all cortical and subcortical speech structures.

Thus the proprioceptive reverse afferentation of the motor components of a speech action becomes the core around which is built up any of the functional units that make up speech as much as thought. Not only does this represent a revival of Pavlov's idea but it also links up with Sechenov's claim that a thought can be viewed as a "psychic reflex with an inhibited terminal segment", that is, without an overt motor component. Let us add that even Hebb recognizes the motor function as an integrating agent by which overt and verbal actions are brought in relation to "various internal codes of thought".

The emphasis on the integrating role of the motor functions in the transition from "thought" to "utterance" enabled AN Sokolov to develop an empirical method of recording electromyographically the "tension" of the speech musculature for different kinds of mental activity.

The muscle tension in the articulatory apparatus (operationalized by Sokolov as speech-motor discharge) increases with the difficulty of the subject's task. Having distinguished between tonic and phasic tension (the latter corresponding to subvocal articulatory motor activity), Sokolov (1971) recorded – in the more difficult among the Raven progressive matrices –

> along with an increase in the general tone of the speech musculature, separate outbursts of speech-motor impulsation similar to those which arise during soundless utterance of words. The subjects firmly stated that sometimes they had "to reason mentally" with the help of certain words or fragments of phrases which they uttered silently: "Yes", "No", "I've found it", "This minus that", "A whole figure" . . . (p 90).

Such condensed utterances are an essential characteristic of (visual) thinking. At the same time, not all thinking must be verbalized in this way; indeed,

> internal speech functions in a highly generalized and fragmentary way, only directing the process of visual analysis and synthesis and introducing certain correctives into them. . . . Such an inclusion of speech into the processes of visual analysis and synthesis transforms them from an act of "unconscious deductions" into a consciously directed and controlled process of logical thought (p 90).

This electromyographic evidence of the existence and nature of "internal speech" induced Sokolov to postulate "kinesthetic codes of thought". A concept of crucial importance for a psychology of language, Sokolov's construct reminds us of an issue widely discussed by psychologists at the turn of the century: the role of mental representations (image vs. abstract idea) in thought and language. Whereas those psychologists quarreled about the notion of representation as the core concept of their respective theories, Sokolov is firmly convinced that the kinesthetic sensations accompanying the child's articulation are correlated with the auditory perceptions of his own and other people's speech, to form the core of the

> various "internal codes of thought" such as soundless word articulation, orienting and watching movements of the eyes, inhibited indicatory movements of the arms and head, strain of the facial muscles, etc. (p 79).

Hebb's notion of phase sequence and Paivio's (1969, 1970, 1971) analysis of imagery as a form of coding unquestionably belong to the same category of views; we shall come to speak of them when dealing with the preverbal and verbal origins of language (Chaps. 11 and 12).

With his electromyographic studies so far reported, Sokolov has shown it to be plausible that thought processes imply to some extent a kind of subvocal speaking (a notion not unfamiliar to orthodox behaviorists). But it is his concept of codes that has direct implications for a psychology of language: inasmuch as the kinesthetic code is an *indispensable* processing stage in the generation (or reception) of the utterance, we may expect an experimental (or pathologic) impediment of this "internal speech" to impair the production or perception of outer speech. In vindication of his presumption, Sokolov reports experiments in which subjects had to listen to texts and remember them while reciting certain verses or syllables. Sokolov discovered that

> such speech hindrance at first greatly impeded the comprehension . . . of the texts read to them . . . The subjects perceived only separate words on the basis of which they tried to guess the general content . . . In our further experiments, when the pronunciation of the verse had become more and more automatized, the subjects began to reproduce the texts more completely . . .; but when more complicated texts were read to them . . ., motor interference again rose . . . (p 84).

When subjects are asked to squeeze their tongue gently between the teeth, such impediment of internal speech is often compensated for "by means of a very rapid and reduced soundless articulation of some *key words* of the given text" (p 85).

What becomes effective in internal speech is a sort of thought plan (which reminds us of James's "thinking is impulsive"), that is, an impulse figure which may assume a more or less condensed form. In highly compressed form there are no more "words in their usual grammatical meaning" in internal speech:

> "the words are rather implied, being replaced by their kinesthetic code which only reminds of an articulation of the key words (p 86).

At this point it is a good time to stop and think how Sokolov's "internal speech" is related to what the generativists describe as deep structure. The two concepts certainly have some elements in common: they postulate that overt language as we observe it in human communication is supported by an underlying covert form of "language"; they both describe characteristic transformations effected in passing from one level to the other. And this is where the analogy ends. The orthodox generativists have proposed a deep structure to streamline their account of certain regularities of surface structure. Sokolov's "internal speech", on the other hand, is the product of experimentation rather than speculation, at least in its essential phenomenal aspects.

A much more interesting comparison emerges if Chomsky's deep structure is replaced with one in Fillmore's sense: we discover a parallel between the dynamic vectors which span the utterance space in qualitatively different directions and the kinesthetic vectors embedded in Sokolov's key words that "act like a quantum generator" (p 91). The matter is taken up again toward the end of this chapter.

In any event, Sokolov's and other Soviet psychologists' contributions to the problem of inner speech offer insights into the processes that precede the utterance, i. e., into a realm that is made accessible to western psycholinguistics practically only through the gate with the inscription "encoding". In a rather peculiar way, Russian psychology of language has established a link with what is developed by western investigators under the heading "nonverbal communication" in relative isolation from the psychology of language. (The relevant body of evidence will be discussed in the next chapter.)

Russian psychology of language conceives of the motor-kinesthetic dimension as an axis along which the transition from the more or less conscious action to the speech act is accomplished.

The evidence offered in support of this conception leaves open a number of crucial questions. We do not know whether inner speech functions as an incipient form of utterances as they appear in everyday language use or whether it exists alongside ordinary utterances. There is considerable vagueness in the idea of transition from inner to outer speech. According to Sokolov's (1967) earlier views the transition consists merely in a "correspondingly stronger excitation of the speech musculature". By 1971 he knows a lot more about "internal speech" and has even less to say about this matter:

> at the moment of a transition to external speech (oral or written), [internal speech] assumes an extended monological form (1971, p 91).

While deploring this vagueness, we may find consolation in the significant contention that the semantic complexes of inner speech are elaborated (verbalized) in different degrees, depending on the circumstances:

> When we convey our thoughts to other people, we, basing ourselves on such semantic complexes, evolve them depending on the given situation, and try to ensure their possibly fuller verbal expression (p 86).

Thus, the degree and nature of the verbalization are determined by the goal pursued by the speaker in the particular communicative situation. Such a view is incomparably more congenial to us than the generativists' conception, according to which the surface structure is reached always by the same flight of stairs and by a fixed number of steps.

The relationship between inner and outer speech has been traced in some detail by AA Leontev (1969a, 1972), who distinguishes between two processes in what Sokolov terms internal speech, namely, inner speaking and inner speech.

Inner speaking is "covert physiological activity of the organs of articulation" (1969a, p 11) as observed in any of two conditions. One is the speech perception condition, and here Leontev calls in the motor theory of speech perception (whose main exponent in the West is Liberman). According to the theory, speech perception relies heavily on the subvocal articulation of what is being heard. This kind of analysis-by-synthesis model is very popular in cognitive psychology

179

nowadays (cf Neisser 1967). But Leontev (1969a, p 11) sees the matter somewhat differently:

> there is reason to believe that not all speech perception takes place in conformity to the scheme proposed by the motor theory[3].

Reinterpreting Sokolov's experiments, Leontev attempts to show that in speech perception inner speaking is not accompanied by inner speech and hence need not be related to "deep seated mental processes". By this token Leontev refuses to accept the enticing prospect offered by the analysis-by-synthesis proponents whereby speech perception and understanding might be envisioned as speech production in reverse.

The other condition in which inner speaking is observed is the non-automatized intellectual act; in this case inner speaking is invariably accompanied by inner speech.

Inner speech is typically observed in problem solving. As inner speech becomes more expanded, it is likely to be accompanied by overt speech. At the other pole of the respective dimension

> is maximally compressed inner speech approaching the simple understanding of speech. According to the available evidence, it is least associated with speaking. The logical culmination of this series is the transition from verbal utterance to discharge of first-signal system stimuli and complete elimination of the intermediate state or stages ... (Leontev 1969a, p 12).

This is how Leontev tries to represent speaking and understanding as *one* dimension of mental activity: perception does go along with maximally compressed speech, in spite of the earlier stated view that perception is accompanied by inner speaking *without* inner speech.

Besides inner speaking and inner speech, Leontev distinguishes a third process denoted as *inner programming*. By this term he refers to the unconscious construction of a schema which becomes the basis for the production of an utterance. Such a schema is specifically developed for a particular utterance, and it contains

> that which is not automatically realized in speech production, which is not contained in the rules of production of any statement in a given language, i. e., the individual characteristics of the given, specific statement that make it possible to select the appropriate words from a lexicon and, from among all possible syntactic structures, that structure which is necessary in the given case (p 12).

This is saying a lot. What is postulated here is – next to, under, and prior to the implementation of automatically operating grammatical rules – a form of existence of the utterance (Leontev speaks of the sentence[4]) most readily conceived as an agglutinative string of meaning in the sense proposed by AN Leontev.

---

[3] Pursuing the suggestion, one wonders what might emerge from an experiment designed to test what kind of utterances are perceived in keeping with the motor theory, and in which conditions, and what other kinds (or parts) of utterances are not. Should Van Lancker's (1975) distinction between propositional and automatic speech be of relevance here?

[4] Strictly speaking, we have no right to use here any of the following terms: sentence, verbal message, or utterance, because nothing of the kind comes into being as long as the stage of inner programming is not followed by that of inner speech.

As has been pointed out before, Leontev regards inner programming as an initial phase in the generation of not only the utterance (outer speech) but also inner speech. Structurally, inner speech resembles inner programming fairly closely, but represents a more developed stage than the latter.

The relationships between the three concepts as pictured by Leontev are shown in Fig. 4.

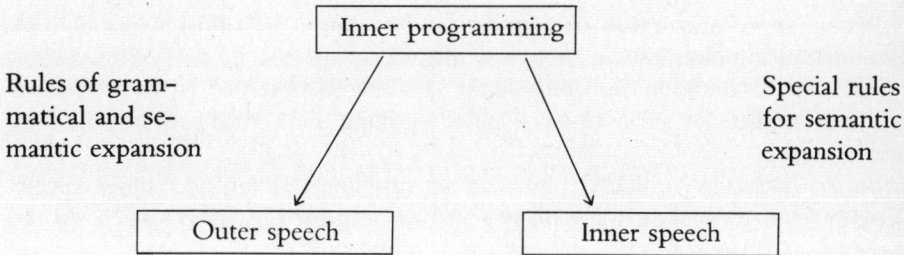

Fig. . Relationships between inner programming, outer speech, and inner speech, according to Leontev (1969a, p. 12)

Thus, inner programming is turned into outer or inner speech by two different expansion procedures. The specific structure of inner programming would be discernible, argues Leontev, if it were not deformed secondarily by the grammatical word sequence required by the particular language. Leontev does emphasize the role of predication, but prefers not to speak of predicative programming

> since predicativeness is essentially a characteristic of a statement as a whole and is associated with the realization (in inner or outer speech) of an inner program. The predicative character of inner speech is a reflection of the minimal grammar contained in the rules for recoding a program into inner speech (p 13).

Later, Leontev (1972, p 7) ascribes even more weight to predication as he sums up the problem by saying:

> Two sets of rules are used in speech generation, following one another, they are the rules of content representation through a system of predicative "utterances" in the inner speech code and the rules translating this system of "utterances" into the code of natural languages.

This seems – to me – to be the utmost in precision attainable in an interpretation of Leontev's views. The question of predicativeness is taken up again a few pages further on. Right now we should try to explore the inner dynamic schema of an utterance by reviewing some of Luria's neurologic investigations.

Luria's central concept is that of dynamic aphasia due to lesions in the posterior frontal region of the left hemisphere (a symptom described in similar manner by Pick and Kleist under the term speech adynamia). The patient is fully in control of the motor and sensory components of speech and has no difficulties in naming objects and in repeating words or even sentences. At the same time, he is unable "to utter independent, expanded statements" (Luria and Tsvetkova 1969, p 26). In less severe cases problems arise only when the patient has to recount a story, describe some situation, or take part in a conversation.

What kind of mechanisms are disordered in cases like these? Luria answers this question by making reference to Vygotsky: the cause is a defect of inner speech. But as we know, inner speech is predicative in character. Hence Luria seeks to interpret the behavior of these aphasics as being due to disturbances in the predicative function.

In doing so, he conceptualizes the predicative element of the utterance as being concentrated in the verb – a view he happens to share with the generative semanticists and contemporary psychologists of language. In one of his experiments (Luria and Tsvetkova 1969) he studies the naming of objects and actions by healthy persons and by patients affected by dynamic aphasia. While the former have no difficulties whatever, the aphasics succeed in naming objects but are unable to name actions demonstrated to them.

What exactly does "deficiency in the predicative function" mean?

A result (of a deficiency in the predicative function of internal speech[5]) may be disturbance in the linear scheme of a sentence, which is necessary for the transition from the initial conception to an expanded spoken utterance (p 29).

Thus our attention is focused on the process of expansion (and contraction) which keeps reemerging as a key issue for the psychologist of language, and which cannot be accounted for by the concept of recoding alone. Vygotsky used to speak of speech being turned into "inward thought", and Sokolov of a reduction to "key words".

How are the processes that take place between "inner programming" or inner speech and outer speech related to Chafe's linearizations and literalizations as discussed in the chapter on generative semantics? And how do they relate to the expansions of child speech by the mother who supplies the missing elements in her child's "telegraphic speech" to ensure its grammaticalness? Although questions of this kind remain unanswered for the time being, their formulation gives us the perspective needed to assess the implications of the Russian studies.

The hypothesis that a defect of the predicative function is due to disturbances in the formation of the linear scheme (by which the original plan is recoded into speech) can be tested in any of two ways. One, the subject is offered the words to be used in the anticipated sentence but not the "linear scheme of the sentence". Two, the opposite procedure is followed.

In Luria and Tsvetkova's experiment, patients with dynamic aphasia were found to be unable to form a sentence from individual words. The results of the other, "positive" experiment were reported by the authors as follows:

We asked a patient with the syndrome of dynamic aphasia to give a sentence expressing a wish ("I am hungry" or "Give me something to drink") or formulating a simple graphic situation (a woman cutting bread, a boy reading a book). After the patient

---

[5] In Luria and Tsvetkova (1969) the term *inner speech* is used in reference to Vygotsky's work and the term *internal speech* in reference to the authors' own work.

demonstrated his inability to compose an expanded sentence, a series of counters was placed on a table. None of the counters carried any additional information, but the number of counters in a row corresponded to the number of words in the required sentence. . . . A patient who had previously been incapable of constructing an expanded sentence was able to accomplish this task by touching each consecutive counter with his finger; when the counters were taken away, he was again helpless (1969, p 30).

The model of a linear sentence scheme was thus used by the patient as a motor aid with which to compensate for the pathologic defect.

It might be useful to revert to Sokolov for a moment, in view of his emphasis on the role of motor functions in language processes. When the aphasic patients were tested electromyographically (by a lead from their lower lip) while preparing for a verbal response without actually pronouncing the sentence, no changes in the background EMG were recorded. According to Luria and Tsvetkova, this shows

that in these patients disturbances do not occur in the motor stage itself, but that the delay in speech impulses is localized in the preliminary stage of the process (p 32).

Quite a different picture emerges if the patient is offered the external support in the form of counters:

In this case, an intention to utter a sentence results in sharp changes in the background EMG and separate EMG outbursts, whose magnitudes correspond to the individual components of the sentence in preparation. It is clear that external supports open a pathway for impulses from the motor speech apparatus (p 33).

The significance of these findings not only for language pathology but also for language psychology in general is self-evident. This is summed up by Luria and Tsvetkova with a quote from Jackson, a nineteenth-century psychiatrist: "To speak is to propositionize[6]."

The view cannot be accepted without an important qualification. Jackson himself observed that language is composed of propositional elements (more susceptible to impairment by lesions in the left hemisphere) and of automatized elements (impaired by lesions in the right hemisphere).

We are thus reminded of Van Lancker's (1975, p 58) thesis that

human language may be viewed as made up of different subsets, which have various relationships to evolutionarily primitive human speech . . . language . . . is heterogeneously processed in the brain.

It would therefore be unreasonable to search those Soviet investigations for evidence of a single path by which all utterances, or elements of utterances, reach the stage of articulation.

From the entire problem of inner speech Luria has singled out the aspect of programming, an aspect studied also by Lashley, though from a different vantage point. Now, what is it actually that is subject to sequential programming or linearization? One might suppose that it is the words that make up the sentence.

---

[6] In the further course of our argument (Chap. 12), the proposition emerges as the core of the utterance developing in the child.

In fact, AA Leontev goes some way toward this particular fallacy in his discussion of inner programming:

> The specific structure of programming is reflected by the "word order" in those cases in which this order is not "deformed" by the grammatical structure of a sentence in the concrete language. Such nongrammatical languages are the spontaneous mimetic language of the deaf-mute, the automatic speech of children, and ordinary children's speech after the lexicogrammatical classes have already been constituted but a grammatical paradigm is still lacking. All these "languages" give the same sequence of "propositional terms": S–At–O–V–Ad [subject–attribute–object–verb–adjective] (1969a, p 13).

While suppressing our delight at the first sentence of the quotation (in which Leontev claims that word order tends to be deformed by grammar), we cannot gloss over the assertion that there is some "natural" sequence of words (in inner speech) prior to the operation of grammar. In effect, the sequence S–At–O–V–Ad would represent a prelinguistic universal common to the human race which is ordinarily blurred ("deformed") by the operation of the particular grammar during the phase of outer speech.

Such an "agglutinative string of meanings" is further processed according to the "rules of semantic expansion". And here we come upon a major inconsistency in Leontev's conception: the "meanings" sequentially arranged by inner programming are static in character, rather than being "directed" structures. Indeed, Leontev clearly refrains from speaking of "predicative programming".

His attitude is all the more perplexing in view of the fact that Leontev positively distinguishes between psychological and linguistic predicativeness and seeks to represent such seemingly nominal utterances as "night, stars" as predication ("it's night, . . .). What, then, is the nature of the "agglutinative string of meanings" arranged in a sequence by inner programming if it acquires its predicativeness only by the operation of some "minimal grammar" and its rules? We ought to bear in mind that we are concerned here with a stage in the genesis of an utterance (or an exemplar of inner speech) which, according to Leontev, occurs prior to its encoding into the words of any particular language ("programming does not depend on the language", p 14). If meaning were to be conceptualized as being expressed in some code, a convenient candidate would be Zhinkin's (1967) "depicting code" comprised by images and schemata.

Our objections to this view are as follows: Is it admissible to construe these wordless meanings – coded in images and motor-kinesthetic schemata – in so static a manner as suggested by Leontev? Is inner programming really necessary to furnish them with the particular sequence (S–At–O–V–Ad), and hence dynamics? Or does the very kinesthetic schema of a verb (e. g., *hit, love,* or *hate*) already comprise a tangible intention toward an object?

The predicate-argument structure of generative semantics, with its internal directiveness, presents itself for this purpose.

Moreover, the now popular concept of (re)coding seems to divert our attention from the inherent dynamic of the pertinent processes. What we mean is the dynamic originating neither in the lexicon nor in the more or less linear sentence schema, but in the speaker with his intention of bringing about a change in the hearer. In spite of its emphasis on motor functions and processes, Soviet psychology of language is much too strongly preoccupied with the concept of levels and what it implies: recoding from one level to the next (or, in a Western manner of speaking, mapping onto the next level). To be sure, the concept may serve a useful purpose, but – as any other layered model – it fails to account for what goes on from one level to the next: a series of cross sections through, say, a muscle does not tell us that it contracts, and how it contracts. From this analogy we realize what the Soviet psychology of language has likewise failed to illuminate – it should suffice to recall Brunswik's longitudinal intentionality.

Eventually, Leontev (1972, p 9) acknowledges the fact that his views are not unlike Fillmore's: "the interpretation of an utterance as a propositional function of 'deep' structure (inner programming – in our interpretation)" is well known from the works of this author, he comments in a footnote.

At this point we readily take advantage of the opportunity to juxtapose two seemingly identical concepts: deep structure as conceptualized by the generativists (the semanticists in particular) and one of the levels of inner speech (e. g., inner programming) as conceived by Soviet psycholinguistics. Should this indeed represent a point of convergence for Chomsky, whose goal is to develop a theory of linguistic competence, and for Leontev, who seeks to develop a theory of utterance generation? And should this also be a meeting point for a number of philosophers of language who seem to discover a certain affinity between Kant's transcendental knowledge and Chomsky's "deep grammar" (we only have to think of Vendler, 1967, and perhaps also of certain aspects of Chomsky's Cartesian linguistics)? Well, it is certainly possible to employ the notion of deep structure in this or that system, but do we know with sufficient precision what deep structure is, in order to know that the same thing is meant here as there? My feeling is that the convergence is spurious: it is like two ships that pass in a stormy night – shouts of "deep structure" from both sides – and here they go.

Even though Leontev's model is marked by certain notions of transformational grammar, it differs from the latter chiefly on two counts (which are seen by the author as its advantages): it possesses an "undetermined, heuristic character", and it is "not algorithmic at all" (Leontev 1972, p 10). The latter statement – which for a western linguist or psycholinguist would be a question of scientific stamina – makes us wish to shake Leontev's hand in gratitude: the language psychologist is also pleased to discuss language in the medium of language.

We conclude our roving tour of Soviet psycholinguistics enriched by a number of insights as well as queries, but also perplexed by the style of the respective writing. Even when exploring the utterance ontogenetically or in its microgenesis, Russian psychologists of language do not take recourse to either the notion of sign or any grammatical element; instead, they keep referring to "speech actions" or activities that go through various stages of planning and execution but need not always result in an overt utterance.

The reviewed Soviet studies in the psychology of language have provided us with interesting cross sections of speech activity; but although we are told how these cross sections follow each other, we do not yet know whether this particular sequence is obligatory or might be reversed in some cases, and what kind of "vertical" mechanism is responsible for the staggering of levels. A similar concept of levels of processing is discussed in Chap. 15, where we are again forced to conclude that the notion of levels cannot do justice to the truly relevant processes which take place across levels and are governed by the speaker's intention as directed to the hearer.

A few more words about Vygotsky, whose point of departure was the correlation of two levels as reflected in the very general question of the interrelations between thought (as embodied in problem solving) and language (as embodied in speech). Vygotsky set out to elucidate this question by a genetic analysis. This has prompted Fodor (1972) to point out that the question entails a still more general one, a question free of either specifically genetic or specifically linguistic presumptions. We may reflect, argues Fodor, about

> the routine ability of higher organisms to interpret information in any one input mode in terms of information from any other. What we see often determines how we take what we hear . . . It is tempting (perhaps it is mandatory) to explain such interactions by assuming that sensory channels transduce stimulus data into a central computing language rich enough to represent visual, tactual, auditory, gustatory, and olfactory information as well as whatever abstract conceptual apparatus is involved in thought. In such a language are performed the calculations involved in evaluating the auditory implications of visual inputs . . . (p 85).

Thus Fodor postulates a kind of metamodal and also metalinguistic central code, but we hesitate to follow him in this categorical statement:

> It is . . . self-evident that the language in which we integrate visual and auditory information cannot be either the language of vision or the language of audition, though it must contain both (p 85).

Such self-evidence has not infrequently led to embarrasing self-repudiations. (And there is some evidence that the processing of visual information encompasses a stage of auditory coding.)

Once we have endorsed this kind of model, we may construe any natural language as a sort of sensory modality

> providing a channel through which input data can gain access to the central information handling system. Linguistic data, like sensory data, are subject to integration and interpretation in light of memory information and current experience (for the integration and interpretation of which they are in turn available). Presumably the computations underlying these integrative processes are effected in the central code. If this is so, then the production and comprehension of speech involve translating between this central code and a natural language (p 85).

Developing his idea Fodor is oblivious of a fundamental fact: that we understand language not in the form of some mysterious central code but – to say the least – as something that is phenomenally a very language-like form. The assumption that language is ultimately translated into some central code represents a highly abstract, formal solution to the problems raised in our argument. Fodor's proposed solution ignores the phenomenal side of the processes, and there is no denying that understanding is a phenomenon as well.

In any case, we ought to remember how great a stride has been made by the psychology of language under Vygotsky's inspiration. Having no access to the seductive and yet unproductive term *coding,* Vygotsky has raised our sensitivity to some of the developments that precede the act of uttering.

These developments – as well as those which range from audition to understanding – will remain in the focus of our attention in the next chapter. Whilst in the present chapter we have been interested in the succession of processes from one (linguistic) level to the next, we now turn to the prelinguistic determinants of the speech act. At this stage, the emergent speech act appears to us as a condensation of something that is not yet linguistic but may already be communicative.

Chapter 11

The Nonverbal Setting of Language

The great variety of (inner and outer) "languages" identified by Russian psychologists of language causes us to raise a question that seemed to be settled for linguistics ever since Saussure and Martinet, if not earlier. This question is: What does the term *language* mean? What do we have in mind when we say an organism, the human being, *speaks?* Where does speaking begin? On examining the ramified implications of the question, we cannot fail to realize that it may involve different (or possibly not quite so different?) readings of *begin:* a phylogenetic, an ontogenetic, and a microgenetic.

The parallel existence of the three aspects has been likewise recognized by Osgood (1971b, p 498), who complains:

> Philosophers and linguists have given precious little attention to prelinguistic cognitive behavior, in any of its three senses – prior to language in the evolution of the human species, prior to language in the development of the individual, or prior to language in the generation of particular sentences by ordinary speakers.

Obviously we cannot base ourselves on the simplistic notion that ontogeny amounts to the replication of phylogeny in a radically shortened mode, or the notion that the same stages of development obtain in the generation *(Aktualgenese)* of an utterance, as in the child's acquisition of language. But we would be well-advised to heed Toulmin's (1971, p 372) postulate that a "theory of language should make biological sense", bearing in mind that language is presumably the most human function of man. Consequently, we would not dare to ignore the insights that might ensue for such a theory from evidence of those biologic processes which have brought the human race to its present position and which are incessantly in operation in the language-using human being.

From our discussion of Wittgenstein's and speech act philosophy and also the Russian psychology of language, it has emerged that the speech act, i. e., the actual utterance, begins long before the speaker opens his mouth.

In the following pages we want to examine the structured relationships that extend between silence, not yet speaking, and uttering.

How can we delineate the field in which a conversation, a request, or a censure is initiated? Taking the question at its face value, we might say: Communicative behavior is anchored in a certain space. That is to say, unless prevented from doing so by external constraints, both sender and receiver are specifically oriented to each other. Their physical spacing as well as the mutual positioning of their heads and bodies is not arbitrary, being dictated by cultural norms and the type of communication intended or carried on. For example, Arab students maintain closer distances to their partners, tend to touch each other and look at each other more frequently than European or North-American students (Watson and Graves 1966). When two American partners approach a rectangular table to engage in a friendly conversation, and one chooses to sit down at a shorter side of the table, the other is apt to sit down at a corner. If their purpose is close cooperation, the two partners will sit side by side at one of the longer sides. When coming together in competition or opposition, they will choose the two longer sides to face each other (Sommer 1965; Cook 1970).

While these may seem to be nothing but amusing observations, a closer look reveals them as tokens of a ramified system of "nonverbal communication" which serves to prepare, support, and codetermine verbal behavior. (For details see von Cranach 1971; Duncan 1969; Mehrabian 1969; Wiener et al. 1972.) We will now try to show how varied in degree and direction this codetermination is. That the matter is of paramount importance for the language psychologist need not be argued any further at this stage. It might be useful however to recall Uhlenbeck's (1963, p 11) "cardinal point":

> every single sentence, also a seemingly trivial sentence, has to be interpreted by the hearer with the help of extralinguistic data.

What seems important here is not only the reference to extralinguistic clues but also to interpretation. Evidently, Uhlenbeck mentions interpretation not in the sense the term carries for the orthodox generativists, namely, the subsequent semantic interpretation of a sentence that is primarily determined by syntax. Uhlenbeck (1967b) is concerned with the fact that "a sentence is not only a linguistic-grammatical act, but also a cognitive act" (p 269) and argues that, in order to grasp this dual position of the sentence, it is necessary to take cognizance of the available (also to the linguist) knowledge of "situational and other extralinguistic factors operative in actual speech" (pp 310–311). It is by an interpretation of situational and contextual factors that the intentional act is endowed with its vector of meaningfulness running in a direction perpendicular to the levels described by Soviet psycholinguists.

Hall (1959, 1966) and Goffman (1959, 1961, 1963, 1964) were among the investigators who first demonstrated the importance of the mutual physical spacing of the interacting partners in this regard. Hall has proposed the name *proxemics* for the respective research domain. His basic hypothesis is that the "admissible" distance between two people involved in a conversation is specified by the norms obtaining in the particular subculture.

> In the United Staates distances of from 6 to 18 inches are typical for intimate interpersonal situations, distances of from 30 to 48 inches are typical of casual-personal interac-

tion, distances of from 7 to 12 feet are characteristic of social-consultative situations . . . (Mehrabian 1969, p 362).

If these are norms, their violation or disregard is bound to have definite consequences. A number of relevant studies are thus summarized by Mehrabian (1969, p 363):

> communicator-addressee distance is correlated with the degree of negative attitude communicated to and inferred by the addressee . . . . . . distances which are too close, that is, inappropriate for a given interpersonal situation, can elicit negative attitudes when the communicator-addressee relationship is not an intimate personal one. . . . the distance between two communicators is positively correlated with their status discrepancy.

How much our behavior is influenced by the nonobservance of such a norm comes into evidence in a variety of situations: experiencing extreme congestion in the elevator, we feel the urge to compensate for the imbalance, either by assuming a suitable expression of the face, or by turning away our gaze, or by making a comment in order to raise the level of intimacy or, on the contrary, in order to stress that the reduced distance has been enforced by external circumstances beyond our control.

Observations of this kind have led Goffman (1963, p 193) to the following generalization:

> the behavior of an individual while in a situation is guided by social values or norms concerning involvement. These rulings apply to the intensity of his involvements, their distribution among possible main and side activities, and, importantly, their tendency to bring him into an engagement with all, some, or none present. There will be then a patterned distribution or allocation of the individual's involvement. . . . we can link the involvement allocation of each participant to that maintained by each of the other participants, piecing together in this way a pattern that can be described as the structure of involvement in the situation.

The resultant structure of involvement in the situation becomes a dynamic base for the verbal communication that follows or continues. The base is dynamic in the sense that the verbal processes originating from it vary from place to place of origination. Owing to the dynamic character of the preverbal base, the ensuing verbal processes acquire at any one time (also at the very first moment) a particular vectorial orientation which helps the speaker to single out from the general background of meaningfulness the particular content he has in mind. Once the hearer has become aware of the dynamic nonverbal base of verbal processes, he is in a position to grasp the intended meaning. Otherwise he persists in a state typically described in these words: "I did hear what he was saying, but I couldn't understand what he meant". The phrase underlines the fact that we understand speakers through the medium of language rather than the sentences of the language.

Taking a more linguistic approach to this interlacement of verbal and nonverbal communication, one is inclined to construe factors such as distance between partners, mutual positioning of head and body, eye contact, etc. as regulators (Ekman and Friesen 1969), that is, as a class of behavior which "seems to serve the unique function of regulating the communication interaction itself" (Wiener et al. 1972, p 202).

It must be realized that with such a juxtaposition of nonverbal and verbal communication some new problems come into sight – provided we look close enough. These problems can be summed up in the following three interrelated questions:

1) When does a regulator still count as communication in this sense; i. e., what is covered by *communication* and what is not?

2) Can we say that something is being "encoded" in such nonverbal behaviors, to be "decoded" by the receiver?

3) To what degree of specificity is it possible to trace the interdependence of verbal and nonverbal processes?

There is a tendency to begin an analysis of these issues with a rather naive identification of *body language, expressive movements,* and *nonverbal communication.* Especially those familiar with the continental-European tradition of the psychology of expression and the theory of projective techniques inspired by psychoanalysis are inclined to include in this study every kind of behavior that might be interpreted by the receiver as indicative of some state in the sender (his mood, his intention, his social status, etc). But can we really ascribe some "meaning" in the "language of the human body" to, say, someone's cheeks reddened by fever? When does a symptom, which by its very existence is associated with an underlying state, turn into a signal deliberately used by the sender "in order to" produce an intended effect in the receiver? And when does it turn into a symbol which by its very essence stands for something else? (See on this subject Bühler 1934, pp 102f., and Hörman 1971a, pp 19f.)

The problem under what circumstances and under what influences purely "informative" behavior is turned into "communicative" behavior has been pinpointed by Wiener et al. (1972). The receiver *may* evaluate, consciously or unconsciously, some informative behavior as a particular clue, e. g., as regulator in the sense proposed by Ekman and Friesen. If in addition we adopt the psychoanalytic position that any behavior expresses some hidden content, "it is seductively easy to make such a transformation" from sign to communication (Wiener et al., p 188) because of the assumption that even "with verbal material it is the latent rather than the manifest content which is taken to be most critical" *(loc. cit.).* For instance, Watzlawick et al. (1967) go so far as to designate as communication any behavior that takes place in the presence of other people. This has its advantages and disadvantages: an advantage is that attention is drawn to the origin of the utterance in social action, and hence to the general background of uncodedness against which each and every coding operation takes place, that is to say, to the fact that speaking must be seen as the continuation of action by alternative means. A disadvantage is the vagueness of the thus accepted notion of communication: if all behavior in the presence of other people is regarded as communicative, what are the scientific returns of designating some behavior as communicative?

Wiener et al. (1972, p 186) are emphatically opposed to an extension of the notion of communication to any situation in which "the observer can make an inference about an individual from his behavior" – in which case they prefer to speak of sign. In contrast,

> communication implies (a) a socially shared signal system, that is, a code, (b) an encoder who makes something public via that code, and (c) a decoder who responds systematically to that code.

Although this kind of definition ensures a neat separation of *communication* from *sign,* it does little to elucidate the relationship between nonverbal and verbal communication; in Wittgenstein's style we might say that a boundary has thus been drawn where there has so far been none. Moreover, the definition pushes quite a few things outside the range of verbal communication that are commonly believed to belong inside. The point is that even in the case of language behavior, the criterion of the speaker's "actively making his experience public via that code" does not always apply in an absolute sense: language processes also serve to "make public" content that may not be consciously present in the speaker's experience and need not be meant for "publication". The criterion of a conscious implementation of a behavior with the express purpose of attaining a definite communicative effect, postulated by Wiener et al., is therefore untenable. Anyone who has asked a speaker why he used this particular sentence rather than any of its possible paraphrases will realize how limited the speaker's awareness is of the exact verbal instrumentation used for the particular communicative purpose.

In formal terms, perhaps the most clear-cut separation of the terms *communication* and *information* has been offered by DM MacKay (1972). An event yields information if it makes us know or believe something we did not know or believe before. "Information-about-X determines the form of our readiness-to-reckon-with-X in appropriate circumstances" (p 8).

Information is thus an interaction between two organisms in the course of which signals from A affect the central organization system of B. This idea shows a certain conceptual affinity with Ajdukiewicz's notion of comprehension as readiness to accept a sentence as valid (see p 153) and also with Deese's (1969) conception of understanding as "the inward sign of the potential for reacting appropriately to what we see or hear".

To turn information into communication, it is necessary, says MacKay (1972, pp 20f.), for B to perceive A as behaving in a purposeful manner in relation to B. A central role has thus been accorded to the intentionality of communicative processes, except that the essential "addition" by which information is turned into communication is not the intention of the sender but the attribution of such an intention to the sender by the receiver!

This kind of discussion on the boundary between information and communication, or between verbal and nonverbal communication (perhaps it would be legitimate to say "nonverbal information" in many a case?), fails as much in unraveling the deeper implications of the problem as the rival approach by which the prestigious term *communication* is used more as a cover for a variety of phenomena than as a device for illuminating them.

No matter how sharp or vague these distinctions are, it will be useful to review a number of studies which bear on the relevant issues (Schönbach 1974; Müller-Eckhard 1974; Terbuyken 1976).

Schönbach (1974) found lengthy, profusely worded utterances in a conversation to convey the impression of politeness. Terbuyken (1976) recorded telephone conversations between student-interviewers and interviewees from different social milieus (clergymen, professors, civil servants, students, friends of the interviewer) and analyzed the transcripts. The way the interviewers phrased their questions (sentence type, number of adjectives, etc.) varied according to the social affiliation of the interviewees. Evidently, the type of sociopsychological situation obtaining between interviewer and interviewee is denoted by certain formal clues which, though attached to language, do not represent part of the linguistic code. Well, do these formal clues form any code at all? Is anything being encoded in this case, is anything being communicated? Very few speakers are aware of the fact that they tend to employ a particular "formal code" when talking to, say, a civil servant.

We are thus reminded that practically all discussions of the interrelations between the concepts *sign, code,* and *communication* have one tacit but far-reaching assumption in common: that it is perfectly feasible and natural to describe and discuss the content "made public" in an utterance in and by the same language game in which the utterance is implemented. Is this correct? It will presently be shown that in very many cases the assumptions underlying the uses of the term *coding* are missing, but this is easily overlooked because the term itself has no precise meaning.

In the frontier area between (purely informative) clues and communication, the concept of code acquires a key position: can we speak of a code as soon as it is used for decoding, i. e., for diagnostic inferencing, or only when its rules are also used (and perhaps consciously used) for encoding, i. e., as a means of transmission?

The aspect of formalization suggested by the very notion of code falls in with that of the deliberate intention of the code user. Accordingly, Ekman and Friesen (1969, pp 55–56) draw the following distinction:

> Informative nonverbal behavior encompasses those acts which have some shared decoded meaning, in that such acts elicit similar interpretations in some set of observers ... Communicative nonverbal behavior encompasses those acts which are clearly and consciously intended by the sender to transmit a specifiable message to the receiver.

And once again Wiener et al. 1972 bring forward cogent arguments against such a distinction: a speaker need not be (fully) aware of his own intention, or else he may be mistaken as to his intention.

How tenuous the boundary is between what is a code and what is not (yet) a code will become apparent from the following discussion.

An approach like Goffman's (1959, p 24), where not only "size and looks, posture, speech patterns, facial expressions, bodily gestures" but also type and placing of the furniture in the living room are treated as clues utilized by a keen observer to assess for instance the status and group affiliation of a person, suggests that no sharp dividing lines can be drawn between clue, sign, sign vehicle, signal, and communication (as conceptualized by Wiener et al.). (Is it not that this lack of sharp distinctions reflects the state of things prevailing at the inception of language?) Should we use the concept of code even at this level? Is it sufficient for such use if only some members of the respective communicative group in some cases report to be guided by these signs or clues when interacting with their partners? Or is it essential for *all* members to utilize them *consistently* in such interaction? That is to say, may a code be called a code only if it is used deliberately for encoding and decoding? If this were so, then we would have no right to designate as code even certain portions of the linguistic code, namely those of which only a few linguists can claim that they are in use.

An alternative, more useful definition of code would require us to shift the emphasis from the conscious intention of the code user to the availability of the sign as such. In doing so we would find it necessary to allow for the fact (thus running into new difficulties) that the transition from purely informative to code-based communicative behavior involves the transition from analogue to digital "representation".

Rather than searching for an "ultimate" definition of code we would do better to indicate the conceptual consequences resulting from the finding that there is a transitional field between the informative and the communicative elements, between what is not quite a code and what *is* a code, a field whose manifest and latent forces influence the emergence of language (in phylogenetic, ontogenetic, and perhaps also in microgenetic terms). It is within this field that Macnamara (1972, p 1) attempts to anchor his theory of language acquisition when he says:

> infants learn their language by first determining, independent of language, the meaning which a speaker intends to convey to them, and by then working out the relationship between the meaning and the language.

This view – which will keep reemerging in the subsequent chapters – implies that the child gradually learns to "articulate" via coding operations what he had got to know earlier – however vaguely – without such operations.

By his tenet, Macnamara raises a problem that seems to carry much more weight for linguistics, and hence also for a psychology of language, than hitherto acknowledged. This problem is: how do we go about discovering structure in language while learning it[1]? Putting it more pointedly: is there a code which allows us to decide which code to use?

The question is considered by Macnamara in its ontogenetic, developmental, and also learning-theory aspects. The same problem may be phrased by the psychologist of perception like this: How does the hearer know *which* code or language game to use at a particular moment, or *when* he should take a turn in speaking, or *when* an utterance is finished? (Verbal signals are not always available for these purposes.) Finally, the language ethnologist who for the first time comes to face a native speaker of an unfamiliar language has to make a similar

---

[1] A *deus ex machina* has been made available for this end by the generativists: the Language Acquisition Device (LAD), a kind of cramming device serving to extract from the samples of language heard by the child the competence rules of this language.

effort to discover, by the application of some code, the structuring of what may at first appear to be an undifferentiated flow of speech and actions. At the same time, he will have to look for clues that might tell him (on the basis of what code?) whether or not the native speaker is about to attack him as a stranger, or is using a code (in relation to "strangers deserving polite treatment", to "barbarians", etc.) that differs radically from the one commonly used in relation to peers or friends.

Evidently, certain processes have to take place prior to any code utilization, processes that are not controlled by the respective code. What are these processes like?

We may try to delineate these processes by following Ploog's (1972) argument that at any early stage of evolution, verbally uncoded communication is focused primarily upon social information, rather than upon information about the non-social environment. The parallel functioning of different subsystems[2], each having its specific code, within a seemingly unitary communicative action, can be accounted for by the controlled stimulation of certain brain areas:

> A modification in the physiologic state of the brain (e. g., by stimulation of circumscribed brain sites) therefore effects changes in the brain systems that share in the generation of the signal. This change is codetermined by the particular group constellation perceived by the animal at the time ... If these two components result in behavior of some information content, the behavior affects the social situation again (Ploog 1972, p 148).

The close reliance of developmentally early forms of communication on social processes noted by Ploog, may likewise inspire a search in another direction. Turning toward the philosophy of language, we are reminded that both Wittgenstein and the speech act philosophers point to the socially conditioned utterances as being the first to move beyond the stream of actions into the realm of symbols. For Wittgenstein it is the imperative "Slab!", defined in its intended meaning by the accompanying action, for Searle it is the performative utterance.

It is precisely in the foreland of encoding and decoding that developments take place which deeply affect the structural framework of language processes. What exactly does take place there? Making the question more specific: what skills or techniques are needed for operating a code? Probably the most elaborate reply to that question has been offered by Garfinkel (1972).

His preliminary evidence resulted from a large-scale analysis of clinic records designed to establish the diagnostic and therapeutic stations passed by patients during their clinic "careers". Suitably trained experts examined some 1500 clinic folders for data which they entered in coding sheets. The clinic records and the coding instructions turned out to be inadequate for the task. Garfinkel explains (1972, p 311):

---

[2] It will be recalled that both Wittgenstein and even more so Ajdukiewicz have pointed out – approaching the issue from a different angle – that any language comprises a variety of languages (or language games) in parallel (see Chap. 9). In neurolinguistic terms, it is possible to distinguish subsets of more or less automated language, as we have learned from Van Lancker (1975).

... in order to accomplish the coding, coders were assuming knowledge of the very organized ways of the clinic that their coding procedures were intended to produce descriptions of. ... such presupposed knowledge seemed necessary and was most deliberately consulted whenever ... the coders needed to be satisfied that they had coded "what really happened" ... no matter how apparently clear coding instructions were. Agreement in coding results was being produced by some other contrasting procedure with unknown characteristics. ... What actual activities made up coders' practices called "following coding instruction"?

The coders were found to employ certain ad hoc techniques (Garfinkel uses the term ad hocing games, which reminds us of Wittgenstein) to assess the relevance (or irrelevance) of the coding instructions in relation to the particular clinic event under coding. Such ad hoc considerations were indispensable – which brings us to the crux of the problem – in deciding

> the fit between what could be read from the clinic folders and what the coder inserted into the coding sheet. No matter how definitely and elaborately instructions had been written and despite the fact that strict actuarial rules *could* be formulated for every item, and with which folder contents *could* be mapped into the coding sheet, insofar as the claim had to be advanced that coding sheet entries reported real events of the clinic's activities, then in every instance, and for every item, "et cetera", "unless", "let it pass", and *"factum valet"* accompanied the coder's grasp of the coding instructions as ways of analyzing actual folder contents (pp 312–313).

By "et cetera" is meant a piece of implicit practical advice to be heeded by the coder in the application of the coding instructions, of the kind: "Read it like this, ... and so forth", which means: "Extend the rule beyond the circumstances and cases mentioned by it". And here we are reminded of Wittgenstein (though Garfinkel does not mention this), who tells us how we explain to someone what a game is (or: what might be encoded as a game): "One gives examples and intends them to be taken in a particular way" (1953, § 71); and elsewhere:

> the words "This is the king" ... are a definition only if the learner ... has already played other games, or has watched other people playing 'and understood' – and similar things (§ 31).

Thus the coder or language user is tacitly assumed to be capable of following a trend merely intimated (not specified) in the coding instructions, beyond what is made explicit therein.

As can be seen from this, language coding is feasible only in the framework of a game that is essentially not fully resolvable in coding operations. Here we have a fundamental property of language processes, whose importance cannot be overestimated: language use invariably implies the utilization of an (one or more?) essentially incomplete, open-ended system which can be employed only if the language user keeps going beyond it. In coding a particular content, the language user must take his bearings against the general background of meaningfulness – which brings us very close to the process of understanding as described in the chapter on sense constancy.

This is born out by the other ad hoc techniques described by Garfinkel: "unless" and "let it pass" refer to the alternative decision not to follow a coding instruction even if required to do so by its literal interpretation[3]. Such a decision may be suggested by considerations

> which any member knows need not and cannot be cited before they are needed, though no nember is at a loss when the need is clear. That is, you presumably can recognize circumstances and cases to which no one in their right (professional) mind would take the rule as applying, though not stated (Garfinkel 1972, pp 312f.).

Garfinkel speaks, characteristically, of the "members of a profession" who are in a position to apply these techniques while coding events known to the profession. That it to say, these supplementary and yet essential elements of knowledge derive from professional practice as a form of life that is a part of the language game.

Knowledge, which is potentially codable, is founded on uncodable skills. Precisely the vagueness of these techniques and the fact that they are not ultimately specifiable and receive their direction from what goes on between and around speaker and hearer (let us recall Ajdukiewicz's "readiness to acknowledgement", which also has such an impetus as a prerequisite) causes such ad hoc considerations to have "irremediable priority over the usually talked about 'necessary and sufficient' criteria" (Garfinkel 1972, p 313) of coding and decoding.

A fair portion of the phenomena subsumed by the term *nonverbal communication* are located in the realm of these ad hocing techniques, i. e., where decisions are made on the application or nonapplication of codes. And since one of the functions of nonverbal communication seems to be the institution of one or another of the ad hocing techniques, nonverbal communication must be seen as a vital prerequisite of language, rather than as a separate, less prestigious system next to the system of language. To be more precise: once again we come to realize that language is not just one system, but is marked by the inevitable interlacement of verbal and nonverbal subsystems. Furthermore, we come to realize that the same things that appear to form a separate subsystem in one aspect (e. g., the subsystem of nonverbal communication), in another constitute the basis of some other system (in this case, verbal communication), a basis which evades perfect systematization. You need the former in order to make use of the potentialities of the latter.

Approaching the issue from one more angle we discover how at the interface of nonverbal and verbal communication the shift takes place from action which refers directly to something, to a level of communication at which precision in conveying and grasping meaning is achieved by having the speaker-hearer's intention refracted through the transparency of a *coded* message. If we may say so, this is where the transition takes place from the speaker-who-means-something to the formalization of his means of expression.

Construing in turn nonverbal communication as an open-ended system, let us have another look at Goffman's structure of a situation in which each participant shows a specific involvement. This involvement structure is codetermined by

---

[3] The fourth of these techniques, *factum valet,* postulates in like manner that "an action that is otherwise prohibited by a rule is to be treated as correct; it happens nevertheless" (1972, p 312 fn.).

what each participant imports into the situation (his age, status, relations with partners, etc.) and by the aims of the situation as they grow out of the interplay of the participants (their intentions and potentialities). The impact of the situation's preverbal structuring upon language behavior in a narrow sense can be traced with particular distinctness (and has been thoroughly studied) by means of the example of forms of address.

In her elaborate study of the ways people address each other in the United States, Ervin-Tripp (1972) identified seven forms of address which differ on formal counts: no particular address, first name, kin title plus first name, Mr/Mrs/Miss plus last name, and title plus last name (special cases, like addressing a clergyman, a president, or a judge, were left out from consideration). The choice of address form is mediated in the proposed model by any of 14 selectors (e. g., kin: yes/no; friend or colleague: of higher rank? 15 years older? married: yes/no;). In her model, Ervin-Tripp makes only a crude distinction between a status-marked and a status-unmarked situation. The number of selectors would increase greatly if we decided to introduce more subtle distinctions by, e. g., specifying the situation as one in which the speaker expects the addressee to do him a favor.

A fact of particular interest to us is that a large proportion of these selectors are represented, or even predetermined, by the nonverbally communicated involvement structure of the situation. Speaker and addressee both belong to externally identifiable groups, or profess to belong to them; the addressee indicates his readiness to enter into an exchange by choosing a suitable distance from the speaker and other people present, and the like.

If we go beyond the particular case of the form of address used into the broader field of discourse, we find that nonverbal clues are used by partners to negotiate a common style for a prospective conversation. Their choice of style may concern questions like dialect vs. standard speech, formal vs. informal style, or restricted vs. elaborated code – called so by Bernstein. But while in his earlier work Bernstein (1964) claimed that the person was a prisoner of the code imposed on him by his class, more recent investigations have cast this claim into doubt. The choice of code is thought to depend on the identity of the discourse partner and the purpose of the exchange as ensuing from the situation. Cazden (1970) found the structural complexity of utterances to grow with personal involvement in the conversation. Rickheit (1975) has shown that differences in the particular code variables in case of narrative, reporting, and descriptive speech cannot be fully accounted for by differences in social affiliation: evidently, the speaker enjoys some freedom in choosing the one code which seems to him most promising with regard to his objective.

Blom and Gumperz (1972) assign such choices of communicative style to a comprehensive theory of behavior which figures prominently in verbal communication:

> The determinants of this communicative process are the speaker's knowledge of the linguistic repertoire, culture, and social structure, and his ability to relate these kinds of knowledge to contextual constraints (p 422).

This reference to knowledge on the strength of which a suitable communicative strategy is chosen, pushes us again toward the notion of competence; in fact, Hymes (1970) called it communicative competence. It has been argued repeatedly in these pages that neither the notion of competence as such nor a multiplication of competences can contribute to a clarification of the problems to be accounted for by a theory of language use. Blom and Gumperz happen to go significantly beyond the postulation of just a norm, as implied by the competence concept:

> Behavioral regularities are no longer regarded as reflections of independently measurable social norms; on the contrary, these norms are themselves seen as communicative behavior (p 432).

The style adopted for discourse need not be regarded as a specific competence; instead, we might construe it as a (general) language game the choice of which is codetermined by the speaker's intention and (social) cognition as well as the repertoire of language games available to that speaker. The notion of language game enables us to take note of the gradual transition from the choice of a particular formal style for the forthcoming discourse to the choice of a "suitable" manner of communication for any individual speech act. As we know, nonverbal communication not only signifies such crude distinctions as between formal and informal style but also makes available clues from which the addressee may infer the intention of the speaker. Someone who approaches within 40 centimeters (1 ft. 4 in.) of me on a parking lot off a superhighway in Holland is more likely to suggest that I buy a watch from him at half price than to ask the way. That is, from nonverbal clues I gather what kind of speech act to expect, what kind of language game is to be played.

The predetermination of the forthcoming speech act by nonverbal information can be examined in terms of form as well as in terms of content. The formal aspect has to do with the segmentation of the speech act from the "stream of behavior", the substantive aspect with the constraints imposed on the choice of type of the prospective speech act. Our attention will now be turned to the formal aspect.

The notion of speech act as it occurs in this context is familiar to us from our attempt to amalgamate psychological presuppositions, intentions, expectations, and the like with the actual utterance into an entity that functions as a building block of communication. Underlining this structural quality of the proposed entity we would like to know how much and in what way nonverbal clues contribute to a separation of the speech act from preceding and subsequent processes.

The question of the temporal structuring and temporal delimitation of an utterance is far more important, and more debatable, in the practice of language use than many a linguist is prepared to admit in his confidence that a sentence starts with a capital letter and ends with a period. Time and again students of oral communication note their surprise – like De Long (1974, p 43) – at

> the incredible amount of sharing that takes place during communication [which] applies not only to the discrete properties (i. e., classes of behavior) but the continuous properties (i. e., the segmentation of the temporal continuum) as well.

It is therefore not so obvious why children of 4 or 5 are already capable of judging that a speaker has arrived at the end of an utterance and expects his partner to take turn, or that the speaker is only pausing to prepare for a further utterance. The boundaries of an utterance are often indiscriminable on purely linguistic grounds, which suggests that the hearer bases himself on some nonverbal clues when identifying the segmentation of the utterance as intended by the speaker.

Some time ago, Condon and Ogston (1966) demonstrated an interaction between the speaker's verbal behavior and the nonverbal behavior of his communication partner in regard to turn-taking, mutual eye contact being of crucial importance in this process. (The latter observation applies to the Anglo-American cultural sphere and may not hold for, say, the Arab world, where totally different norms of eye contact obtain – see Hall, 1966.) Kendon (1967) discovered a regularly recurring gaze pattern in a dyadic conversation: speaker A tends to look more and more at his partner B while approaching the end of his utterance; he is apt to maintain his gaze while B is starting to speak. At the same time, B begins to speak with his eyes turned away.

In case of a fault in this pattern, as for instance when A concludes his utterance without gazing at B, a marked delay in the conversation tends to ensue, or B may fail to respond altogether.

> Kendon found that speech while looking is faster and more fluent, and that gaze behavior at juncture pauses (defined grammatically) is distinctively different from that at hesitation pauses. Speakers tended to look at their interactants just before and during the first part of juncture pauses, but tended to look away during hesitation pauses. The listener complements this behavior by doing about half his looking during the speaker's juncture pauses (Duncan 1969, p 131).

On the basis of his investigations, Kendon has come to identify four functions of eye contact:

1) Cognitive: the speaker looks away in the case of difficulties with encoding

2) Monitoring: the speaker looks at his partner to indicate the termination of a unit of thought and to make sure that his partner is ready to take over

3) Regulative: eye contact serves either to spur the partner or to dissuade him from speaking

4) Expressive: gazing at the partner may communicate the speaker's excitement or involvement.

The four functions of eye contact described by Kendon may be again interpreted as four different but partially interwoven subsystems of communication.

In his study of kinesic activity in preschool children, De Long (1974) went far beyond the bounds of eye contact. He found a highly significant intensification of head, arm, hand, finger, and similar movements toward the termination of utterances, but not prior to or at the beginning of utterances. (The desire to speak is evidently signaled by postural shifting.) Such termination signaling consists mostly of downward and leftward movements. Much weaker kinesic activity indicates the termination of a phrase within an utterance than the end of the utterance itself. This means at the same time that such movements serve to signal the internal structure of a longer utterance, thus offering the hearer important clues for the segmentation of the utterance. In the same area falls Kendon's discovery that the interconnectedness of a string of words within an utterance is indicated by keeping the head motionless, i. e., in a nonverbal manner.

When discussing language acquisition in the next chapter, we shall realize how important it is for the construction proposed by Macnamara (1972) that the child can avail himself of such "auxiliary devices" in order to attribute the perceived structure of the utterance to what he has previously established, independent of language, as the meaning intended by the speaker.

A singularly attractive prospect emerges from one of De Long's secondary findings. Having divided the child's utterances into primarily other-directed and essentially self-directed ones, De Long (1974, p 65) compared the amount of kinesic activity at the ends of these utterances:

> As previously found, kinesic activity tends to increase significantly toward the ends of utterances, but only in the case of other-directed speech. Self-directed utterances did not display this characteristic!

One could scarcely think of a more eloquent example of the function of nonverbal regulators in verbal communication.

The importance of nonverbal regulators is even more striking in cases of verbal communication so primitive that it must be accompanied by supportive nonverbal communication in order to be effective. Rule (1967, pp 160–161) points to the fact that

> the least evolved human groups, e. g., the natives of the Kalahari desert, simple food gatherers and hunters, have a vocabulary estimated at eighty words, and their communications system is so embedded in posture and gesture that they have difficulty communicating in the dark[4].

Surveying the diverse examples of nonverbal communication, we seem to recognize that in most cases they comprise movements that impose temporal patterning on speech. We want to keep this in mind as we come "closer to language" in the further course of our argument.

When discussing the role of nonverbal factors in verbal processes we have repeatedly made the suggestion – however preposterous it may sound – that there is a smooth, gradual passage from the nonverbal to the verbal phenomena, and that it would be impossible (or at least impracticable) to draw a sharp dividing line between the linguistically coded, the nonlinguistically coded, and the entirely uncoded substance. Proceeding to discuss pausing phenomena, we would like to stress that only a very small step separates the above discussed movements-as-clues from the pauses interspersed in the flow of speech.

How important these pauses are in verbal communication follows from the fact that they take up from 40 to 50 per cent of the total duration of speaking and that variations in rate of speaking result overwhelmingly from changes in number and duration of pauses and only marginally from alterations in rate of articulation.

---

[4] For this reference I am indebted to Professor WF Angermeier of Cologne.

In the foregoing pages we examined the importance of nonverbal information for an identification of the (predominantly social) situation in which language events occur. While highly informative for the hearer, pauses tell him less about the social than the psychological or even physiological determinants of the speech event.

Before we go into the question of the information conveyed by pauses in speech, we must first find out what exactly gives rise to these pauses.

The relevant data have been supplied chiefly by Goldman-Eisler. Pauses observed in spontaneous speech obviously represent those segments of the total language event that are used for planning and selection, i. e., for generation of information. Depending on the number and duration of pauses, the rate of speaking is related to the probability structure of the words which precede the pause and those which follow it. This provides the first indication (to be supplemented with more compelling evidence) that it is in the course of these pauses that the kind of verbal planning takes place which the Russian psychologists of language have come to call "inner programming" or expansion of the time-compressed stage into the stage of either inner or outer speech.

How "far down" the structural determinants of pauses are anchored can be seen from a study by Goldman-Eisler (1967) in which rhythmic alterations of faster and slower speaking were recorded in what was generally slow speech (i. e., speech where pauses comprise more than 30 per cent of the time). Goldman-Eisler comments:

> It would seem therefore that even the most fluent passages of an output in rhythmic speech are under some kind of inhibitory restraint as compared with the fluent passages of non-rhythmic speech. This may indicate that here a negative feedback operates even after the executive phase, whereas in the non-rhythmic samples the acceleration is more absolute, the action impulsive, and the process seemingly uncontrolled (p 131).

Goldman-Eisler interprets the distinction between rhythmic speech (with alternating fluent and hesitant passages) and nonrhythmic speech by drawing an analogy with the distinction between movements that can be adjusted by feedback or afferent control while in progress and so-called ballistic movements which are set off by a brief and predetermined force to be executed in a fixed manner.

Encouraged by this analogy, we feel entitled to indulge in a speculation also suggested by some of our earlier arguments. As pointed out in Chaps. 6 and 7, the units in terms of which an utterance is "encoded" and "decoded" vary greatly in size: in some cases we have to fall back on a "word lexicon", in some other cases (e. g., idioms) the unit is made up of a word sequence that may not be further decomposed. Could the deep-rooted "anisotachy" of speaking be due to the incessant shifting from one level of analysis to another? Are "prefabricated", ready-made, molar sayings ("George is on the wagon") pronounced as a whole, i. e., in a "ballistic" manner, at one breath? Bearing in mind the work of Soviet psychologists of language on the one hand and the arguments of Craik and Lockhart (see Chap. 15) on the other, we seem to discern here a promising line of research. But for the time being we would rather stay on more familiar ground.

In her subsequent investigations, Goldman-Eisler (1972) succeeded in demonstrating an even closer dependence of pauses on the utterance's linguistic structure. She winds up by pointing out that

> the speaker who thinks on his feet organizes his message in highly cohesive sentence units with a clear hierarchical structure whereby constituent clauses are temporally integrated into the sentence frame, if by this we mean uttered with fluency, to a far greater extent than sentences are into the whole discourse. The degree of this temporal integration ... diminishes as we move from relative subordinate [who, which, whose], other subordinate [because, which, since, if] to coordinate clauses [and, but, or, therefore] (p 110).

The fact that transitions between sentences are nearly always marked by pauses

> indicates that a basic property is involved, marking sentences as distinct units of speech, occupying in the general stream of discourse a figure to ground position (p 111).

This conceptualization of the sentence in terms of figure to ground promises insights that by far exceed the context of the original formulation.

The figure-to-ground model of the sentence developed by Goldman-Eisler on the basis of her research on the distribution of pauses in the production of utterances invites further elaboration in the light of other, more "language-related" findings, whereby the particular productivity of this model might be demonstrated. The fact is that the rhythmic structure of the utterance comes into evidence not only in the varying rate of articulation and distribution of pauses but also in the alternation of stressed and unstressed syllables.

The most general finding is that the temporal distribution of the syllables produced within an utterance depends on what has preceded the given syllable as well as on the utterance as a whole. (A Markoff model would therefore be out of place here.) At the same time, the temporal organization of the utterance is dominated by its stressed elements. According to JG Martin (1972), these elements receive priority in planning, where

> planning means at least selecting the time at which syllables will be actualized ......
> one might think of accented syllables as the main targets in the organization of the articulatory program (p 499).

Martin maintains that the programming of the basic thematic structure of the sentence takes place during this early phase, a suggestion which opens up the prospect of cross-reference to the Soviet findings on the early phases of inner speech. Bearing in mind the arguments brought forward in Chap. 8 on the subject of generative semantics, one is tempted to elaborate Martin's ideas in more concrete terms as follows: Formed in line with the speaker's intention, the utterance's predicate-argument structure prescribes the upper branches of the tree diagram of rhythm[5] at a very early stage in the generation of an utterance, whereas the lower branches (which end up in function words) obtain their organization at some later point.

We are confronted here with an important line of development in the psychol-

---

[5] Martin shows in great detail how the accentuation is distributed over the sequence of interconnected units (either sounds or syllables) as decreed by the tree diagram.

ogy of language. Leaning heavily on Miller's chunk concept, NF Johnson (1965a) construed the planful organization of the utterance as a hierarchic process of coding by which higher-order units (phrases) are transposed into lower-level units down to the level of articulation. His model was subsequently revised and specified by Engelkamp (1973), who found these units to be of a semantic rather than syntactic nature: they can be more adequately described in terms of predicate-argument structure than in terms of syntactic deep structure.

Now we seem to discover a purely formal side of such semantic structure, and this consists in the distribution of accentuation over time.

Boomer and Laver (1968) showed that slips of the tongue in the form of reversals of syllables occurred most often with pairs of accented syllables, less often with pairs of unaccented syllables, and rarely with an accented and an unaccented syllable. From this and other evidence, Martin (1972, p 501) comes to the conclusion that "there is extensive information available at the rhythmic level that can be used by the listener".

In the light of these arguments we must recognize prosodic structure as a vital construct that might help us in bridging the gap which separates the child's understanding of the *speaker* from his understanding of the speaker's *utterances*. This has been convincingly shown in a study by Wakefield et al. (1974).

In the experiment, two groups of subjects listened to 16 test sentences in an unfamiliar language (Korean). Each sentence was presented twice: once with a pause interrupting a structural component (word or phrase) and once with such an interruption between components. The subjects were asked to identify the version of each sentence that "sounds more natural". Before the testing, subjects in group A listened for 27 minutes to a 3-minute recorded story (repeated nine times) in Korean, and subjects in group B to a similar story in Chinese (another unfamiliar language).

Result: Group A identified the natural segmentation pauses of the test sentences significantly better than group B. That is to say, listening to an unfamiliar language for even a limited period of time proved helpful in an identification of the components of this language. Furthermore, sentence constituents were more accurately identified than words. Evidently, these organizational units are of no lesser importance in the acquisition of a language than the content-carrying word units.

At this point, direct connections with Höpp's deliberations on the ontogeny of language present themselves, as well as with Bever's strategies of language acquisition; both issues will be discussed in the next chapter.

The crucial role of temporal segmentation effected by nonverbal clues in both the production and understanding of language is also recognized by AA Leontev (1969c, p 41): Full command of a nonnative language presupposes the assimilation of the peculiarities of nonverbal behavior that accompany language.

One is even more impressed by the experimental evidence offered by Ertel and Bloemer (1975) to the effect that verbal material is more effectively assimilated when accompanied by commensurate hand movements, while incommensurate movements interfere with verbal learning (for details see pp 58f.).

Let us sum up the insights gained from the analyses of pauses and accentuation for our general line of argument. Like any other human action, an utterance is subject to temporal patterning, and this runs parallel to a figure-to-ground segmentation of the constituents of this utterance (or indeed any action), i. e., a differentiation in their importance. The basic similarity of all types of actions in this respect (meaning their temporal organization as dictated by their respective functions) lies at the root of the fact that one kind of action may be substituted for another kind of action and that one may function as the sign of another.

When speaking of similarity in the temporal segmentation of verbal and nonverbal actions we certainly do not have a perfect synchronization in mind.

This correspondence – and area of transition – between nonverbal and verbal structures was long ago recognized by Wundt as an essential relationship: the sentence was viewed by him as possessing "psychological reality" and was thought of as a transformation of a simultaneous global representation *(Gesamtvorstellung)* into a sequential structure of words. In this way, Wundt took note of the seemingly unaccountable and certainly elusive transition from one temporal dimension to another, that subtle interlacement of what-we-have-simultaneously-in-consciousness and what is subject to sequential and hierarchic articulation. (The same interlacement is present in the transitions from one level of speech to the next as conceived in Soviet psycholinguistics.) This interlacement comes into evidence in the anisotachy of the flow of speech: its segmentation by pauses and stresses makes it possible to grasp simultaneous states of consciousness. We grasp meaning because the speaker-hearer's intention forces us to transgress the various temporal horizons of the utterance in search of the underlying message.

When approaching the utterance in terms of figure to ground, or identifying therein figures against a ground, we are back again to the relation between the general horizon of intelligibility and the portion particularized by the given utterance.

"Figure to ground" brings one more thing into view. The evidence contributed by physiologic and perception psychologists shows that the static figure-ground phenomenon is the product of highly dynamic processes, not of stationary conditions (the reversible figures being a case in point!). While employing this concept in our exploration of language processes in virtue of its formal and structural convenience, we must make sure that in the subsequent, predominantly thematically oriented chapters our attention is focused not on relations between static phenomena (as for instance sign/signified, or expression/expressed) but on the dynamic which a speaker directs at the hearer, or the hearer at the speaker, the very dynamic which underlies quasi-stationary phenomena of the figure-ground kind as an indispensable condition.

Chapter 12

The Genesis of Language

In the preceding chapter we tried to picture in rough outline how the processes of language unfold from a variety of essentially nonlinguistic (informational and communicative) processes, the latter being the supportive, structuring, and guiding matrix of the former. In doing so we chose a rather formal approach, culminating in a formal characterization of this relationship, namely, in figure-ground terms. In the present chapter we approach the same issue in terms of substance rather than form. Accordingly, we shall concern ourselves with the content or quality of what now begins to move from the stream of action into the space or medium of language. As before, the matter will be explored from a distinctly developmental perspective.

On more than one occasion we took care to balance the pitfalls underlying the study of the "genesis of language" against the insights to be gained from it. The fact is that, being in possession of linguistic "competence" like any adult, we stand little chance of learning anything of value about the substance or the "core" of an utterance if we fail to explore this core at a relatively early stage, i. e., before it is totally overwhelmed by what tends to build up around it in the course of development. In saying this we must bear in mind that our view as expressed in the foregoing sentence is based on a string of assumptions and hence stands or falls on the insights it might hopefully yield.

The following seems to be a singularly promising line of attack. On examining with Bronowski (1967, 1970) the various distinguishing marks commonly considered in the debate on "Do animals have a language?", we discover that most of these criteria are of little use in drawing a sharp dividing line between animal and human language – whereby we are reminded of Lenneberg's arguments as quoted in Chap. 3. Still, one of Bronowski's (1967, p 375) criteria is of particular relevance on account of its general validity:

> the signals that animals make are (like most animal reactions) too direct and total, too immediate, to make them capable of the constructive assembly which characterizes human speech and thought.

In effect, the ability to insert a delay between the arrival of the signal and the issuance of a (verbal or nonverbal) response constitutes for Bronowski "the central and formative feature in the evolution of human language" (p 381).

This emphasis on temporal delay as a constituent of language is important in a number of ways. For one, it signifies a total rejection of any S−R model of language learning (which does not provide for any "temporal buffer", except perhaps by the hazy concept of mediation). The same kind of delaying and shifting device is implied by Wundt's concept of sentence, which posits a transformation of a simultaneous "global representation" *(Gesamtvorstellung)* into a word sequence. A similar emphasis, based on arguments not unlike Bronowski's, can be found in ideas expounded by proponents of Korzybski's General Semantics, who view their construct as a precondition for the humane use of human language. Finally, there is the repeatedly mentioned aspect of delay: the bringing to conscious awareness of signal-*cum*-response.

According to Bronowski, this delay has resulted in or has been the result of:

(a) The progressive separation of emotional charge from the content of the message

(b) Prolongation, i. e., the ability to refer backward and forward in time (to propose action in the future)

(c) The internalization of language (Vygotsky), by which language becomes an instrument of reflection

(d) The capacity for analysis as well as synthesis, or reconstitution from parts which do not exist in advance.

Thus the ability to disengage, if only for moments, from the incessant flow of stimuli and responses constitutes a basis for the characteristically human "creative", reconstitutive uses of language.

From which it follows that the study of animal communication is most likely to tell us something – if anything at all – about the functions and functioning of *human* language in cases where the capacity for such a delay is vested already in the neurophysiology of the animal, i. e., in the primates. It is in primates that we find the disengagement from the immediate stimulus, as manifested in curiosity.

A further corollary of Bronowski's reasoning is that the communicative behavior of primates ought to be investigated in a manner that would encourage and prompt their capacity for delay, on the understanding that the investigation would be primarily aimed at exploring *human* language rather than at studying the "normal" modes of communication in primates (an interesting topic in its own right, no doubt). In the present context we would like to know how primates may be induced to communicate in conditions that enforce delay and provide them with a suitably tailored means of communication.

And so we come to speak of the two young females: the Gardners' Washoe and Premack's Sarah.

In view of the failure of earlier efforts to teach apes to speak (Kellogg, Hayes), the Gardners deemed it wise to bypass the apparent bottleneck, i. e., the apes' articulatory apparatus, and to rely instead on the chimpanzee's remarkable manipulatory abilities. They began to teach American Sign Language – as used by deaf-mute persons – to Washoe, a young female chimp. This "teaching" was effected in much the same way as in the case of children: every day, for long hours, Washoe was in the company of a person who tried to communicate with her, commenting on what she was doing, putting questions, and reacting to her "utterances". This procedure proved successful to an extent neither fully anticipated by the Gardners nor even remotely admitted, in their worst nightmares, by those linguists who shared Chomsky's view that "acquisition of even (the) barest rudiments (of language) is quite beyond the capacities of an otherwise intelligent ape" (1968, p 59). After a time, Washoe was found to communicate, also spontaneously, with her environment, and after three and a half years she could use something like 85 signs in combinations up to five in succession. From that moment no one could seriously claim that the capacity for language is present either all-of-a-piece or not at all (see the discussion in Chap. 3).

In order to obtain some evidence bearing on the question raised at the outset of this chapter (namely: What exactly is subject to this progression from the realm of actions into the medium of language?) we shall have to examine in some detail Washoe's communicative feats. What exactly did she learn?

Free-living chimpanzees make use of their various means of communication chiefly to signal their affective and motivational states. Nothing is known about "cognitive performance" that would enable them to segment their environment into elements or aspects and label the isolated elements with definite names.

This is precisely what the human child does (in his *Psychology of Early Childhood,* originally published in 1914, William Stern described the child's realization that each thing has its name as the most important discovery of his life). And this is what Washoe is able to do. She learned the sign for *open* initially in relation to a particular door. Without specific training she immediately began to apply the same sign to other closed doors, and also to closed containers, briefcases, drawers, and eventually also to make people open a bottle of lemon juice or turn on the water-tap for her.

The phenomenon of "word generalization", clearly unaccountable in terms of conventional learning theory, has thus been observed in Washoe, an ape raised in a strictly controlled environment.

Evidently, Washoe is able to anchor the newly acquired sign in something that has existed in her before; for lack of a better term, let us call this "something" her *cognitive structure.*

The problem at hand has been commonly approached the other way around, of course. Investigators have been in the habit of inquiring: How does the child (or perhaps the animal) form the concept that corresponds to the given word? Or else: How does a child learn the meaning of a word? We now realize that the problem ought to be rephrased like this: A particular cognitive structure (e. g., *open*) seems to pervade in preverbal form much of what can and needs to be opened. That is to say, the action of opening and its cognitive counterpart have come to form an entity by being isolated preverbally from the flow of events. Hence we ought to put the question with Nelson (1974, p 268) in the following way: "How does the child [or, in this case, Washoe] match words to his concepts?"

We might also try to express the same reversal of the problem in the terminology of generative linguistics by asking: How does the child assign utterances to meanings? Such a formulation presupposes the primacy of *semantic* deep structure. This in turn underlines the importance of a "generative semantics" which, by conceiving deep structure as being semantic, paves the way to a sensible psychological discussion of language acquisition. We have come to realize this already in our inquiry into nonverbal communication, and the same will become apparent in the following pages; indeed, the arguments advanced in the present chapter could not be formulated without the work of the generative semanticists.

Once we assume the preverbal existence of a unitary cognitive structure *(open)*, we are in a better position to understand how a word used as a label for one particular instance of the structure (a token of the given type) comes to match the entire structure with all its particular instances at once.

Such a *preverbal nucleus* of what subsequently, at a later stage of development, will come to be identified as *meaning,* forms undoubtedly the initial phase in Macnamara's (1972, p 1) model of language learning, where it is claimed that

> infants learn their language by first determining, independent of language, the meaning which a speaker intends to convey to them, and by then working out the relationship between the meaning and the language.

In advocating thus the primacy of cognitive over linguistic structures, one is compelled to give some thought again to the controversial issue of *nativism vs. empiricism,* which has been repeatedly raised in these pages (see Chap. 3).

The logic followed by the extreme nativists can be most aptly illustrated by Katz's (1966) reasoning:
1st premise: There are linguistic universals.
2nd premise: There are no psychological or sociological factors cutting across all human cultures and languages that could be held responsible for the observed uniformities of human learning. Conclusion: All linguistic universals are therefore part of man's genetic endowment.

A few years later, McNeill (1970, p 2) wrote in much the same vein that

> virtually everything that occurs in language acquisition depends upon *prior* knowledge of the basic aspects of sentence structure. The concept of a sentence may be part of man's innate mental capacity.

Well, this is how you arrive at the conclusion that the concept of a sentence (a linguistic concept, no doubt) is vested in man's biologic constitution.

The principal weakness of the inference lies in what is posed above as Katz's second premise. The point is that man's development *is* codetermined by certain psychological factors; these factors, though underpinned by innate mental dispositions (but not necessarily linguistic ones), are crucially dependent upon learning and maturation. Having taken note (at the end of the preceding chapter) of the parallelism between cognitive and linguistic structures – identified already by Wundt – we find it natural that these primarily cognitive structures should eventually acquire a linguistic character; indeed, such an assumption eliminates the discomfort felt at the suggestion that the sentence might be part of our genetic endowment.

There is a valid reason for dampening the more radical claims of the nativists: A thorough examination of human psychological development (in ontogeny as well as phylogeny) reveals that some more or less universal linguistic structures need not be fully determined by biology, being rather the outgrowth of cognitive structures that take shape in the course of the child's interaction with his environment against the background of his dispositions[1].

That the development of cognitive, and hence also linguistic structures is largely, but not wholly, determined by the human genetic endowment has been argued for decades by Piaget. An interaction of native and empirical factors can be traced even in his conception of the earliest, preverbal stage of cognitive development known as "sensorimotor intelligence".

Extending roughly from the 6th to the 18th month of life, this stage is marked by a progressive coordination of sensory and motor acts. An external event, after transformation into sensory data, becomes the input into an internal schematic structure which thrives on the "assimilation" of the data. The motor output of the schematic structure produces an "accommodation" in the external event. Thus the child learns about the world by interacting with it. An exploratory interaction with what gradually emerges as object and action produces modifications in the internal schema controlling the interaction. For instance, an infant sucks the nipple, and he tends to apply the same schema to other objects (finger, pillow, etc.). Such an assimilation of new objects into the schema already represents a kind of amplification of the genetically determined category of "suckable" objects. On the other hand, assimilation results inevitably in an accommodation of the action itself: the motor actions involved in sucking the finger are not the same as in sucking the nipple.

Such an amalgamation of reception and action is likely to have formed around a genetically-founded core in the form of some figure/ground distinction, or some reflex, but the core itself is subject to modification by experience. The progressing coordination of perception and activity, as expressed in progressively perfected actions, is construed by Piaget as intelligence, or the earliest form of knowledge.

Much the same function is attributed by Bruner (1972) to the play of primates and infants. Examining in detail the great variety of integrated manipulations and perceptions that enable the chimpanzee to familiarize itself with a tennis ball, Bruner (1972, p 10) comes to this conclusion:

---

[1] The problem in question runs in linguistics and psycholinguistics under the heading "strong or weak linguistic universals", ever since this distinction was proposed by McNeill (1970). A strong universal points to a specifically linguistic ability which need not be related to any (more general) cognitive ability; in the case of a weak universal, a given cognitive ability is a necessary and sufficient precondition for the particular linguistic universal. That such "weak linguistic universals" do exist is taken a matter of course by the psychologist today. As argued by Lakoff (1973, quoted after Wasow 1973), the issue whether there are strong universals or not is of little concern to the generative semanticist, for whom the deep structure of the sentence is primarily a semantic, and hence cognitive (e. g., Chafe), structure.

These initial acts are then modified in a systematic manner to fulfill further requirements of the task. The acts themselves have a self-rewarding character. They are varied systematically, almost as if in play, to test the limits of a new skill.

Referring to a stage in which there is as yet no distinction between *knowing how* and *knowing that,* the key term *skill* provides the link between Piaget's theoretical work and what has been repeatedly stressed in the pages of Chaps. 9 and 11: that the nucleus of the knowledge, or cognition, from which language emerges is contained in *the perception- and action-based act.*

These time-spanning sensorimotor coordinations presuppose the child's (or Washoe's) ability to construct a "neuronal model", or a kind of memory representation of the stimulus, as conceived by EN Sokolov (1960, 1963).

The neurophysiologist Sokolov has developed this notion to account for the genesis of the orienting reflex: once an appropriate neuronal model has been formed, an oft-repeated stimulus no longer evokes the orienting reflex; the reflex reappears in case of some modification in the stimulus, e. g., a rise in its intensity.

A mentalist counterpart of this neurophysiological concept can be traced in William James' remark that the exclamation *Thingumbob again* marks a fundamental human (though presumably also a primate) ability – the ability to identify the recurrent elements of the environment. The human being (and Washoe) is capable of constructing permanence out of the flow of events, later also the flow of linguistic events. The phenomenon has been termed *establishment of constancy* (Hörmann, 1971a, pp 275f.), in an effort to stress that this is a process determined at least partially at will. (The more familiar notion of memory implies a more automatic encoding and storing.) A constancy established in this way may be subsequently revoked or cancelled.

Bronowski seems to have a similar thing in mind when he speaks of *prolongation* as an essential characteristic of human language.

In Piaget's theory we find for this the term *object permanence.* In the stage of sensorimotor intelligence the child gains the ability – as a result of his experience with the *groupes de déplacements,* i. e., the coordinated modifications in action and perception – to make rapid shifts of focus in his interactions with the environment; in all these shifts, one thing remains constant: the particular object. This is how the genetically determined biologic groundwork of the process becomes elaborated with the accumulation of experience.

Taking sides in the great nature-nurture controversy, the Gestalt psychologists of the Berlin school were inclined to attribute greater importance to the biologic groundwork, in contrast to, say, Hebb (1949) who regards the figure/ground distinction as innate, but the development of phase sequences as due to learning. However the case may be, here lie the sources of the

human capacity for analyzing and manipulating the environment in the mind by sub-dividing it into units that persist when they are moved from one mental context into another (Bronowski and Bellugi 1970, p 673).

This capacity for structuring seems to be closely related to the figure-ground articulation discussed in the preceding chapter. But whereas the latter-type segmentations are *enforced* by the physical properties of the stimulus and the physiological mechanisms of the brain, we are now concerned with the kind of structuring a human being acquires through his successful interactions with the world. And there is always an element of arbitrariness in these interactions.

This underlying capacity is not a human monopoly: it is likewise present in Washoe, and in Sarah. As pointed out by Premack (1970), Sarah is in a position to arrange the plastic tokens (each representing one word) into meaningful sequences because

> the word ... reflects some of the most basic features of experience, among them the consensus that perceptual experience can be divided into stable elements (p 110).

Asserting, on the other hand,

> We are not free in how to divide this situation. We are free to choose the situation but not free in our choice of how to divide it (p 112),

Premack is certainly right at the "lowest level". The forefeet of an animal (Quine's example!) are more likely to merge into a figure than a part of a forefoot plus a portion of the ground, for no other than purely physiological reasons. But what about Washoe's *open?* Would this cognitive structure have arisen in an environment totally deprived of things that could be opened? How far does our freedom go in subdividing reality? Is the distinction between useful plants and weeds anything other than a human way of looking at vegetation? At this point many similar questions come to mind:

1) Is the freedom to impose an alternative structure on events in the environment (including language events) by any chance a distinctive mark of human language as contrasted with "animal language", including Washoe's and Sarah's? (If so, then animals would not be able to make the choice between idioms and literal meanings.)

2) How are these problems related to the Whorfian hypothesis and the issue of "systematic" and „accidental" gaps in the vocabulary? (cf. Chap. 5).

Be that as it may, object permanence emerges as a first invariant (Sinclair-de Zwart 1969), as the earliest form of knowledge, from the sensorimotor act. The schema of a persistent object is constituted as the representation of a thing, and this representation may in turn become the point where a semiotic function becomes entrenched through the matching of words to concepts[2].

With his notion of object permanance, Piaget happens to restrict the applicability of this all-important process to an uncomfortable degree. The establishment of constancy is by no means limited to *objects:* it applies to *actions* in equal measure. In the same way that an object retains its identity after a *groupe de déplacements speciales,* so does an action even when undertaken in a new (spatio–temporal) situation. Not only does the object *milk bottle* acquire its permanence in space and time; the same can be said of *sucking* as an action. Nothing

---

[2] The emergence of sensorimotor invariants and the controlling function of such invariants are also stressed in JJ Gibson's theory of perception. For instance, the stimulation that corresponds to a three-dimensional visual percept does not consist of a particular stimulus but rather of some invariant relations between otherwise variable stimuli (cf. Gibson 1950, 1966).

short of such an expansion of the scope within which constancy is established will enable us to comprehend – at a later stage – semantic relations (of the agent–action–object type, for instance).

While it is perfectly possible to have an action established as a constancy at one or another point of a sensorimotor act, man's physiological constitution obviously gives preference to those entities that are made up of simultaneous, and not only of successive configurations. There are two constancies that tend to emerge from the flow of events at a very early stage: the *agent of action* and the goal, or *object of action*.

The use of nouns *(agent, goal, object)* might suggest that the constancy thus formed relates static objects, and that it derives its (formal) dynamic from some other source. Nothing would be farther from the truth. What is in fact meant is that a particular role played in a particular action becomes constant and so becomes useful in other actions, too. This idea is not unlike certain constructs proposed by linguists: Fillmore, for instance, employed the drama allegory to state his case for case. We disagree with linguists, however, as long as they claim – as does Chomsky and the other LAD champions, notably McNeill – that grammatical relations (whereby they mean syntactic relations, of course) are already predominant in the first utterances of the child. The inevitable conclusion of this claim is that the underlying grammatical skills are innate, i. e., are part of the Language Acquisition Device (LAD). In substantiation of this position it can be further asserted that in view of the inadequate input into LAD, the child lacks the opportunity of acquiring grammar by learning (no learning theory being able to offer a reasonable account of the process). The spurious character of this argumentation has been cogently demonstrated by Schlesinger (1971 b).

Those who postulate the primacy of linguistic form cannot escape the awkward question as to how the child "entering" his language environment might succeed in associating a linguistic form with the underlying action role. As we know, LAD stands or falls on its *linguistic* input, there being no question of any preverbal knowledge or preverbal structuralizations[3].

Taking a different path, we want to join company partway with those investigators (to name but Schlesinger, Macnamara, Bloom, and Nelson) who see these roles not in primarily linguistic terms, but in terms of cognitive and act psychology. Under this approach, the various action roles are not endowed with the corresponding linguistic forms until the child has learned to employ linguistic designations and syntactic relations for marking the conceptual vectors of the interactions between speaker and hearer.

Assuming a primarily semantic determination of early child utterances (by concepts such as agent, action, direction, patient, location,) we have to face up to the problem of how the child acquires the ability to refer to these intentions and relations through the medium of the linguistic structures that characterize the

---

[3] The evolution of the LAD concept has been superbly described by Levelt (1975), who also points out the strict correspondence between LAD and the notion of competence.

utterances of the older child and adult. In such a framework there is no longer a place for the argument that the unavailability of an adequate learning theory (classical and operant conditioning being just as useless for the purpose as imitation) precludes the possibility that learning *is* taking place.

Fillmore, Chafe, and others have offered linguistic evidence of the nature of such invariant role concepts. Piaget has demonstrated – without going into the problems of language – how the genesis of cognitive concepts may be construed by the psychologist. At present we are turning for further evidence to the psychology of language acquisition, or "developmental psycholinguistics".

The kind of concepts that are of special interest to us are *intrinsically relational;* these are concepts that need not be interrelated by some content-free, purely formal (syntactic) mechanism. The question raised at the beginning of this chapter may now be specified as follows:

a) What evidence is there of the various conceptual roles?

b) How does a conceptual role relate to its linguistic manifestation in an utterance?

Before learning to speak, the child learns to understand language. Well, how? We know Macnamara's (1972) answer to this question almost by heart by now: the child first learns to determine what the speaker means and only then can he use these intentions as a key to his eventual command of the linguistic code. The speaker's intentions thus represent the input in this particular model of language acquisition. Schlesinger, one of the most influential proponents of the model, has formalized this input as Intention (I) marker – in analogy to the P markers of the orthodox generativists. Such I-markers serve to describe concepts in their mutual relations. Let us test the approach by examining the intentions contained in an (adult's) utterance addressed to a child, such as:

JOHN IS CATCHING A RED BALL.

The most general intention is to describe or report (even more generally: to direct the child's attention to) something that is going on right then, in other words, to bring to the hearer's awareness a particular event. Thus, to produce the utterance contrasts with two other possibilities: to abstain from directing the child's awareness to anything (i. e., to say nothing), or to direct his awareness elsewhere. In most general terms, the speaker's intention is first of all of an imperative kind: he wishes to direct the hearer's awareness to a particular object or event.

Having thus arrived at a crucial juncture in the genesis of language, we feel entitled to pursue the matter further by putting the question: Does language start with an imperative? An affirmative answer seems justified by the following arguments:

a) the deliberations of Macnamara and Schlesinger (adduced above)

b) Höpp's (1970) investigation of the evolution of language and reason.

For Höpp, the evolution of language starts with what he calls *Einerspruch*[4]

---

[4] The term *word* sounds too much like an assembly part (Höpp) to use it in a discussion of the origins of language. *Einerspruch* is conceived by Höpp as a self-contained unit of language of the lowest order.

("one-say"). The "one-say" is man's acoustic tool "with which individual contributions to consonant or labor-sharing actions are mobilized" (1970, p 7).

This is where Höpp concurs with Wittgenstein (1953, p 3), who singles out the exclamation "Slab!" from the action game shared by two builders, and also with Vygotsky and his Marxist followers.

The imperative "one-say" is complemented by an equally imperative proper name. The latter is used to attract attention and summon the addressee; subsequently, it serves to exclude all other hearers from the conveyed message and hence to adjust the language processes to the division of labor.

In order to understand how the "two-say" *(Zweierspruch)* came into being we have to follow Höpp in his analysis of an individual's behavior and to distinguish with him between two identifiable components: the releasing sensory impression, and the movement of the human subject relative to the object, i. e., the action itself. The same division is applicable to labor-sharing cooperation: the speaker may confine himself to the sensory impression and – rather than entirely foregoing the consequent action – delegate its execution to the addressee. At this stage the speaker's own movement is substituted by communication:

> Under this form of action the speaker is able to act "indirectly" without changing his own position in that he confines himself to the non-exchangeable part (the sensory impression) and employs communication to shift the execution of the exchangeable part to another person (1970, p 14).

Höpp's fascinating conception is not unrelated to Bloomfield's knotting together of the two action components (practical and verbal). But its main relevance for us lies in the emphasis on the action-structuring processes of nonverbal and preverbal communication as discussed in the preceding chapter.

Thus it is the imperative nature of the earliest utterances that paves the way to the dualization of object and action – which is to be seen as an important elaboration of Piaget's concepts of object and self. Moreover, here we have the beginning of that dualization of the world-as-reflected-in-language into entities and events/states/processes upon which Chafe has based his semantic structures.

Most importantly, however, we note here the intentionality and directionality of human actions as crucial elements of language acquisition, though unlike Höpp we would regard the imperative less as an intervention in the addressee's actions than as an attempt at influencing his conscious awareness. For there is always an element of injunction in language communication: "This is what I want you to think".

Now back to early language acquisition. The preverbal child is able to grasp the speaker's intention insofar as he can follow the situation in which both action and utterance take place. The child is able to follow the situation, and fall in with it, because he is guided by the pattern of pauses and accentuation that serves to separate the important from the unimportant for the child, and which endows the situation with a goal gradient. (The findings by Goldman-Eisler and JG Martin discussed at the end of the preceding chapter are highly relevant here.) Try to read to the child an isolated sentence from a book, and you'll find that he can make no sense of it.

Going further into the intentions of the speaker of our specimen sentence, we realize that the utterance was meant to communicate to the child that John is involved in a particular action performed on an object (ball). The child may grasp this intention only if he is in possession of a sensorimotor schema that is sufficiently articulated to make him discriminate between two entities of which one plays the more active and the other the more passive role[5]. The agent of an action can be fairly easily identified as a figure standing out against an undifferentiated ground. One reason is perceptual: it is associated with the fact that a moving object is perceived as a figure precisely because it is moving as a whole. Another reason is the communicative counterpart of the latter phenomenon: people tend to speak primarily of what has just changed, or is in the process of changing, rather than of what has been constant for some time. (Cf. Nelson 1974, p 281, and also Osgood's study of "simply describing", discussed in Chap. 13.)

The differentiation between an (active) agent and a rather passive object, as the goal of the action, is rooted in the processes singled out by Piaget in his analysis of object genesis. That the differentiation reaches a very advanced level in comprehension before coming into evidence in language production, was demonstrated by Huttenlocher, Eisenberg, and Straus (1968) in their study in which young children were induced to act out with toys sentences like

THE GREEN TRUCK IS PUSHING THE RED TRUCK
THE RED TRUCK IS PUSHED BY THE GREEN TRUCK.

In this kind of task one of the toy trucks is fixed while the other is to be moved in relation to it. The children were found to perform much better when they had to move the truck described as the agent in the sentence than when the action had to be performed on the object of the sentence.

Much of what has been said about the concept *agent* so far applies in principle also to the concept *object-of-action*. The respective development has been traced by Nelson (1974, pp 277f.) on the example of *ball*, starting with the stage at which the child is in the process of establishing the constancy of an object around which his interaction with the environment centers, in this case with the mother. (Naturally, object is one of several possible centers of interaction, alternative centers being agent and action.) In neurophysiologic terms, the entire process rests on some hitherto unexplored mechanisms of attention focusing.

In one of the interactions with a ball, Nelson (1974, p 277) made the following observation:

Out of this interaction emerge the following actions and relationships:

$$
\text{Ball}_1 \begin{bmatrix} \text{In living room, porch} \\ \text{Mother throws, picks up, holds} \\ \text{I throw, pick up, hold} \\ \text{Rolls, bounces} \\ \text{On floor, under couch} \ldots \end{bmatrix}
$$

---

[5] Höpp distinguishes between action word (which embodies the sensations produced by our own movements) and object word (which comprises both the distance-induced and the contact-induced sensations).

The formation of the *ball* concept begins with the emergence of a cognitive map (Tolman) made up of dynamic relations between the particular object and the child himself, or the mother, or various locales and developments. All these relations tend to covary, by which the reciprocal delineation of the diverse roles is facilitated. What remains constant from this particular vantage point is the object, but its constancy is always relational, i. e., it is the object of a particular action, not object per se.

Nelson does not fail to stress that at this early stage a concept emerges always from the child's interactions with the world. It is only by such a stabilization that the child acquires the means of recognizing things when they recur, to compare them across space and time, and to utilize them in the further delineation of roles. Once the child has entered upon his cognitive map the data extracted from another situation with a ball:

$$\text{Ball}_2 \begin{bmatrix} \text{On playground} \\ \text{Boy throws, catches} \\ \text{Rolls, bounces} \\ \text{Over ground, under fence} \ldots \end{bmatrix}$$

the process is one of reciprocal delineation of the *different* balls and their *integration* into the concept of ball.

This kind of concept has a functional core. In Nelson's (1974, p 278) own words:

> from the child's interactions with people and objects, specific concepts emerge, each of which is composed of a functional core synthesized from the various relationships and acts into which each concept enters[6].

The finding that the functional core of a concept contains relational information may well prove useful, at a later stage, in exploring the relationship between word and sentence.

Having followed the process by which concepts such as *agent of action* or *object of action* are constituted, from the flow of the child's global activity, as dynamic centers of action, we can easily conceive how other concepts of this early type emerge in the course of actions. Cross-language comparisons have revealed a marked consistency in the underlying semantic relations. In Bowerman (1973, p 208) we find the following list:

> agent-action, action-object acted upon, object located-location, possessor-possessed, and demonstrator-demonstrated.

Among the primary "stabilizations" are also spatial ones, as shown by the case of a child whose first five words included *up*. Taking note that, on the very day the word appeared in the child's vocabulary, *up* was used for every vertical movement performed by the child or by any object, we are immediately reminded of two things:

---

[6] Personally, I would prefer to say: ". . . synthesized from the various relationships and acts in which each concept functions", in order to articulate the fact that prior to such relationships and acts the concept does not exist.

a) that Washoe was able to apply the sign for *open* without special training to a variety of situations that fitted this conceptual structure, and

b) that the emergence of such relational links is accounted for by Piaget by the interaction between the self and the environment, and less by passive observation of the environment.

Nelson (1974, p 281) comments on this issue:

> Thus the child would use the word *[up]* to name and identify a function, but the actors and objects involved in the function would neither be part of the concept nor would they be separately named – they would act as part of the ground for this conceptual figure.

What seems certain at this stage is that before the child can start to use language actively he must go through a stage of cognitive development in the course of which he employs preverbal procedures to single out, from the flow of events in which he is immersed and engaged, what for him are the recurring points of reference. It remains to be seen how the child succeeds in picking from the linguistic input those designations of language that conform to the identified points of reference.

To accomplish the feat, the child has to identify the intention of the (adult) speaker, argues Schlesinger. A prerequisite for this, and also for Macnamara's progression from the meaning conveyed by the speaker to the relation between meaning and language, is the explicitness of the speaker's intention. And indeed, the speaker's intention *is* quite explicit in all those situations where any language learning takes place (in the early stages of language acquisition). The young child might be exposed for hours and days to, say, conversations on political developments in an exotic country without the slightest profit for his language skills. There is presumably a kind of filter that eliminates from the child's linguistic input all that is not really addressed to him (cf. Ervin-Tripp 1971).

In fact, utterances addressed to children differ radically from those addressed to adults, as research on maternal style has shown (Snow 1977). In a study of the language of parents, Drach (1969, quoted after Ervin-Tripp 1971, p 192) found the mother of a young child to employ over two and a half times as many passive constructions, conjoined phrases, and subordinate clauses in her address to adults as to her 2-year-old son. Speech directed to children is markedly lacking in hesitations, false starts, and errors, while abounding in repetitions, either in identical or in paraphrased form.

Moreover, clause boundaries are emphasized and intonation is "overdone". Eve Clark (according to Levelt 1975) found virtual conversation games being diligently and thoroughly practiced by parent and child.

As we combine these findings with what was said in the preceding chapter about the steering devices of nonverbal communication, the inescapable conclusion is that adults construct their utterances to language-learning children in such a way as to ensure that the structure of the intention can be easily recognized in the structure of the utterance[7]. Practically everything that is said to the young

---

[7] This notion contrasts sharply with the concept of LAD, where it is assumed that the speech

child is so intimately tied up with the current flow of events that the utterance itself carries little information. To the extent that the situation is understood by the child (who is now past the early stage described above) he is free to use his understanding in his attempts to grasp the linguistic code. *It is because the child knows what the speaker means that the utterance becomes meaningful.*

At this early stage of language learning there is a distinct asymmetry between the acts of meaning and understanding: the child must first learn to grasp the meaning intended by the speaker by "looking through" the latter's utterance before he can start to convey, by means of language, his own intended meaning. Bloom (1973, pp 55–56) says accordingly:

> Children learn that objects are acted upon, that people or movable objects do things, that objects and events exist, cease to exist, and recur. This is the basis of perceptual-cognitive experience in the early years, and so it should not be surprising that these are the kinds of things that children talk about in early speech. But whereas children need to learn a linguistic code for talking about such phenomena as relations among objects and events in the world, knowledge of the code is not necessary for their understanding such relations.

The enormous redundancy of child-directed adult utterances is thus a prerequisite for the child's grasping of the relations between the speaker's intention and the utterance made in this situation. Since he knows what the speaker means, the child may explore the relation between intended meaning and utterance in order to learn how to express his own intended meaning in the medium of language. As Schlesinger puts it, the child grasps the situation in terms of I-markers and now has to learn the realization rules by which these I-markers are transformed into verbal utterances.

A characteristic feature of adult speech to children is the high frequency of comprehension-promoting questions and orders. Whereas in ordinary family conversation questions account for from 1 to 25 per cent of utterances, in utterances directed to young children the share of questions may come to as much as 50 per cent. Bearing in mind the dovetailing of action and language, we come to realize that it is through this "original word game" so elegantly described by Brown (1958b) that names are assigned to those "enclosures" of dynamic entities whose genesis we tried to depict in the preceding pages.

It was just stated that the redundancy of an utterance is needed and utilized by the child to identify the linguistic realization of the speaker's intended meaning. Hence the child must be in possession of a cognitive "meaning" in order to be able to acquire the corresponding linguistic form (word or construction). (Here a reminder of the typical view: "The child has to learn the meaning of words.") If this is so, then enormous difficulties must arise if the learner is forced to start his language learning (whether it is the first, the second, or a foreign language) with

---

to which a child is exposed represents a random sample from the corpus of spoken language. And since ordinary spoken language is said to be full of errors, nothing else but LAD can ensure that the linguistic competence is filtered out from the error-burdened samples ... Cf. also Levelt (1975).

meaningless linguistic structures. Compelling evidence to this effect has been offered in two studies.

In one, Moeser and Bregman (1972) had college students learn an artificial language that formed a miniature system of phrase structure rules with nonsense syllables as "words". The authors linked their study to Chomsky's (1965, p 33) claim that

> semantic reference may greatly facilitate performance in a syntax-learning experiment, even though it does not, apparently, affect the *manner* in which acquisition of syntax proceeds.

Subjects learned the artificial language in one of four conditions. In the first condition, the "words" of the language referred to nothing whatsoever. In the second condition, each sentence referred to a picture created out of geometric forms, but the association of words with pictorial features was arbitrary. In the third condition, there was the same kind of pictorial reference, while the words belonging to a particular syntactic class referred to items belonging to the same visual class. The fourth condition was like the third but, in addition, the syntactic constraints in the sentences mirrored the logical constraints in the pictures. Moeser and Bregman obtained clear-cut results (p 759):

> Learning of complex features of syntax was possible only when these reflected properties of, or constraints in, the reference field.

Contrary to Chomsky's claims, the *manner* of learning was found to depend on the presence or absence of semantic reference. The authors reported the following (p 769):

> In the semantically empty condition, words are mapped directly onto sentence positions (position learning strategy); in the semantic reference condition, words are associated to relevant aspects of the reference field and the field is structured into a meaningful organization, and then this semantic information is used in the mapping process. . . . it is only when the elements in the reference field mirror the syntactic constraints of the language that complex grammatical conditions are easily acquired.

Perhaps even more striking is the second piece of evidence, quoted here after Ervin-Tripp (1971, p 195). A self-instructional program for learning Russian was administered over seventeen weeks to students (members of the armed forces), with no meanings being given for the first month. Instead, there were drills in writing, discrimination, and imitating syllables and phrases in Russian. Late in the program meaning clues were added to the workbook incidentally. At the end of the program the students scored below chance on the Army language achievement test for Russian. Thereupon, the students entered the usual intensive program for learning Russian along with other students with no experience at all in Russian. The students initially trained without meaning "remained worse throughout the program and never were able to learn as well as the neophytes", writes Ervin-Tripp.

With our (perhaps overoptimistic) attempt at demonstrating the plausibility of the thesis that the formation of cognitive entities and relations must precede the acquisition of linguistic designations, we run the danger of underestimating the epistemological pitfalls of the problem under discussion. When challenged with the question: "How can you tell what the child's actual knowledge of language is?", investigators have diligently dug up evidence of the child's use of one-word sentences, on the assumption that the child's own production is the best indicator of his (tacit) knowledge of language.

The notion of *one-word sentence* (or holophrastic utterance) implies that the child's earliest utterances are not just single words – for instance, serving to name objects – but that they reflect the presence of the concept of sentence (by which we are reminded of McNeill's position), a concept that cannot, however, be fully realized because of limited processing capacities. In other words, the competence is there, but performance is lacking. The thesis that the child's one-word utterance is already a sentence implies, of course, that the child has already learned to express relations, but does so, for the time being, in an "inaudible" form. The fact is, however, that relations such as agent of action and object of action can be reliably reported to exist only when the utterance itself contains a structure capable of holding a relation – which cannot be the case with utterances composed of less than two words! Only here may the presence of, say, a particular word order be interpreted as evidence of the respective structure. But are we entitled to arrive at the same conclusion from a one-word utterance[8]?

Bloom (1973) has rightly argued that there may be alternative interpretations of early one-word utterances. For instance, the child might have first acquired a lexicon without any grammar.

The following is Brown's (1973) exemplification of the problem. Suppose we watch a child filling a cup with juice and handing it over to mommy, again and again. As long as this action remains unaccompanied by an utterance, the psycholinguist may feel disinterested. But suppose the child says *juice,* or *give,* or *mom,* or *cup.* In this case we are free to paraphrase the child's intention as being, for instance: "I'm handing mommy a cup of juice". But would we not impute too much (or perhaps too little?) intention to the child? The question is not of minor significance.

For Brown (1973), the question is the key to what he feels to be a crucial problem of the psychology of language. The reason why it is so acute a problem for him is that he seeks to keep meanings clearly separate from grammatical relations.

His implicit assumption is that an intended meaning is expressed, among other things, in the grammatical relations of words in a sentence. For example, the object of the predicate *(bites the dog)* is a grammatical relation which tells the hearer that the object *(dog)* is the passive recipient of the action *(to bite)* mentioned in the sentence.

All these grammatical relations are for Brown "peculiarly linguistic" (p 201), even if they are used to express *semantic* relations or intentions of a preverbal kind. But how and where do these grammatical (or syntactic) relations originate?

---

[8] In our use of the term *one-word sentence* we merely refer to an utterance of MLU = 1 (mean length of one word) without going into the theoretical dispute whether it is a sentence of incomplete, or compressed, or secondarily reduced (e. g., by deletion rules) form.

Construing meanings in contrast to syntactic relations, Brown (1973, p 201) is willing to follow Piaget:

> I mean ... to suggest that these meanings [deriving from sensorimotor intelligence] probably are universal in humankind but not that they are innate. I mean, in addition, to suggest the possibility that these meanings probably are not *exclusively* human even as sensorimotor intelligence is not.

Still, how are these meanings brought into relation with each other? Do children have a "presyntactic knowledge of grammar" at the one-word stage? (to use Bloom's formulation). Could Washoe and Sarah possess the same kind of knowledge? Here we have an aftereffect of the notion of competence ("knowledge of grammar"), and at the same time we can see why Brown became interested in Washoe's feats only when she started to *combine* signs into *sequences of two* and more (Brown 1970).

Is the advance from one to two and more signs tantamount to a progression from mere *semanticity* – present to some extent in certain animal species – to *productivity,* i. e., the capacity of constructing new utterances to express fresh experiences and novel meanings?

Again: what is "mere semanticity"? Are we entitled to assign unequivocally at this stage the concept of actor or agent residing in *daddy* – an utterance referring to the ball-throwing father – to semantics rather than to syntax, i.e., grammar? Evidently, one's approach to the problems we are discussing in reference to Brown and Bloom crucially depends on one's views concerning the nature and boundaries of semantics, syntax, grammar, productivity, surface and deep structure, and related concepts[9].

To what extent these problems depend on definitions may be seen from the following juxtaposition of Brown's (1973) and Bloom's (1973) views: Brown seems to be willing to accept a smooth progression from sensorimotor intelligence as described by Piaget to semantic intentions, but he fails to see any solid link between the latter and grammatical relations. For Bloom both semantics and syntax are linguistic categories, the critical distinction running between linguistic categories and cognitive categories (the latter being the "mental representation of experience").

The more one tends to conceive meaning in terms of vectors (e. g., agent is one), the less there remains of Brown's problem. Conversely, the more static our view of "meaning", the stronger the need for "additional" relations – to be supplied by a grammar whose presence in the one-word utterance is by no means certain.

However, one should not be misled into believing that the entire problem is merely a dispute over definitions, and hence of little relevance to the real issues at stake. After all, our ability to figure out how language is actually used by humans

---

[9] Anyone working with Fillmore's case grammar may find, for instance, that radically different semantic (deep-structure) roles can function as subjects in the surface structure of a sentence: "John opened the door", "The door opened", "The key opened the door". Where does the child's one-word utterance come in here?

depends on our faculty of reasoning and arguing about language in a language of well-defined concepts. Bloom (1973, pp 19–20) has the following to say on this issue:

> Whether or not children do have any pre-syntax knowledge of grammar may well be unknowable; that is, it is not clear that any amount or kind of evidence can demonstrate convincingly that children know about sentences before they say sentences. Why, then, should one bother to dispute the claim that they do? Essentially, the argument is worth pursuing because one would like to be able to explain . . . why it is they begin to use syntax when they do, and . . . what it is they do know at this age – if *what* they know is not grammar.

Our interest in the border area of semantics and syntax, and the progression from the not-yet-sentence (or crypto-sentence?) to the sentence, is motivated by yet another aspect of the problem. As we have seen, one of the possible approaches is subsumed by the question: Is the "one-word sentence" an *incomplete* mirroring of fully developed semantic relations and intentions? The question itself presupposes that a sentence serves to mirror or "represent" something. Well, are there any grounds for this assumption? In any event, there is always the chance that the tacitly accepted concept of "representation in language" is totally misleading and hence responsible for the emergence of many a spurious problem.

Continuing our inquiry, we shall now not only try to find evidence of those "semantic intentions" by which the one-word utterance is turned into a verbal manifestation of a preverbal (sensorimotor) action schema, and also evidence of some formal relations between the various levels and stages of the global situation surrounding the one-word utterance; but above all we want to trace the different aspects of the process of learning and development, in the course of which the child learns to transpose his nonverbal intentions and experiences into regular language. At the same time, we must be prepared to scrutinize carefully and critically the play on such words as cognition, intention, transformation, or incomplete mapping onto syntax. Much is to be gained not only from Brown's and Bloom's arguments about presyntactic language but also from Greenfield's illuminating studies of prelinguistic syntax.

Let us start with a finding that serves as a rough analogy. Stokoe (1974, p 121) argues that if an ape shows fear and simultaneously points to the cause (e. g., a snake),

> there is *in ovo* what generative semanticists would term a semantic structure, e. g., "dangerous that". . . . Or stated in Fillmore's case grammar, "threatening to me that".

Is the connection between symptom and deixis in this case essentially grammatical or semantic? The question is unresolvable, not only because there is obviously no sequential ordering between the two signs (this being a rudimentary criterion of syntax); the instance also reveals an aspect commonly ignored by the sign-theory-minded linguists and psychologists, namely, that certainly the notion of syntax and probably the notion of semantics (more accurately: semantic relations) imply that the sign is freely available to the sender. But for one thing, a *symptom* is not freely available by definition (Bühler). And how sure can one be that the *symbol* which stands for a semantic relation *is* freely available to Washoe

223

or to the young child? Is the child free to decide which portion or aspect of a sensorimotor action schema is to be verbalized and which not?

To what extent the child's earliest symbols are anchored in the flow of the global action has been demonstrated by Piaget (1953, Observ. 180) with the following example:

Having practiced the filling and emptying of pails and other containers before, Lucienne (1; 4) found it easy to retrieve a small chain put by Piaget into a semi-closed matchbox: the girl either turned the box upside down or used her finger to fish out the chain. Next, Piaget made the opening in the box small enough to prevent Lucienne from inserting her finger or the chain from falling out by itself when the box was turned upside down. Manipulating now with the box, Lucienne suddenly stopped, opened and shut her mouth several times, each time a little more, and then pushed the box open.

For Piaget, this was an instance of preverbal motor symbolism. But is it really a symbol that is involved here? Abiding by the customary definition of symbol (as a sign standing for something other than itself), we run into difficulties again: opening the mouth does not stand in the same way for opening the box as Washoe's ASL sign *open* stands for opening the door. Opening the mouth is a token of the cognitive schema *to open* (where the schema functions as a type). But it is a *displaced* token, the displacement being from box opening to mouth opening. The reason for the displacement is that the child's action is now dominated by the intention of opening something, and it happens to be executed on the mouth because the child finds it easier to open her mouth than the box – and also easier than uttering the word *open*. This case offers a magnificent exemplification of Höpp's earlier discussed view of how the components of a primitive expression come apart.

According to the sign theory of language, our next question would have to be: Is there a minimal magnitude of such a displacement, and a minimal intention behind it, to make it into a "semantic relation" between the sign and the signified? So long as there is no answer to this question – which is unanswerable – there is likewise no answer to Brown's question of how much "semantic intention" might be legitimately imputed to the child's or Washoe's one-word utterance. For Brown's semantic intention bridges precisely the distance over which the sign has been displaced from the signified. How far can the young child displace the sign from the signified into the medium of language? It depends on our judgment of the child's *ability* ("knowing how") to freely articulate the action schema and to control all its components whether or not we attribute to him any *knowledge* of semantic and/or grammatical relations.

Under an alternative approach, we might interpret Lucienne's behavior as an attempt to communicate to her father the intended meaning with increased precision, in which case the message need not be translated into any code since it consists of an action. Unlike the sign-theoretic approach, the present interpretation does not seek to account for the ability to speak (knowledge how to speak) in terms of *knowledge* of language (the origins of the latter remaining a mystery); rather, it proposes to *derive language knowledge from the ability to speak, and the ability to speak from the ability to act and interact with other people.*

The integral nature of ability (knowledge how) and knowledge (that) as revealed in Lucienne's behavior entails a philosophical problem a discussion of which would inevitably lead us back to Wittgenstein. Once established in the maturing human being, this integration is taken for granted: it does not come to our notice until it is disturbed in a pathologic condition. In certain types of aphasia, for instance, the patient is unable to produce the word for pencil though he may have access to its functional core, which he attempts to paraphrase by saying "for writing". In some cases the word *pencil* may reappear in the event that the patient is prompted to use a pencil as an instrument of action. The present evidence suggests a reinterpretation of Luria's experiment reported in Chap. 10; there, a patient who did not know how to form a sentence from words made available to him (dynamic aphasia) was presented with a linear scheme of the sentence, which enabled him to construct sentences such as "I am hungry" or "The woman is slicing the bread." Discussing the problem in the context of Russian psychology of language, we spoke of the interrelation of the sentence scheme with motor behavior. In effect, we came to regard the linear sentence scheme as a kind of protosyntax: in dynamic aphasia, this syntax is impaired, while individual words are available to the patient. Now we are in a position to specify: what is affected (and may be compensated for by the linear sentence scheme) is not an empty syntactic pattern into which the available words (conceived of as static units) can be fitted, but the functional aspects of the word's meaningful core.

Our next step is of considerable importance: leaning on evidence supplied by Greenfield and her co-workers, we shall argue that even at a stage where the child is as yet unable to employ suitable word combinations, his actions are governed by rules that could be readily called grammatical if only accompanied by verbal processes. Obviously, it is again a "mere analogy"; but is it not that our understanding of the world benefits greatly from analogies that are then found to be inadequate in one way or another?

Greenfield et al. (1972) set out to demonstrate something that does not exist for Chomsky, that does exist for Piaget, and that possibly exists for Brown: "a general isomorphism between language and other forms of cognition" (p 292). But unlike Bloom, Schlesinger, and others who chose semantic relations (agent, patient, . . .) for the purpose, Greenfield et al. proceeded to investigate nonverbal action strategies in search of grammar-like programs of action. They watched 64 children aged from 11 to 36 months playing with seriated (nested) cups. The experimenter would place five cups of different sizes in front of the child and would then nest the cups by means of a particular "strategy".

When the children were thereupon allowed to play freely with the cups, 54 of them (from the total of 64) followed one particular strategy during the trials, and it was not necessarily the strategy demonstrated by the experimenter (i. e., presumably the most advanced one). The choice of this strategy was unaffected by either the arrangement of the cups in front of the child or by the features of the cup with which the child was induced to start. Only the age of the child was found to determine his or her choice of strategy at the first trial. The simplest of these strategies (involving one or more pairings of objects, each accomplished by moving one of the cups toward the other) apparently derives from an earlier "motor rule", which, however, did not suffice for the child to solve the problem. As recounted by Greenfield et al. (1972, p 299):

> (In) the preceding stage . . . the baby's two hands are limited to symmetrical manipulation. At that stage, two objects can be banged together at the midline [of the table], but differentiated interaction is impossible. . . . When differentiated hand-use does appear at about 11 months, it seems that once a cup has become the acting or moving cup by virtue of being picked up by the child, he treats it as an extension of his hand. This relationship of cup and hand is particularly apparent when the child puts one cup into a second and immediately withdraws that cup without ever letting go. This form of strategy was used by all 11-month-old and seven out of eight 12-month-olds.

Up to the age of 12 months the child has a binary concept of size, i. e., one is the big cup, all others are small. Then comes a developmental stage during which five cups can be seriated by size, and yet the child is unable to construct a series proceeding from a sixth, medium-sized cup. The latter can be achieved only when the child has acquired the operation of reversibility (Piaget), i. e., can identify one and the same object as bigger in relation to some, and as smaller in relation to other things, in quick succession.

Further on, Greenfield and co-authors quote evidence from the literature to the effect that the same developmental sequence as discovered for cup-nesting is followed in the acquisition of grammatical structures (the common criterion being structural complexity), with a delay of several months, of course. Greenfield et al. (1972, p 308) conclude:

> rather than think of linguistic capacities as causing cup strategies or *vice versa,* and looking for a temporal relationship to prove it, we prefer to consider both as behavioral manifestations of underlying internal forms of organization which have many other concrete applications as well.

Taking into account what has been said above, we are led to believe that among the "internal forms of organization" acquired by the child at a relatively early stage there is the ability to act with one object (treated as an extension of the hand) upon another; the emerging Agent-Patient relationship is closely associated with tool manipulation.

The study by Greenfield et al. (1972) has one more interesting aspect, which is not discussed by the authors. The experimental situation in which the child is watched at play is not a communicative situation! The child already seems to be following rules at this early stage, even though he is not intent upon achieving anything by doing so. Under these circumstances, one might expect him to follow a different strategy at each trial. His adherence to one strategy can be accounted for if we imagine that a certain type of action has been endowed with constancy long before it can benefit language communication.

We can claim to have gained two insights from the foregoing. One would be that the use of language comprises a number of highly differentiated, more or less linguistic components, the other, that Toulmin (1971) is right – in his dispute

226

with Chomsky (Chap. 3) – that human language has an evolutionary history insofar as it comprises many capacities that are discernible at a prelinguistic stage.

The growing child seems to acquire rules of behavior that may yield no immediate benefit. Could this tendency toward rule acquisition be the starting point for the emergence of universal rules that can subsequently serve communication purposes because they are universal? The *grammar of action* conceptualized by Bruner (1971) and exemplified by Greenfield and co-authors has been traced by Goodnow and Levine (1973) in young children's copying of geometric figures: here too motor regularities come into evidence that "actually are not necessary" but then tend to become relevant as we proceed from mere movement to the perception-coordinating and perception-constituting movement *rule,* as postulated for instance in Hebb's theory of phase sequences.

An interesting view of the interaction of such regularization with the verbalization factor is offered by Greenfield (1972) in her study of "playing peekaboo with a four-month-old". A smiling response only regularly sets in when the mother adds some utterances to the game; inanimate objects are particularly unlikely to elicit the response, unless accompanied by some speech cues. Accompanying speech evidently serves to accentuate the course of a global action, thus helping the child to understand what the parent means. This again draws our attention to the bearing of temporal segmentation on the acts of meaning and understanding. In the preceding chapter we became aware of the nonverbal segmentation of the global (and thereby also of the linguistic) course of events; now we are confronted with the verbal segmentation of the (also nonlinguistic) course of events. Without such an integration the young child would never learn the language in the manner outlined by Macnamara.

From Greenfield's prelinguistic rules let us once more move closer to language processes, mindful of our question as to whether the child's one-word utterance is but a relationless designation, or whether it expresses some semantic relation, or perhaps is even a syntactically integral sentence that is subject to compression because of the child's limited processing capacity or the like, and let us for the time being ignore the far-reaching implications of the notion of *expressing*.

Here we ought to mention in first place Eve Clark's (1973a) study, which shows how the child goes about analyzing adult utterances with the aid of an already existing cognitive (but nonlinguistic) structure. We shall discuss this important investigation later in this chapter, once we have explored the underlying notion of strategy.

A differentiation of semantic intentions in one and the same word was discovered by Menyuk and Bernholtz (1969) in a study of prosodic features in the speech of 18-month-old children. The authors recorded five words which appeared to carry three different intentions: declarative, interrogative, and emphatic; they based their judgment on both context and prosodic features of the words. At first glance this could be one of those projective interpretations whose dangers have been pointed out by Brown (1973). Learning of the next step of the investigation, however, we are reassured: the authors produced spectrograms of the five word triplets in which differences between the three intentional "modalities" were clearly discernible. The regular occurrence of word-plus-prosody combinations appears to demonstrate the presence of those relational intentions we have been looking for. In an alternative interpretation, we might make reference to the notion of speech act by saying: we understand what the child is saying because (and if) we realize how he is saying it – as interrogation, declaration, or emphasis. The relation upon which this interpretation focuses is not a strictly semantic one, such as between the sign and the signified, but rather between means and end.

We may move onto more solid ground by turning to one-word utterances that can be conceived not as making reference to an object but as being "essentially relational". Washoe for instance used the sign *more* at first for tickling and soon afterward also for other pleasant experiences (brushing, swinging), and later also for extra amounts of candies. Allison Bloom (at the age of 16 months) used *more* first for another helping, two days later to make the babysitter give her another tickle, and then to designate the second shoe (the first was *shoe*). Bloom (1973) states explicitly that Allison used *more* (and words like *there, stop*) in relation to many more objects and events than were represented in her vocabulary at the time; the concept of *more* had come to represent a relationship independently of the particular things related. (But is this claim warranted? Does not *some* thing come in by definition?)

Is there any answer to this question? And would not either an affirmative or a negative answer immediately require us to specify what "some" thing means? Once again we run the risk of regressing, when trying to elaborate our findings and interpretations. Have we again reached the periphery of the language game in which we may talk about language[10]?

The occurrence of words such as *ball* and *hat* is not so easily interpretable as in the case of inherently relational words. When and under what circumstances are the former words uttered? If a word is uttered by itself, the specific function of the utterance cannot be unequivocally determined. Bloom (1973, p 97) reports:

> at 14 months, Allison and I were walking in the early evening and Allison looked up from her stroller at the moon. She said "moon", and several minutes later, "Mimi". Her babysitter (Mimi) had pointed out the moon to her on other walks ... What was the function of "moon" – was the word used simply to name it ... or, was "moon" somehow inextricably bound up with Mimi in Allison's mind when she said it? Further along in that same walk ... the words "moon", "Mimi", and "Mama" occurred often as we moved along and stopped at each intersection. At one intersection, Allison looked up to the moon ... and said "stop". That night at the dinner table, she reported the events of her walk to her father ... and said, quite clearly, "moon stop".

Was it impossible for Allison (aged 14 months) to discriminate her own movement in the stroller from that of the moon[11] so that the moon really seemed to

---

[10] The question of "inherently relational" words is raised once more later on in this chapter, in connection with a discussion of the genesis of their comprehension in the context of the concept of strategy.

[11] Such a differentation presents considerable difficulties in conditions of passive movement, as shown by, e. g., Held (1965).

stop at every intersection? Bloom points out that there is no way of telling whether *moon* functioned as agent or as object in those one-word utterances.

But how about *Daddy, Mama,* and *Mimi?* As soon as these words have appeared at the age of approximately 10 months, they are used either to "announce" persons as they enter the room, or as a "greeting", when Allison would come into the room. Are these two genuinely different forms, and is it absolutely essential for the child and the investigator to decide in favor of one of them? The matter is not much different with Bloom's (p 99) following account:

> When she reached out for a package that Mama was opening, there was little doubt that she wanted to do the opening. But, her utterance "Baby" in such a situation could have represented the desired location for the package (in Allison's hands), the goal of Mama's action (giving to Allison) as well as the desired agency of an action (Allison opening), etc.

Bloom lists these alternatives to show that the question of whether the child's one-word utterances carry any semantic intentions remains open. Well, is it really necessary for the child to differentiate categorically between these three semantic intentions – a task that may pose some problems even for an adult? – And why should we require the child to entertain just one of the three semantic intentions before granting him any at all? Here we face a danger inherent in the notion *semantic intention:* both Brown and Bloom hold semantic intention to be something that is either present or not, and, if present, to be of a definite quality or kind. Consequently, if present, a semantic intention must be mirrored in, say, a suitable syntactic construction.

Would it not be more sensible to construe semantic intention as something that is *done* rather than as something that one *has?* This view would help us to understand that the child might refrain from differentiating between semantic intentions in the event that he is able to cope with the situation without such differentiation (an intention that exists might persevere even when not needed).

The next step brings us closer to two-word utterances and hence also to the resolvability of the Brown – Bloom problem: it is the phenomenon of successive one-word utterances.

The following example from Bloom (1973, p 41) will illustrate the point:
Allison (at 18 months) is eating a peach handed out by Daddy.
Daddy had cut a piece of peach that was in
the bowl of a spoon, with a knife. Allison
ate both pieces, then picked up another
piece of peach and held it out to Daddy   *peach / Daddy /*
Allison picking up the spoon   *spoon /*
Allison giving peach and spoon to Daddy   *Daddy / peach / cut*

Judging by their prosodic and temporal patterns, these are successive one-word utterances, not just a succession of designations. Verbalizing in quick succession the various aspects of her action schema, Allison must have been aware of the entire schema right from the start.

The same problem may be approached from a different angle. As reported by Bloom, Allison produced the (two-word) utterance *Mommy sock* in two quite different situations: when looking at her mother's socks and when mother was putting Allison's socks on. Thus one and the same surface structure can be employed for the realization of two different deep structures (genitival or possessive in one, and an Agent–Object type in the other case). In all likelihood, such a convergence of *different* deep structures into *one* surface structure may also be present, in principle, at the one-word stage.

Rather than construing the progression from the one-word "sentence" to the two-word "sentence" in terms of a sudden emergence of a structure previously unavailable to the child, we would prefer to say (in consonance with, e. g., Schaerlaekens 1973) that, in employing the two-word sentence, the child *tends* to make use of a particular word order to express a particular semantic function; yet judging by instances like *Mommy sock,* even at the two-word stage not every distinction is signalized in the utterance. Hearing the child say *Mommy sock* on seeing mother's socks, we may feel more certain in judging that the child is referring to the Possessor–Possession relationship than in the case of a one-word utterance. If the child says *Mommy sock* while having her socks put on by mother we may feel *more certain* in assuming that the utterance represents an Agent–Object relationship. But has the child said anything *more* than at the one-word stage? That is, does the utterance express more of what we have come to call the child's intention or cognitive grasp of the world? In what way does the present stage differ from the one-word stage at which Allison may have said simply *Mommy* in the very same situations? Even then she would have been *understood* by the adult, and her communicative achievement (not particularly consequential at this age) would have been of comparable magnitude. But now the hearer feels *more* certain about it, receives *more* guidance, is supplied with *more* reliable cues.

If one succumbs to the tendency of construing word order in the child's utterance as an indication of the dominant order of the underlying concepts, one should bear in mind what Slobin (1970) has shown in his cross-linguistic investigation: that knowledge of intentional structures is universal, but not linguistic knowledge of what is a syntactically admissible word order.

What is meant is – to an increasing degree – specified or "made precise" by what is said. This relationship between what the child says and what he talks about is usually conceptualized by claiming that what is being meant is more and more fully *represented* in the utterance. Is this still a useful proposition? Let us now consider some ideas contributed by Garfinkel.

Garfinkel (1972) asked his students to report common conversations by writing on the left side of a sheet what the parties actually said and then try to explain on the right side "what they and their partners understood that they were talking about."

The latter task turned out to be an exceedingly difficult one, notably when increasing precision was demanded from the students in their right-side accounts. Eventually, they gave up. What was the reason for their failure?

Embarking on their task, the students were well aware that the recorded conversations were extremely sketchy and hence incomprehensible for an outsider. (In a sense, their situation was similar to that of the investigators of child language.) They thought it necessary, writes Garfinkel (1972, p 318),

> to look elsewhere than to what was said in order (a) to find the corresponding contents, and (b) to find the grounds to argue for ... the correctness of the correspondence.

In their striving to give an exhaustive account of what was talked about on the basis of the record of what was said, the students had to fall back on their knowledge of the correspondences obtaining between linguistic representation and semantic content. This in turn presupposed thorough knowledge of what was talked about. In an effort to get all this across in their accounts, reports Garfinkel (p 318),

> the students would invoke their knowledge of the community of understandings, their knowledge of shared arguments, in order to recommend the adequacy of their accounts of what the parties had been talking about.

There we have the presuppositions, or tacit assumptions, without which there can be no communication by language. To enumerate all these presuppositions turns out to be an endless task. Employing our notions again, we would say that the students, in trying to specify in ever greater detail the relationships between what was said and what was talked about, made the sense-constituting background recede step by step. "The way of accomplishing the task multiplied its features", they complained, having discovered that each presupposition entails some metapresupposition, and so on. Invoking our discussion in Chap. 7 once again, we might explain the students' difficulties by the inevitable failure of any attempt to transform all of the necessary distance between information and sense (necessary to establish meaning) into information. Knowledge of what is being talked about cannot be fully explicated on the grounds of what is said.

Eventually, Garfinkel suggests a radically different approach:

> suppose we drop the assumption that ... we must at the outset know of what the substantive common understanding consists. With it, drop the assumption's accompanying theory of signs according to which a "sign" and a "referent" are, respectively, properties of something said and something talked about, and that in this fashion proposes sign and reference to be related as corresponding contents (pp 318–319).

Complying with Garfinkel's suggestion, we would have to abandon an idea that pervades the thinking of many investigators of child language (Brown and Bloom included), i. e., the conviction that the investigator's prime task is to explore those "correspondences" (between sensorimotor schema and semantic intention, between semantic intention and syntactic representation, between cognitive category and linguistic category, etc.) which the growing child has to master in the process of learning the language.

Thus we have come face to face with a problem of great importance:

a) The associationists produced the following answer to the question "What is acquired by the child?": associations between sign and referent (but how – they could not tell)

b) The generativists answered the same question by saying: knowledge of grammar (and having likewise no idea how such knowledge could be learned, they devised LAD)

c) Now the question is different (more vague and hence less suggestive of the answer): "What changes in the child in the course of learning the language?" (or: "in the course of language acquisition?").

In pursuit of this problem, let us revert once again to Macnamara's (1972) idea that the child starts by grasping the meaning which a speaker intends to convey to him and then works out the relationship between the meaning and the speaker's utterance. From what we now know, the relationship should not be construed in terms of correspondence between two entities (i. e., between what is said and what is talked about), but rather as the relation between means and end. With his utterance, the speaker instructs the hearer on how to understand him. But this instruction is never complete and final, in the sense that it would indicate a terminal point for the processes released in the hearer[12]. Even at the stage of one-word utterances the adult hearer always has many other clues to rely on in addition to the child's utterance; these clues are embedded in the situation, as are the clues that enable the child to understand the adult. Still, the situational clues have some important shortcomings: for one thing, they often lack in specificity, and, for another, people also talk about things that refer to past or future situations. It is because of this essential limitation of situational determinants as clues for understanding that more and more comprehension-inducing and comprehension-guiding elements have to be included in both the utterances of the maturing child and in the adult utterances addressed to the child. Such is the essence of the changes occurring in the language learning child.

How does the child go about extracting more and more from adult utterances? A preliminary answer would be something like this: The child tends to discover new rules by focusing his attention, by way of experiment, on various aspects or portions of the utterance and by establishing them as determinants for comprehension. The child applies to the language addressed to him the kind of strategies he has learned to use for his nonverbal action (as demonstrated in the study by Greenfield et al.).

The notion of strategy in the child's language understanding was explored by Bever (1970) in a significant study. A strategy is a sort of "prescription for action". Bever illustrates this with an example from visual perception: in order to judge which of two arrays of dots displayed on paper contains the most dots, the adult may employ any of three strategies: (1) he may count the dots in each array and compare the numbers obtained in this way; (2) he may decide for the larger array, on the assumption that a larger number of dots is bound to occupy a larger area; (3) or he may decide for the array of greater density, on the understanding that density increases with numerosity.

---

[12] Brown (1973) offers a suitable example: Eve says "Mommy lunch". Her mother expands this utterance as far as seems necessary to her for ensuring immediate understanding: "Yes, Mommy is making lunch." She feels no need to say, for instance: "Yes, today, February the 4th, Mommy has been busy preparing lunch for the past hour by ..."

The second or third strategy is likely to be chosen if the child either cannot count, or does not think if worth the effort, or has not enough time to do it. This would indicate that the notion of strategy subsumes organismic capacity factors as well as factors anchored in the scale of the task and in the exigencies of the situation. Bever does not go into this issue; nor does he specify whether he regards these strategies as innate or as taking shape in the course of the child's attempts to cope with the linguistic input. Bever is inclined to believe "that the child may extract particular perceptual strategies by selective induction over his early linguistic experience".

Before going into the individual perceptual strategies, let us see what Bever has in mind when he says that

> the child's systems for talking and listening partially determine the form of linguistic structure even as the structure is being learned and used by the child. Thus, the way we use language as we learn it can determine the manifest structure of language once we know it (p 281).

The strategies Bever has in mind are thus procedures by which the principles of language perception are brought to the service of language acquisition. Bever does not go beyond the realm of language and so fails to benefit theoretically from the fact that the boundary between verbal and nonverbal actions is exceedingly tenuous. Such a restricted notion of strategy is of little use to us. For Bever, it is perhaps useful as an instrument with which to make LAD somewhat more open to experience. How strongly his thinking is tied up with the structure-mapping concept can be seen from the following quotation:

> The child will accept as linguistically relevant data those surface sentences for which he can understand the internal structure, and he will form perceptual inductions over those internal/external structure pairs.

Our argument is better served by another, less stringent formulation from the same author: The child will first learn those linguistic structures that are most easily handled by his perceptual system. In fact, the child's perceptual system deals most effectively with those linguistic structures that have their counterparts in the structures of nonverbal or preverbal actions.

Such a formulation subsumes, on the one hand, much of what has been argued in these pages about the projective nature of perception and speech comprehension and, on the other, does justice to our propositions concerning the gradual blending of nonverbal and verbal actions, the importance of temporal segmentation and related factors, etc.

Our thesis is that both non- and prelinguistic strategies of action are instrumental in the child's analysis of adult utterances and hence, potentially, in language acquisition as well. The operation of such strategies in the nonverbal realm has been demonstrated by Greenfield and co-workers and by Goodnow and Levine; these strategies seem to be correlated with the processes of language acquisition. We now turn to a study by Eve Clark which shows the actual conjugation of nonlinguistic strategies and linguistic hypotheses by means of an example of child analysis of linguistic information in terms of cognitive (nonlinguistic) structures.

Investigating the child's comprehension of relational terms, Eve Clark (1973a) had children aged 18 months and older perform simple verbal instructions, such as: "Put the doggie *in* the box", "Put the pussie *on* the trunk", "Put the crocodile *under* the table," etc.

The youngest children did the following: When the goal of the action was a container (box, trunk, etc.), they followed *each* instruction as if it contained *in,* irrespective of the actual preposition. When the goal was an object with a flat surface, each instruction was followed as if it contained *on.*

Clearly the child acts in accordance with a nonlinguistic strategy when performing the order expressed in the given sentence, and he does so, says Clark (p 169), "in the virtual absence of comprehension". From our point of view, however, the child understands by and large what the adult means; he or she obeys the order given by the adult to a high degree, only the fine details are not yet understood. Hence we would prefer to speak of "virtual comprehension", not virtual absence of it. Eve Clark, for her part, maintains that the prepositions *(in, on, under,* etc.) were being understood as locatives, by which she moves into the vicinity of Herbert Clark's view (discussed in Chap. 6), which states that there is an ontogenetically determined order by which the child acquires the various features of a word (e. g., + Polar markedness).

The more fully a nonlinguistic strategy (available to the child) dovetails with a particular verbal construction, the quicker can this construction be expected to turn up in the child's acts of meaning and understanding. It is in this sense that we follow Eve Clark in claiming that some meanings (e. g., *in)* are cognitively simpler than others (e. g., *under);* in the former case the child finds it easier to develop a linguistic hypothesis from his nonlinguistic procedure than in the latter.

Eve Clark's proposition (which seems congenial to Herbert Clark's feature theory) that the order of acquisition of particular linguistic forms depends on the relative complexity of underlying cognitive structures (the growth of cognitive complexity, in turn, being due to maturation, as claimed by Piaget), is, however, subject to qualification on the evidence supplied by Kuczaj (1975). Though the child does interpret contextual information while building the meaning of words, this process is codetermined, notably in the young child, by many environmental factors, which leads to marked individual differences. The subsequent trend toward uniformity of language acquisition is due to the fact that at later stages the child's semantic system develops increasingly under the influence of linguistic factors.

Let us now go back to Bever's strictly linguistic strategies. The major language acquisition strategies are given by Bever as follows:

1) Group together anything that is pronounced in one go (i. e., is not separated by pauses)

2) Pay attention to accentuation

3) Judge word combinations by what appears most plausible in the light of the word meanings and your knowledge of the world

4) Pay attention to word order.

It becomes immediately obvious that language understanding and language production involve the use of more than one strategy at a time (surely even in the case of young children!).

A detailed discussion of the segmenting strategy would require us to repeat more or less what has been said in the preceding chapter about the segmentation of an utterance by psycho- and physiological factors (figure/ground differentiation) and by nonverbal regulators (eye contact, accentuation, pauses).

The accent-sensitive strategy is an excellent illustration of what Bever means by "shortcuts": unable to grasp all that comes in by ear, the child will concentrate on the stressed elements of the message.

The word combination strategy falls back, in one way, on what we have argued about the semantic core of a word, and, in another, embodies *in nuce* the operation of sense constancy. Picking out from an utterance the words *daddy, cookie,* and *eats,* the child may decide that the most sensible interpretation is "Daddy eats the cookie", considering that *daddy* is the only word that might function as agent and *cookie* the only one acceptable as patient (or object of action). Thus the recipe runs: make sense of it in the simplest way suggested by your knowledge of the words and of the world.

That the strategy is often used by older children as well can be seen from the following findings. Required to pick from among a number of pictures the one corresponding to a particular sentence, children find this task more difficult in the case of a passive construction: "The horse was followed by the cow" poses more difficulties than "The cow followed the horse". Now, there is no such difficulty gradient between active and passive sentences in the case of semantically non-reversible sentences (Slobin 1966): "The dog ate the cookie" is not any easier to understand than "The cookie was eaten by the dog".

The child's knowledge of the world is here the decisive factor: the dog may well eat the cookie, but not the other way around. This being so, the child understands the sentence even if it is in the passive voice. For any syntax-centered interpretation, this finding is the source of endless problems, insofar as *all* passive constructions differ from their active counterparts by one and the same feature, namely, passive transformation. And if the syntactic factor, i. e., the additional transformation, were to be regarded as the source of the difficulty, then *every* passive sentence would have to be more difficult than the corresponding active sentence.

In our interpretation, the same finding bears out the notion that the child tends to understand not what is said, but what is meant. The child in the above example certainly does not understand the passive transformation rule, but he does understand enough of what the speaker means to act appropriately. "Understanding is the inward sign of the potential for reacting appropriately to what we see or hear" – this definition by Deese (1969, p 516) has been quoted before.

The extent to which knowledge of language is determined by knowledge of the world, and not conversely, is demonstrated by one of Bever's (1970, pp 305 f.) experiments. Bever tested the understanding of sentences such as (a)

The mother pats the dog, and (b) The dog pats the mother, by having children of different ages act out the respective scenes with toys. What he found was that 2-year-olds did not perform any worse on (b) sentences than on (a) sentences, whereas older children were much better at acting out (a) sentences than (b) sentences. Obviously, we cannot go along with Bever when he says:

> The implication of this is to invalidate any theory of early language development that assumes that the young child depends on contextual knowledge of the world to tell him what sentences mean, independent of their structure (p 306).

Instead, we would rather follow Macnamara's reasoning: Because older children know more about the world, they realize that the situation described in sentence (b) is highly implausible, which is enough to interfere with their acting it out. It is here that probability of occurrence seems to enter the scene again, long after Miller's attempts to account for it – though now we are concerned with the probability of events in the world, not with the probability of words (or letters) occurring in a text.

For all that, a simple reversion of Bever's conclusion will not do; it can only be claimed that an utterance is understood by the child as a specification of what is meant by the speaker. When trying to follow the instruction conveyed by sentence (b), the older child will marshal his knowledge of the world only to find it clash with what the syntax of the sentence suggests. The principle of sense constancy makes the child suspect that the speaker is saying something he does not mean, and this discrepancy is responsible for the delay in acting out the sentence (conflicting response tendencies being known to delay a response).

Bever's finding has one more interesting aspect for us. Discussing the concept of lexicon, we reviewed the ways in which investigators have sought to represent the "knowledge" implied in a word. The most popular way is by isolating the semantic features of a word. A word can be semantically defined by enumerating the features belonging to it. Examining Herbert Clark's feature concept, we ran into difficulties when trying to establish the order in which the features of a word are acquired.

The present context serves to multiply the difficulties: the child's growing experience seems to modify the probability of a particular feature assuming relevance for the meaning of the given word. For very young children one of the features of *dog* is apparently the possibility that the dog might pat the mother. We now know that the subjective probability of this eventuality tends to decline with age. How should such a decline (or rise) in probability of relevance of semantic features be accommodated within the lexicon concept[13]? The basic conceptual apparatus of generative grammar as comprised by syntax plus lexicon reveals its inadequacy once again, and Clark's feature theory becomes even more vulnerable to questions like this: Does the child learn the features that belong to a word, or does he learn the word that labels a concept (construed, if you like, as an aggregate of features)?

---

[13] The problem is evaded by linguistics with a pseudosolution: the knowledge of the probability with which a word or word combination occurs, or a feature becomes relevant, in the particular situation, is said to be stored not in the lexicon but in the encyclopedia.

Les us now return to the strategies used by the child in handling the linguistic input. Not all the sentences heard by the child can be dealt with through the application of a semantic strategy of the kind described above. Though the young child may not need to discriminate between "The dog ate the cookie" and "The cookie was eaten by the dog", he has to learn the distinction between "The boy struck the girl" and "The girl struck the boy". The child must learn to extract from his linguistic input the information about the agent, or patient, etc., of an action even in cases where the particular role is not an essential characteristic of the given word. In other words, on hearing *boy, dog,* and *strike* in one sentence the hearer may legitimately expect these concepts to be interrelated in a manner concurring with the patterns established in his consciousness; consequently, "The boy struck the dog" is the most probable interpretation. But the speaker is likely to instruct the hearer also quite often about less probable events. In case of *boy, girl,* and *strikes* going together, the hearer cannot do without an additional instruction as to who of the two is to be cast as actor and who as patient. Such an instruction may be supplied, for instance, by the order in which the words appear in the sentence. This is where Bever (1970, p 298) adds his fourth, the sequential labeling, strategy:

Any *Noun–Verb–Noun* (NVN) sequence within a potential internal unit in the surface structure corresponds to *"actor–action–object"*.

After a comprehensive survey of studies into what we would call the "problem of the role of word order in understanding", Brown (1973, p 160) comes to the conclusion that

word order in its role as evidence of relational intentions and as the first aspect of the syntax of the expressive medium to be learned is confirmed.

In his survey, Brown is concerned with the reception side of language learning, and this is where Bever's strategy is frequently used. Judging by such formulations as "first aspect of the syntax of the expressive medium", Brown relies heavily on an assumption which will be presently shown to be tenuous. By claiming that in his decoding performance the child shows some kind of syntactic competence, Brown goes definitely beyond the available data: the notion of competence implies, as it is, that the child should be capable of using his syntactic competence also in *producing* language. Accordingly, Brown undertakes to track down the "second aspect" of his syntactic competence as revealed in the word order of the language samples produced by the child. He expects that the child would fall back on word order not only when extracting the relations which the speaker has embedded in his utterance, but also when trying to convey such relations to the adult (or any other) hearer. And this is precisely where the evidence is highly contradictory. Even one and the same child – a bilingual girl speaking Serbo-Croat and Hungarian, for that matter – may use complex locative constructions in one language and fail to use the corresponding constructions in the other language in what is effectively the same situation; obviously, she does not lack the necessary cognitive capacity. Having surveyed numerous studies covering a great variety of languages, Brown speaks of an "extravagant variation in the data" and continues (p 157):

> It is evidently not the case ... that human children everywhere find some single order sensible for cognitive reasons having to do with the order in which attention might be captured by an agent, an action, and an object. It is evidently not the case that human children will limit themselves to the orders that are dominant in the speech they hear from their parents. ... [or] that [they] will always probability-match the orders they hear ...

We have to reconcile ourselves to the fact that young children, while using word order in adult utterances to extract additional information about the speaker's intentions, do not employ the same means ("syntax") consistently for the same purpose in their own speech over a long period. At what point and to what extent word order begins to be actively employed for the purpose, depends to a large extent on how much weight the particular language assigns to this factor.

The available evidence strongly contradicts the notion that a person either does or does not possess one grammatical competence. There is one further aspect of the issue to which Brown draws our attention; it is "the child's lack of concern with making himself clear or ... his assumption that if he speaks at all he will be understood" (p 167).

Clearly the child begins to be interested in the specification of meaning much earlier in the case of understanding than in the case of speaking. Serving two different purposes, the acts of meaning and understanding are not symmetrical manifestations of one and the same knowledge; the different purposes or goals they serve are not equally important, and each requires different means to be attained. Our search for manifestations of one and the same syntax in both aspects of language use may have blinded us to this insight.

Thus we are led back to what is already a familiar point of view: the emphasis on the *functions of language*. The child does not use utterances in the same way in both the act of meaning and in that of understanding. Utterances are means to an end, but these means are not equally required for understanding as for meaning something. His goals in speaking are on a different scale from his goals in understanding: in the latter case the child may be already interested in learning something about the not-here and not-now aspects of what the adult has in mind, insofar as parents tend to refer to things past and future, or to what is neither in sight nor within reach. At the same stage the child is not yet interested in informing his hearers of the not-now and not-here aspects of what he has in mind with a precision that might compensate for the possible absence of some or all of the situational and probabilistic determinants of the utterance. The child lacks such interest for the simple reason that his semantic intentions do not reach that far. Language being the continuation of action with alternative means, the child does not feel the need to elaborate his utterances as long as his actions remain embedded in the current situation.

Our interpretation seems to be far more consistent with the empirical evidence than the rival view, which postulates a unitary syntactic competence and yet fails to account for the fact that this competence is brought into play in some but not in other circumstances.

With this in mind we dare not overlook another finding made in the realm of the productive uses of word order: while it has not been possible to identify any cross-individual or cross-linguistic rules of productive word order uses, some such rules can be traced in the utterances of every individual child. "What all children do," writes Brown (p 244), "is concatenate *in some order* the words relevant to the semantic intention they seem to have."

Here we are reminded of Greenfield's finding that every child also follows some strategy in the preverbal realm. There seems to be a universal tendency to submit ever new aspects and segments of communication to such strategies or rules, although the benefit from an early application of the rules would not be great enough to stimulate a regular developmental progression in the acquisition of rules across all children. At later stages of language acquisition the child is perhaps less preoccupied with learning how to make use of (e. g., syntactic) rules to ensure adequate precision in conveying the intended meaning, than with another important task which is thus described by Brown (p 245):

> a major dimension of linguistic development is learning to express always and automatically certain things (agent, action, number, tense, and so on) even though these meanings may be in many particular contexts quite redundant. The child who is going to move out into the world as children do, must learn to make his speech broadly and flexibily adaptive. It may be that automatizing a certain number of meanings leaves the human's limited central channel capacity free to cope with the exigencies of particular communication problems, which require that one say what is necessary, omit what is not, and use a lexicon and syntax familiar to the particular audience.

In line with our functionalist approach to language, we cannot fail to notice the frequent overdetermination of what is the goal of language use. Instead of treating speaking as representation of knowledge in action, we prefer to see it as an intricate complex of interrelated means of action that are used in highly variable ways for purposes of conveying and grasping meaning.

Chapter 13

Utterances Are Ego-Centered

From what has been said so far it should be clear to the reader that by *understanding* we mean the process of "instancing", or concretization of a particular segment, within a preexistent scaffolding of sense. In child–adult interaction, the adult seeks to convey some meaning to the child and does so by indicating within the latter's rather vague scaffolding of sense a point to which the child is meant to direct his consciousness. Carried initially by the dynamic of the common strivings of adult and child, this process of meaning is in need of further specification once the child has sufficiently widened his horizon of sense to make it difficult for the adult to ensure a perfect fit between what is meant and what is understood. The specification of what is meant by the adult is effected by what he says; the specification of what the child understands of what is meant by the adult is accomplished as the child learns to extract from the adult's utterances the clues that point to what the speaker has in mind. And since the acts of meaning and of understanding are older than language itself, we are fully in accord with Macnamara when he says that language learning (to be exact: learning to understand) can be viewed as the extraction of linguistic meanings from the speaker's utterances. Adult utterances carry meaning for the child insofar as the child has a presentiment of what the speaker means.

Searching in the preceding chapter for the nucleus and starting point of the child's understanding and subsequent production of speech, we came upon simple cognitive relationships of the object-of-action type. Originating in the prelinguistic stage, these relationships come into being as the child's global behavior, his perceptions, and then also his utterances are grouped and organized into dynamic entities by virtue of biologic factors and the child's endeavors and intentions. This intention-induced dynamic segmentation of the interactional structures that have built up between the child and the world, and subsequently between child and adult, entails in many cases a more or less spontaneous figure–ground differentiation; the latter assumes some degree of constancy in the course of time, as a result of the developmental processes described by Piaget. It

240

is by these processes that Object, Agent, and Action are constituted as cognitive relationships linking the child's ego with developments around him. In the course of language acquisition these relationships assume a linguistic, semantic, and symbolic character.

The process of conversion into language is essentially a process of regularization: certain aspects of behavior come to be governed by rules. An overall tendency toward regularization is noticeable even in prelinguistic behavior (Greenfield). The rules are endowed with a communicative function by being applied, as kinds of patent shortcuts (strategies), to the linguistic input, in an effort to ensure as much understanding as quickly as possible by what might be described as a near-stochastic procedure (Bever, Slobin).

Whereas such an interpretation may suffice to characterize the origins of language acquisition and language use, it is certainly inadequate when it comes to accounting for what goes on in adults as they focus attention on a complex sentence (one never heard before), in order to identify the underlying intentions and cognitions of the speaker or writer. We cannot possibly hope to make the long step needed at this point without abandoning the developmental vista in favor of a thorough analysis of the ways in which both (adult) speaker and hearer actually *use* language.

But first, let us try to express our intention in the conventional language game of grammar: our purpose would be to explore chiefly and "simply" the motivation of syntax. For example, what is chosen to function as the sentence subject, and why so; how does this subject interact with the predicate? Again, the question *Why* can be examined in terms of very different language games: we may say that it is the noun dominated by S (sentence symbol) in the tree diagram that is chosen as subject; or else, using a different language game, we might say that the subject serves to identify the theme concerning which a predication is made in the sentence. Thus a global reference to syntax (as defining the particular sequence of words or signs) does not adequately characterize our psychological approach to the problem. We must employ a much more powerful enlarger or magnifying glass to discern the processes responsible for a particular sequence of words or signs. In the present chapter we are primarily concerned with the centering of the utterance around the speaker's ego.

In the preceding chapters, the act of using language has repeatedly revealed its advantages as a basis of analysis. There is likewise no reason why we should restrict our present analysis to intralinguistic (syntactic) relationships. Indeed, we shall deal extensively with the fundamental fact that the utterance is produced by a speaker, is destined for a particular hearer(s), and is perceived by the hearer(s); moreover, we shall try to reckon with the far-reaching implications of this fact.

The cognitive relations described in Chap. 12 are, as we know, distinctly centered around the ego. The first "object" to emerge in Piaget's sensorimotor stage (through assimilation and accommodation) is a schema inseparably tied up with the child's ego. The first object is not just an object, but an object-of-my-action. The first agent is the child himself. Brown fails to notice the relation to the ego in the one-word utterance because this anchoring of the utterance in the ego is a matter of course for the child and as such need not be given any linguistic expression. Putting it in Bühler's terms, we would say that the *origo* (point of origin) of the language field is marked by the child with the very fact of producing the utterance.

It would be totally wrong to assume that the young child feels the need to express in language first the thing that is most important to him. On the contrary, we are inclined to suggest that the central action enters the utterance (as a verb) at a relatively late stage precisely because the child is fully immersed in it. The object, on the other hand, and possibly the agent other than the child himself, is more likely to be verbalized – and indeed must be verbalized – since there is no other convenient way of directing the hearer's attention to it. And this is why the linguistic specification of the *origo* – with the aid of the three deictic words *now, here,* and I (= *me*) – enters the child's *active* language use with considerable delay compared with his *comprehension* of the same words. There is no need for the child, in his relations with adults, to verbalize the demand "me here now", which Bühler (1934, p 102) paraphrased in the following way: "look at me as a sound phenomenon, and accept me as a time token for one thing, as a place token for another, and as a sender token for the third." This finding does not call into question the rudimentary and persisting presence of what Bühler called the "system of coordinates of subjective orientation in which all partners of the interaction are implicated and continue to be so". Naturally, the psychologist of language cannot fail to take note of this system.

The foregoing argument fortifies our view that the groundwork of language communication is constituted neither by the lexicon as a register of symbolic designations for things, nor by any set of rules for stringing together these designations, but by the ego engaged in an incessant confrontation with a world of human beings. Anchored in the conscious ego as the *origo* of the phenomenal field (at the intersection of *me/here/now,* which the young child fails to verbalize as yet) are

> the deictic words ... (which) serve to guide the partner in a purposeful fashion. The partner is addressed by them, and his searching gaze, or, in more general terms, his searching perceptual activity, the receptive alertness of his senses, is being referred, by the deictic words, to aids, gesture-like aids and their equivalents[1], which serve to improve and round off his orientation in the circumstances of the situation (Bühler 1934, pp 105–106).

This quotation directs our attention once more to the fact that the initial function of language use consists in "improving and rounding off" our orientation, as compared to what could be achieved by nonlinguistic and prelinguistic means. Moreover, it also bears out the fact that in his intention to guide and influence the hearer, the speaker exerts "illocutionary force" and reaches his goal only if there is an "Archimedean point" to serve as support. This point is provided by the ego.

In the case of the young child, the Archimedean point is given with the mere

---

[1] Cf. our discussion of nonverbal communication.

fact of the utterance; the adult speaker employs in the same capacity the sounds of speech as acoustic signals of communication. In Bühler's words (p 109):

> Nothing is more natural for a seeing receiver of signals than turning toward the source of the sounds. In the case of language communication, the source of the signs is the speaker and its location is that of the speaker's. The *here* and the *me* combine to demand, or at least suggest, this reaction. To that extent they are identical in their function as deictic words. But then they tend to diverge in the conveyed intention (or interest): in one case it is the position and the environmental conditions of the sender, in the other it is the sender himself that is registered with a physiognomic . . . gaze.

The *now*, it will be added, serves to position the *origo* in time, and it is in relation to this point in time that designations such as *earlier, later, before, after, recently,* and *then* play their deictic roles.

That each utterance has its origo (point of origin) comes into evidence as soon as a shift in point of origin is undertaken for reasons related to the partner's communicative intention. Let us consider two examples.

As rightly argued by Bühler, he who faces a row of athletes will issue his commands *(left, face!)* in keeping with the orientation of the addressees. The same thing is brought home with singular force in the following sentence interpretation experiment conducted by Ertel (1977).

Subjects were handed a picture in perspective showing a speaker (who utters a sentence inscribed in a bubble) standing in front of a fence; there were also two girls in the picture: one (Gisela) standing on the same side, and the other (Inge) on the far side of the fence. The subject's task was to tell which of the two girls the speaker was referring to with a sentence, e. g., "I am going to fetch the girl who is standing in front of the fence." As could be expected, the vast majority of subjects decided that "in front of the fence" referred to Gisela.

A characteristic shift in interpretation occurred when the same sentence was described as being uttered by a speaker (Hans) standing on the far side of the fence: some 58 per cent of the subjects thought the sentence referred to Inge and about 42 per cent continued to interpret it as referring to Gisela. Evidently, for the majority of subjects the *origo* as the point of origin for "reckoning" was transferred to Hans as the speaker of the sentence, though a substantial proportion of subjects clung to their own perspective.

Ertel's evidence confirms Bühler's claims about place designation. Yet Bühler's claims also covered the designations *me (I)* and *you*. These are, in the same way as *here* and *now* and *in front of* and *behind,* signals with properties varying from case to case, "for anyone may say *I,* and whoever says *I* is referring to a different object from anyone else" (Bühler, p 103); they are not symbols involving what-designation *(Wasbestimmtheit)* – and only this would qualify them for inclusion in a categorized lexicon. Both *I* and *you* point to the actors in any act of speech. These are not assigned their roles once and for all, but are designated specifically by the given speaker for the particular occasion. *I* serves to direct the hearer's attention expressly to the speaker. *You* (when used evocatively: *you, look here!*) is a prelude to an act of direct communication, a prelude by which the roles in the emergent speech act are assigned. In much the same way as a proper name, *you* is

243

used to attract attention and summon the addressee to the exclusion of all other possible hearers (Höpp 1970, pp 11–12).

Instructions for role assignment and indications as to the proposed direction of the intended communication are evidently among the crucial elements of any communication by language. It was by deliberate choice that Bühler gave priority in his book to deictic signals over representational symbols. The deictic moment, i. e., the act of indicating or pointing out, was very important for him. But what does *pointing out* mean in actual fact? When pointing to a passing car, I do not touch the car with my finger; I merely point with my arm *toward* the car. Thus, the pointing is anchored in my ego; it is not an attention-catching token affixed to the object in question. In linguistic terminology we might say that the term *pronoun* is a misnomer in that pro-nouns are not proxies of nouns employed whenever the noun (as a name for a thing or person) might not be available or sound awkward; instead, they precede the respective nominal designations in temporal development. Consequently, Bühler plots out a special field of language in which to accomodate such words: the deictic field *(Zeigfeld)*; the latter is contrasted with the symbol field of language in which nouns proliferate.

Unlike in Chap. 5, where the notion of field served to determine the "belonging together" of words, it is used here to characterize the functioning of words: it makes us aware of the fact that individual words *(you,* or *there,* or *here)* as well as individual sentences are never used in isolation, but that by the mere fact of being uttered they are referred to some meaningful context and, by this token, are brought into relation with the ego of the speaker. This is where we must take note of the important contribution made by the speech act philosophers who stressed the meaning-constitutive function of the act of uttering; stating the same idea in the framework of our argumentation, we would say that a model of *language as used by human beings* cannot be based on words construed merely as lexicon entries or on signs conceived without reference to their actual uses.

The utterance is related through its context not only to the speaker's ego but also to the situation encompassing both speaker and hearer. The processes of meaning and of understanding are guided by the situation and all the constraints imposed by it, much as in the prelinguistic infant. Let us recall: the concretization accomplished by the specification of a particular area within the general scaffolding of sense is a constraining process; by understanding the speaker's utterance we gain a more precise notion of what he means. It is in this sense that Rommetveit (1968) speaks of the "deictic anchoring of an utterance". It is a remarkable feature of utterance dynamics that the deictic elements of a sentence are immediately deleted from memory if the sentence is presented in isolation, that is, if it is free of any context to which the deictic elements could be related. The recall score for deictic elements is twice as high in a situation that provides suitable bearings for the test sentences: only then can deictic elements become truly functional (Brewer and Harris 1974).

The situation supplies us with clues which serve to organize the material and which perform an attention-directing function; it is upon these clues that the linguistic clues of the utterance are built up. Bühler (1934, p 171) explains it by arguing that

> it is for the user of language signs an established habit to devote all his attention to what the language signs stand for as symbols, and to address himself to the same goal with his internal, creative, or recreative activity as speaker or hearer. ... One ... allows his constructive and reconstructive internal activity to be guided to a large extent by the object itself, an object one is familiar with already, or an object indicated and elaborated by the text.

For the time being let us note that the use of language is conceptualized by Bühler as falling into the realm of man's established habits (or way of life – *Lebensgewohnheiten*), which guide the processes occurring in the hearer. This reminds us of Wittgenstein and our own concept of the speaker's intention of bringing about a change in the hearer.

This influence exerted upon the hearer's consciousness by the linguistic signals issued by the speaker is located by Bühler primarily in the deictic field of language, which is centered, as we have seen, upon the ego. It is at the interface of the deictic field and the symbol field that Bühler locates the anaphoric uses of deictic words and the imagination-guided deixis. Words like *this* or *that* and *here* or *there* are also used to designate "places in the structuring of speech" (Bühler, p 121) and, in this case, places in the realm of recollections and imagination. Anchored in a present or imagined *me here now,* the signals that act as signposts in these realms can function effectively if speaker and hearer

> have enough concordant orientation in common, an orientation in a framework in which the thing to be pointed out has its place (Bühler, p 124).

This concordance in orientation on the part of speaker and hearer dovetails neatly with what has been argued in the chapter on sense constancy about the common groundwork that is a prerequisite if any communication by language is to take place.

Turning to the symbol field, Bühler is looking for alternative organizing and place-assigning clues, and he hopes to find them among the "purely linguistic mediators" (p 115), on the understanding that within the symbol field, the ego *(I, me)* hands over its organizing and centering role to syntax, or to the relations between the syntactic and the lexical aspects of language. We shall now try to show, in contrast to Bühler, that the centering and organizing role of the ego looms large on both sides of the dividing line between the deictic and the symbol field of language, a line blurred anyway by imagination-guided deixis and by ellipsis.

The point is that the step taken by the introduction of the concepts of anaphora and imagination-guided deixis is greater than suspected by Bühler.

Although Bühler realizes full well that any anaphoric use of deictic words presupposes that the speaker and hearer both have the entire discourse in view and are able to make backward and forward reference to any of its parts, he forestalls any further analysis of the problem by commenting that the underlying operations of immediate memory are familiar to the psychologist (p 122). Imagination-guided deixis with its forward and backward roaming far beyond the temporal location of the utterance itself brings into focus a realization of paramount importance for our knowledge of language processes: that these are intimately bound up with memory processes. We shall come back again to this problem on more than one occasion.

But what do we actually mean by "having the entire discourse in view?" The first and foremost answer is: we mean a state of consciousness which at any given moment embraces elements of the past and of the future. And since it is the consciousness of the speaker or hearer, this state is centered around a core from which all "seeing", reckoning, rating, and thinking is done. This core is, of course, the speaker's (or hearer's) ego. It does not make much difference whether the pointing is effected within the realm of recollections, or imagination, or in a book, or in story telling: *some* ego is always the reference point, except that the ego need not have its *now* and *here* coordinates as origin.

The ego emerges therefore as much more than a mere *now* and *here;* it forms the center of the utterance, not only in physical space, but also in the cognitive space of memory and imagination. The way an utterance is understood depends on the state of the apperceiving consciousness. And this holds not only for deixis, not only for *you* and *here* and *before.* It holds even in the nonlinguistic realm: when thinking of the slaying of the babes of Bethlehem I do not adopt a bird's-eye view; when I recall the sight of the Alpine peak Matterhorn my gaze tends to turn upward. Thus, even in pure imaging the ego functions as the point of origin for its own projections, own thinking, and own actions. That self-consciousness is an integrating agency for all our experiences has been argued by, e. g., Eccles (1970; cf. also Popper and Eccles 1977). The same idea can also be traced in Wundt, who viewed the sentence as an "evolution in time" *(Entfaltung-in-der-Zeit)* of a simultaneous global representation *(Gesamtvorstellung),* the latter being always centered around one's own consciousness.

In view of the pervasive nature of ego-centeredness as a characteristic of the human mind, we can scarcely expect its influence in language to be limited to deixis. Rather, we would expect the "meaning" or "value" of an utterance (any utterance, not only one with a deictic function) to be anchored in the ego of the speaker and, hence, to be a function of the current state of that ego. Insofar as any utterance is issued by some ego, the actual "meaning" or "value" of the utterance also depends on the state of the ego. This is why we are also bound to reckon with the ego-centered character of an utterance, when exploring the meaning of representational symbols such as nouns and verbs.

In stating this, we contradict the traditional view that nouns and verbs are largely "self-contained" symbols possibly codefined by other words of the same semantic field, and that, being symbols, i. e., signs for objects or events, they lack a specific relation to the speaker. Bühler's classical distinction between symbol and symptom, or between representation and evocation (appeal), rests squarely on the assumption that such a dividing line can be drawn with great precision. This assumption seems to be lacking in realism: it is not only when we "understand" the feverish flush on someone's cheeks that a relation is established between this flush and the "owner" of the flushed cheeks; in understanding words

246

(ordinarily classified as symbols) the world–speaker relationship is likewise of paramount importance, because the ego is always the primary reference point (origin) of both the produced and perceived utterance. The empirical evidence for the validity and theoretical productivity of this concept has been provided by Hörmann and Terbuyken (1974).

The basic hypothesis of the study stated: If it is true that the meaning of a word is anchored in the current state of the speaker's or hearer's ego, then this meaning should also be influenced by the way the person conceptualizes the situation in which the word is uttered: a change in conceptualization should result in a shift of meaning.

The hypothesis was tested by having different human figures appear on cartoons, two figures on each drawing. All these figures had been rated by subjects on the Semantic Differential in an earlier phase of the experiment, each figure being rated high (or low) on one of the three dimensions (Activity, Potency, Evaluation) and medium on the other two dimensions. In the second phase, 36 other subjects rated on the Semantic Differential the verb of a short sentence (e. g., I *beg* you) appearing on the cartoon as being addressed by one of the figures to the other. In addition, the same verbs were subsequently (by a third group of subjects) rated separately, i. e., without reference to any drawing.

The results of the study were summarized by Hörmann and Terbuyken (1974, p 307) as follows:

> The . . . connotative meaning of an utterance as assessed by the Semantic Differential is determined not less by the persons perceived in the verbal intercourse than by what is said.

For example, a speaker (figure) rated + Potent endows his utterance with a high loading on the Potency factor, even if the pertinent verb had scored low on Potency in an asituational rating. Or, a word rated + Active in isolation will lose much of its Activity features when uttered by a speaker who scored low on Activity.

This finding can be viewed from a number of angles. For one thing, it sheds "negative" light on the linguists' conventional idea of an internal lexicon: evidently, the meaning of a word cannot be conceptualized as a fixed intersection of a fixed set of semantic dimensions (each with a fixed indifference point), in the way described in Chaps. 5 and 7. What is even more important in the present context is that the uttered sentence (rated by our subjects) functions as an entity in a consciousness that cannot be neutral, being exposed, at any one moment, to varying influences of biographic, situational, and contextual types. In Chap. 15 we shall come back to the constitutive factors of this global semantic situation.

Generally speaking, an utterance is invariably implicated in some action, and its effect is always situation-conditioned, even if the subject (as in the reported study) is specifically required to rate solely (the verb of) the utterance. Hörmann and Terbuyken (1974, pp 308–309) reported:

> In our experiment, the subject, when asked to rate the word on the SD, is not able to discriminate the "parts" of his consciousness which are traceable to the "word per se"

from those which are due to his perception of the situation. He therefore ascribes the unitary characteristics of his momentary conscious experience to the word.

In view of the transparency of language, we are unable to tell with any precision where meaning is situated and what is its source. In its capacity as an Archimedean point, the conscious ego makes its valid contribution to the place and process of the utterance. The experiment by Hörmann and Terbuyken has shown that this contribution may consist in a kind of shift of the neutral point of, say, the connotative semantic dimensions used in the Semantic Differential. Those subjects who notice a sturdy (+ Potent) speaker on the cartoon are differently oriented from subjects who see a frail person in his place. The knowledge carried by people into the acts of meaning and understanding, i. e., their cognitive (not linguistic!) presuppositions, affect crucially even a process that seems to be largely independent of circumstances, namely, the determination of word meaning. The matter will be further examined in Chap. 15.

The influence of the cognitive point of origin can be seen with the naked eye, so to speak, when it comes to choosing words and word order.

Our next task is therefore to examine the ways in which the *formulation* of an utterance is affected by the current cognitive state of the speaker's ego. For this purpose, we now turn to a study by Osgood which, for its lucidity and originality, ranks among the classic works of the psychology of language. Osgood (1971b) puts the simple question: "Where do sentences come from?."

The investigator is concerned here with the "language of simply describing": adult subjects are asked to describe, in terms comprehensible to "a six-year-old boy just outside the door," what they observed during a short eyes-open period.

Step 1: An orange ring is placed in the middle of the table while the subjects keep their eyes closed. After taking a look at the table, the subjects say, for instance:

AN ORANGE RING IS ON THE TABLE, or
THERE IS AN ORANGE RING ON THE TABLE.

In this case, sentences like

THE RING ON THE TABLE IS ORANGE

almost never occurred.

Step 2: While the subjects keep their eyes closed, the experimenter removes the ring and now stands holding a black ball in front of him. On opening their eyes, the subjects usually say:

THE MAN IS HOLDING A BLACK BALL.

Step 3: The ball is now on the table. The subjects say:

THE BLACK BALL IS ON THE TABLE.

Step 4: The ball has been removed, and the experimenter now holds a red cup in front of him. The subjects say:

THE MAN IS HOLDING A RED CUP.

Step 5: A green cup is now on the table. Subjects typically say:

THE CUP ON THE TABLE IS GREEN

248

But they never say sentences analogous to the one in Step 3:

THE GREEN CUP IS ON THE TABLE.

The first conclusion emerging from this sequence of demonstrations is formulated by Osgood (1971 b, p 498) as follows:

> It is obvious that nonlinguistic, perceptual antecedents can create *cognitive presuppositions* in the same way that previously heard or uttered sentences do and that these presuppositions influence the form that descriptive sentences take.

By this momentous statement the reader is immediately reminded of Katz and Fodor's semantic theory which refuses, in principle and absolutely, to consider any nonlinguistic knowledge as a component of the model and which is therefore unable to explain why sentences are the way they are. Osgood's thesis is that

> any theory of language behavior ... must inquire into the antecedents of S (sentences) and relate these antecedents to the forms and contents of particular sentences (p 498).

Under this approach, the goal of generative linguistics (to account for the well-formedness of sentences) becomes a subgoal in a much more comprehensive program. Among the antecedents of a sentence are presuppositions (also) of a nonlinguistic kind. The presuppositions Osgood has in mind range from the global figure/ground differentiation of phenomena, and object permanence, to the psychological "happiness conditions" observed in the performance of, say, the speech acts of promising and reproaching. Schlesinger's intentions and Fillmore's cases can likewise be viewed from this angle: in Osgood's investigation, events featuring *the man* as agent are described in 84 per cent of the instances with a sentence in which *the man* is used in the agentive case, while the same case is used in only 8 per cent of the sentences describing events in which "the man" is not the agent.

Presuppositions are thus believed to provide the framework in which an utterance is constructed, produced, addressed, received, analyzed, and understood. One particular aspect of this framework consists in the expectations implied by it. In one of his experiments, Osgood (p 514) found subjects to use adverbs in their descriptions to the extent that the situation they were describing deviated from "norm" (i. e., from their cognitive presuppositions):

THE BALL IS ROLLING ON THE TABLE.

Watching the ball roll on the table for the first time, subjects used adverbial modifications in only 8 per cent of the cases. The next time when the ball was rolling more slowly on the table, the subjects added *slowly* in 68 per cent, and other "manner" expressions in 11 per cent of the cases.

Once again we are made to realize how much our linguistic output is affected by the cognitive (nonlinguistic) referencing system within which communication is taking place – a system which the speaker assumes he shares with the hearer. The *origo* of the utterance field varies in response to changes in the situation and the speaker's developing experience; these variations in the *origo* are sensibly taken into consideration by the speaker.

In addition to the effect of experience, situation, and context, Osgood also recorded consistent person-specific predilections in time reporting. He found subjects to refer their descriptions to a subjective "time-zero," which revealed itself in the tense of the verbs. Some subjects showed a predilection for time-zero coinciding with the termination of the perceived event, while others consistently used the time of reporting the event as time-zero.

The formation of reference systems is a psychological principle which extends far beyond the realm of language processes. Analogous phenomena can be traced in the adaptation level dynamic described by Helson, as well as in the fact that it is the discrepancy between the neuronal model proposed by EN Sokolov (as a kind of temporary reference system) and the current stimulus input which evokes an orienting reflex. The general rule is to communicate (whether by language or some other information transmission system) that there is something that does not fit the pattern, which is what matters in communication. At the same time, the neuronal model has some affinity with Piaget's schema: our mental experience is pervaded with schematic representations of actions and states of the world. Trying to describe these actions and states of the world we call the hearer's attention to the deviations from the schema in order to bring about the desired modification in the hearer's consciousness.

Osgood's subjects address their descriptions to an imaginary "six-year-old boy standing just outside the door." The sequential effects observed in successive descriptions reveal what the subjects believe to be going on in their imaginary hearer. They assume, for example, that the hearer is able to remember certain identifications and may use the stored information in identifying the subsequent events. In other words, they presume the hearer to follow the same rules or strategies they would be following in a comparable situation. This presumption must be seen as a projection of human confidence in the intelligibility of the world, a confidence without which human beings would not be able to function in this world (cf. Chap. 7).

How closely the speaker follows in his utterances the image he has formed of the current cognitive state of his hearer can be read from Olson's (1970) cognitive theory of semantics.

Olson begins his argument by rejecting the referential theory of semantics. In choosing the words to be used in an utterance, the speaker is guided above all by the anticipated effect they would exert on the hearer's cognition, rather than by any fixed relationship between the word and its referent (because such a fixed relationship does not exist). Thus the referential moment is replaced in Olson's theory by the intentional moment. Olson (1970, p 264) illustrates his view with the following example:

A gold star is placed under a small, wooden block. A speaker who saw this act is then asked to tell a listener, who did not see the act, where the gold star is. In every case, the star is placed under the *same* block, a small, round, white, . . . one. However, in the first case there is one alternative block present, a small, round, *black* one. In the second case, there is a different alternative block present, a small, *square,* white . . . one. In a third case there are three alternative blocks present, a round black one, a square black one, and a square white one. . . . In these situations, the speaker would say for Case 1 "It's under the *white* one", for Case 2 "It's under the *round* one" for Case 3 "It's under the *round, white* one".

In effect, one and the same block is being referred to in three different ways, depending on its surroundings (as thought to be perceived by the hearer). Olson defines meaning correspondingly as *information that permits a choice among alternatives* (p 265). His formulation sets forth in bold relief the deictic and guiding aspect of language communication, to which we have repeatedly referred in these pages. At this stage we are in a position to specify: rather than itemizing *all* properties of the object mentioned ("physical body of wood, covered with paint . . ., showing traces of . . ."), an utterance identifies only those relevant in the particular context (where the idea is to guide the hearer in his search for the gold star).

Considering that by reference to the critical attributes, the utterance reveals by implication which attributes may be left out of consideration (saying "under the round one," the speaker implies that color is irrelevant), the hearer may extract more information from the utterance than from the visual perception of a physically indicated block. Though in the latter case the hearer has no doubts that this particular block is meant, it is only in the former case that he learns *why* it is the block referred to by the speaker (because it is round). Olson's claim that linguistic deixis is thus superior to gestural pointing is even more valid in the case that the various alternatives are inaccessible to visual inspection, being merely stored in memory. A growing complexity of the alternatives mentally available to the hearer requires the speaker to elaborate his utterance to the point where he can hope to make it clear to the hearer which alternative he means. Osgood (1971b, p 512) has the same in mind when he says:

> If the entity is presumed to be novel to the listener, and hence must be identified ("established" as a referent . . .), the speaker is under pressure to elaborate the noun phrase; if it is presumed to be familiar already, and hence need merely be recognized (. . .) by the listener, economy dictates stripping the noun phrase to the bare nominal bone.

Olson's paradigm ascribes to the speaker not only presuppositions as to the hearer's ability to discriminate between white and black, round and square, . . ., but above all presuppositions as to the hearer's intentions (that he wants to find the star that he knows is under one of the blocks). It is against the background of presumed knowledge that the symbols uttered by the speaker function as signals for the hearer. This border area between signal and symbol (as conceived by Bühler) will be examined at a later point.

For the time being, let us discuss some attempts, predominantly linguistic, to come to grips with how the speaker's state of mind influences the utterance. The conceptual frameworks developed for this purpose are typically marked by a striving to attribute a particular function to the grammatical subject (cf. also Ertel 1974b, 1977). A widely known conception along these lines is that of Hockett (1958). Starting with the observation that in European languages the subject of the sentence as a rule introduces or designates the thing or person about which something is stated while the predicate specifies what is new about that thing or person, Hockett proposes the terms *topic* and *comment* to distinguish between the Given and the New. Considering the sentence as the largest unit, the author runs

251

into trouble when trying to make out what is New and what is Given in the *isolated* sentence. As cogently argued by Lyons (1968, pp 334f.), if the sentence *John ran away* answers the (explicit or implicit) question "Who ran away?," then *John* is the comment and *ran away* the topic; if the question was "What did John do?," then *John* is the topic and *ran away* the comment, in the same answer. Originally developed to account for dependencies that reach byond the sentence, text linguistics has failed to cope with this difficulty so far. This is not particularly surprising if one considers that to do so would require the introduction of presuppositions concerning not only antecedent utterances but also the content of consciousness (in speaker and hearer alike). Hockett is prepared to replace grammatical categories (subject and predicate) with what he claims to be purely logical ones (Given and New), but he is not willing to enter the realm of psychological processes (what is *present* in consciousness and what is *added* to it).

More concern with this psychological aspect has been shown by the Prague school with its *theme/rheme* dichotomy. Halliday (1970, p 161) says:

> The theme is another component in the complex notion of subject, namely the "psychological subject"; it is as it were the peg on which the message is hung, the theme being the body of the message.

Now, what is "the body of the message"? The theme is a "point of departure for the message" also because it usually appears at the beginning of a sentence. But it is not always the case that theme specifies the Given and rheme the New. As pointed out by Halliday (p 162),

> the association of theme with given, rheme with new, is subject to the usual "good reason" principle ... – there is freedom of choice, but the theme will be associated with the "given" and the rheme with the "new" unless there is good reason for choosing some other alignment.

Halliday's rather diffident final remark provokes the following comments. For one thing, this diffidence reflects the difficulties encountered in attempts to assign a single, logical or psychological principle to the grammatical subject. On the other hand, whereas the theme (or topic) does exert some influence on what is chosen to figure as subject in the sentence, the communicative role termed *mood* by Halliday (declarative, interrogative, imperative, etc) is also a frequent determinant of this choice. How multifaceted the contingencies of subject assignment are transpires from a study by Flores d'Arcais (1973b) devoted to the perceptual determinants of sentence production.

Subjects were asked to rate the adequacy of sentences describing simple scenes *(A man is smoking a pipe)*. The object chosen for the topic of the situation was found to be typically assigned first place in the surface structure of the description. In addition, topicalization depended on such factors as size of object and direction of action: with the action running from left to rigth, the object on the left stood a better chance of becoming the topic of the sentence, being presumably construed as agent.

The influence exerted by perceptual factors on what goes on in the sentence reminds one of the figure/ground differentiation, disclosed by Goldman-Eisler and JG Martin in their studies of segmentation in the communicative situation, and also of Osgood's above reported contribution to the question "Where do sentences come from?."

Summing up his comprehensive analysis of the sentence subject issue, Ertel (1977) concludes that the choice of the grammatical subject is affected by several classes of determinants:

a) Immediate processual antecedents, among them intensity and/or priority of attention

b) Persistent situational antecedents, such as salience and valence of the nominal unit (noun) to be used.

Precisely this overdetermination in the choice of the subject[2]

might account for facts which have long since puzzled linguists:

- that subjects more often are agents than recipients, but that they are not always agents;
- that the subject represents more often the given than the new, but it does not always represent the given;
- that the subject more often represents the topic than the comment, but it does not always represent the topic;
- that the subject noun mostly precedes the object noun, but this again is not always the case (Ertel 1977).

In following Osgood's invitation to inquire into the antecedents of utterances we would be ill-advised to look for simple and clear-cut relationships between specific antecedents and some particular attributes of the utterance. In fact, more often than not we have to put up with relatively vague clues. Ertel (1974b), for instance, interprets the grammatical subject of a sentence as "an ego-near point of reference for anchoring the relations within the sentence."

The ego as a foothold in the field within which the utterance is structured has been a central notion of our inquiry for some time. But it is not only in the deictic field that the hearer-instructing signals are moored in the speaker's me-here-now *origo;* even in the symbol field the same function is performed by signs that carry the speaker's personal mark and which owe at least some of their value to this mark. The ego provides a firm support for the speaker's intentions to bring about a change in the hearer; this fact is one of the presuppositions considered by both speaker and hearer in their interactions.

Other presuppositions consist – as demonstrated by Osgood and Olson – of the speaker's reckoning with what the hearer knows already and with what his strivings are. Being thus provided with its bearings, the utterance may be reduced to an ellipsis of the kind used when booking your ticket ("straight ahead"); a mere "under the round one" is enough for Olson's subject to communicate his instruction, because the utterance is an intrinsic component of the dynamic field extending between speaker and hearer.

Olson's theory of semantics is restricted to a speaker who is aware of his partner's strivings. There are situations, however, in which the person's inten-

---

[2] A word of caution is in order: as pointed out by Uhlenbeck (1967b, p 269), much confusion is caused by the fact that the same terms (e. g., *subject, predicate*) are employed in both a linguistic and a cognitive analysis of an utterance.

tions are not sufficiently articulated to warrant a reduction of the utterance to diacritical marks indicating which one from among the alternatives is meant. It is not in every case that the hearer's intentions (or the speaker's beliefs as to these intentions, to be exact) can carry the bulk of the communicative burden.

This is particularly so when the hearer himself lacks definite intentions in the matter at hand. Whereas we are not prepared to abandon our thesis that language communication originates in action and that it represents the continuation of action by alternative means, we cannot overlook the fact that this (linguistic) means is also used in cases where the link with any action (a preceding or a subsequent one) is too tenuous to be noticed and utilized in the acts of meaning and of understanding. Such is the case whenever the hearer has no wish to act, but merely to learn something. As in all other instances mentioned so far, the speaker's intention is likewise to bring about a change in the hearer's state of mind, but the intended change has no direct bearing on the hearer's actions. If the speaker's intention is merely to add something to the hearer's knowledge without exerting direct influence on the latter's actions, the utterance obviously lacks the character of a figure on the ground of intended actions. Well, how can the hearer understand messages that are not meant to guide his actions? Olson's theory fails to supply an answer to this question. How do we understand messages unrelated to our interests, i. e., communications of which we merely "take note"? We understand them by, for instance, letting ourselves be guided by the syntactic instructions with which the speaker distinguishes the Given from the New. This brings us to an investigation examining the comprehension aspect of what was studied by Osgood (1971 b) in its production aspect.

Regardless of its undefined correspondence to the grammatical subject/predicate dichotomy, the distinction between the psychological categories of Given and New is of considerable importance in the formation of a system of reference. Haviland and Clark (1974, p 512) have shown it to be plausible with their experimental study that

> the listener, in comprehending a sentence, first searches memory for antecedent information that matches the sentence's Given information; he then revises memory by attaching the New information to that antecedent.

Bearing this in mind, the speaker may avail himself of a variety of devices to distinguish syntactically between the Given and the New. For example, the sentence

THE JOKES HORACE TELLS ARE AWFUL

begins with a relative clause *that Horace tells* which is a common device for conveying Given information. In the sentence

IT WAS EINSTEIN WHO SEARCHED IN VAIN FOR THE UNIFIED FIELD,

the New information is introduced by *it is*.

The hearer cannot successfully employ the above described "strategy" unless he succeeds in tying in the Given information with what is stored in his memory. When unable to locate the respective antecedents in his memory (by calling them to mind), he must either construct a kind of "peg," or approach all the input

254

information as New (whereby quite significant modifications may occur), or else, he might undertake a revision of the Given/New segmentation.

Arguing in much the same way, Hornby (1974, p 537) concludes that

> several different surface structure features of English can be employed to distinguish between one part of an utterance that is presupposed and another part that is focal, and when used in combination these features produce a strong tendency for the listener to accept part of the utterance as true and to question or search for information relevant to the truth of only the focal assertion. The presupposition, being taken for granted, is not likely to be questioned by the listener.

Once again we come to realize that the speaker seeks to "manipulate" the hearer, or to effect a change in him, and in pursuit of his goal the speaker may avail himself of a variety of devices, possibly in parallel, to distinguish, for instance, between presupposition and assertion in his utterance. These devices grow in importance with the decline in the degree to which the utterance's intended meaning ensues from situational constraints.

On noticing this "deliverance of language from the situation," one feels a strong urge to follow Bühler in his sharp distinction between speech actions *(Sprechhandlungen)* and "language-works" *(Sprachwerke,* meaning the products of language). In the case of a speech action, the speaking expires by the time, and to the extent that, it has accomplished its task of solving the practical problem shared by speaker and hearer. In contrast,

> the language-work *per se* has to be available for inspection and has to be examined in emancipation of its position in the individual life and experience of its maker (Bühler, 1934, pp 53–54).

Bühler speaks characteristically of a "deliverance" *(Entbindung),* and a few pages further on even of a "release *(Erlösung)* of linguistic structures (in terms of their functional value) from the constraints of the particular speech situation" (p 57). Indeed, nothing else but the autonomous, i. e., independent of speaker and situation, "language-work" (in its purest form: as a verbal work of art) is for Bühler the product of the human language capacity. He extols this deliverance as "an act of emancipation that might count among the most decisive in the evolution of human language" (p 366), and designates it as

> emancipation from situational supports, . . . the progression from essentially empractical speaking to largely synsemantically autonomous (self-sufficient) products of language (p 367).

We have our doubts whether there is really so much of a new quality, because we have witnessed the developments engendered by such a sharp distinction between the products and the acts of language: we are familiar with the trend nourished by Saussure's influential distinction between *langue* and *parole,* the implications and consequences of which were discussed in the first few chapters of the book.

But there is one more respect in which the emancipation of the linguistic product from the constraints of the particular speech situation cannot be achieved otherwise than asymptotically. Even in the case of an utterance which seems to exist independently of any situation, we cannot hope to grasp its full meaning without having established its broader relationships. Here we are referred back to the notion of presupposition.

Suppose you find a scrap of paper with the following question written down by a soccer fan:

DID BAYERN MUNICH PLAY AGAINST REAL MADRID?

We cannot even read it aloud without making certain presuppositions: should we stress the first word *(did)* on the assumption that a match of the two teams had been pending and the writer wanted to know whether or not it had occurred on this occasion, or should we stress the name of one of the two teams, etc. (cf. Chap. 8).

Even a seemingly context-free sentence cannot function without certain presuppositions: to render precise by the intended meaning and to safeguard its understanding, suitable relationships with what lies clearly outside the utterance itself must be established.

There can be no doubt that in order to understand an utterance in full, we need a point of departure (Uhlenbeck 1967b, p 295), but there is no agreement among the authors employing the notion of presupposition as to the location of this point and as to the direction to be followed from that point:

a) For GA Miller (see also the end of Chap. 6), the meaning of a word belonging to the field of verbs of motion can be identified by interpreting it as a specification of a focal presupposition shared by all words of the same field: *to run* is a specification (indicating speed in this case) of the presupposed "travel from one position to another." The presupposition refers us to the midpoint of a field, and the specification establishes a relationship from a particular point in this field to the midpoint.

b) Osgood's "language for simply describing" (as discussed earlier in this chapter) yields a different picture: the way an utterance is phrased is affected by what the speaker has learned before the utterance and what he believes to know in common with the hearer. *The cup on the table is green* will occur only if there has been a cup and also another color beforehand. Unlike Miller, who places the reference point in a lexicon subdivided into semantic fields, Osgood (and also Olson) ascribes it to the individual's familiarity with preceding events.

c) A somewhat different idea emerges from an instance borrowed from Chafe (1971b, pp 65–66). The sentence

I SAW THE FALSE TEETH THAT WERE WORN BY GEORGE WASHINGTON

is semantically well-formed, whereas the quite similar sentence

I SAW THE SHOES THAT WERE WORN BY GEORGE WASHINGTON

is not, because our knowledge of the world tells us that a person may be happy during his lifetime with just one set of false teeth, but not with one pair of shoes.

Thus, from a *linguistic* perspective, the term presupposition is a catch-all for quite disparate relationships. It is only in a psychological framework that it can be shown to stand for a uniform concept. As we see it, the presupposition represents a vector from which the hearer may read the channeling of the utterance into a particular meaning and thus understand the utterance. If presupposition and assertion, topic and comment, and theme and rheme evade attempts at linguistic interpretation, it is so because they refer to mental processes in the language user; as such they are of little use to those whose goal is to describe (or even to grasp the essence of) *language-in-itself*. The fact is that language is always "for me" (or for him); each utterance is bound up in some broader context from which it takes its bearings, and it can be understood only with reference to an intelligible, meaningful world.

A presupposition may thus be pictured as an anchor mooring the given utterance in the current cognitive framework of the language user. To what extent the processing of utterances is affected by such anchoring can be seen from a study by Olson and Filby (1972).

Contrary to the assertions of orthodox generativists that passive sentences are more difficult to process than the corresponding active sentences (as the former have to be subjected to an additional transformation), Olson and Filby were able to show that the rate of processing sentences depends on the manner of coding the (pictorially presented) situation to which the sentence refers. When focusing on the agent in a picture scene, the subject is quick at verifying the corresponding active sentence. But when his attention is focused on the recipient of an action, the subject is quicker in processing the corresponding passive sentence.

Now back to Bühler's "deliverance of the language structure from the situation." We have come to the conclusion that there can be no question of a complete emancipation, because some kind of situation is inevitably implied by the knowledge required for processing an utterance. Nevertheless, this knowledge is subject to an incessant rearrangement in the process of time-spanning and time-bound communication. What the actual presupposition of a given utterance is can be told only from the utterance itself. In many cases the content of consciousness at time t will turn out to be the presupposition of an utterance heard at time $t+1$. Though the speaker may hope to have freed himself from the situational supports of the *here,* he will continue to be encased by the *now,* his speaking being at all times the continuation of some previous action (even if it were silence). Neither the distinction between speech actions and "language-works" nor any other can invalidate this fundamental fact.

From our psychological analysis of presupposition it follows that understanding can be conceived as a motion originating in a definite cognitive state. The speaker who means something may be said to implant certain magnetic points in the hearer's presupposed cognitive field in an effort to modify it in the desired manner.

This implanting of magnetic points, which together produce the vector of understanding, can be effected by a variety of devices; deixis and the imperative are presumably the oldest among them. While having no sympathy with Bühler's categorical distinction between speech action and "language-work," we cannot refuse to acknowledge the fact that a certain shift in emphasis ensues from the progressive loosening of the interrelation between utterance and accompanying action noted in ontogenetic development. The difference between the speech of the child and the speech of the adult is characterized, among other things, by a progressive freeing of speech from dependence on the perceived conditions under which it is uttered and heard, and from the behavior which accompanies it (De Laguna 1927; quoted from 1963, p 107).

Although there is no need for a new, qualitatively different approach to language processes with the gradual devaluation of situational and actional clues, it stands to reason that the relative absence of these clues must be compensated for by the emergence of other determinants of meaning and understanding. Bühler (1934, p 144) describes it as inevitable

> that language *(la langue)* should abandon in some measure the stage of amoeba-like plasticity[3], from one speech situation to the next, to grant the speaker productivity in a new respect at a higher level, with partially solidified, petrified implements.

At a stage where the situation-, speaker-, and hearer-induced dynamic exerts a diminishing influence upon the acts of meaning and of understanding, language communication becomes a difficult affair insofar as the hearer's voluntary attention, hitherto guided by both situational dynamic and utterance, has now to be steered predominantly by the utterance alone. We remember Olson's contention that even the situation-bound utterance can be more informative than gestural pointing; evidently, the informational value of an utterance is bound to grow in parallel with the "freeing" of attention by the diminishing importance of the situation. In effect, the utterance itself may receive more attention; indeed, it *must* receive more attention if the communicative function is to be upheld.

The greater the extent to which the acts of meaning and of understanding are determined by the utterance alone, the more determinants must be built into the utterance. Simple action schemata of the actor-action-object type will no longer do the trick. Having repeatedly claimed that the utterance is a continuation of action, we may now construe the growing complication of the utterance in analogy with the gradual complication of actions. The utterance may gain autonomy because it becomes a kind of multiple action: different subroutines, or simple action patterns, are intermeshed in various ways; the utterance becomes a skilled act of the kind described by Bruner, and, earlier still, by Lashley, in the preverbal realm. As noted by Bruner (1972, p 6),

> one is struck repeatedly by the extent to which such activity grows from the mastery of specific acts, the gradual perfecting of these acts into what may be called a modular form, and the combining of these into higher order, longer range sequences. Flexible skilled action may almost be conceived of as the construction of a sequence of constituent acts to achieve an objective (usually a change in the environment) while taking into account local conditions.

An instructive analogy: we are struck by the heterogeneous composition, on the one hand, and the concentration upon the goal, on the other. When Bruner speaks of a change in the environment aimed at by the composite action, we recall our statement about the intention of bringing about a change in the hearer's consciousness. Again, the constituent acts described by Bruner are of great diversity

---

[3] ... under the round one, ... under the white one.

in the case of the utterance: the presupposition which the speaker presumes to exist in the hearer and which is planted by him in the con-text, the inherent dynamic of certain verb categories and of predication in general (to be discussed in the next chapter), and also transitional probabilities encountered in, for instance, conventional phrases.

The compositional heterogeneity of the utterance makes the employment of these "prefabricated elements" both feasible and necessary: they are needed as a base for the vectors of meaning and of understanding, and they are useful in that they assist the language user in handling the more complex utterances. The flexibility and diversity of speech acts with which one and the same goal can be attained testifies to the overdetermination of linguistic structures which we owe to the concatenation of many constituent acts. Continuing his argument, Bruner says:

> The flexibility of skill consists not only of this constructive feature but also of the rich range of "paraphrases" that are possible: for a skilled operator, there are many different ways of skinning a cat; and the word paraphrase is not amiss, for there is in this sense something language-like about skill, the kind of substitution rules that permit the achievement of the same objective (meaning) by alternative means.

From the heterogeneity and overdetermination of the situationally emancipated utterance arises the possibility of paraphrasing and eventually of linguistic productivity (in the direction of the verbal work of art, as phrased by Bühler). The declining dynamic of situational supports creates the need for new "Archimedean points," from which the processes of meaning and of understanding can operate; in Bühler's words, there is need for new "solidified, petrified implements."

In incipient meaning and understanding the "core of crystallization" has been shown to lie in the emergence of entities, in the figure-on-ground structuring, in the gradually stabilized concept of object-of-action, and the like. The formation of these entities is known to be strongly codetermined by the physiologic properties of our apperceptive apparatus (as postulated by Bierwisch, cf. Chap. 5), and also by genetic development and individual experience. In the present chapter the emphasis has rested on one aspect of this process of entity formation and differentiation: the centering around the language user's ego. The importance of verbally coded signals and instructions has been found to grow with the declining influence of the situation. This tendency is to be further examined in the next chapter, in an inquiry into the interaction and grouping of words in the sentence.

Chapter 14

What Goes on in a Sentence

The sentence is an aggregate of words organized according to a variety of principles and rules (though not every such an aggregate is a sentence!). On account of the manifold relations obtaining between the words, the sentence possesses a characteristic stability, and it is this stability that provides the bearings for the hearer's understanding of the utterance. The vast overdetermination of the utterance thwarts all attempts at constructing a unified psychological theory of the sentence. Hence the psychological factors operating in a sentence can be described only by enumeration. Whereas every utterance is governed by some rules, no sentence follows all these rules at the same time.

The term *organized aggregate of words* is meant to underline the fact that the various elements of a sentence are interlocked in different ways, in different measure, and for different reasons. These elements come to form larger entities (chunks, units), which again show manifold interrelations. This is how directions, gradients, and tendencies build up in a sentence. A number of possibilities are created in this way while many other possibilities are ruled out in the process. A peculiar feature of these tendencies, feasibilities, and constraints is their simultaneous presence in the utterance and in the consciousness of the speaker-hearer who produces the utterance while "being in it" for a time.

The elements of an utterance become "organized" into higher-order units and as such acquire new functions. The psychological dynamic involved in these processes is of the same kind as the dynamic encountered in the prelinguistic cognitive realm. In earlier chapters we studied this dynamic in linguistic terms (e. g., Fillmore's case theory, in Chap. 8) and from a developmental angle (in Chap. 12). In the present chapter we want to begin with processes in the prelinguistic realm again, but now we shall consider "cognition as such," i. e., unrelated to particular persons or categories of persons. This will allow us to study the dynamic obtaining between the verbal elements of a sentence. In doing so we must take care not to think merely in terms of *ergon* (work), but to bear in mind the *energeia* (activity) of man's language behavior.

The conception of cognitive entities, each endowed with a dynamic organization and capable of combining with others into higher-order units by a similar dynamic, forms the central theme of Heider's theorizing and experimentation.

Fritz Heider originally studied perception in the framework of Gestalt psychology. Investigating the dynamic of perceptual processes focused upon the person as object of perception, Heider (1930) found the observer to structure the developments in his environment in terms of mutually delineated and reciprocally operating action units. We are by now familiar with this kind of figure/ground distinction. Furthermore, in his earlier investigations, Heider has demonstrated (similar to, e. g., Michotte 1963) that there is a tendency in the observer to center these action units around an agent who is acting under some kind of motivation (even in the case of geometrical figures in motion). The observer may say for instance when watching a cartoon film: "The red circle pushes the blue square aside." Thus the circle is linked with the action of pushing. In Heider's terminology: unit U is formed between the cognitive element p (circle) and the cognitive element x (push): pUx, i. e., p does x, and in this case: the circle pushes; p becomes the agent of action x. While applicable even to a geometrical figure the description acquires particular significance in the case of p's being a person.

The notion of *phenomenal causality* thus implied affirms in the first place that the observer presumes object p to be acting in a purposeful way; he does so by projecting this schema upon events in the world. This construction links up with the agent-action schema of the developmental psychologists, on the one hand, and with Fillmore's notion of case and Chafe's ideas, on the other: they all assert that the world is (conceptually) organized by a built-in cognition. At the same time, we are led back to an idea proposed in Chap. 7: that all human actions are pervaded by man's basic tendency to regard developments in the world as intelligible, i. e., as making sense. Thus we have linked up with Arnheim and von Allesch (cf. Chap. 1).

The principle that people consider developments around them as consisting of purposeful actions performed by social agents was subsequently applied by Heider (1958) to real-life social processes as they occur between real persons. To this end Heider set up a second principle, that of the sentiment relation. The relation obtaining between a person and the things the person likes differs from the relation to things the person does not like: the former condition favors the development of a unit *(pLx,* standing for *p likes x)*, while the latter does not yield a unit *(p-Lx)*.

Heider is further interested in the dynamic processes arising when the same elements (e. g., p or x) appear simultaneously in two qualitatively different mutual relationships.

In pursuit of these questions, Heider developed his most seminal concept: the *principle of balance:* Suppose p is perceived as forming a unit with x *(pUx)* and at the same time p is perceived as disapproving of x *(p-Lx)*. As we know, the latter implies that p does not like to be linked with x; the result is an incongruence or contradiction. For example, p pushes *(pUx),* but p does not like to push *(p-Lx)*.

Balance is a dynamic factor, that is, there is a tendency to establish a balance or to maintain an existing balance. In our case, the sentiment p-Lx and the unit pUx are brought into balance by changing the sign of any of the two units in pursuit of consonance. That is to say, if p dislikes pushing, the pushing may not take place at all, or: having pushed, p will tend to like pushing.

Considering the matter at a higher level of complexity:

Person p is building house x *(pUx)*

Person p likes person o *(pLo)*

Person o does not like house x *(o-Lx)*

Here we have a case of imbalance again. A balance for the triad p, o, x could be obtained if p were to dislike o, who does not like house x, or if o would come round to liking house x after all.

Heider's major contribution consists in having made commensurable in one comprehensive system two qualitatively different relations: the sentimental or affective relation pLx (or p-Lx) and the unit relation pUx (or p-Ux). The processes involved in the system derive their dynamic precisely from this balance (or imbalance, to be exact); the perceiving person feels compelled to alter one or both of the constitutive relations in order to restore a balance, or consonance, between them. Much the same dynamic underlies the earlier described phenomenon of sense constancy, and it is this dynamic that lays the foundation of the theory of (cognitive) dissonance or consonance, so popular since Festinger.

Heider's model, where quasi-stationary states (having a house built, liking someone, disliking a house) give rise to a dynamic which presses for changes, or the preservation of an existing consonance, has exerted an especial influence on social psychology. A series of congruity models have been proposed in this domain as well as in the psychology of language. The most important in the latter domain is the model by Osgood and Tannenbaum (1955), initially designed for predicting attitude change.

Osgood conceptualizes the meaning of a word or concept in terms of *mediating response,* as we know. If two words or concepts in a sentence become interrelated (the nature of this interrelationship needing specification), then the two participating mediating responses are subject to modifications intended to preserve or restore a balance.

There are a number of ways in which two or more words in a sentence become interrelated. The simplest way is by merely stringing them together; more complex relationships develop when the successive words have different roles to play in the sentence.

Let us begin our discussion with the relatively simple case when the word sequence itself is functionally effective (at first glance, in any event). Even in the seemingly straightforward enumeration of, for instance, personal attributes, the order of the adjectives used has been found to affect the hearer's image of the person described (e. g., Asch 1946). This goes to show that, in order to operate in the relevant domain, we must bear in mind the important fact that the psychological processes occurring at any given moment around any single "element" of an utterance are frequently determined only by subsequent developments. The same kind of asynchrony (or anisotachy, to use a more elegant term) in the processing of utterances was noted in our discussion of the Russian psychology of language and Goldman-Eisler's studies of pauses in speech.

It is in this context that Uhlenbeck (1963, p 13) speaks of the "principle of sustained memory," which holds that a certain number of (sentence) elements

> may remain unconnected and kept present, until an element or elements appearing in the utterance much later can be connected with them.

In a phrase containing a noun and one or more modifiers (e. g., adjectives), some of the modifiers may appear before, and others after, the noun.

Rommetveit and Turner (1967) presented their subjects with curved lines and with sentences describing these lines. There were, for instance, two sentences referring to one such line:

a) *A leftward, jaggedly descending broken curve*
b) *A jagged, broken curve descending leftward*

The subjects were asked to identify the curves from such descriptions and then to reproduce these descriptions.

Prenominal adjectives resulted in improved recall and better differentiation of the objects. This finding has been further elaborated by Dolinsky and Michael (1969) who found the recall of a string of adjectives to depend on whether the adjectives were followed by a noun or not. The noun evidently acted as a postintegrative factor, causing the preceding adjectives to "close" with it into a new entity; such an entity had a functional effect on recall.

At this point we realize that an order of sentence constituents originally regarded as purely linear may become a hierarchic order. Arranged in a particular sequence, these elements reveal certain dominance structures; the building blocks of these structures are either the elements themselves or the higher-order units formed from these elements.

The close affinity between sequential and hierarchic structures can be readily exemplified by means of modifier groupings again. Linguists distinguish between coordinate and subordinate endocentric phrases: in the former case each of the two (or more) modifiers acts upon the head noun independently of the others *(a chilly, humid morning);* in the latter case the first modifier acts to change the second modifier, and the thus affected second one acts upon the head noun *(the wide open door).* Now, is there a psychological match of this difference in linguistic structure?

Degermann and Mather (1972) have obtained results which make a positive answer quite plausible. In their experiment, they asked subjects to draw spatial representations of the two types of phrases: the diagrams depicting subordinate word sequences revealed a higher multiple ordering than those supplied for coordinate sequences. A multiple ordering of this kind represents both the hierarchic and sequential information contained in subordinate phrases.

Once again we come to realize how small a step separates mere sequential ordering from supra- and subordination.

The matter served as a point of departure for a research trend which, after some impressive findings, found itself in a blind alley because its goal had been wrongly set. GA Miller attempted (prior to his *Language and Communication,*

1951) to subsume under one heading both kinds of information: that about the sequential ordering of elements and that about the interdependencies of elements. He construed transitional probabilities between successive elements as depicting both the ordering in, and the psychological processing of, the utterance. In spite of its amazing productivity, this approach was bound to run aground for a number of reasons. One was the reduction of the rules of grammar to "nothing but" transitional probabilities. Another was its discordance with the psychology of communication: the modification effected by an utterance in the consciousness of the hearer does not always tend toward what is most probable. Finally, the third reason was entailed by the fact that the notion of *element* (indispensable for any operation with transitional or joint probabilities) can be unequivocally defined only in a sequential but not in a hierarchic sense; a hierarchy comprises interlocking units of different sizes.

As usual, the baby was thrown out along with the bathwater, not without Miller's effective assistance. Once generative grammar had made its appearance, every kind of probabilistic thinking was discarded as being in principle out of place in psycholinguistics. This explains why even today the psychology of language lacks a conceptual apparatus capable of handling the internal chaining and automaticity of conventional phrases and idiomatic expressions, with which our everyday language is pervaded to an amazing extent. That this is so can be seen from the neurolinguistic evidence surveyed by Van Lancker (1975), who postulates that such "prefabricated" entities are processed in a specific manner.

In order to account for the internal dynamic of a sentence, we must therefore start by construing the mutually independent existence of hierarchic and sequential information, and then try to trace their interaction. Attempts to explore the interlocking of the dependency and sequential aspects of planning in a sentence go back to Lashley's (1951) discussion of serial order in behavior, a study of remarkable impact on psychology as a whole. Lashley asserted that an idea which is to be expressed in language is initially represented in the brain in some nontemporal manner[1] (e. g., in terms of space) and that this representation is then scanned and transformed into a succession; it is in this process that the morphemes needed to express the idea in linguistic form are selected and arranged linearly in a sentence.

In language processes this interplay of sequence and hierarchy is particularly evident in the realm of "preferred adjective order." A number of grammatical rules have been proposed by linguists to account for this (e. g., Vendler 1963); other linguists have rejected these rules as mistaken (e. g., Katz 1964). In contrast, JE Martin has advanced a more psychological hypothesis, which seeks to do justice to the processual nature of the phenomenon. According to Martin (1969, p 698):

> the order of adjective production is habitually the inverse of the order of adjective choice. Adjectives produced closer to the noun (are) chosen prior to adjectives produced further from the noun. ... in the case of normally ordered adjectives, the main antecedent of order of adjective choice is differential adjective accessibility.

---

[1] The same thing has already been claimed by Wundt.

The degree of accessibility varies with the relation obtaining between the meaning of the adjective-modified noun and the attributes designated by the adjective. This relation comprises a normative element, as illustrated by the following example. A quarter-dollar piece may be described either as *large* or as *small,* depending on the noun modified by the adjective: in the case of *coin,* a more appropriate designation would be *large,* but in the case of *disk* it would be *small* (a quarter-dollar piece is a large coin but only a small disk). Back in 1967 Bierwisch observed that it depends on the noun whether, and to what extent, a norm is implied by the noun-modifying adjective. The interlocking of noun and adjective and the implication of a norm can be exemplified by the following confrontation:

THE AIRPLANE IS HIGH
THE INTERIOR IS HIGH
THE ROOM IS HIGH

In each case the noun implies a scale of standard in accordance with which *high* receives a specific interpretation. For *room,* this standard is certainly defined with greater precision than for *interior:* a high room can be visualized more easily than a high interior, which may be the interior of a box, a room, a church, and many other objects. Thus the accessibility of an adjective should depend also on the speed with which the respective standard becomes available for mental inspection. At the same time, we realize from our example that the particular standard scale needed to understand the given sentence becomes available only with the formation of the adjective-noun entity; this scale is implied neither by the adjective nor by the noun alone. The newly formed entity provides us with additional information – which issue will be considered in detail in the further course of our argument (chiefly in the next chapter).

The scanning or selection procedure proposed by JE Martin in imitation of Lashley will activate all adjectives – in keeping with the thus defined accessibility – at one stroke, so to speak, as long as the adjectives appear in their customary or conventional order *(the large, red, Chinese shawl; dear old grandmother).* But what about an unconventional adjective order? What are the conditions for producing *the Chinese red large shawl* or *old dear grandmother,* and what states are evoked by these utterances in the hearer?

The remarkable thing about such an unconventional word order is certainly the insertion of a pause between the two adjectives. In the light of Goldman-Eisler's findings (see end of Chap. 11), a pause like this can be interpreted as marking the formation of a new entity (cf. also O'Connell et al. 1969). JE Martin (1969) maintains that, unlike the case of a conventional word order, a recycling of the scanning is taking place: during the first cycle the adjective close to the noun is chosen, while during the second cycle the thus formed entity *(large shawl, dear grandmother)* is expanded by the other adjective, which now affects the entity rather than the noun alone.

The significance of these arguments goes beyond the problem of adjective order and its psychological correlates: the structural peculiarities of the utterance are accounted for by differences in the underlying structuring *processes.* This is a familiar "figure of thought" for the generativists, of course. For a psychology of subjective experience the process of recycling and its pauses is of interest on account of its attention-rousing function. (A similar thing occurs in metaphor, where the hesitation over an apparent incongruence spurs attention and furthers understanding; cf. Hörmann 1973.) Pauses generate attention, and increased attention generates pauses – as demonstrated in the study by O'Connell et al. (1969).

Attention effects cannot be sensibly discussed without going into the intentions of the subject. We shall therefore have to go beyond the realm of language-immanent factors in our account of adjective ordering; a suggestion along these lines was contained in Bierwisch's postulate of reckoning with the reference standard that is part of the language user's knowledge of the world. In their study of prenominal adjective order, Danks and Schwenk (1972) proceed from the assumption that the attention-inducing adjective is placed first in a series of adjectives. If the speaker wants the hearer to discriminate between, say, two red cars, one large, the other small, he is bound to order the adjectives in the conventional fashion *(the large red car)*. But if the hearer's attention is to be drawn to the distinction between two large cars, one red, the other blue, the speaker is likely to say *the red large car*.

In their experiment, the two authors presented the subjects with a set of four *pictures,* for instance:

LARGE	small
RED	brown
CAR	scissors
small	large
gold	green
key	car

Thereupon subjects heard two word sequences (in this case, *the large red car* and *the red large car*) and were asked to tell which of them "would better enable a listener to identify the criterion object from the set" (the criterion object being in the upper left-hand corner). The results confirmed the authors' "pragmatic communication rule," which says that the more discriminating adjective is placed first.

This finding dovetails neatly with Olson's (1970) cognitive theory of semantics: it depends on the perceptual context of the object what kind of verbal description the speaker will choose to ensure effective communication. When so required by the goal of communication, the speaker will not hesitate to "violate" a convention which, in many cases, is proclaimed as a grammatical rule only because it reflects the preponderant usage.

We have dealt so far with adjective-noun sequences, finding that the very "stringing" of words produces certain semantic effects and results in the formation of hierarchic subunits within the utterance. Certain words or sentence elements, however, have built-in specific instructions on how to enter into such entities or units. The dynamic of unit formation in the sentence is considered in the next few pages, and the reader is requested to bear in mind our arguments concerning the generation of units and the dynamic disclosed in this process (see the chapters on generative semantics and the acquisition of language).

An elementary example of a "built-in" instruction for the formation of units in the sentence is the transitive verb.

As we try to picture the kind of lexical representation entailed by these verbs, we seem to discover in a transitive verb some sort of "pointer" to the subsequent nominal phrase; intransitive verbs lack such a pointer. Hence an isolated intransitive verb enjoys a greater "autonomy" than an isolated transitive one. Accordingly, Polzella and Rohrmann (1970) found that isolated intransitive verbs were recalled better than isolated transitive ones. While negatively affecting recall, this kind of "semantic incompleteness" causes transitive verbs used as stimuli in the association test to associate more quickly and with a greater number of nouns than is the case with intransitive verbs.

Transitivity vs. intransitivity are relatively general and, shall we say, rather superficial designations for a verb; they cannot account, by themselves, for the central role of the verb in the sentence process. Back in the chapter on generative semantics, we discussed a theory which proposes the notion of predication (or the formation of a verb-argument structure, or of a proposition) as a conceptual tool for dealing with this type of unit formation.

Making now a fresh approach – a more psychology-oriented one than in the chapter devoted to linguistics – to the circumstances and implications of verb-centered unit formation in the sentence, we might start again with the earlier mentioned study by Hörmann et al. (1975), from which we know that in conditions of perceptual masking, the verb is more difficult to identify than any other sentence element.

Once the verb has been made out, the probability of a correct identification of both subject and object is raised; there is no such facilitation in the other direction, however: the perception of either subject or object does not raise the probability of verb identification. Evidently, the verb (predicate) gives guidance in understanding the sentence; it instructs the hearer how to put together and organize the word-conveyed concepts and pieces of information in the predication.

Predication has been repeatedly mentioned in these pages; at present we want to examine this concept in its linguistic, logical, and psychological aspects, substantiating the heuristic productivity of such a comprehensive approach by empirical evidence.

Predication can be understood as "stating something about something" (a conception which goes back to Aristotle). The acceptance of this logical relation by linguistics is based on two tenets. One asserts that the physical world is made up of things that have certain properties, initiate or undergo certain processes, stand in a certain relationship to one another, or have a certain extension or location in space or time (Lyons 1968, p 271). The other tenet states that the structure of language corresponds to this (logical) structure of the world and that thus the world can be reflected by language.

There is no need to enlarge here on the many logical and psychological difficulties ensuing from the interlocking of logic and syntax, but we ought to mention the interesting distinction between substantial and instrumental universals proposed by List (1974). If it can be claimed that in the argumentation that follows we move "closer to psychology", it is principally in the sense that our attention is focused not on the thing about which a predication is made, but on the verbalized action by virtue of which persons and things are brought into mutual relation.

Hence, in general terms, predication interrelates verbalized states or events of the world. Whereas in the case of adjective stringing we were confronted with the mere addition of characterizations, predication is essentially an act of judging. In its simplest form it amounts to an assertion of the kind

X is a Y, or *X has a Y.*

In terms of the psychology of communication such an assertion consists in the verbalization of a certain "existential" relation between two states of the world; the speaker who verbalizes this relation usually assumes that the hearer is not aware of it. Suppose you enter a forest at spring time and tell your companion, "The trees are green." You cannot claim to have passed on any information to your companion unless he is blind. What you actually seek to achieve with your utterance is to establish in the mind of your hearer the same kind of relation (between *trees* and *green*) that exists in your own consciousness. The predicative utterance is thus meant to lead to the formation of a certain entity in the mind of the hearer. Such an entity is formed not by addition, as in the case of the modifier sequence, but by the process of judging, asserting, or predicating.

In following this line of reasoning we shall be well advised not to confuse predication, as a psychological act of judgment or assertion, with the syntactic predicate – an error we have been warned against by Uhlenbeck (1967b). Such a fallacious identification may easily give rise to the claim that it is always the verb that states something new about the subject.

Being expressed in the form of predication, the entity thus formed implants a vector, or direction, in the consciousness of the hearer. The place from which this vector of understanding takes its beginning depends, among others, on the presuppositions built into the act of communication and on the centering of the utterance upon the ego (i. e., the centering of the communicative action around an origo). A number of conceptual tools could be used in exploring the position and direction of this vector. For the time being, we will make use of the balance or congruity principle developed by Heider and by Osgood and Tannenbaum. Osgood exemplifies his thesis with the sentence

TOM IS A THIEF

For the policeman who caught Tom in the process of stealing, this sentence represents a "congruent" assertion, insofar as the presuppositions underlying the statement are congruent with its formulation. If the same sentence is uttered to Tom's mother, who holds her son in high esteem, there arises an incongruence between *Tom* and *thief* in her consciousness. The intrinsic tendency to maintain or restore a balance calls for modification: either Tom's mother refuses to accept the statement, or she arrives at the classical judgment, "You are not my son any more," or else, she concludes (in a more up-to-date manner), "Everyone does some stealing these days."

Whether in the case of the policeman or in the case of Tom's mother, the processes of unit formation and the resultant restructuring dynamic owe much of their determination to the fact that the (uttered) predication is brought into relation with some existing cognitive content (with which it "fits" or not). Both the formulation and the implications of the predicative judgment do not always (or not entirely) depend on the relationship with the existing, unverbalized cognitive content however. The relationships between the *verbalized* states of the world as they become interrelated through the act of predicating are also very important. The latter circumstance has certain philosphic aspects that ought to be mentioned here.

Predication has just been described as "stating something about something," and we may now add that the relationship linking one "something" to the other "something" may differ in kind. In one case, the predication may contain no *new* information about its subject, bringing instead a specific aspect of that subject to mind. In philosophy, this kind of predication is called analytic judgment *(the circle is round),* and its purpose is to specify the meaning of the word *circle.* The predication contained in most utterances is of a different type, in that it adds some information to the existing content *(the circle is green).* In philosophy, this kind of predication is called synthetic judgment.

Considered in terms of logic, the relationship between what is predicated and the subject of predication provides a perspective from which we may examine the truth value of a sentence. This approach leans heavily on the notion of synonymity: if *bachelor* is synonymous with *unmarried adult male* then the sentence THE BACHELOR IS MARRIED cannot be true (unless a suitable shift of meaning has been effected by the mechanisms of sense constancy as discussed in Chap. 7). Whether synonymity does occur or not is another matter, to be determined empirically. The truth value of synthetic sentences (BILL IS A BACHELOR or A BACHELOR HAS AN EASY LIFE), on the other hand, depends on extralinguistic circumstances.

Turning again, after that excursion into philosophy, to the psychology of language, we feel obliged to represent "specification" and "addition" as the two basic modes of predication in a kind of model that would illuminate the psychological nature of the underlying processes (redundant vs. informative). With this goal in mind we now turn to Steinberg (1970).

In his study of analyticity and syntheticity, Steinberg seeks to make subject and predicate compatible by relying on the semantic features of the two sentence parts. He is concerned solely with the kind of predication where two nouns are linked by an *is a* relation (see Chap. 6), and where both nouns share the same feature sequences – except for the minimal difference of the notorious *differentia specifica:* THE MAN IS A HUSBAND. (And it is only thanks to this restriction that his feature paradigm allows Steinberg to develop a model of specification and addition as the two basic processes of predication.)

To achieve his aim, Steinberg has elaborated the feature concept – commonly employed in a dichotomous manner – in an important way. Prior to specifying the sign of the given feature (+ or −), it has to be established whether the respective semantic dimension does apply to the given word or not. In other words, a dimension may assume values other than plus or minus, namely:

v (+ or −, but not both), or
x (neither + nor −), or
O (either v or x, but not both).

Hence it has become possible to judge the relevance ot the respective dimension in terms of feature codings. For example, *man* is coded in the following way:

Animateness (A)	+
Humanness (H)	+
Sex (male) (S)	+
Marriage (M)	v
Engaged (E)	O

Husband shows these features:

Animateness (A)	+
Humanness (H)	+
Sex (male) (S)	+
Marriage (M)	+
Engaged (E)	x

Next, Steinberg contends that the meaning of the subject–predicate unit subsumed by the predication can be construed as a particular interaction of the feature sequences of subject and predicate term, for synthetic sentences in any case. Thus the sentence

THE MAN IS A HUSBAND

yields the coding pairs

(A)	+	+	specified as	+
(H)	+	+	specified as	+
(S)	+	+	specified as	+
(M)	v	+	specified as	+
(E)	O	x	specified as	x

The specification takes the following course: if a less definite feature (e. g., v or x or O) is joined by a more definite feature, then the latter determines the respective dimension. For M (Marriage) there is still the alternative *(v)* between married (+) and unmarried (−), and for E (Engaged), between E relevant and E irrelevant; in either case the indefiniteness is resolved by the predicative unit formation (The man *is a* husband): M is now definitely plus and E definitely x.

Steinberg's construction is quite impressive at first glance, but a number of questions are left open. Remaining with our example, why should the dimension Married have relevance for *man* while being undetermined in value, whereas the dimension Engaged is indeterminate in its relevance? What makes for the determination of relevance? One possible answer is offered by Engelkamp (discussed further below).

Another thing: Steinberg has restricted himself to one form of predication, i. e., two nouns linked by an *is a* relation. How about other, more common kinds of predication? For example, the kind where a predicative adjective is used to state something about a subject marked with an attributive adjective: THE AFFABLE GIRL IS TALL. Can we expect here the same dynamic adjustments to occur as suggested by Heider's balance principle and Osgood–Tannenbaum's congruity principle?

We could hope to identify relevant modifications in the grammatical subject only if both the two adjectives and the noun acted upon were amenable to description within one semantic system – or else we could not hope to trace the formation of the functional unit that makes up predication. The only empirically founded and empirically measurable semantic system available for the time being is Osgood's connotative space, with its three dimensions Evaluation, Potency, and Activity as comprised by the Semantic Differential technique. Let us see how this instrument can serve to account for the dynamic processes occurring in sentences such as THE AFFABLE GIRL IS TALL or THE NICE XYZ IS SUBMISSIVE.

Osgood's initial view was that an adjective–noun combination is equivalent to the respective noun–predicative adjective combination: HONEST TOM can be fully neutralized by the predication ... IS DISHONEST. This view is based on the perfectly viable working hypothesis that even in the case of predication the combination is effected by mere addition. But in the study discussed in the previous chapter Osgood (1971b) was able to show that in nonconnotative terms the attributive adjective and the predicative adjective cannot be viewed as equivalent. In describing an event involving a red cup with which the hearer is already familiar, the speaker is bound to use *red* attributively, not predicatively: THE MAN IS HOLDING THE RED CUP, rather than THE CUP HELD BY THE MAN IS RED.

We tried to construe this determination of adjective mode (attributive or predicative) as being due to differential states of the speaker's consciousness (or of the hearer's consciousness as assessed by the speaker), i. e., as being the effect of a cognitive presupposition. If it is true that the mode of the adjective depends on cognitive presuppositions, can it be claimed that these different presuppositions have no effect on the way in which the noun is influenced by the respective adjectives?

Engelkamp and Merdian (1973) have devoted an empirical study to this problem. Three competitive hypotheses were given consideration:

a) The effect of the congruity or balance principle does not depend on attributive vs. predicative adjective mode

b) The attributive mode of the adjective is used only for referencing, and the predicative mode introduces the genuinely new content, as suggested by Osgood's (1971b) findings

c) An attributively used adjective exerts a stronger influence on the noun than a predicatively used one – a hypothesis implied by the results of a study by Carr and Kingsbury (1938), frequently quoted in personality psychology, in which the attributively described trait (HELPFUL OTTO) is thought to hold for a longer time (has more temporal validity) than a trait described predicatively (OTTO IS HELP-FUL, or OTTO HELPS).

In their experiment, Engelkamp and Merdian gave their subjects sentences of the type:

THE NICE BIV IS DISGUSTING,

instructing subjects to rate the (anonymous) grammatical subject on the Semantic Differential. The use of various control groups served to cancel out effects of order etc. Engelkamp and Merdian (1973, p 176) concluded that

> the resultant noun meaning is not arrived at by means of the congruity principle. The mutually contradictory, distinctly polarized meanings of the attributively and predicatively used adjectives do not cancel each other out completely . . ., rather, they cause the rating of the grammatical subject to take over the sign of the predicative adjective and to show less polarization than the latter.

In sentences of this type, the predicate performs a "concept-modifying" function, as Engelkamp and Merdian put it. Treading more softly, we would prefer to speak of a modification effected in the speaker-hearer's consciousness.

The study by Engelkamp and Merdian has shown that the integration of the connotative meanings which the adjectives "project" upon the subject depends on the role these adjectives perform in predication. There we have further evidence of the multifarious determination of the processes occurring in the sentence and, all the more so, in the speaker-hearer's consciousness. The above quoted study has also revealed an entirely different factor which intervenes in adjective-noun interaction: the investigators found evaluatively negative predicates (i. e., predicates negatively rated on Evaluation) to have a stronger effect than positive ones. They further discovered a sequence effect: initially positive information is subject to stronger negative modification by subsequent negative information than the reverse.

To account for this finding we shall have to consider a notion which Engelkamp and Merdian failed to bear in mind when interpreting their results; we refer to Boucher and Osgood's (1969, p 1) "Pollyanna hypothesis," which states that

> there is a universal human tendency to use evaluatively positive (E+) words more frequently, diversely and facilely than evaluatively negative (E−) words. . . . humans tend to "look on (and talk about) the bright side of life".

Substantiated by the authors with various evidence derived from a number of languages, this linguistic (or cognitive?) universal makes the finding reported by Engelkamp and Merdian, and also by some other investigators, seem quite plausible. Since evaluatively positive information has been found to occur with greater frequency, thus being of higher probability, than negative information, the latter, when appearing (especially after positive information), is apt to exert a stronger influence on the connotative meaning of the grammatical subject.

In speaking of predication as the formation of a functional entity within the sentence, we have restricted ourselves to *is a* and *has a* relations; the actual formation of an entity has been inferred from modifications in the connotative meaning.

Our next step is to advance our argument in two ways: 1) We must try to go beyond the confines of *is a* and *has a* statements (which are of considerable interest, notably for the logician, but which strike the psychologist of language as somewhat sterile) into the wide and chequered landscape of ordinary verbs that determine, in all their richness, the specific quality of the entity within which the elements of the utterance become integrated by the act of predicating. 2) We shall seek to trace the effects of predication (its various types) as revealed in not only the connotative meaning of the grammatical subject but also other aspects of utterance processing.

The psychologists' favorite index of unit formation, or integration, has long been association in memory.

The typical pattern of thought is as follows: in the case that stimulus word X evokes predominantly word Y and only infrequently word Z as response, XY is more likely to function as a unit than XZ. The same basic pattern underlies an experimental paradigm involving recall: in the case that word X comes to mind whenever word Y is recalled but rarely when word Z is recalled, XY is more likely to be a unit than XZ.

The most widely known attempt to trace in this fashion the structure of a sentence as stored in memory was undertaken by NF Johnson (1965a, 1965b). (This study is discussed in detail by, e. g., Hörmann 1971a, pp 245 ff.; Weisberg 1971; Engelkamp 1973.) Johnson assumed that when trying to remember a sentence, we tend to group its constituents in chunks of different sizes and at different "hierarchic levels." Each chunk is coded in memory as a node, and each word within the chunk associates with this node, rather than directly with any adjoining word. The sequence and rank order of these chunks is likewise stored in memory. This principle of segmentation is illustrated in Fig. 5.

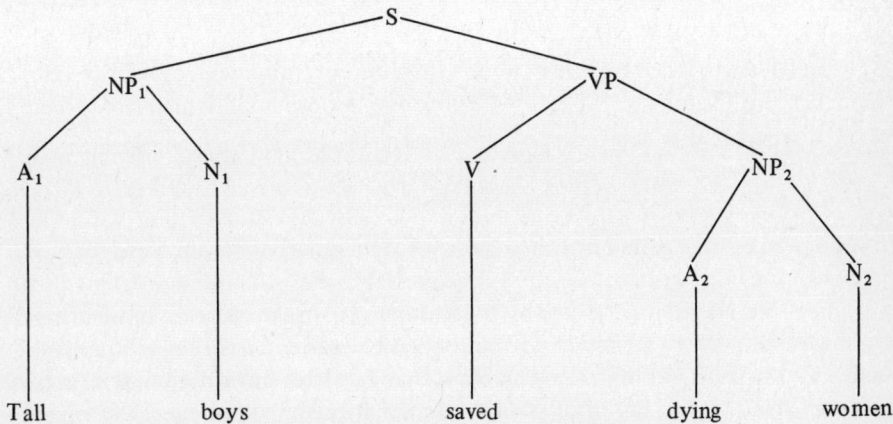

Fig. 5. The structuring of a sentence as proposed by N. F. Johnson

The verb *saved* is here part of the verb-phrase unit (VP) which also comprises NP_2. Coding in memory apparently follows the surface structure postulated by the generativists. (It is likewise possible to devise models which relate coding to the deep structure of the memorized sentence, entirely in line with Johnson's coding principle; cf. Weisberg 1971.)

Johnson's approach proved successful to the extent that he was able to predict with some accuracy the probability with which a subject recalling a particular word (e. g., *boy*) would recall other words (e. g., *tall,* or *saved*). In this case, the subject is more likely to remember *tall* than *saved,* since the latter is linked with N_1 (boy) by the higher-level node S, whereas *tall* is connected with *boy* by the lower-level NP_1. These transitional error probabilities reflect the internal structure of the sentence.

This reflection is of a very rough kind, however. As demonstrated by Weisberg (1971), intrasentence word associations are not as symmetric as postulated by the model. The response to V as stimulus is much more often N_2 than A_2; N_1 as stimulus evokes V twice as often as A_1, contrary to Johnson's predictions.

The evidence contributed by Weisberg has made it equally clear that the boundaries of the coding units established by this paradigm do not coincide with the deep structure of the sentences. From Weisberg's study, and even more so from Engelkamp's investigation, it would appear that nothing but the two main phrases of the sentence (NP and VP) do actually function as memory chunks in this way. At the same time, the two studies reveal that the formation of units in the process of sentence memorization is governed by semantic rather than syntactic considerations (the latter being Johnson's assumption).

So this would be the right moment to bring in the arguments put forward in our discussion of the formation of semantically determined units – which leads us back to the process of predicating, but this time without restriction to auxiliary verbs. The reader should bear in mind that the predication in question is not the same thing as the "predicate" in the grammar employed by, e. g., Johnson. Our view is that *predication* is a judgment by which a relationship is established in the consciousness of the language user.

How can we imagine the formation of such *semantically* determined units? We shall now report an idea expounded by Engelkamp (1973) with reference to certain post-Chomskyan developments in linguistics, notably the notions contributed by Fillmore, Langendoen, and Chafe (see Chap. 8). These authors all concur in the view that "every sentence . . . is built around a *predicative* element" (Chafe 1970, p 96). The predicative core of a sentence serves to integrate aspects of states or events with aspects of things (i. e., physical objects, and also reified abstractions). States and events are represented by the verb, things by nouns. *The verb is central;* functioning as the predicate, the verb governs the nouns as its arguments. In Chap. 8 we discussed Fillmore's case theory as an example of such a system.

Engelkamp assumes that by conceiving the predicate of a sentence, the language user has at the same time made available, in outline, the arguments opened by the verb in this particular case. Having heard *cut,* the hearer prepares to make available the arguments belonging to *cut:* a Patient to be cut, an Agent who does the cutting, and an Instrument to cut with. In other words, the hearer becomes aware of the criteria the respective nouns have to satisfy by their semantic features.

The verb *implies* its arguments, says Engelkamp. To explain how this is accomplished, he avails himself of Steinberg's design as described a few pages back, according to which we must first establish the relevance of a feature dimension and only then the polarity or sign revealed by the particular word on this dimension. The arguments actually used to fill the open places (e. g., *bread*) serve to specify the general information implied by the verb *(to cut)* – in this case, that the material to be cut must be fairly solid, but not too hard or liquid[2].

In predication, the verb implies its arguments; the words actually used in the open places serve to modify the verb. On the other hand, when I hear that it is bread which is to be cut, I also learn something about the manner of cutting. The verb and ist arguments form an entity – and this must also come into evidence in memory processes.

If this is how a predicate implies its arguments, then a recall experiment should show that a subject who has remembered the predicate is more likely to recall any noun that functions as the verb's argument in the sentence than any other noun in the same sentence. For example, in a sentence containing the predicate *cut* and the nouns *knife* and *cloud* a subject who recalls *cut* should be able to retrieve *knife* more easily than *cloud*.

The same does not hold in the opposite direction. A predicate does imply its arguments, but the arguments do not imply the predicate[3]. Thus we are reminded of the dominant position of the verb, which comes into evidence here as much as in the earlier discussed experiment by Hörmann et al. (carried out after Engelkamp's study).

Furthermore, a sentence with a greater number of thus conceived units should be more difficult to remember than a sentence with fewer such units. THE MAN WITH THE DOG WAS DRIVING THE CAR should pose more difficulty than THE MAN WAS CUTTING THE BREAD WITH THE KNIFE, because the latter sentence comprises only one predicate–argument unit, while the former contains two.

Relying on this kind of semantic determination of units, Engelkamp made predictions concerning different aspects of sentence storing, and these predictions were verified in his experiments with much greater precision than was the case with Johnson's predictions made on a syntactic basis.

---

[2] In imitation of Steinberg, Engelkamp construes the integration of the feature sequence implied or made available by the verb with the feature sequence contributed by the argument-noun as a kind of logical addition of the features from the two sequences. He is thus exposed to all the difficulties which arise when we operate with a lexicon or dictionary that provides for only two places (+ and −) on each dimension. Thus we realize again that predication cannot be reduced to one function, or explained by one mechanism.

[3] In this way, Engelkamp precludes an approximation of his conception to the notion of association: associations are by definition symmetric. At the same time, he does justice to the directional nature of the process of predicating – a point stressed by Fillmore and even more so by Chafe.

Engelkamp (1973) was able to show in his study that in understanding and storing a sentence, we use the semantic, morphological, and syntactic instructions contained in the utterance to construct and store in memory the basic semantic relations (directions and units) of the sentence.

Thus the organization of the material of the sentence in predicative units constitutes a basic property of the process of understanding. The critical importance of the formation of these structures was likewise revealed in experiments with text reading (i. e., reading of a string of sentences). Kintsch and Keenan (1973) found that the time needed to read a text grew as the number of propositions[4] increased, even though the number of words or syllables remained constant.

Evidence of the kind contributed by Engelkamp and Kintsch has brought our notions of what goes on in the language user during the processing of sentences closer to the well-known findings on memory. Psychologists have known for some time that the processes by which material is committed to long-term memory are of limited capacity, i. e., that only a limited number of units can be stored at any one time in short-term memory. In his "magical number" paper, GA Miller (1956) was able to show that the only way for our short-term store to work on larger amounts of material was by arranging this material into larger chunks, the number of these chunks being the limiting factor. As demonstrated by Mandler (1967), a marked improvement in recall of isolated verbal material is obtained if the subject is offered *in advance* clue words that enable him to categorize the material: the category designations function as nuclei around which structures are built up, and structuring is known to facilitate the storing of material. (Cf. also Bock 1978.)

Predication as the formation of a unit becomes functional in terms of memory and in other ways – this is one of two aspects of interest to us. The other is the internal directedness of the unit, its dynamic as implied by the underlying semantic relation. The issue of directedness covers, of course, Fillmore's cases, and this is what comes in for discussion right now.

It will be in order to recall that Fillmore's cases did not emerge from psychological investigations, and hence it is impossible to tell whether Patient, Instrument, etc. are psychologically effective cases or not. There are good grounds for believing in the Agent's psychological relevance, however; suffice it to go back to the developmental evidence reviewed in the preceding chapters. According to Shafto (1973), both Agent and Experiencer possess more psychological reality than Instrument and Object. But here we feel the need for a more differentiated approach.

Having subjects quickly answer questions about some relational aspects of sentences they had just heard, Suci and Hamacher (1972) assumed that the latency period of the answers would reveal the hierarchical nature of sentence processing.

---

[4] What we have come to know as predication, or verb–argument structure, is called *proposition* by Kintsch: "Propositions are n-tuples of word concepts, one of which serves as a predicator, and the remaining ones as arguments, each fulfilling a unique semantic role" (Kintsch et al., 1975, p 196).

They tested the hypothesis that the primacy of the grammatical subject is based, not on its (syntactic) role in surface structure, but on whether or not the subject plays some action role in semantic deep structure, as conceptualized by Fillmore and Chafe. Suci and Hamacher (1972, p 37) concluded that

> the processing of a noun-adjective relation is a function of the action role of the noun ... rather than of the position or grammatical category in the sentence. Relations with agent nouns are processed more rapidly than the relations with patient nouns.

The verb–argument structure affects not only the rate of processing. In the already quoted paper, Shafto (1973, p 561) reported that

> sentences with the same underlying predicate structure were relatively more confusable in a running recognition task than were sentences with identical surface subjects and objects or sentences which simply used the same nouns.

In other words, what is understood and stored by the hearer is the semantic structure that lies behind (or underneath) the surface of the sentence.

In treating propositions (or predications, or verb–argument structures) as the organizing cores of sentence understanding and storing, we have come to realize that these units are endowed with an internal directedness in terms of Agent, Patient, and other relations as described in Fillmore's case grammar and also by some investigators of language acquisition.

The internal directedness of the predication may likewise interact with the concepts that serve as arguments of the verb in quite a different manner than discussed so far.

Let us begin with what may appear a ludicrous question. When hearing the sentence

JOHN BENDS PAPERCLIPS

we cannot be sure how many paperclips are involved. Generally speaking: Does the verb in such sentences offer implicitly some information about the numerical or other size of the category referred to in the grammatical object? Take the two sentences:

JOHN BUYS VEGETABLES
JOHN LIKES VEGETABLES

What is meant in the first sentence is that John buys perhaps a few varieties of vegetables; in the second sentence it is asserted however that John likes most kinds of vegetables, if not all.

The finding that in predication some verbs do quantify the grammatical object has inspired further investigations (Gilson and Abelson 1965; Kanouse 1972). Kanouse was able to distinguish between classes of verbs in terms of their quantifying effect; he found "manifest" verbs (search, collect, make, find, destroy, attack, damage, etc.) to apply to a smaller proportion of the given object class than "subjective" verbs (love, trust, understand, admire, despise, fear, ignore, etc.): when saying *he ruins shoes,* we invariably mean fewer pairs of shoes than when saying *he likes shoes.*

Very clearly, integration in the unit of predication has some other effects in addition to those discussed so far (adjustments in connotative meaning and formation of chunk-like organizing nuclei). This reminds us of an important insight, arrived at on several occasions: the linguistic or psychological "mechanisms" identified in language use (e. g., predication, or stringing of modifiers) have diverse and varying functions to perform. The functions of any "mechanism" differ from situation to situation.

Leaving aside the issue of predication, we turn now to another aspect of unit formation which looms large in the sentence and presumably also in text, i. e., to pronominalization.

Lesgold (1972) had his subjects remember sentences like

> THE AUNT ATE THE PIE AND SHE WAS SENILE
> THE AUNT ATE THE PIE AND ALICE WAS SENILE

Recall was tested after presentation of a cue consisting of either the first noun, or the second noun, or the verb, or the adjective. The investigators recorded superior recall for sentences with pronouns than for sentences with two separate propositions. Lesgold (1972, p 320) concluded:

> Pronouns can be conceived of as sentential cues that indicate the sharing of lexical items by more than one underlying proposition.

Pronouns act as signals for the hearer to store an input as an integrated unit. If that is so, then a sentence containing two propositions brought into relation by a relative pronoun should be more easily stored than a sentence with the same propositions side by side:

> THE DOG CHASED THE CAT WHICH WAS YELLOW

should be better recalled than

> THE CAT WAS YELLOW AND THE DOG CHASED THE CAT.

Lesgold's findings have confirmed this assumption. The kind of relation obtaining between the two predications (coordinate conjunction versus subordination by relative pronoun, or unit formation by personal pronoun) was found to affect recall. Pronouns seem to perform a deictic function in the process of understanding (and/or in retrieval); they direct our attention and comprehension to a particular place, or in a particular direction, much as the verb's argument vectors serve as signposts in predication. Located by Bühler in the *Zeigfeld* (deictic field) of language, deixis plays an equally crucial role in the symbol field of language. In either case our consciousness is guided by the clues contained in the words and in the functional units arising from these words in the sentence.

These clues retain their validity for only as long as needed; they are forgotten as soon as they have fulfilled their function: on arrival in Athens we no longer remember whether in Corinth there had been any road sign to indicate the way or not, and, if so, what it looked like. The analogy carries considerable weight for any psychological theory of language use, in that it conveys the idea that the syntactic form of a sentence is less well recalled than its "content," which is the opposite of what would follow from the orthodox generativists' notion that semantic interpretation is an appendix to the primary syntactic processes.

A brilliant demonstration of the primacy of the semantic element in memory was offered by Sachs (1967), who presented her subjects with stories of approximately paragraph length. After each story, subjects heard a test sentence and had to tell if this sentence had occurred verbatim in the story or not. The test sentence was identical with the critical sentence, or was a syntactic variation, or contained some semantic modification of the sentence.

For instance, the critical sentence in the story was HE SENT A LETTER ABOUT IT TO GALILEO, THE GREAT ITALIAN SCIENTIST, its syntactic variation was A LETTER ABOUT IT WAS SENT TO GALILEO, THE GREAT ITALIAN SCIENTIST, and the semantic modification was GALILEO, THE GREAT ITALIAN SCIENTIST, SENT HIM A LETTER ABOUT IT.

If the test sentence was presented immediately after the critical sentence in the story, subjects had little difficulty in identifying the two modifications. But if it came after the second part of the story which ran over 80 more syllables, the subjects had serious difficulties in identifying the syntactic variation, whereas the semantic modification was pretty well identified even after a story extension of 160 syllables.

It follows from Sachs's investigation that it is wrong to speak of "retention of sentences" in general. What is ordinarily recalled of a sentence is its "content" or "meaning," i. e., the message carried by the utterance. That the message is grasped and stored is due, among other things, to the syntactic clues which are deleted from memory as soon as they have fulfilled their role. (Similar findings have been reported by Fillenbaum 1966, and Foppa and Wettler 1967.)

From Engelkamp's and Shafto's experiments we concluded that in processing an utterance the hearer arrives at its semantic structure, which is what he stores in his memory. Taking note of the evidence contributed by Sachs, we may now go one step further by asking: If semantic structure is stored *without* the syntactic "signposts" used to identify it, how do we go about retrieving the stored "content" and reproducing it verbally? What is involved is some kind of reconstruction, no doubt; Bartlett looms in the shadows.

Flores d'Arcais (1974) seems to be aware of this as he sums up his thorough survey of the relevant literature and his own experiments in the following way.

Even after a very brief interval following its presentation, a sentence is not recalled in its original form, nor in the form of a "transform" obtained through grammatical rules of transformation. "What is preserved is the main semantic information present in the original sentence: who has done what to whom and under what conditions" (p 54). On examining the errors and intrusions we find that the semantic information has been stored in rather abstract form rather than by way of storage of specific lexical entries. The sentence produced by the subject in a recall test is a new construction based on the semantic information retrieved from memory. It is precisely the reconstruction postulated by Bartlett for recall.

Leaving a detailed discussion of this issue to the next chapter, we now address ourselves to the essential and yet elusive clues that serve to guide us in processing an utterance. Do these clues serve us all the time in the same way? We have had many reasons to suspect that this is not the case. A few pages back it was argued that the functions of predication may vary from situation to situation. This "indeterminacy" of the acts of meaning and understanding also comes into evi-

279

dence in a study which examines the issue from another angle, yielding equally impressive results.

In the earlier reported study by Engelkamp (1973) we saw how the verb is integrated with its arguments into a functional unit; the nouns which the verb implies as its arguments are more easily available than those not integrated into this unit. Being familiar with the verb *to cut,* we know that it implies some instrument and an object with specific properties. He who does not share this knowledge is excluded from this language game. We have learned of the memory characteristics of such unit formation. We shall now consider the perceptual effects of this kind of unit formation.

Rosenberg and Jarvella (1970) have investigated the effect of the semantic integration of sentences on the perception of these sentences. A semantically well-integrated sentence has its subject, predicate, and object originating from the same (linguistic and nonlinguistic) context, whereas in a semantically poorly integrated sentence those three elements derive from different contexts: e. g., THE DOCTOR CURED THE PATIENT belongs to the first, THE DOCTOR REPAIRED THE SWORD to the second category.

In the experiment, subjects were required to repeat sentences they heard on tape, one by one. Some subjects heard the sentences in normal conditions, others under noise which reduced intellibility by about 50 per cent. The first finding was that there were no differences between the two integration classes in normal conditions. Under noisy conditions, however, the poorly integrated sentences posed more difficulties (notably toward the end of each sentence) than the well-integrated ones; obviously, this was due to the relative unavailability of contextual clues.

The second finding is even more important for us: Tested unexpectedly for (incidental) recall immediately after a series of 12 sentences, subjects hearing the sentences in normal conditions performed equally well on the two sentence classes. Under noisy conditions, poorly integrated sentences were definitely less well recalled, whereas the well-integrated sentences were better recalled both absolutely and relative to the normal condition.

Considering that the subjects had not been asked to remember anything, we are led to the conclusion that the noise interference had caused subjects to process the verbal material in ways differing from those under normal conditions.

Here we come upon a new factor in our study of language use. Having begun with an analysis of "language-inherent" factors and continuing with a discussion of the language user's knowledge of the world and his intentions, we now come to realize that the processing of linguistic material both in the act of meaning and in that of understanding takes place at different levels and in different ways. The outcome of this processing (e. g., in terms of duration of storing) will depend on the "program" chosen by the language user for the particular occasion. We have repeatedly stressed the importance of the language user's own activity in the course of meaning and of understanding, notably when discussing the concept of sense constancy. In the next chapter we have to focus upon this activity again, before rounding off the picture.

Chapter 15

Levels and Vectors of Understanding

In the course of the preceding chapter we saw the emphasis shifting gradually from the opening question "What goes on in a sentence?" to what might be phrased as "What does the hearer do with a sentence?" The latter question is not really new; for quite some time students of memory have supplied us with the stock reply "The hearer (en- or de)-codes the sentence."

And this is where we want to resume our argument, in view of the apparent similarity between the process of coding and the act of understanding.

It is with reference to the hypothetical processes of encoding, possibly recoding, and eventually decoding that investigators have sought to account for the difference observed, for example in a recall experiment, between the material initially offered for retention and the material eventually reproduced by the subject. As suggested by the term *code,* the idea is that some kind of translation is effected from one "language" into another, for instance, from the auditory "dialect" of initial sensory perception into the "dialect" of cognitive schemata, in which the perceived material is stored for longer periods of retention. The order in which the various codes are employed one after another has been construed – in line with the conceptualizations of general psychology – as a biological or anthropological "universal" of the human being. That is to say, it has been considered as certain that the coding proceeds in a fixed sequence of stages, irrespective of kind of input or the subject's intentions[1]. For example, the view has prevailed that auditorily as well as visually presented verbal material is stored in auditory form for some time. The psychology of memory has accordingly developed models comprising a succession of stores, each disclosing specific properties (VSTM, STM, LTM); the transfer of material from one store to the next has been construed as involving a recoding procedure. Under this concep-

---

[1] Such is certainly the case with the first coding stages in the perception of language. But if the notion of coding is extended to embrace the construction of schemata in long-term memory, there can be no question of a complete determination of stages.

tion, neither the succession of stages nor the temporal characteristics of storing are granted any variability.

Right from the start the theory revealed a number of flaws, but these were generally ignored, if only because it was the only workable theory of memory at the time[2]. Since then, the theory has been questioned and revised in numerous ways. Let us mention three of these objections:

a) Verbal material of a certain kind (i. e., words designating concrete things) is stored in an essentially different form from some other material (words designating abstract concepts)

b) The reproduction, and perhaps also the perception and understanding of verbal material, involves predominantly constructive, rather than analytic and interpretive, processes

c) The concept of (perceptual) strategy (as discussed in the latter part of Chap. 12) is based on the assumption that the speaker-hearer enjoys a certain amount of freedom in adopting the procedure by which to convey meaning or attain understanding.

If we are to pursue our argument by discussing (a), we might start with the study by Sachs (1967, mentioned at the end of the previous chapter). Sachs has demonstrated that the exact wording of an auditorily presented sentence is available for recall only for a very brief period, following which only the "semantic structure" of the sentence is stored, and it is the latter structure that serves as a basis for reproduction (recall) in the course of what is a constructive process. Important evidence as to the form in which the "semantic structure" is stored in memory has been contributed by Paivio and his associates. Paivio ventured onto ground that had been taboo for behaviorism over decades: the role of images in the processing of words and sentences (see Paivio 1970 for a concise resumé of the problem). Nonverbal images, says Paivio (1969, p 243)

> are regarded as symbolic processes which are linked developmentally to associative experiences involving concrete objects and events ... The mediational function and arousal of imagery are theoretically coordinated to an abstract-concrete dimension of stimulus meaning, which is defined in terms of directness of sensory reference ...... it can be understood as extending from abstract nouns to concrete nouns to pictures and objects ...

The sentence THE FAT BOY HIT THE GIRL evokes in the hearer an image of the event in which the meaning of the whole sentence is unitarily contained. (In construing the processes by which the image is evoked, Paivio draws heavily on associationism, by which he comes very close to Osgood's mediation model.) Thus, any such "concrete" sentence is transposed into an imaginal code "in which the information is stored spatially, in parallel, rather than sequentially as a string of words" (Begg and Paivio 1969, p 821). The information contained in an "abstract" sentence, however, is not amenable to recoding into the imaginal code and is hence stored in a form resembling the original verbal sequence. Accordingly, Begg and Paivio (1969, p 821) predict

---

[2] For example, the fact that faces are well remembered is incompatible with Glanzer's verbal loop hypothesis.

that the most effectively coded, stored, and retrieved aspects of a concrete sentence will be those related to the sentence as a whole unit, such as its meaning or general theme. In abstract sentences, on the other hand, the specific words will be relatively better retained.

In their study Begg and Paivio furnished an enormously interesting specification of Sachs's findings. Whereas Sachs (1967) had postulated that semantic information lasts longer than the original wording in the case of all sentences, Begg and Paivio (1969, p 825) observed

> that changes in meaning were more often recognized than changes in wording in concrete sentences but that the reverse was true in abstract sentences.

Since abstract sentences are coded in the form of word–concept schemata, a change in their wording is more easily discovered during the recall test than in the case of concrete sentences that are stored in imaginal form.

Known as the *dual coding hypothesis,* the idea developed by Paivio has strongly influenced subsequent researches in the psychology of language. In the following pages we shall go into some of its implications.

One implication is that the hearer can process verbal material in (at least) two different ways, and this alone argues distinctly against the notion of a unitary lexicon or dictionary in which "word meanings" are stored by their "semantic features". If it is true that THE FAT BOY HIT THE GIRL is recoded into *one* image and stored as such, then there is no longer a place for the operation of, say, the features attaching to the word *boy* (Animal+, Human+, Male+, Adult−, etc.), as elaborated by a succession of authors from Katz to Engelkamp. Should we nevertheless opt for retaining the feature concept – which seems to offer, for the time being, a fairly convenient solution to a number of problems – it will be necessary to postulate two different phases in the processing of verbal material: one, during which the pertinent features are activated as a basis for meaningful understanding, and another, during which an image is evoked. The process of understanding evidently comprises two qualitatively different components or phases, which need not take place in succession but might equally well run in parallel.

Another implication of the dual coding hypothesis is of a more general kind: If it is true that the language processing human can avail himself of two different coding mechanisms, how free is he to choose between the two? Is the sentence THE FAT BOY HIT THE GIRL always coded as an image simply because these words invariably evoke a particular image due to their intrinsic linguistic qualities, or could the same sentence be coded and stored in the alternative, abstract-literal manner if required by the circumstances (e. g., the hearer's condition, notably his intentions)?

At the core of Paivio's theoretical position is the process of coding. Concrete sentences are easier to understand, are more reliably remembered, and their modifications are more easily identified than in the case of abstract sentences because the former are coded in the form of images. We now turn to arguments which modify this causal sequence by focusing upon the process of understanding rather than on coding for recall. Such arguments have been advanced in particular by Bransford. In a series of studies, Bransford and his collaborators have contributed evidence from which our insight into the process of understanding has benefitted more than from most other findings.

As we did in the case of Paivio, we may start again with Sachs's finding and the resultant query as to the particular form of the "semantic structure" that plays such a crucial role in storing and recall. Although Bransford does not altogether discard this "interpretive" approach (which owes its inspiration to generative grammar), he considers it insufficient to account for the processes of recall. In Bransford et al. (1972, p 194) we read:

> An alternative to the interpretive approach to sentence memory is one in which sentences are not viewed as linguistic objects to be remembered. Instead they are viewed as information which subjects can use to construct semantic descriptions of situations.

Bransford's reference to *semantic descriptions of situations* in place of the *semantic structure of sentences* signifies a refusal to accept the linguists' claim to guidance. Rather than speaking of processing some input – thus implying that the outcome of this processing is exclusively or chiefly determined by the material quality of the input – the protagonists of the new trend prefer to speak of *construction* on the basis of an input (or perhaps even "on the occasion of an input"?).

An enormously important expansion is taking place in this way, an expansion which the linguistically oriented psychologists of language have been unable to achieve: the incorporation of nonverbal information in the processing of verbal input. Since comprehension involves not only analytic or interpretive processing of the input, but also construction on the basis of the input, the constructive descriptions of situations convey more information than is contained in the verbal input itself. Whether in comprehension or in the seemingly simple task of recalling a previously heard utterance, the language user himself contributes something to the process, i. e., he constructs something from the available data. Bransford considers the incoming sentence as a kind of instruction for the construing of semantic descriptions which subsequently serve as a basis for recall. Similar suggestions were contained in Bühler's notion of deixis and in many other conceptions reviewed in these pages, including the concept of instruction for the formation of units discussed in the preceding chapter.

Bransford exemplifies his idea with the following sentences:

a) THREE TURTLES RESTED BESIDE A FLOATING LOG, AND A FISH SWAM BENEATH THEM

b) THREE TURTLES RESTED ON A FLOATING LOG, AND A FISH SWAM BENEATH THEM.

These two sentences do not differ in deep structure (except for the specification of the "lexical" units *on* and *beside*), whereas the semantic situations underlying the two sentences are clearly different. Sentence (b) suggests that the fish was under the log, but we would look in vain for this suggestion in any of the linguistic constituents of the sentence. The suggestion ensues from our knowledge of the spatial relations obtaining in the world – knowledge which is activated in some general way by the sentence.

This line of reasoning is supported by Bransford et al. (1972) with the following experiment. Should the subject have stored solely linguistic information when presented with one of the two sentences (a or b) for recall, he would notice in either case a difference in a test sentence (c) presented for recognition:

c) THREE TURTLES RESTES BESIDE/ON A FLOATING LOG AND A FISH SWAM BENEATH IT.

Quite different predictions ensue from the "contructivist" theory. When relying in their judgment on the semantic description built up on the basis of the input of the initially presented sentence (either (a) or (b)), rather than on the linguistic input alone, the subjects who had processed sentence (a) should recognize sentence (c) as nonequivalent, while subjects who had heard sentence (b) should fail to identify the difference. The point is that the semantic description developed for sentence (c) is identical with that built up for sentence (b).

Having found support for his hypothesis in the results of this experiment, Bransford could now proceed to test the validity of his constructive theory also at levels above and below the sentence. Is the understanding of single words and of entire texts also affected by such input-induced and world-knowledge-supported constructions?

The first issue, "Has context any effect on the semantic storing of a *word?*" is of the greatest importance for any theory of the lexicon. All current linguistic theories lean squarely on the assumption that a word possesses invariant semantic properties (whether they are called markers, or features, or implicit associative responses, or just images). Although such invariance dovetails neatly with the dimensionality of a suitably tailored lexicon, it is totally out of tune with the kind of semantic flexibility observed in the variable interpretation of the word *piano* in the following sentences:

$$\text{THE MAN} \left\{ \begin{array}{l} \text{LIFTED} \\ \text{SMASHED} \\ \text{TUNED} \\ \text{PHOTOGRAPHED} \end{array} \right\} \text{THE PIANO}$$

The first sentence is oriented, by its verb, upon the heaviness of the piano, the second upon the piano's "woodiness", the third upon its sound qualities, and the fourth upon its characteristic shape. Thus each sentence serves to activate a different feature from among those attaching to the word *piano*. That is to say, the word *piano,* rather than acting *as a whole* to call forth the respective global concept from the hearer's lexicon, activates some particular feature (of the word), depending on the context.

In a study pursuing this issue, Barclay et al. (1974) were able to show that a subject who had heard the first sentence was much more likely to recall the word *piano* when prompted with "something heavy" than with "something with a nice sound", whereas the latter prompt proved much more effective in the case of the third sentence.

In their interpretation of these results, the authors are not content with making the cogent if vague statement: "word plus its context form a 'higher-order unit' or gestalt in memory". They argue (1974, p 479):

the way in which an unambiguous noun was psychologically instantiated was governed by the relevance of each of its semantic properties to the event described by the sentence as a whole. For example, given the event "lifting", the heaviness of a piano is relevant, while the sound it can make is not. We suggest that the contextually determined relevance of each of a word's semantic properties is somehow indicated in the encoded representation of that word.

The process may be construed as a kind of activation, or instigation, or prompting. And immediately we are led to inquire into the apparent similarity between this selective activation of particular semantic features of a word by the semantic dynamic of its context and the conceptualization proposed by Engelkamp in reference to Steinberg's study (cf. the preceding chapter). Engelkamp asserts that the verb implies its arguments in a global way; he bases his thesis on the finding that nouns which function as arguments of the verb are more easily remembered than other nouns. For Engelkamp, a noun is either an argument of the verb or not, i. e., the noun functions as a whole, whereas in the study by Barclay et al. it is the argumentative aspects or properties of the noun that serve to relate it to the verb and hence are subject to activation in recall.

Thus the interlocking of predicate and argument, or even of the generally activated meaningful background and the specifically uttered content, emerges with increasing clarity as a fundamental characteristic of the processes underlying communication by language. The sentence uttered activates something in the hearer that forms – together with the utterance – an entity for recall. This integration of the uttered and the activated content does not proceed automatically; instead it represents a goal-directed construction effected by the hearer immersed, as he is, in a particular situation – which issue will be elaborated further on.

For the moment we have to describe Bransford's third approach to the problem. In his above reported experiments Bransford made it plausible that in comprehending and storing single sentences and single words, the subject constructs semantic descriptions while drawing on elements of nonlinguistic knowledge. Proceeding to analyze text comprehension and storing, he assumes analogously that a sequence of interrelated sentences converge to yield a common semantic description which is then stored as a whole. Empirical support for this assumption has been supplied by Bransford and Franks (1971). What a subject understands of an utterance, and how he goes about it in the process, depends on the relations obtaining within the semantic description developed for this occasion. Bransford et al. (1972, p 206) illustrate as follows:

> For example, suppose someone communicated the following situation: "There is a driveway on the right, a tree on the left, and a baby sitting between the two". Now suppose another piece of information is added to this description; namely that "a dog sat directly to the right of the baby and licked the baby's face". This latter statement allows a considerable amount of information about the relation of the dog to other objects; namely that the dog is to the left of the driveway and to the right of the tree. These latter two propositions did not have to be provided linguistically, yet this information appears to spontaneously be "filled in".

The point we have now reached is of such significance that we feel the need to halt for a while and take stock. This kind of progression from sentence to text is distinct from the one discussed earlier. For instance, in Chaps. 8 and 13 we learned that the preceding utterances affect the understanding of the incoming utterance by offering the presuppositions necessary to understand the latter. There, the text effect (if we may speak of anything of the sort) involved the projection of the past upon the present. Now we have become familiar with a text effect that apparently projects from the present into the future. The "whole" formed by the convergence of diverse pieces of information thus acquires emergent properties that contain more information than offered by the sum total of its components. Here we have a fundamental principle of Gestalt psychology. How difficult it is to conceptualize this *generation of information* in terms of information theory can be seen from the fact that in the above quoted passage the three authors employ phrases such as "allows information" and "information appears to be filled in". Once again it is brought to our attention that information is not something we discover in the outside world, perceive, and store (possibly for subsequent communication to others), but that it is something we generate by our own activity whenever "allowed" to do so by circumstances and wherever we can find a place among the facts of the world to project it upon. After all, it is man who imparts sense to the world around him, making the world pregnant with information. Accordingly, in the paper by Bransford et al. (1972, p 207) we read:

> In a broader sense the constructive approach argues against the tacit assumption that sentences "carry meaning". People carry meanings, and linguistic inputs merely act as cues which people can use to recreate and modify their previous knowledge of the world.

This view is largely in accord with the position outlined in the present book; though we would prefer to regard meaning not as something that is "carried" by people but as something that is "made" by people (in the process of meaning and of understanding).

According to Bransford, the hearer integrates the information extracted from the linguistic input with the information contributed by his knowledge of the world to construct the "semantic description" of the situation. Examining Bransford's specimen sentences, however, we have reason to suspect that these descriptions might be identical with the images evoked in the hearer by "concrete" sentences (as suggested by Paivio). Hence it is an essential question for Bransford whether or not these integrative and constructive processes are likewise evoked by "abstract" sentences. Inquiring into this issue, Franks and Bransford (1972) presented abstract texts to their subjects and found them to integrate "partial meanings"[3] and store "wholistic representations of the complete ideas".

Although these results do not invalidate Paivio's dual coding hypothesis, it cannot be denied that the "wholistic" tendency (which Paivio ascribes to his imaginal code) is likewise present in the case of abstract material. Consequently

---

[3] Regardless of his above quoted declaration, Bransford continues to speak of "partial meanings" of individual sentences, or sentence components, or text components.

we are faced with the question: If it is not the facilitated storing of the wholistic image that makes for superior recall of "concrete" as compared with "abstract" sentences – what factor is responsible for the difference in recall (observed also by many other authors)?

The issue has been pursued by Bransford from an angle which is of considerable interest to us. Unlike Paivio, who believes that his subjects were equally successful in understanding concrete and abstract sentences and that the differential recall data are due to differences in *storing,* Johnson et al. (1972) suggest that abstract sentences are harder to *understand* and therefore yield poorer recall than concrete sentences. Attributed by Paivio to memory, the processes in question are located by Bransford in the sphere of understanding. Elaborating the issue, we might ask: Does integration fall within the sphere of understanding, or does integration follow understanding in that the assimilated material is integrated (in images, chunks, etc.) for purposes of storing and eventual retrieval?

To decide the question, a subject has to be furnished, in addition to the verbal input submitted for processing, with knowledge that would affect the comprehension of the test material. Bransford and Johnson (1972) provided such additional information in the form of a drawing depicting the situation to which the verbal input referred. Subjects who were shown the corresponding drawing either before or during the presentation of the text were more successful in understanding and storing the text than subjects shown the drawing subsequently or not at all. Evidently, a picture provides the semantic context (rather than acting merely as a "headline" or "theme") by which text comprehension is essentially affected.

Thus we are led back to what was said before, in Chap. 7, that in order to endow a particular utterance with sense, there must exist a scaffolding of presuppositions, or a wider horizon of sense, a particular segment of which is addressed by the utterance. An utterance makes sense only if the hearer succeeds in perceiving it as a particular realization of the global structures by which human actions and the world at large become intelligible.

The idea that some kind of organizing center must be in existence before any new material can be assimilated has been voiced in psychology on numerous occasions and in different contexts: Bartlett (1932) spoke of schemata, and so did Piaget; similar arguments were advanced by Arnheim; Ausubel (1962) used the notion to develop a cognitive learning theory; Mandler (1967) has demonstrated the importance of such organizing cores in recall.

The integration of imagery and verbal information into a "semantic description" serving as a basis for further verbal actions (e. g., in recall) deserves to be examined in the light of evidence contributed by investigators whose work has already been discussed in these pages, albeit from other angles. Perhaps the most sweeping statement on this subject has originated from Fodor (1972, p 85), who postulated (as mentioned before, in Chap. 10) the existence of a cross-modal central code that is responsible for

> the routine ability of higher organisms to interpret information in any one input mode in terms of information from any other.

288

Unfortunately, this approach is crippled by the imprecision of the two key terms *interpret* and *code;* in particular, it cannot explain how new information is *generated* through the integration under discussion.

The interaction of pictorial and verbal information was again discussed in connection with the study by Hörmann and Terbuyken (1974, cf. Chap. 13), where it was demonstrated that the particular meaning ascribed to a word depends on the hearer's understanding of the situation in which the word was uttered. This finding serves to underline the role of the semantic situation in the promotion of understanding.

The integration of information stemming from different sources may proceed along lines other than those suggested by Hörmann and Terbuyken. Loftus and Palmer (1974) had subjects watch a filmstrip showing two cars colliding and then tested these subjects with the following question in which the final verb was varied from case to case: "About how fast were the cars going when they smashed/collided/bumped/hit/contacted?"

The speed estimates given by the subjects showed that the verb used in the question significantly affected their judgment: those who heard "smashed" rated the speed roughly 10 mph higher than those who heard "contacted".

Moreover, asked one week later whether they had spotted any broken glass in the car crash displayed on the film, those subjects who had heard "smashed" were much more inclined to reply "yes" than those who had heard "hit" – even though there had been no glass around. Interpreting these findings, Loftus and Palmer (1974, p 588) propose

> that two kinds of information go into one's memory for some complex occurrence. The first is information gleaned during the perception of the original event; the second is external information supplied after the fact [in this case it was supplied by the subsequent question – H. H.]. Over time, information from these two sources may be integrated in such a way that we are unable to tell from which source some specific detail is recalled. All we have is one "memory".

This is how the psychology of language has benefited from a traditional trend in the study of memory (Bartlett, Carmichael, Katona, etc.) that conceptualized the processing and storing of material in terms of the construction of schemata. Loftus, however, seems to keep these two kinds of information too far apart. Furthermore, it might be necessary to explain in what way the information conveyed by *smashed* differs from that conveyed by *hit*. Are we here anywhere near the ideas advanced by GA Miller (1972) in his analysis of verbs of motion (see Chap. 6)?

Having argued in rather general terms that understanding language involves the integration of verbal information with previously available or concurrently supplied "background" information, we ought now to describe several attempts at elaborating this global notion.

The finding that verbal and nonverbal information combine to form a semantic description gives rise to the question as to the relative share of the two "components", and as to the factors that might possibly modify the sharing.

Among these factors is the generality vs. specificity of the two kinds of information and the distance separating the one kind (pictorial) from the other (verbal)
along this dimension. Some research on sentence negation will be quoted as
illustration.

Hörmann (1971 b) and Engelkamp et al. (1972) found facility of recall to vary
with the type of negation. For example, the predicate negation
(PN) THE POLICEMAN DID NOT STOP THE TRUCK
is easier to recall than the subject negation
(SN) IT WAS NOT THE POLICEMAN WHO STOPPED THE TRUCK
(the original German version sounded simpler than that: Nicht der Polizist hat
den LKW angehalten, i. e., it was not a cleft sentence) or the object negation
(ON) IT WAS NOT THE TRUCK THAT WAS STOPPED BY THE POLICEMAN
(German original: Der Polizist hat nicht den LKW angehalten).

The authors interpreted this finding by arguing that predicate negation is of a
more general type than the other negations and that with the negation of the
action itself the hearer was supplied with conclusive information, whereas in
subject negation (SN) and object negation (ON) the hearer felt the need for
additional information (*who* was it that stopped the truck, or *what* was it that was
stopped, respectively).

The three kinds of negation may be seen as inducing different presuppositions
in the hearer (cf. Wason and Johnson-Laird 1972). Though complete in terms of
syntax, SN and ON sentences are incomplete in a communicative sense; PN
sentences, on the other hand, may function by themselves. On account of their
underlying presuppositions, SN and ON sentences are inadequate as answers.

If such is the reason for the varying recall scores of the different negations, then
it should be possible to make up for the inadequacy of SN and ON sentences by
adding pictorial information that would fill the "gap" in the respective situations.
We might, for instance, complement the SN sentence IT WAS NOT THE POLICEMAN
WHO STOPPED THE TRUCK with a picture showing a hitchhiker stretch out his
hand. Now we would expect the recall advantage of the corresponding PN
sentence to disappear.

This expectation was largely confirmed in an experiment by Engelkamp and
Hörmann (1974): rounded off by suitable pictures, "communicatively" incomplete sentences of the SN and ON type were no harder to recall than PN sentences.

Putting it in general terms, we would say that the more specific the presupposition of an utterance and the less the utterance "fits" the presupposition, the
more essential it is for the hearer to be supplied with additional information
before he can construct a relevant "semantic description". In other words: additional specifying information is taken into consideration in order to close the gap
in an "open" situation and thus make it more intelligible.

Considered in this way, the process of understanding consists of establishing a
balance between the vague generality of the more or less persistent overall horizon of sense and the specificity of what is conveyed by the given utterance. An
utterance establishes the link between the general background of intelligibility

and the particular instance invoked by the utterance; the instance is "put under the authority" of the general.

Some insight into the "trade-off" taking place between the generality and the specificity of information on the way to comprehension can be gained from the findings reported below.

A kind of specificity vs. generality interaction between verb and noun as object has been revealed by Engelkamp (1975). A specific verb combined with a general object *(to adopt a child)* showed superior recall compared with specific verb plus specific object *(to adopt a girl),* and conversely, a general verb plus specific object was easier to recall than a general verb plus general object.

This peculiar trade-off between verb specificity and object specificity in determining recall might be taken to mean – by a stretch of the imagination – that there is such a thing as an optimum of utterance specificity, at least as far as mnestic performance goes.

The idea seems to be borne out by the results of a further picture experiment (Bock and Hörmann 1974). Whereas in the studies by Bransford and by Engelkamp and Hörmann the additional information resulted in an elaboration and complementation of the sentences, Bock and Hörmann were able to demonstrate the effect of integration on the pictures used in the experiment. They presented unambiguous sentences together with pictures that referred to the test situation in an ambiguous way (example: THE BOY HAS SMASHED THE WINDOWPANE was accompanied by a drawing showing *two* boys and a broken window). While the picture did not affect the understanding or retention of the sentence, the imperfect agreement between sentence and picture was found to affect *picture* recall. Because of its ambiguity in relation to the sentence, the picture was particularly well recalled. Bock and Hörmann (1974, pp 356–357) came to the conclusion that

> verbal and pictorial information ... is processed jointly and thereby brought into relation with each other. Thus it will depend on the semantic analysis of the sentence if and at what place pictorial information is included, provided any such information is made available by the pictorial context. Conversely, it will depend on the semantic analysis of the [pictorial] situation (which happens to be mostly triggered and guided by the utterance) whether or not additional verbal information is taken into consideration in processing (e. g., for recall).

Having adopted this point of view, we are committed to another step in the same direction: we must conceptualize an "agency" that would decide in any one case whether or not additional information is needed and possibly should be searched for. It would have to be an agency capable of deciding at what stage the semantic description of the situation is sufficiently explicit to abandon the search for further information (whether originating from perception or from our knowledge of the world). Such an agency was proposed and discussed in some detail in Chap. 7 under the heading "sense constancy." The integration observed in the experiments reported above converges upon dynamic points of gravity in our consciousness that may be denoted as "making sense" and "intelligibility."

Processes resembling the "construction of a semantic description of a situation" are also descernible in the internal operations of someone reading a text or listening to a story or a conversation. Arguments for the constructive rather than analytic nature of understanding as a process (and as an outcome of the process) have been contributed by a number of recent investigations.

These investigations were based on the following observations, as recounted by Frederiksen (1975):

When asked to reproduce a text presented to them by ear or by eye, subjects respond by

a) paraphrasing the original,

b) condensing the material, thus offering overgeneralized information,

c) offering inferences derived from the text and from previously available knowledge (as in the case of Bransford's research reported above),

d) elaborating the content beyond what is implied by the text.

Now, what is the source of these departures from the original? Is it the subject's faulty memory and his striving to fill the gaps during the retrieval phase, or do the deviations reflect what goes on during the processing of the text?

Attacking this issue, Frederiksen assumed that ordinarily the speed of presentation is such that subjects are unable to process and store all the information contained in a complex text. Hence they resort to selective processing of the input.

For example, the passage

Circle Island is located in the middle of the Atlantic Ocean north of Ronald Island. It has good soil but few rivers and hence a shortage of water

may be reproduced as

Circle Island is a small island in the Atlantic that has only a few rivers and hence a shortage of fresh water.

The omission of "in the middle" and "north of Ronald Island" constitutes an overgeneralization, i. e., the subject leaves out certain details of the text. The information that there is a shortage of *fresh* water represents the subject's own inference.

Both overgeneralization and additional inferencing may have taken place during the phase of processing and/or during the phase of retrieval. Frederiksen put the issue to the test by tracing the subject's errors when the same text was repeated and reproduced a second, third, and fourth time. If it is true that these errors originate in the processing phase, then – being an integral component of the "semantic description of the situation" stored by the subject – the number of errors should remain the same in successive reproductions. But should the errors be made during retrieval, when the subject tries to fill the gaps in his reproduction, then we would expect their number to decrease from trial to trial.

From Frederiksen's experiments it follows clearly that the errors revealed in overgeneralizations and elaborations originate in the structures formed during text processing. Having obtained evidence in support of the above interpretation, Frederiksen (1975, p 168) points out that

as the subject builds up a semantic structure for a text, the derived information becomes an integral part of the subject's understanding of the text.

The material derived by the subject from the text as well as from his knowledge of the world, Frederiksen argues,

> is maintained as a part of the subject's knowledge structure, even when the subject is given opportunities to eliminate such derived information by comparing his semantic interpretation to the textual input.

We have thus arrived at conclusions which go far beyond the realm of the psychology of language. Here they are:

1) Understanding is to be conceived, not as coding (or recoding) of linguistic input, but as a process in which existing elements of knowledge, actualized (made conscious) by virtue of the linguistic input, are integrated with the incoming verbal information to form a unitary yet differentiated semantic description of what we comprehend as text.

2) Once such understanding has been attained, there is no need to revise it by comparing it against "reality"; understanding as an outcome presents itself again as a gratifying condition that ends any further processing of the input (or any additional input). Once "brought home", the situation need not be scrutinized further.

Interpreting the understanding of text in terms of the construction of a semantic description of the verbally depicted situation, the evidence contributed by Bransford, Franks, Frederiksen, Engelkamp, and Hörmann has served to elucidate chiefly the subjective component of this semantic unit construction. Approaching the issue from a different angle, we want now to inquire into the composition and effects of the emerging structure.

A major determinant of the structure is naturally the content of the processed text, but what does *content* mean in this case? The question reminds us of a problem that has been repeatedly raised in these pages: What is actually "stated" in an utterance or text? (Let us think of the work by Ziff and Garfinkel.) Considered on a methodological plane, this problem turns up in all those experiments in which text comprehension is studied by testing recall or reproduction.

> There is, of course, more to memory for text than just the memory for its meaning, with important concerns ranging from memory for surface features of a text to the pragmatic aspects of the communication act ... (Kintsch et al. 1975, p 196).

Finally, in order to account fully for the constructive processes that enable the hearer to understand a text, the psychologist of language will have to work out an elaborate description of text structure.

Kintsch (1974) and his collaborators (1975) have gone some distance toward developing such a system for the description of text structure. The basic unit of meaning is for Kintsch the proposition, i. e., a configuration of word concepts one of which is the predicator and the other are the arguments (cf. Chap. 14). The predicator specifies the kind of relation obtaining between the arguments. The word concepts themselves are defined by the propositions in which they occur. The meaning of a text is represented by interrelated, ordered lists of propositions (called text bases). The essential task of a text psychology is to explore the type of interrelations and the degree of orderedness obtaining within a text base. The question of ordering is handled by Kintsch in that he assumes that one proposition is subordinated to another if it shares an argument with the first one.

Kintsch begins by trying to cope with problems that may be said to lie on the periphery of his central issue. One such problem is how text retention is affected by the number of argument types that occur in a text built up from propositions. Investigating this issue, Kintsch et al. (1975, p 206) made the following finding:

> It is easier for readers [and also for hearers – H. H.] to process and retain in memory a proposition that is built up from old, already familiar elements, than to process propositions which introduce new concepts into the text.

An additional processing stage is required to deal with propositions which introduce new concepts. Besides deducing (construing) the proposition from the text and storing it as a component of the emerging text base, the subject has to make any new concept available in memory by a special encoding process. Familiar concepts need not be coded in this way, since they can be retrieved by reference to the previously coded memory trace.

Leaving aside Kintsch's arguments for a moment, we find ourselves at a point where we may survey the breadth and scale of the problems at hand. The following questions arise:

a) How does the "encodedness" of an already available concept stand in relation to its presence in consciousness?

b) What is the decaying rate of this "encodedness" in the case that the given concept does not occur in the text, and how does such occurrence affect the state of encodedness?

c) Is there a capacity limit on the number of arguments simultaneously available in their encodedness for the processing of a text?

d) Does the encoding of a concept result in easier access to related concepts, so that the subsequent encoding of the latter might take less time than otherwise?

With these questions in mind, we now return to Kintsch's findings and address ourselves to his proposition concept.

Kintsch found the time needed for reading a text to depend on the number of propositions comprised by the text. Thus propositions act as organizing cores of the kind discussed in the preceding chapter. The data obtained by Kintsch have served to reveal some other structures too: superordinate propositions are better recalled than subordinate ones, irrespective of their relative positioning in the text (superordinate propositions are known to occur more frequently at the beginning than at the end of a text). Moreover, Kintsch has obtained evidence to the effect that the superiority of higher-order propositions is expressed not only in the encoding phase (as could be expected from the work by Bransford and Frederiksen) but also in the storing and retrieval phase, superordinate propositions being retained for longer periods.

Examining the reported studies in retrospect, we discover quite significant differences between them.

Kintsch deals only with more or less literal reproductions, whereas Frederiksen also accounts for generalizations, elaborations, and for the reconstructive aspect in general. Taken together, the two investigators have elucidated the process of

294

understanding in several important ways, in particular by describing the active sorting out of propositions that come to function as organizing cores, the actualization of word concepts as arguments of these propositions, and the active perseverance of the concepts within a hierarchic structure that builds up in the course of text processing.

The notion that something may be understood on one of many different levels is, of course, not new. It ought to be supplemented with the contention that the process of understanding involves the setting up of different levels, a hierarchy of relations within the content of consciousness.

Thus, an inevitable ambiguity is present in the notion of levels of understanding (processing). From what we have learned so far, both the formation of units and the building up of a hierarchy are determined by the kind of material processed by the language user. Earlier in this chapter we realized that, in the process of understanding, information supplied by the verbal input is integrated with information derived from other sources (knowledge), to form a semantic description as an entity with emergent properties. This is not the only possible process, however. In a different kind of task, i. e., in a different intentional framework, there may be a much stronger emphasis on analytic processes. In a verification experiment, for instance, the subject is required to assess the correspondence between a verbal statement and a picture. The relevant processes can be accounted for most satisfactorily by the model proposed by Carpenter and Just (1975).

According to this model, both representations (verbal and pictorial) are decomposed into their constitutents, and these are retrieved pairwise for comparison[4]. The sequence of constituents is determined by the propositional structure of the sentence. In the case of incongruence between the corresponding constituents of sentence and picture, the process of comparing is resumed from the start (after a change of sign).

In a verification task, and also in dealing with "implicitly negative" words (forget, except for, different, other, etc.), with counterfactual statements, and with quantifiers, the subject takes a much more analytic and detailed approach than in the experiments described by Bransford. The find-and-compare operations devised by Carpenter and Just involve a series of elementary comparisons, and the time needed to perform these is proportional to the number of comparisons (this being the author's principal finding).

Looking at the matter from a distance, we discover that some findings can be readily accounted for by a model of the Carpenter-Just type while others are better served with the kind of procedure followed by Bransford, Engelkamp, Hörmann, Frederiksen, and Kintsch. The process of understanding is of a kind that cannot be explained by one or other model alone. Indeed, it seems to refer to

---

[4] The model falls, in a way, into the large class of congruence models which we associate with the names of Heider and Osgood. But in contrast to the latter authors, who were interested in the consequences of congruence or incongruence, Carpenter and Just focus on the act of comparing itself.

a plurality of procedures that may substitute for each other, but which might possibly run in parallel in one and the same act of understanding. If so required by the task, or perhaps also by some other factors, any input can be decomposed into a series of propositions, or constituents, or even features, and in this form made available for subsequent storing. But the same input may be also (or alternatively) integrated with already available or concurrently incoming information into a unitary semantic description through a series of generalization and assimilation processes.

The familiar question as to what is being stored: *an integrated unit with emerging properties,* or *a matrix of more or less abstract elements of information,* has lost its validity by now. Rather than speaking of "understanding a sentence and storing what has been understood," we ought to conceive of understanding, storing, and retrieval for further uses, as different aspects of an integrated process in which it is possible to identify different but not necessarily mutually independent phases. Some of these phases may consist of periodic iteration (as for instance in the find-and-compare procedure postulated by Carpenter and Just) while others may provide for an integration of information derived from different sources (Bransford). Which phases and what orders are involved depends evidently as much on the "structure of our perceptual apparatus," or the structure of our memory, as on the operation of many other factors. (Cf. on this issue the study by Brockway et al. 1974.)

And this is where the notion of *strategy* acquires its true significance as an account of the process under consideration: In dealing with a linguistic input, the language user enjoys a certain degree of freedom when choosing one or more from among a number of available procedures. We shall address ourselves to this freedom of choice, bearing in mind our guiding question: What does the hearer do with what he hears?

Important evidence has been contributed by experiments in which subjects were required to perform tasks at different levels.

Bobrow and Bower (1969) displayed sentences visually and asked their subjects either to verify the spelling of one of the words or to disambiguate this word with reference to the sentence. Subsequently, the subjects were unexpectedly tested for retention of the grammatical object of the sentence. The authors recorded much better recall for sentences that were analyzed for their meaning than for sentences searched merely for a spelling error. In another experiment, the same authors obtained evidence to the effect that sentences to which subjects were required to produce continuation sentences were recalled better than sentences read three times in succession. Furthermore, subjects could remember two nouns for which they had to devise a sentence better than they could the same nouns appearing in a sentence presented merely for reading.

These simple findings make it clear that it is the task orientation with which the subject approaches the linguistic material that is responsible for the quality of recall – even if the task does not specifically require such recall. At the same time, our attention is directed to the problem of understanding: in all these cases the subjects could not have failed to understand the test sentences – but do they understand them in the same way? Do we understand a sentence read for the purpose of discovering a possible spelling error in the same way as a sentence we formulate on the theme of two nouns? Calling to mind Deese's (1969, p 516) definition of understanding as "the inward sign of the potential for reacting appropriately to what we see or hear", we cannot fail to notice one more facet of this heterogeneous concept: Deese refers in his definition to different kinds of understanding as implied by the particular task of the hearer. Once we have crossed the formal boundary drawn by Deese, understanding is revealed, not as a homogeneous process or state, but as a class of varying potential and different states of consciousness. How should we go about exploring further the various degrees or levels or types of understanding (as both process and terminal state)?

Pursuing the issue, Mistler-Lachman (1972) made use of the well-known fact that ambiguous sentences are more difficult to process, and hence more time-consuming, than unambiguous ones.

She presented her subjects with three comprehension tasks, recording the performance time for each type: (a) judging the meaningfulness of a sentence, (b) judging whether the target sentence followed "appropriately" from a preceding "context" sentence, (c) making up a sentence which followed "reasonably" from the target sentence. The latter sentence could be either ambiguous or unambiguous, ambiguity being either lexical (*glasses* – to drink from or to be worn for better seeing), or surface-structural (SMALL BOYS AND GIRLS ARE EASILY FRIGHTENED), or deep-structural (I WAS FEEDING HER DOG BISCUITS).

The first conclusion reached by the investigator was that each task was addressed to a different "type" of understanding: the mere judgment as to the meaningfulness of a sentence remained entirely unaffected by the ambiguity status of the sentence, i. e., the subject was simply searching for a possible anomaly in the sentence and paid no attention to (the more time-consuming) ambiguity.

And yet it is not the type of task alone that determines the kind, and hence duration, of the search procedure: a further determinant is the type of material processed. The author would have obtained longer processing latencies for semantically anomalous sentences of the type used by, e. g., O'Connell et al. (1969), as well as for metaphors interspersed between anomalies.

In her remaining tasks (judging semantic correspondence between two sentences and producing sequel sentences) Mistler-Lachman apparently induced her subjects to comprehend the target sentences more deeply. Commenting on her production task, Mistler-Lachman (1972, p 621) says:

If deep comprehension involves considering the joint consequences of multiple propositions, then the subject must generate additional propositions for himself, unless they are given.

Very clearly, this comment refers to the kind of constructive process postulated by Bransford, a process that signifies "deeper" understanding.

Having arrived at the key notion of *depth of understanding,* we must bear in mind that it has appeared here in the context of the concept of strategy and thus implies freedom of choice: you may choose to go deeper in your understanding of what you hear, or not. The notion of depth induces us to have another look at the various models of processing and memory. Should "deeper" indicate that the processing is continued across a number of stores or levels? Depth of processing may serve as a vague alternative to a multistore model.

The credit for juxtaposing a depth-of-processing approach and a multi-store approach goes to Craik and Lockhart (1972), who came out with the concept of levels of processing as a framework for memory research. A fundamental concept of their theory is (Craik and Lockhart 1972, p 675) that

> trace persistence is a function of depth of analysis, with deeper levels of analysis associated with more elaborate, longer lasting, and stronger traces. Since the organism is normally concerned only with the extraction of meaning from the stimuli, it is advantageous to store the products of such deep analyses, but there is usually no need to store the products of preliminary analyses.

As suggested by the evidence reviewed earlier in these pages, depth of processing does not always involve a progressive differentiation or elaboration of the original input; rather, it often refers to the kind of elaboration achieved by virtue of constructive processes, by an integration of the verbal input with information obtained from other sources and from previously available knowledge.

If it is true that trace persistence (i. e., retention) depends on depth of processing, what are the factors determining depth of processing? Craik and Lockhart enumerate (p 676): (1) "amount of attention devoted to a stimulus" – itself a resultant of the task facing the subject, (2) compatibility of the input with the "analyzing structures" responsible for the processing, and (3) "the processing time available."

Craik and Lockhart construe the perception, processing, and storing of verbal messages (and possibly also nonverbal perceptions) as a "continuum of analysis" (p 676) – though "analysis" must be a slip of the tongue in view of the fact that the two authors believe this continuum to be dominated by synthetic rather than analytic processes.

For purposes of a scientific description – Craik and Lockhart concede – this continuum may be subdivided into stages or segments (e. g., sensory analyses, pattern recognition, stimulus elaboration), whereby we are again reminded of a multistore model that would assign separate stores to the three stages (VSTM, STM, LTM). Quoting plenty of empirical evidence, Craik and Lockhart discuss with considerable discernment the advantages and disadvantages of these two "language games." Eventually they opt for *depth of processing* as a continuum across which separate levels may be identified solely for purposes of description. Their approach carries, nevertheless, one unfortunate implication: that a certain depth of processing may be reached only after passing through the "shallower" levels. In other words, their theory does not envisage the possibility of "skipping" some of the shallower levels in favor of a "deep" processing right from the start, should such be the language user's desired strategy. Craik and Lockhart overemphasize the dimensional character of their model and hence fail to notice the active role of the language user in choosing the level at which the processing should start, the rate at which it should gain depth, and the point at which it should be discontinued. Elaborating Craik and Lockhart's model, Mistler-

Lachman (1974, p 105) explicitly refers to such a possibility as she accounts for her results by suggesting that

> the system immediately enters a processing level appropriate to the task demands. Deeper tasks are handled at deeper levels, and deeper levels are characterized by better memory for the input.

Posed by Mistler-Lachman as a possibility, the idea was submitted to empirical verification by Green (1975). This investigator aurally offered sentences which his subjects were instructed either to repeat verbatim or to complement with sequel sentences. But before they could perform their task, the subjects were given a probe noun and had to tell if the noun had appeared in the sentence or not. The probe nouns were either identical with the target nouns, or phonologically similar, or semantically related to the latter.

Green found the task instruction to affect the semantic, but not the phonological, sentence representation developed by the subject. When the subject was set to produce a sequel sentence, the latency of his response to the probe noun was more strongly affected by its semantic similarity to the entire sentence than by its similarity to the noun in the sentence. When the subject was set upon veridical memorization, however, the latter similarity was the decisive factor in the test. Thus it would appear that the meaning of the probe word is checked against the semantic description of the sentence constructed at the deepest level of processing reached on this occasion. Such an interpretation stands in glaring contrast to earlier views (e. g., Garrod and Trabasso 1973) which postulate that the subject starts by developing a surface representation of the sentence and only then, realizing its inadequacy, proceeds to deeper levels of analysis. Green's experiment bears out the idea underlying Bransford's investigations, namely, that the subject constructs a unified semantic description for the sentence.

From the evidence supplied by Mistler-Lachman and Green it follows that the processing system may become engaged directly at the level required by the particular task or situation. Such is unquestionably the case when the subject acts under the pressure of time. Accordingly, Carpenter (1973, p 513) hypothesized that

> such processes as comparison and inference making are initiated as soon as the sentence is read, and this processing will occur without any prior simplification of grammatical structure.

In her experiments, the investigator used counterfactual sentences like JOHN WOULD HAVE DIED IF THE DOCTOR WOULD HAVE LEFT. These "parent" sentences were either accompanied or followed by clauses like THE DOCTOR LEFT, and the subjects were required to tell if the latter were true or false. It turned out that under pressure of time the "parent" sentence immediately received a complex representation: predication plus negation, i. e., (neg [THE DOCTOR LEFT]). But when there was more time, subjects would convert this representation into a simpler one (THE DOCTOR STAYED). If required, such a conversion strategy may be adopted right from the start.

We are faced here with two "adjacent" levels, and we already know of one factor (pressure of time) responsible for the choice of one rather than the other level of processing for the particular task. This suggests that the processing of sentences is a limited-capacity activity, i. e., that the resources of processing are limited in time, but may be distributed – within the global amount available at any one time – over different levels of processing, the "cost" of processing varying from level to level.

Speculating along these lines, Carpenter (1973, p 520) finally says:

> The conclusions of these studies suggest a multistage model of sentence processing that distributes processing capacity to various stages depending upon the amount of time permitted by external conditions.

Pressing the issue still further, we would say that this limited processing capacity cannot be distributed quite freely, and with equal efficiency, over the different phases or levels; certain priorities result from the flow of communication, and there are optimal points in time for the actualization of the particular factors that come into play. The relevant evidence can be gleaned from a study by Bock (1976). The work reported in this paper recalls a familiar subject: meaning considered as a set of elementary features (primitives). When discussing this approach, we became aware of the difficulties ensuing from a decomposition of meaning into static, brick-like components. Now we are aware that it is the *process* of decomposition that makes for the depth of understanding and hence also for the quality of retention.

In his study, Bock had his subjects run down a list comprising 15 bird and 15 tool designations; group A subjects were instructed to mark all words belonging to the category Birds (or Tools), and group B subjects all words belonging to the category Animate (or Inanimate). In a subsequent recall test the author found that group B subjects had retained fewer words than group A subjects (irrespective of whether the recall test had been announced in advance or not). The author concluded that the A instruction resulted in the activation of a greater number of features than the B instruction. That the decisive factor of retention was the subject's intention of understanding the items on the list, follows from the fact that no improvement in recall could be obtained by informing group B after the experiment (but before testing for recall) that all the animate objects had been birds (and all the inanimate objects tools). Obviously, the semantic depth to which the process of understanding was driven cannot be changed in retrospect. Thus the "accessibility" of the words from the list (all of them stored away in memory long before) is established in the course of processing the list: an intention involving the activation of many semantic features makes for better retention than a task calling for the activation of fewer features.

As pointed out before, Bock's investigation underlines the importance of the language user's intention. Guided by his intention, the language user starts processing at the appropriate level; in a sense, he is set to function at a certain level of meaning and understanding.

The same picture emerges from a study by Jörg (1978), which in some respects represents an advance over Bock's investigation. Bock was concerned with how the retention of a sentence is affected by the level at which the sentence is processed; Jörg focused upon the effect of sentence processing level upon nonverbal percepts (pictures) that were either referred to in the sentence or not.

In the experiment, subjects were shown plates with four (outline) pictures each. One plate displayed, for instance,

flower   butterfly
coin   car

(the flower could also be called a tulip, the car a VW, etc.).

Subjects in a control group were merely told in advance that they would be tested for recall. Subjects in two experimental groups were additionally given a sentence in which two of the four objects in the plate were related to each other, either in their specific or in their general form. Group A heard for instance THE PEACOCK (butterfly) IS NEXT TO THE TULIP, and group B heard THE BUTTERFLY IS NEXT TO THE FLOWER. These sentences always preceded the pictures.

In the recall test that followed, each of the four objects (whether mentioned in the sentence or not) was shown in the original version as well as in five other versions of increasing dissimilarity. Subjects were asked whether they had seen the pictures before or not.

The results of the experiment were summed up by Jörg as follows:

The antecedent verbal description reduces – in a degree that varies with the level of the verbal category used – the subject's ability to discriminate between the modified pictures. Following a sentence with specific concepts (tulip, peacock), subjects are fairly successful in discriminating between picture versions more closely resembling the original, but fail in differentiating the picture versions of greater dissimilarity to the original. Subjects who heard sentences with general concepts (flower, butterfly), on the other hand, pay little attention to slight departures from the original, but manage to differentiate between the more dissimilar versions.

Evaluating this evidence, we seem to discover an effect of the limited-capacity factor. The subjects may be said to possess a limited supply of differentiation resources, and it depends on the type of sentence heard as to how they choose to allocate these resources. Our repeated contention that the utterance serves to guide the consciousness of the hearer has been borne out and further specified by the present evidence: the generality (category level) of the nouns used determines the allocation of the available differentiation resources.

Another finding of Jörg's study is that the pictures to which no reference was made in the preceding sentence were processed in each case in the same manner as those referred to.

Thus the linguistic form of the sentence determines the storing and recognition not only of the pictures mentioned in the sentence but also of the remaining pictures (for which neither general nor specific designations were provided). The processing of an utterance is apparently an activity that is not restricted to that utterance. The "instructions" extracted by the subject from the experimental situation, and from the sentence in particular, serve to guide him *in general,* not only in processing the sentence-designated pictures.

Once again we realize how strongly integrated verbal and nonverbal processes are. As shown by Bransford and some other authors, the understanding of the "semantic description" of a sentence is accomplished under the guiding influence of the sentence as well as the perceptual and other elements of the global situation. From Jörg's study we gather that the "semantic description" applies not only to the utterance but also to the nonverbal components of the current content of consciousness.

Quoting Polanyi (in Chap. 3), we discussed linguistic transparency, or the act by which the hearer "sees through" the phonemes, syllables, words, and sentences to identify what the speaker "means." And because the speaker is only "subsidiarily aware" of these phonemes, syllables, words, and sentences, they can direct the focus of his consciousness. How and to what end this focus is directed is shown by the process of understanding going on in the hearer; the evidence supplied by Jörg indicates that understanding is an act that transcends the linguistic input.

It has to be realized that the limited-capacity processing system, which serves to bring things to our consciousness, cannot be viewed as a model of every kind of process involved in language use. Van Lancker's arguments concerning automated speech illustrate the issue. Posner and Warren (1972, p 34) postulate that "many complex mental operations that are learned and that require time" can be performed outside the system which handles conscious processes. Indeed, they do not hesitate to make a further step which is as interesting as it is dangerous from a theoretical point of view:

> For our purposes the use of this system becomes the central definition of a "conscious process" and its non-use defines what is meant by "automatic".

Having conceptualized *understanding* as a vector of consciousness subject to determination by a variety of "instructions," we now find this construction imperiled again, once we admit that consciousness ceases to be determined by understanding alone and is itself a determinant of understanding. We feel like Bunter when he says to Lord Peter Whimsey:

> My lord, facts are like cows. If you look them in the face hard enough, they generally run away. (Dorothy L Sayers 1958, *Clouds of Witness,* p 74).

Chapter 16

Conclusions

Human language is language because it is used by people for a purpose, namely, to live with other people. The purposeful use of language is embodied in acts of meaning and of understanding; in these acts the essence of language is integrated with the condition of man. The nature of language as a goal-directed activity cannot be disregarded by anyone seriously concerned with developing a theory of language as used by people. Any theory of language knowledge must therefore have its antecedent in a theory of language use.

The notion of competence as introduced by Chomsky, and backed up by his grand achievement, applies to the knowledge of the *ideal* speaker-hearer, a construct exempt from the frailties and vacillations of human attention and human memory, a device that produces utterances for art's sake, that is, for the sake of well-formedness. This restriction contrasts strongly with the extravagant claim that language as conceived by generative grammar is identical with the language used by people in the real-life acts of meaning and of understanding. The claim has revealed itself as an idle promise; the fact is that a theory of language developed on purely rational grounds, as is the case with generative transformational grammar, discloses its inadequacy as soon as it is exposed to the crucial test of its predictive power, i. e., the power to predict events as they occur in everyday life.

The notion of competence might become *psychologically* acceptable, and might even prove productive and seminal, once we decide to discard the dehumanized anthropology in the framework of which Chomsky construes his ideal speaker-hearer. Such a radical revision would obviously entail a thorough restructuring of the relationship between competence and performance.

The futility of efforts to distinguish between "knowledge that" and "knowledge how" becomes apparent as we scrutinize the various attempts to account theoretically for the "meaning of words" by proposing a lexicon, or dictionary, as a store of language knowledge. The major problem of the lexicon in purely linguistic terms is its internal structure; the proponents of this kind of lexicon conceptualize the structure so as to achieve a significant reduction in complexity, oblivious of the fact that the multiplicity of word meanings is a fundamental characteristic of the human vocabulary and as such parallels the complexities that characterize the mind of the language user.

As we review the controversy over the lexicon (noting the extreme positions held by authors like Katz and Fodor versus Bierwisch), we are forced to discard the view that the structures of the lexicon are predominantly, or perhaps exclusively, structures of language – in favor of the conception that lexical structures duly reflect the more general cognitive structures which serve human beings in their verbal *and* nonverbal interactions with the world. In effect, the analogy beween lexicon and memory acquires a theoretical potential that acts against the sharp distinction between linguistics and psychology.

The manner in which the structures of the lexicon articulate our vocabulary is mirrored psychologically in the "belonging together" of lexical units. By refining progressively the grain of their lexical analysis, authors like Miller, Fillenbaum and Rapoport, and Clark have made it clear that a lexicon derived from this kind of analysis would lack the stability postulated (or implied) by linguistics and psycholinguistics. The inevitable conclusion is that it depends on the circumstances and the purposes of the communicative act which elements of the lexical store are employed by the language user.

Trying to elucidate the ways in which the elements of the lexicon, or word store, are activated in the process of language use, we come upon an underdetermination involved in the representation of word meaning by a matrix of semantic features: for no obvious reason the language user employs a matrix fully in some cases and only partially in others. From psychological studies, as well as from Chafe's linguistic analysis (notably in application to idioms), it transpires that the constitutive elements of an utterance do not possess the kind of fixed potential that would allow us to compute the meaning of the utterance as the sum total of the meanings of its components. Thus, in addition to semantic elements (or their matrices), we must postulate the operation of a higher-order factor which determines the way the matrices, and indeed the entire lexicon, are *handled* on each particular occasion by the language user. There is overwhelming evidence against the notion of a lexicon as a store of lexical units which, activated under the command of syntax, add up to yield the meaning of the sentence. The only alternative is to endow the material stored in the lexicon with more indeterminacy, in order to account for the undeniable effects of context, situation, and intention.

One implication of this approach is that the *processes* of meaning and of understanding must be interpreted, to some extent at least, teleologically, that is, with respect to their ultimate objective, which is to enhance the intelligibility of the world. Guided by this objective, the language user searches for ways and means that would enable him, for example, to take an ostensible semantic anomaly for what it actually is: an eloquent metaphor. At this point, our attention is turned to the phenomenon of sense constancy and its workings.

Making sense of an utterance must be seen, not primarily as an outcome of its analysis, but as the setting of bearings for such a meaningful analysis. Rather than being put together through a laborious decoding or interpretation of signs, the intrinsic, general intention of an utterance is available even before its piecemeal analysis has begun. Understanding is older than meaning *by language*. In order to understand an utterance we must establish its relationship to an invariably present scaffolding of sense. This process gives rise to what Deese has called the "potential for reacting appropriately to what we see or hear."

The hearer's "instancing" of some particular portion of the overall horizon of intelligibility may be addressed at the wrong place, of course, i. e., it may miss the speaker's intended meaning. The understanding achieved in this case is, from the speaker's viewpoint, a misunderstanding. The fact that one and the same event may be seen in two contrasting ways underlines the importance of the autonomous, nonlinguistic factors involved in the process.

Implicating a speaker and a hearer, and hence taking place against the background of a particular cognitive situation, an utterance is therefore to be conceived as *a specifying instruction issued by the speaker for the benefit of the hearer, with the intention of effecting a modification in the consciousness of the latter.*

By this token we break with the view that communication by language consists in the exchange or transmission of information; the view could be upheld only at the expense of the precision embodied in the notion of information. What is taking place between speaker and hearer is an act of guidance, the object of guidance being not so much the hearer's knowledge as the momentary content of his consciousness. The speaker acts so as to modify the momentary consciousness, and hence also the current behavior, experiences, thoughts, etc. of the hearer.

By construing language as an *instrument with which the speaker may affect the consciousness of the hearer* we discover a way out of the blind alley into which the issue of meaning has been pushed by the speculations about *reference* and *structure*. This way leads through an elaboration of Wittgenstein's idea that meaning is embodied in the use of language. Our account of language must begin with an examination of its functions rather than its elements considered in abstraction of their uses. Inextricably bound up with other human activities, language is a major component of the unitary language game that embraces the speaker, the hearer, and the situation.

Combining these philosophical inspirations with the psychological insights mentioned, we view an utterance as an organized and situation-related set of instructions for the hearer. Here our views converge with SJ Schmidt's "instruction semantics."

What are the instructions like? By adopting this question as a leitmotif we reduce the danger of focusing upon language in itself; you cannot possibly talk of modifying or guiding without keeping in mind *what* is being modified and in which direction. As it is, the problem can be approached from a number of angles: the guidance provided by such instructions may be assumed to come into effect no lower than at sentence or utterance level, by the interaction of elements that have no guiding effect by themselves (i. e., are not "impulsive," as James would have said). Alternatively, we might trace the guidance down to the core of the processes (in ontogeny and microgenesis alike) that lead up to the utterance. Searle's speech acts have their origin at a molar level, while Fillmore's cases are more related to a molecular level. Russian psychology of language and Chafe's linguistic model are concerned, each in its own way, with the processes taking place between the core and the surface, between the inside and the outside. The generation of an utterance has to be considered from every possible angle – and each of these angles has to be held simultaneously in perspective.

Our basic contention that language serves to influence the hearer's consciousness suggests that it might be useful to conceptualize the actual use of language as proceeding across several different levels. The entire process receives its impetus from the speaker's intention, as argued by Brunswik. Intention is ultimately responsible for the transparency of language: we understand an utterance by attending, right through the language as medium, to what the speaker means.

As we approach the problem in terms of levels, we come upon highly interesting processes occurring at the interface between the nonverbal and verbal levels. Discovering the extent to which verbal behavior is regulated by nonverbal factors, such as proximity, kinesics, eye contact, and silence, we are fortified in the view that communication by language is a continuation of human action with other means. Having established a bridge between language processes and human actions and cognition in general, we become skeptical about the formal definitions furnished by linguistics and psycholinguistics for concepts such as information, communication, and code.

The essential inability of people to decode completely their own verbal code, demonstrated by Garfinkel, lies in the realm where language starts from nonverbal and protolinguistic processes. Thus we become aware of the inevitability of the interplay between the definable and the never-fully-definable, as between making sense and understanding.

Valuable hints as to the roots of language can be gleaned not only from the border area of nonverbal and verbal communication, however. Observations and experiments on primates and children have shown that cognitive structures (e. g., Washoe's *open,* or the cup–nesting strategies described by Greenfield) serve to structure behavior as well as knowledge in the prelinguistic period, being provided with a word label at a later stage. The child learns gradually to differentiate knowledge as it emerges from skills. Long propounded by Piaget, this contention reminds us of Wittgenstein's ideas. The first entities formed as a result of the young child's interaction with things and events do not refer to physical objects, however, but rather to the roles identified by the child through his actions: Agent, Patient, Instrument, Location, etc. Construed as elementary linguistic categories by generative semantics, these entities are conceived by us primarily as cognitive-conceptual vectors.

Consequently, in terms of learning, the question is as follows: How does the child learn to refer to these roles and intentions with the linguistic means employed by his environment? Macnamara gives this pointed reply: First an infant understands what the speaker means and then works out the relationship between the (intended) meaning and the utterance.

This is how developmental psychology has elaborated the conception of the acts of meaning and understanding as represented in these pages: the primary thing is the action involving two partners, and it is in the framework of this interaction that the verbal acts of meaning and of understanding emerge. The adult speaker's verbalization of what he means is for the infant initially but a signal to focus his attention upon the interaction. In the course of time the child learns to identify in the utterance specific indicators of the to-be-conveyed meaning; eventually, the child learns to grasp the not-now and not-here.

At first such learning proceeds by what might be called patent shortcuts: the child imposes a particular strategy upon the current verbal and nonverbal interaction, and it is upon this interaction that he may pin his attention. Here we realize why in ontogeny the two acts of meaning and of understanding do not emerge fully in parallel. A fairly differentiated knowledge is employed by the child in the course of understanding, at a time when no such knowledge is available to him in his own act of meaning. At this early age the two acts differ in their functional value; indeed, in this period language contributes so little to meaning and understanding that the functional core of the emerging concepts can be symbolized in a play-like atmosphere in which there is no need to differentiate between knowledge and skills. Knowledge of language can be acquired because understanding is older than language use.

Stressing the function of language as a means for coping (behaviorally and cognitively) with the world, we finally part with the view that the only communicative function of language is to mirror the world. When using language, the adult speaker invariably seeks to influence the consciousness of the hearer, and the attainment of this goal is assured by an overdetermination, in a variety of ways, of the processes serving this end. Any use of language is a case of multiple action *(Mehrfachhandlung)* – a term coined by the early German psychologists.

This statement has important methodological implications. The fact that a goal may be pursued and reached by a variety of means (e. g., a negation can be signaled by syntactic, lexical, prosodic, and/or gestural devices) is bound to thwart attempts at designating invariable relationships between means and end whenever the grain of such an analysis is below a critical value. In order to be successful in our investigation of language as a means used for a particular purpose we must preserve a certain distance from the object of our analysis, a distance that ensures a sufficiently broad perspective.

In our search for invariable relationships between the means of language and the communicative goals pursued by those means – a search instituted at a convenient level of moderate generality – we take a lead from the ideas about the core, or nucleus, of linguistic structures voiced by generative semanticists and developmental psychologists. Our analysis shows that practically all utterances are anchored in a frame of reference for which the speaker's ego provides a center of gravity. Since language invariably involves interpersonal instruction, it is always blended with deixis. The point of origin of deixis (Bühler's *origo*) keeps shifting with the situation and the intention of the communicative act. Measurable along the dimensions of Osgood's semantic space, or in terms of the knowledge-induced presuppositions, this shifting position of the *origo* determines the choice and functional value of the constituents of an utterance.

The centering around a core as the origin of deixis and instruction is not the only organizational principle operating in the utterance. The desire to impart meaningfulness to our relations with the environment is the source of the dynamic that pervades the acts of meaning and of understanding. The same desire becomes operational in the phenomenon of sense constancy, and the course of its action is designated by a number of vectors.

One of these vectors ensures the intimate interaction of speaker, utterance, and the world. This vector carries the familiar name *predication,* and it has been recognized for some time as the center of organization in the utterance. As a central element of the utterance, the verb entails certain preferences in the choice of arguments. At this point our attention is attracted by the hierarchic structures which Fillmore's theory of case describes in linguistic terms, and Brown's and Bloom's analysis of child utterances in psychological terms. Now we come to recognize the sentence-organizing function of these structures. It is in relation to these hierarchic structures in the sentence that the language user produces or perceives, e. g., the nouns which point to a particular place in the preexistent scaffolding of sense; when examining earlier the same process from quite a different angle, we spoke of the shift from the generally meaningful background to the particular object of understanding.

We must now transfer our discussion onto a different plane if we want to deal with the overall organization owing to which the internal processes of the utterance become interlocked with those induced by the situation in which the utterance is issued. From the manner in which language is processed in both production and reception, we conclude that the acts of meaning and of understanding do not solely depend on the inherent dynamic of the utterance, but that they are the products of a language user's constructive activity embedded in a language-transcendent situation. Here again we are induced to consider the utterance as conveying a set of instructions for the hearer to construct a cognitive "image," though the utterance itself is certainly not an image and need not associate with any imagery. Following these instructions, the hearer carries out operations on certain cognitive elements he has stored in memory; these elements are neither constituents of the utterance itself nor "symbolized" by the utterance in the sense that they are represented by these constituents.

Thus the utterance in itself does not convey any information to the hearer; it only guides the hearer in creating the information for himself. That the hearer knows how to do this, and that he is able to follow the instructions built into the utterance, is the outcome of his incessant striving to *make* the world and all events around him fully intelligible. The criteria which the hearer sets for himself in terms of the explicitness and precision of his action depend on the task he is facing.

The depth to which the hearer chooses to process the utterance in the projective-constructive act of understanding varies with the demands of the task and the standards the hearer himself has set for the explicitness of his understanding of the world. In his penetration of successive levels of what Brunswik has called *Tiefenstaffelung* (staggered in depth), the hearer is driven by the intentionality of his process of living-into-the-world. As he passes from one level to the next, the sounds, words, and sentences of the language become transparent; they fade away to make room in his consciousness for the meaning meant.

References

The Journal of Verbal Learning and Verbal Behavior is abbreviated JVLVB

Abraham W (1971a) Stil, Pragmatik und Abweichungsgrammatik. In: Stechow A von (ed) Beiträge zur generativen Grammatik. Vieweg, Braunschweig, pp 1–13

Abraham W (1971b) Vorwort (Preface). In: Fillmore C (1971) Kasustheorie (German translation of The case for case). Athenäum, Frankfurt

Abraham W (1973) Zur Linguistik der Metapher. Mimeographed paper, Rijksuniversiteit, Groningen

Ach N (1932) Zur psychologischen Grundlegung der sprachlichen Verständigung. In: Kafka G (ed) Bericht über den 12. Kongress der Deutschen Gesellschaft für Psychologie. Fischer, Jena, pp 122–133

Ajdukiewicz K (1934) Sprache und Sinn. Erkenntnis 4:100–138

Ajdukiewicz K (1935) Die wissenschaftliche Weltperspektive. Erkenntnis 5:22–30, 165–168

Allesch GJ von (1909) Über das Verhältnis der Ästhetik zur Psychologie. Z Psychol 54:401–536

Allesch GJ von (1942) Über das Verhältnis des Allgemeinen zum realen Einzelnen. Arch Ges Psychol 111:23–38

Alston WP (1964) Philosophy of language. Prentice-Hall, Englewood Cliffs

Anglin JM (1970) The growth of word meaning. MIT Press, Cambridge, Mass.

Apel K-O (1973) Ch. W. Morris und das Programm einer pragmatisch integrierten Semiotik. Introduction to Morris CW (1973) Zeichen, Sprache und Verhalten (German translation of Signs, language and behavior). Schwann, Düsseldorf

Apostel L (1972) Illocutionary forces and the logic of change. Mind 81:208–224

Argyle M (1973) The syntaxes of bodily communication. Int J Psycholinguist 2:71–90

Argyle M, Alkema F, Gilmour R (1971) The communication of friendly and hostile attitudes by verbal and non-verbal signals. Eur J Soc Psychol 1:385–402

Arnheim R (1947) Perceptual abstraction and art. Psychol Rev 54:66–82

Asch SE (1946) Forming impressions of personality. J Abnorm Soc Psychol 41:258–290

Austin JL (1957) A plea for excuses. Proc Arist Soc 57:1–30

Austin JL (1962) How to do things with words. Harvard University Press, Cambridge, Mass.

Ausubel DP (1962) A subsumption theory of meaningful verbal learning and retention. J Gen Psychol 66:213–224

Bar-Hillel Y (1954) Logical syntax and semantics. Language 30:230–237

Bar-Hillel Y (1973) On Habermas' hermeneutic philosophy of language. Synthese 26:1–12

Barclay JR, Bransford JD, Franks JJ, McCarrell NS, Nitsch K (1974) Comprehension and semantic flexibility. JVLVB 13:471–481

Bartlett FC (1932) Remembering. Cambridge University Press, Cambridge, England

Baumgärtner K (1956) Linguistik als Theorie psychischer Strukturen. Sprache im technischen Zeitalter 13–16:1362–1370

Baumgärtner K (1966) Die Struktur des Bedeutungsfeldes. In: Moser H (ed) Satz und Wort im heutigen Deutsch. Schwann, Düsseldorf, pp 165–197

Begg J, Paivio A (1969) Concreteness and imagery in sentence meaning. JVLVB 8:821–827

Bendix EH (1966) Componential analysis of general vocabulary: The semantic structure of a set of verbs in English, Hindi and Japanese, Part II. Int J Am Ling 32/2

Bernstein B (1964) Elaborated and restricted codes: Their social origins and some consequences. Am Anthropol 66/6:55–69

Berry-Rogghe G (1971) The scope of semantics. Linguistics 73:5–16

Bever TG (1970) The cognitive basis for linguistic structures. In: Hayes JR (ed) Cognition and the development of language. Wiley, New York, pp 279–352

Bever TG (1971) The nature of cerebral dominance in speech behavior of the child and adult. In: Huxley R, Ingram E (eds) Language acquisition: Models and methods. Academic Press, London, pp 231–255

Bever TG (1972) The limits of intuition. Found Lang 8:411–412

Bever TG, Fodor JA, Weksel W (1965) Is linguistics empirical? Psychol Rev 72:493–500

Bierwisch M (1966) Aufgaben und Form der Grammatik. In: Zeichen und System der Sprache, vol III. Berlin, pp 28–69

Bierwisch M (1967) Some semantic universals of German adjectivals. Found Lang 3:1–36

Bierwisch M (1969) On certain problems of semantic representations. Found Lang 5:153–184

Bierwisch M (1970) Semantics. In: Lyons J (ed) New horizons in linguistics. Penguin, Harmondsworth, pp 166–184

Bierwisch M (1971) On classifying semantic features. In: Steinberg DD, Jakobovits LA (eds). Semantics (1971) Cambridge University Press, Cambridge, England, pp 410–435

Blom JP, Gumperz JJ (1972) Social meaning in linguistic structures: Code-switching in Norway. In: Gumperz JJ, Hymes D (eds) Directions in Sociolinguistics. Holt, Rinehart & Winston, New York, pp 407–434

Bloom L (1973) One word at a time. Mouton, The Hague

Bloomfield L (1933) Language. Holt, Rinehart & Winston, New York

Blumenthal AL (1966) Contribution to the discussion of Wales RJ, Marshall JC (1966) The organization of linguistic performance. In: Lyons J, Wales RJ (eds) Psycholinguistics papers. Edinburgh University Press, Edinburgh, pp 80–84

Blumenthal AL (1967) Prompted recall of sentences. JVLVB 6:203–206

Blumenthal AL (1970) Language and psychology: Historical aspects of psycholinguistics. Wiley, New York

Bobrow SA, Bower GH (1969) Comprehension and recall of sentences. J Exp Psychol 80:455–461

Bock M (1974) Kodierung als Merkmalsselektion. In: Tack WH (ed) Bericht über den 29. Kongreß der Deutschen Gesellschaft für Psychologie. Hogrefe, Göttingen, vol 1 pp 174–176

Bock M (1976) The influence of instructions on feature selection in semantic memory. JVLVB 15:183–191

Bock M (1978) Wort-, Satz-, Textverarbeitung. Kohlhammer, Stuttgart

Bock M, Hörmann H (1974) Der Einfluß von Bildern auf das Behalten von Sätzen. Psychol Forsch 36:343–357

Bolinger DL (1965) The atomization of meaning. Language 41:555–573

Bolinger DL (1968) Aspects of language. Harcourt, Brace, Jovanovich, New York

Bolinger DL (1976) Meaning and memory. Forum Ling 1:1–14

Boomer DS, Laver JDM (1968) Slips of the tongue. Br J Disord Commun 3:2–12

Boucher J, Osgood CE (1969) The Pollyanna hypothesis. JVLVB 8:1–8

Bower G (1967) A multicomponent theory of the memory trace. In: Spence KW, Spence JT (eds) The psychology of learning and motivation, vol 1. Academic Press, New York, pp 229–325

Bowerman M (1973) Structural relationships in children's utterances: Syntactic or semantic? In: Moore TE (ed) Cognitive development and the acquisition of language. Academic Press, New York, pp 197–213

Braine M (1971) The acquisition of language in infant and child. In: Reed C (ed) The learning of language. Appleton-Century-Crofts, New York, pp 7–95

311

Bransford JD, Franks JJ (1971) The abstraction of linguistic ideas. Cogn Psychol 2:331–350

Bransford JD, Johnson MK (1972) Contextual prerequisites for understanding: Some investigations of comprehension and recall. JVLVB 11:717–726

Bransford JD, Barclay JR, Franks JJ (1972) Sentence memory: A constructive versus interpretive approach. Cogn Psychol 3:193–209

Brekle HE (1972) Semantik. Fink, Munich

Brentano F (1955) Psychologie vom empirischen Standpunkt. Meiner, Hamburg (original publication 1924)

Brentano F (1973) Psychology from an empirical standpoint (translated by Rancurello AC, Terrel DB, and McAllister LL) Routledge and Kegan Paul, London.

Brewer WF, Harris RJ (1974) Memory for deictic elements in sentences. JVLVB 13:321–327

Brewer WF, Lichtenstein EH (1974) Memory for marked semantic features versus memory for meaning. JVLVB 13:172–180

Bridgman PW (1959) The way things are. Harvard University Press, Cambridge, Mass.

Brinkmann H (1962) Die deutsche Sprache. Schwann, Düsseldorf

Brockway J, Chmielewski D, Cofer CN (1974) Remembering prose: Productivity and accuracy constraints in recognition memory. JVLVB 13:193–208

Bronowski J (1967) Human and animal languages. In: To honor Roman Jakobson, vol 1. Mouton, The Hague, pp 374–394

Bronowski J, Bellugi U (1970) Language, name, and concept. Science 168:669–673

Brown R (1958a) How shall a thing be called? Psychol Rev 65:14–21

Brown R (1958b) Words and things. Free Press, Glencoe

Brown R (1970) Psycholinguistics: Selected papers. Free Press, New York, pp 208–239

Brown R (1973) A first language: The early stages. Harvard University Press, Cambridge, Mass.

Brown R, McNeill D (1966) The "tip of the tongue" phenomenon. JVLVB 5:325–337

Bruner JS (1957) Going beyond the information given. In: Bruner JS, Brunswik E, Festinger L et al. Contemporary approaches to cognition. Harvard University Press, Cambridge, Mass., pp 41–69

Bruner JS (1967) The ontogenesis of symbols. In: To honor Roman Jakobson, vol 1. Mouton, The Hague, pp 427–446

Bruner JS (1971) Competence in infants. Paper delivered at Soc Res Child Dev, Minneapolis

Bruner JS (1972) Nature and uses of immaturity. Am Psychol 27:1–22

Bruner JS (1975) From communication to language: A psychological perspective. Cognition 3:255–287

Brunswik E (1934) Wahrnehmung und Gegenstandswelt. Grundlegung einer Psychologie vom Gegenstand her. Deuticke, Leipzig

Bühler K (1927) Die Krise der Psychologie. Fischer, Jena

Bühler K (1932) Das Ganze der Sprachtheorie, ihr Aufbau und ihre Teile. In: Kafka G (ed) Bericht über den 12. Kongress der Deutschen Gesellschaft für Psychologie. Fischer, Jena, pp 95–122

Bühler K (1934) Sprachtheorie. Fischer, Jena

Campbell PN (1973) A rhetorical view of locutionary, illocutionary and perlocutionary acts. QJ Speech 59:284–296

Carmichael L, Hogan HP Walter AA (1932) An experimental study of the effects of language on the reproductions of visually perceived form. J Exp Psychol 15:73–86

Carpenter PA (1973) Extracting information from counterfactual clauses. JVLVB 12:512–521

Carpenter PA (1974) On the comprehension, storage, and retrieval of comparative sentences. JVLVB 13:401–411

Carpenter PA, Just AM (1975) Sentence comprehension: A psycholinguistic processing model of verification. Psychol Rev 82:45–73

Carr HA, Kingsbury FA (1938) The concept of traits. Psychol Rev 45:497–524

Carroll JB (1953) The study of language. Harvard University Press, Cambridge, Mass.

Carroll JB (1959) Review of Osgood CE, Suci GJ, Tannenbaum PH (1957) The measurement of meaning. Language 35:58–77

Cassirer E (1953) The philosophy of symbolic forms. I: Language (translated by Manheim R). Yale University Press, New Haven

Cazden CB (1970) The situation: A neglected source of social class differences in language use. J Soc Issues 26/2:35–60

Cerf W (1966) Critical Notice on "How to do things with words." Mind 75:262–285

Chafe WL (1970) Meaning and the structure of language. Chicago University Press, Chicago

Chafe WL (1971a) Directionality and paraphrase. Language 47:1–26

Chafe WL (1971b) Linguistics and human knowledge. Georgetown University Series on Languages and Linguistics 25:57–69

Chomsky N (1957) Syntactic structures. Mouton, The Hague

Chomsky N (1959) Review of Skinner BF (1957) Verbal behavior. Language 35:26–58

Chomsky N (1962) Explanatory models in linguistics. In: Nagel E, Suppes P, Tarski A (eds) Logic, methodology and philosophy of science: Proceedings of the 1960 International Congress. Stanford University Press, Stanford, pp 528–550

Chomsky N (1965) Aspects of the theory of syntax. MIT Press, Cambridge, Mass.

Chomsky N (1966) Cartesian linguistics. Harper & Row, New York

Chomsky N (1967) The formal nature of language. In: Lenneberg EH Biological foundations of language. Wiley, New York, pp 397–442

Chomsky N (1968) Language and mind. Harcourt, Brace, Jovanovich, New York

Chomsky N (1971) Deep structure, surface structure and semantic interpretation. In: Steinberg DD, Jakobovits LA (eds) Semantics. Cambridge University Press, Cambridge, England

Clark EV (1970) How young children describe events in time. In: Flores d'Arcais G, Levelt WJM (eds) Advances in psycholinguistics. North-Holland, Amsterdam, pp 275–284

Clark EV (1973a) Non-linguistic strategies and the acquisition of word meaning. Cognition 2:162–182

Clark EV (1973b) What's in a word? On the child's acquisition of semantics in his first language. In: Moore TE (ed) Cognitive development and the acquisition of language. Academic Press, New York, pp 65–110

Clark HH (1969a) Influence of language on solving three-term series problems. J Exp Psychol 82:205–215

Clark HH (1969b) Linguistic processes in deductive reasoning. Psychol Rev 76:387–404

Clark HH (1970a) Word associations and linguistic theory. In: Lyons J (ed) New horizons in linguistics. Penguin, Harmondsworth, pp 271–286

Clark HH (1970b) The primitive nature of children's relational concepts. In: Hayes JR (ed) Cognition and the development of language. Wiley, New York, pp 269–278

Clark HH (1973) Semantics and comprehension. In: Sebeok TA (ed) Current trends in linguistics, vol 12. Mouton, The Hague, pp 1291–1428

Clark HH, Card SK (1969) The role of semantics in remembering comparative sentences. J Exp Psychol 82:545–553

Clark HH, Chase WG (1972) On the process of comparing sentences against pictures. Cogn Psychol 3:472–517

Clark HH, Clark EV (1968) Semantic distinctions and memory for complex sentences. Q J Exp Psychol 20:129–138

Clark HH, Lucy P (1975) Understanding what is meant from what is said: A study in conversationally conveyed requests. JVLVB 14:56–72

Collins AM, Quillian MR (1969) Retrieval time from semantic memory. JVLVB 8:241–248

Collins AM, Quillian MR (1972) Experiments on semantic memory and language comprehension. In: Gregg LW (ed) Cognition in learning and memory. Wiley, New York, pp 117–138

Condon WS, Ogston WD (1966) Sound film analysis of normal and pathological behavior patterns. J Nerv Ment Dis 143:338–347

Connolly KJ, Bruner J (eds) (1974) The growth of competence. Academic Press, London

Conrad C (1974) Context effects in sentence comprehension: A study of the subjective lexicon. Mem Cognition 2:130–138

Cook M (1970) Experiments on orientation and proxemics. Hum Relat 23:61–76

Cornish ER (1971) Pragmatic aspects of negation in sentence evaluation and completion tasks. Br J Psychol 62:505–511

313

Coseriu E (1967) Lexikalische Solidaritäten. Poetica 1:293–303

Coseriu E (1970) Einführung in die strukturelle Betrachtung des Wortschatzes. Narr, Tübingen

Coseriu E (1973a) Semantik und Grammatik. In: Moser H (ed) Sprache der Gegenwart, vol 20. Schwann, Düsseldorf, pp 77–89

Coseriu E (1973b) Die Lage in der Linguistik. Innsbrucker Beiträge zur Sprachwissenschaft, Vorträge 9, Innsbruck, pp 5–15

Craik FIM, Lockhart RS (1972) Levels of processing: A framework for memory research. JVLVB 11:671–684

Cranach M von (1971) Die nicht verbale Kommunikation im Kontext des kommunikativen Verhaltens. In: Jahrbuch der Max-Planck-Gesellschaft zur Förderung der Wissenschaften. Vandenhoeck & Ruprecht. Göttingen, pp 105–144

Danks JH (1969) Grammaticalness and meaningfulness in the comprehension of sentences. JVLVB 8:687–696

Danks JH, Schwenk MA (1972) Prenominal adjective order and communication context. JVLVB 11:183–187

Deese J (1962) On the structure of associative meaning. Psychol Rev 69:161–175

Deese J (1967) Meaning and change of meaning. Am Psychol 22:641–651

Deese J (1968) Association and memory. In: Dixon TR, Horton DL (eds) Verbal behavior and general behavior theory. Prentice-Hall, Englewood Cliffs, pp 97–108

Deese J (1969) Behavior and fact. Am Psychol 24:515–522

Deese J (1970) Psycholinguistics. Allyn & Bacon, Boston

Degerman R, Mather RS (1972) Spatial representation of noun phrases. JVLVB 11:66–72

Dittrich O (1903) Grundzüge der Sprachpsychologie, vol 1. Niemeyer, Halle

Dolinsky R, Michael RE (1969) Post-interpretation in the recall of grammatical and ungrammatical word sequences. JVLVB 8:26–29

Donaldson M, Wales R (1970) On the acqusition of some relational terms. In: Hayes JR (ed) Cognition and the development of language. Wiley, New York, pp 235–268

Drach K (1969) The language of the parent: A pilot study. Working Paper No. 14: The structure of linguistic input to children. Language behavior research laboratories, University of California, Berkeley

Duncan S (1969) Nonverbal communication. Psychol Bull 72:118–137

Eccles JC (1970) Facing reality. Springer, Berlin Heidelberg New York

Efron D (1941) Gesture and environment. Columbia University Press, New York

Ekman P, Friesen WV (1969) The repertoire of nonverbal behavior: Categories, origins, usage, and coding. Semiotica 1:49–98

Elias CS, Perfetti CA (1973) Encoding task and recognition memory: The importance of semantic encoding. J Exp Psychol 99:151–156

Engelkamp J (1973) Semantische Struktur und die Verarbeitung von Sätzen. Huber, Bern

Engelkamp J (1974) Psycholinguistik. Fink, Munich

Engelkamp J (1975) The interaction of semantic features of transitive verbs and their objects. Psychol Res 37:299–308

Engelkamp J, Hörmann H (1974) The effect of non-verbal information on the recall of negation. QJ Exp Psychol 26:98–105

Engelkamp J, Merdian F (1973) Die konnotative Bedeutung des Satzsubjekts als Funktion widersprüchlicher Adjektivbedeutungen. Arch Psychol 125:166–183

Engelkamp J, Merdian F, Hörmann H (1972) Semantische Faktoren beim Behalten der Verneinung von Sätzen. Psychol Forsch 35:93–116

Ertel S (1967) Allgemeinqualität und Relation. Arch Psychol 119:26–56

Ertel S (1970) Selbstbeurteilung, Semantik und Persönlichkeit. Psychol Forsch 33:254–276

Ertel S (1974a) Interferenz beim deduktiven Denken durch konzeptuelle Anisotropie polarer Adjektive. In: Klix F (ed) Organismische Informationsverarbeitung. Akademie-Verlag, Berlin, pp 282–296

Ertel S (1974b) Satzsubjekt und Ich-Perspektive. In: Eckensberger LH, Eckensberger US (eds) Bericht über den 28. Kongreß der Deutschen Gesellschaft für Psychologie, vol 1. Hogrefe, Göttingen, pp 129–139

Ertel S (1975) Gestaltpsychologische Denkmodelle für die Struktur der Sprache. In: Ertel S, Kemmler L, Stadler M (eds) Gestalttheorie in der modernen Psychologie. Steinkopff, Darmstadt, pp 94–107

Ertel S (1977) Where do the subjects of sentences come from? In: Rosenberg S (ed) Sentence production: Developments in research and theory. Erlbaum, Hillsdale

Ertel S, Bloemer WD (1975) Affirmation and negation as constructive action. Psychol Res 37:335–342

Ertel S, Prodöhl DG (1969) Akzentuierung nichtperceptiver Größenschätzung. Psychol Beitr 11:3–22

Ertel S, Theophile I (1966) Ein Versuch zur Messung richtungsspezifischer Aktivierung. Psychol Forsch 29:241–263

Ervin-Tripp S (1971) An overview of theories of grammatical development. In: Slobin DI (ed) The ontogenesis of grammar. Academic Press, New York, pp 189–212

Ervin-Tripp S (1972) On sociolinguistic rules: Alternation and co-occurrence. In: Gumperz JJ, Hymes D (eds) Directions in Sociolinguistics. Holt, Rinehart & Winston, New York, pp 213–250

Feltkamp HW (1971) On idealizing native speakers. Neophilogus 55:234–245

Fillenbaum S (1966) Memory for gist: Some relevant variables. Lang Speech 9:217–227

Fillenbaum S (1969) Words as feature complexes: False recognition of antonyms and synonyms. J Exp Psychol 82:400–402

Fillenbaum S (1971) Psycholinguistics. Annu Rev Psychol 22:251–309

Fillenbaum S, Rapoport A (1971) Structures in the subjective lexicon. Academic Press, New York

Fillmore CJ (1968a) The case for case. In: Bach E, Harms RT (eds) Universals in linguistic theory. Holt, Rinehart & Winston, New York, pp 1–88

Fillmore CJ (1968b) Lexical entries for verbs. Found Lang 4:373–393

Fillmore CJ (1969) Types of lexical information. In: Kiefer F (ed) Studies in syntax and semantics. Reidel, Dordrecht, pp 109–137

Fillmore CJ (1972) Subjects, speakers and roles. In: Davidson D, Harman G (eds) Semantics of natural language. Reidel, Dordrecht, pp 1–24

Flores d'Arcais GB (1973a) Cognitive principles in language processing. Rijksuniversiteit Leiden

Flores d'Arcais GB (1973b) Some perceptual determinants of sentence construction. Report E 036–1973. Psychological Institute, University of Leiden, Leiden

Flores d'Arcais GB (1974) Is there a memory for sentences? Acta Psychol 38:33–58

Fodor JA (1971) Current approaches to syntax recognition. In: Horton DL, Jenkins JJ (eds) Perception of language. Merrill, Columbus, pp 120–139

Fodor JA (1972) Some reflections on LS Vygotsky's Thought and language. Cognition 1:83–95

Fodor JA, Garrett M (1966) Some reflections on competence and performance. In: Lyons J, Wales RJ (eds) Psycholinguistics papers. Edinburgh University Press, Edinburgh, pp 135–179

Foppa K, Wettler M (1967) Psychologie des sprachlichen Lernens. Schweiz Z Psychol 26:24–30

Forguson LW (1968) "It's raining but I don't believe it". Theoria 34:88–101

Foss DJ, Swinney DA (1973) On the psychological reality of the phoneme: Perception, identification, and consciousness. JVLVB 12:246–257

Franks JJ, Bransford JD (1972) The acquisition of abstract ideas. JVLVB 11:311–315

Franks JJ, Bransford JD (1974) A brief note on linguistic interpretation. JVLVB 13:217–219

Frederiksen CH (1975) Acquisition of semantic information from discourse: Effects of repeated exposure. JVLVB 14:158–169

Frege G (1879) Begriffsschrift. Nebert, Halle

Frisch K von (1965) Tanzsprache und Orientierung der Bienen. Springer, Berlin Heidelberg New York

Fromkin VA (1971) The non-anomalous nature of anomalous utterances. Language 47:27–52

Frye M (1973) Force and meaning. J Philos 70:281–294

Gardner RA, Gardner BT (1969) Teaching sign language to a chimpanzee. Science 165:664–672

Garfinkel H (1972) Remarks on ethnomethodology. In: Gumperz JJ, Hymes D (eds) Directions in sociolinguistics. Holt, Rinehart & Winston, New York, pp 301–324

Garrett M, Fodor JA (1968) Psychological theories and linguistic constructs. In: Dixon TR, Horton DL (eds) Verbal behavior and general behavior theory. Prentice-Hall, Englewood Cliffs, pp 451–477

Garrod S, Trabasso T (1973) A dual-memory information processing interpretation of sentence comprehension. JVLVB 12:155–167

Geckeler H (1971) Strukturelle Semantik und Wortfeldtheorie. Finke, Munich

Gibson JJ (1950) The perception of the visual world. Houghton, Boston

Gibson JJ (1966) The senses considered as perceptual systems. Houghton, Boston

Gilson C, Abelson RP (1965) The subjective use of inductive evidence. J Pers Soc Psychol 2:301–310

Glanzer M (1963) The verbal loop hypothesis: Binary numbers. JVLVB 2:301–309

Goffman E (1959) The presentation of self in everyday life. Doubleday, New York

Goffman E (1961) Encounters. Bobbs-Merrill, Indianapolis

Goffman E (1963) Behavior in public places. Free Press, Glencoe

Goffman E (1964) The neglected situation. Am Anthropol 66/6:133–136

Goldman-Eisler F (1967) Sequential temporal patterns and cognitive processes in speech. Lang Speech 10:122–132

Goldman-Eisler F (1968) Psycholinguistics: Experiments in spontaneous speech. Academic Press, London

Goldman-Eisler F (1972) Pauses, clauses, sentences. Lang Speech 15:103–113

Goldman-Eisler F, Cohen M (1970) Is N, P, and PN difficulty a valid criterion of transformational operations? JVLVB 9:161–166

Goodnow JJ, Levine RA (1973) The grammar of action. Cogn Psychol 7:82–98

Green DW (1975) The effects of task on the representation of sentences. JVLVB 14:275–283

Greenberg JH (1960) Concerning inferences from linguistic to nonlinguistic data. In: Hoijer H (ed) Language in culture. University of Chicago Press, Chicago, pp 3–19

Greenberg JH (1966) Universals of language. MIT Press, Cambridge, Mass.

Greenfield PM (1972) Playing peekaboo with a four-month-old: A study of the role of speech and nonspeech sounds in the formation of a visual schema. J Psychol 82:287–298

Greenfield PM (1973) Who is "Dada"? Some aspects of the semantic and phonological development of a child's first words. Lang Speech 16:34–43

Greenfield PM, Nelson K, Saltzman E (1972) The development of rulebound strategies for manipulating seriated cups: A parallel between action and grammar. Cogn Psychol 3:291–310

Greenfield PM, Smith JH (1976) The structure of communication in early language development. Academic Press, New York

Greimas AJ (1971) Strukturale Semantik. Methodische Untersuchungen. Vieweg, Braunschweig

Grice HP (1957) Meaning. Philos Rev 66:377–388

Gründer K (1975) Sokrates im 19. Jahrhundert. In: Fromm H, Harms W, Ruberg U (eds) Verbum et signum, vol 1. Fink, Munich, pp 539–554

Habermas J (1971) Vorbereitende Bemerkungen zu einer Theorie der kommunikativen Kompetenz. In: Habermas J, Luhmann N (eds) Theorie der Gesellschaft oder Sozialtechnologie. Suhrkamp, Frankfurt, pp 101–141

Hall ET (1959) The silent language. Doubleday, New York

Hall ET (1966) The hidden dimension. Doubleday, Garden City

Halliday MAK (1964) Syntax and the consumer. Monograph Series on Languages and Linguistics (Washington) 17:11–24

Halliday MAK (1970) Language structure and language function. In: Lyons J (ed) New horizons in linguistics. Penguin, Harmondsworth, pp 140–165

Hampshire S (1967) JL Austin. In: Rorty R (ed) The linguistic turn. University of Chicago Press, Chicago, pp 239–247

Hare RM (1952) The language of morals. Clarendon Press, Oxford

Hare RM (1970) Meaning and speech acts. Philos Rev 79:3–24

Harman GH (1967) Psychological aspects of the theory of syntax. J Philos 64:75–87

Harvey N (1973) The semantics of high-low continua. Br J Psychol 64:51–54

Haviland SE, Clark HH (1974) What's new? Acquiring new information as a process of comprehension. JVLVB 13:512–521

Hayes C (1951) The ape in our house. Harper & Row, New York

Hebb DO (1949) The organization of behavior. Wiley, New York

Hebb DO (1960) The American revolution. Am Psychol 15:735–745

Heider F (1930) Die Leistung des Wahrnehmungssystems. Z Psychol 114:371–394

Heider F (1944) Social perception and phenomenal causality. Psychol Rev 51:358–374

Heider F (1958) The psychology of interpersonal relations. Wiley, New York

Heider F (1959) On perception and event structure and the psychological environment. Psychol Issues 1:1–123

Heider F (1967) On social cognition. Am Psychol 22:25–31

Heinroth O (1910) Beiträge zur Biologie, insbesondere Psychologie und Ethologie der Anatiden. In: Verhandlungen des V. Intern. Ornithologischen Kongresses, Berlin

Held R (1965) Plasticity in sensory-motor systems. Sci Am 313:84–94

Henley NM (1969) A psychological study of the semantics of animal terms. JVLVB 8:176–184

Herrmann T (1974) Über Benennungsflexibilität. In: Tack WH (ed) Bericht über den 29. Kongreß der Deutschen Gesellschaft für Psychologie. Hogrefe, Göttingen, vol 1 pp 168–173

Herrmann T, Deutsch W (1976) Psychologie der Objektbenennung. Huber, Bern

Hockett CF (1958) A course in modern linguistics. Macmillan, New York

Höpp G (1970) Evolution der Sprache und Vernunft. Springer, Berlin Heidelberg New York

Hörmann H (1971a) Psycholinguistics: An introduction to research and theory (translated by Stern HH). Springer, Berlin Heidelberg New York

Hörmann H (1971b) Semantic factors in negation. Psychol Forsch 35:1–16

Hörmann H (1973) Semantische Anomalie, Metapher und Witz. Folia Ling 5:310–330

Hörmann H (1974) Psycholinguistik. In: Koch WA (ed) Perspektiven der Linguistik, vol 2. Kröner, Stuttgart, pp 138–156

Hörmann H, Lazarus G, Lazarus H (1975) The role of the predicate in sentence perception. Manuscript, Ruhr-Universität, Bochum

Hörmann H, Terbuyken G (1974) Situational factors in meaning. Psychol Forsch 36:297–310

Holborow L (1972) Review of Searle JR (1969) Speech Acts. Mind 81:458–468

Hornby PA (1972) The psychological subject and predicate. Cogn Psychol 3:632–642

Hornby PA (1974) Surface structure and presupposition. JVLVB 13:530–538

Husserl E (1970) Logical investigations (translated by Findlay JN). Routledge & Kegan Paul, London

Huttenlocher J, Eisenberg K, Straus S (1968) Comprehension: Relation between perceived actor and logical subject. JVLVB 7:527–530

Huxley JS (1948) Evolution: The modern synthesis. Allen & Unwin, London

Hymes D (1970) Linguistic theory and the function of speech. In: Proceedings of the International Days of Sociolinguistics. Istituto Luigi Sturzo, Rome

Hymes D (1972a) Models of interaction of language and social life. In: Gumperz JJ, Hymes D (eds) Directions in Sociolinguistics. Holt, Rinehart & Winston, New York, pp 35–71

Hymes D (1972b) Toward communicative competence. University of Pennsylvania Press, Philadelphia

Ingram E (1968) Recent trends in psycholinguistics: A critical notice. Br J Psychol 59:315–325

James W (1890) Principles of psychology, vol 1. Holt, New York

Jarvella RM (1974) Memory for the intentions of sentences. Mem Cognition 2:185–188

Jarvella RM, Herman SJ (1972) Clause structure of sentences and speech processing. Percept Psychophys 11:381–384

Jerspersen O (1933) Essentials of English grammar. Allen & Unwin, London

Jörg S (1978) Der Einfluß sprachlicher Bezeichnungen auf das Wiedererkennen von Bildern. Huber, Bern

Jörg S, Hörmann H (1978) The influence of general and specific labels on the recognition of labeled and unlabeled parts of pictures. JVLVB 17:445–454

Johnson MG (1970) A cognitive-feature model of compound free associations. Psychol Rev 77:282–293

Johnson MK, Bransford JD, Nyberg SE, Cleary JJ (1972) Comprehension factors in interpreting memory for abstract and concrete sentences. JVLVB 11:451–454

Johnson NF (1965a) Language models and functional units of language behavior. In: Rosenberg S (ed) Directions in psycholinguistics. Macmillan, New York, pp 29–65

Johnson NF (1965b) The psychological reality of phrase structure rules. JVLVB 4:469–475

Kanouse DE (1972) Verbs as implicit quantifiers. JVLVB 11:141–147

Katona G (1940) Organizing and memorizing. Columbia University Press, New York

Katz JJ (1966) The philosophy of language. Harper & Row, New York

Katz JJ (1967) Recent issues in semantic theory. Found Lang 3:123–194

Katz JJ (1973a) Interpretive semantics meets the zoombies: A discussion of the controversy about deep structure. Found Lang 9:549–596

Katz JJ (1973b) On defining "presupposition". Ling Inquiry 4:256–260

Katz JJ (1964) Semantic theory and the meaning of "good", J Philosophy, 23:739–766

Katz JJ, Fodor JA (1963) The structure of a semantic theory. Language 39:170–210

Kellogg WN (1968) Communication and language in the home-raised chimpanzee. Science 162:423–427

Kellogg WN, Kellogg LA (1933) The ape and the child: A study of environmental influence upon early behavior. McGraw-Hill, New York

Kendon A (1967) Some functions of gaze-direction in social interaction. Acta Psychol 26:22–63

Kessel FS (1972) Imagery: A dimension of mind rediscovered. J Psychol 63:149–162

Kintsch W (1970) Recognition memory in bilingual subjects. JVLVB 9:405–409

Kintsch W (1974) The representation of meaning in memory. Erlbaum, Hillsdale

Kintsch W, Keenan J (1973) Reading rate and retention as a function of the number of propositions in the base structure of sentences. Cogn Psychol 5:257–274

Kintsch W, Kozminsky E, Streby WJ, McKoon G, Keenan JM (1975) Comprehension and recall of text as a function of content variables. JVLVB 14:196–214

Klix F (1971) Information und Verhalten. Huber, Bern

Köhler W (1956) The mentality of apes (translated by Winter E). Routledge & Kegan Paul, London

Kolligs M (1942) Optische Figuren im Entstehen und die Entwicklung ihrer Bedeutung. Arch Ges Psychol 111:39–116

Korzybski A (1941) Science and sanity. International Non-Aristotelian Library, Lancaster, Penn.

Kuczaj SA (1975) On the acquisition of a semantic system. JVLVB 14:340–358

Laguna GA De (1927) Speech: Its function and development. Yale University Press, New Haven (Reprinted by Indiana University Press, Bloomington 1963)

Lakoff G (1971a) On generative semantics. In: Steinberg DD, Jakobovits LA (eds) Semantics, Cambridge University Press, Cambridge, England, pp 232–296

Lakoff G (1971b) Presupposition and relative well-formedness. In: Steinberg DD, Jakobovits LA (eds) Semantics Cambridge University Press, Cambridge, England, pp 329–340

Lakoff G (1972) Hedges: A study in meaning criteria and the logic of fuzzy concepts. In: Papers from the 8th Regional Meeting of Chicago Linguistics Society. University of Chicago Linguistics Department, Chicago

Lakoff G (1973) Deep language. Letter to the New York Review of Books 20:1

Lancker D Van (1975) Heterogeneity in language and speech: Neurolinguistic studies. Working Papers in Phonetics 29, Los Angeles

Langendoen D (1970) Essentials of English grammar. Holt, Rinehart & Winston, New York

Langer S (1942) Philosophy in a new key. Harvard University Press, Cambridge, Mass.

Lashley KS (1951) The problem of serial order in behavior. In: Jeffress LA (ed) Cerebral mechanisms in behavior. Wiley, New York, pp 112–136

Laucken U (1974) Naive Verhaltenstheorie. Klett, Stuttgart

Leise E (1953) Der Wortinhalt. Seine Struktur im Deutschen und Englischen. Quelle & Meyer, Heidelberg

Leisi E (1962) Englische und deutsche Wortinhalte. Wirkendes Wort 12:140–150

Lenneberg EH (1967) Biological foundations of language. Wiley, New York

Lenneberg EH (1969) On explaining language. Science 164:635–643

Leontev AA (1969a) Inner speech and the process of grammatical generation of utterances. Sov Psychol 2/3:11–16

Leontev AA (1969b) The psychological structure of meaning. Sov Psychol 2/3:37–38

Leontev AA (1969c) Language, speech and speech activity (in Russian). Prosveshchenie, Moscow [German translation (1971) Sprache, Sprechen, Sprechtätigkeit. Kohlhammer, Stuttgart]

Leontev AA (1972) Soviet psycholinguistics – New trends. Paper at 20th Intern. Congress of Psychology, Tokyo

Leontev AN, Luria AR (1956) Introduction to Vygotsky LS (1956) Selected psychological investigations (in Russian). Izd APN RSFSR Moscow [German translation (1958) Z Psychol 162:165 205]

Lesgold AM (1972) Pronominalization: A device for unifying sentences in memory. JVLVB 11:316–323

Levelt WJM (1972) Some psychological aspects of linguistic data. Ling Ber 17:18–30

Levelt WJM (1975) What became of LAD? De Ridder, Lisse

Liberman AM, Cooper FS, Harris KS, MacNeilage PF (1963) A motor theory of speech perception. In: Fant GM (ed) Proceedings of the Speech Communication Seminar. Royal Institute of Technology, Stockholm

Liberman AM, Mattingly IG, Turvey MT (1972) Language codes and memory codes. In: Melton AW, Martin E (eds) Coding processes in human memory. Winston, Washington, pp 307–334

Lipps T (1923) Leitfaden der Psychologie, 3rd edn. Engelmann, Leipzig

List G (1974) Syntagmatische Sprachpsychologie. Kohlhammer, Stuttgart

Loftus EF, Palmer JC (1974) Reconstruction of automobile destruction: An example of the interaction between language and memory. JVLVB 13:585–589

Long AJ De (1974) Kinesic signals as utterance boundaries in preschool children. Semiotica 11:43–73

Lorenz K (1935) Der Kumpan in der Umwelt des Vogels. J Ornithol 83/2–3 pp. 137–213 and 289–413

Lounsbury FG (1964) The structural analysis of kinship semantics. In: Lunt HG (ed) Proceedings of the 9th Intern. Congress of Linguists. Mouton, The Hague, pp 1073–1093

Luhmann N (1971) Sinn als Grundbegriff der Soziologie. In: Habermas J, Luhmann N (eds) Theorie der Gesellschaft oder Sozialtechnologie. Suhrkamp, Frankfurt, pp 25–100

Luria AR, Tsvetkova LS (1969) Neuropsychological analysis of the predicative structure of utterances. Sov Psychol 2/3:26–33

Lyons J (1968) Introduction to theoretical linguistics. Cambridge University Press, Cambridge, England

MacKay DG (1972) The structure of words and syllables: Evidence from errors in speech. Cogn Psychol 3:210–227

MacKay DM (1972) Formal analysis of communication processes. In: Hinde RA (ed) Non-verbal communication. Cambridge University Press, Cambridge, England, pp 3–25

Maclay H (1971) Overview. In: Steinberg DD, Jakobovits LA (eds) Semantics, Cambridge University Press, Cambridge, England, pp 157–182

Macnamara J (1971) Parsimony and lexicon. Language 47:359–374

Macnamara J (1972) Cognitive basis of language learning in infants. Psychol Rev 79:1–13

Mandler G (1967) Organization and memory. In: Spence KW, Spence JT (eds) The psychology of learning and motivation, vol 2. Academic Press, New York, pp 327–372

Marshall JC (1970) Introduction: A note on semantic theory. In: Flores d'Arcais GB, Levelt WJM (eds) Advances in psycholinguistics. North-Holland, Amsterdam, pp 189–196

Martin JE (1969) Semantic determinants of preferred adjective order. JVLVB 8:697–704

Martin JG (1967) Hesitations in the speaker's production and listener's reproduction of utterances. JVLVB 6:903–909

Martin JG (1972) Rhythmic (hierarchical) versus serial structure in speech and other behavior. Psychol Rev 79:487–509

Martinet A (1960) Eléments de linguistique générale. Colin, Paris

Mathesius V (1964) On the potentiality of the phenomena of language. In: Vachek J (ed) A Prague school reader in linguistics. Indiana University Press, Bloomington, pp 1–32

May JE, Clayton KN (1973) Imaginal processes during the attempts to recall names. JVLVB 12:683–688

McCawley JD (1968a) Concerning the base component of a transformational grammar. Found Lang 4:243–269

McCawley JD (1968b) The role of semantics in a grammar. In: Bach E, Harms RT (eds) Universals in linguistic theory. Holt, Rinehart & Winston, New York, pp 125–169

McCawley JD (1971) Where do noun phrases come from? In: Steinberg DD, Jakobovits LA (eds) Semantics, Cambridge University Press, Cambridge, England, pp 217–231

McNeill D (1970) The acquisition of language: The study of developmental psycholinguistics. Harper & Row, New York

Mead GH (1934) Mind, self, and society. Chicago University Press, Chicago

Mehler J (1963) Some effects of grammatical transformations on the recall of English sentences. JVLVB 2:346–351

Mehrabian A (1969) Significance of posture and position in the communication of attitude and status relationships. Psychol Bull 71:359–372

Menyuk P, Bernholtz N (1969) Prosodic features and children's language productions. MIT Research Laboratory of Electronics, Quarterly Progress Reports 93:216–219

Meyer DE, Schvaneveldt RW, Ruddy MG (1974) Functions of graphemic and phonemic codes in visual word recognition. Mem Cognition 2:309–321

Michotte A (1963) Perception of causality. Methuen, London

Miller GA (1951) Language and communication. McGraw-Hill, New York

Miller GA (1956) The magical number seven plus or minus two. Psychol Rev 63:81–97

Miller GA (1965) Some preliminaries to psycholinguistics. Am Psychol 20:15–20

Miller GA (1968) Linguistic aspects of cognition: Predication and meaning. Mimeographed paper, Rockefeller University, New York

Miller GA (1969) A psychological method to investigate verbal concepts. J Math Psychol 6:169–191

Miller GA (1971) Empirical methods in the study of semantics. In: Steinberg DD, Jakobovits LA (eds) Semantics, Cambridge University Press, Cambridge, England, pp 569–585

Miller GA (1972) English verbs of motion: A case study of semantics. In: Melton AW, Martin E (eds) Coding processes in human memory. Winston, Washington, pp 335–372

Miller GA, Galanter E, Pribram KH (1960) Plans and the structure of behavior. Holt, Rinehart & Winston, New York

Mistler-Lachmann JL (1972) Levels of comprehension in processing of normal and ambiguous sentences. JVLVB 11:614–623

Mistler-Lachmann JL (1974) Depth of comprehension and sentence memory. JVLVB 13:98–106

Moeser SD, Bregman AS (1972) The role of reference in the acquisition of a miniature artificial language. JVLVB 11:759–769

Moore GE (1947) Ethics. Oxford University Press, London

Moran LJ, Mefferd RBJr, Kimble JPJr (1964) Idiodynamic sets in word association. Psychol Monogr 78/579

Morris CW (1946) Signs, language, and behavior. Prentice-Hall, Englewood Cliffs

Morton J (1969) Interaction of information in word recognition. Psychol Rev 76:165–178

Moscovici S (1967) Communication processes and the properties of language. In: Berkowitz L (ed) Advances in experimental social psychology, vol 3. Academic Press, New York, pp 225–270

Mounin G (1963) Les problèmes théoriques de la traduction. Gallimard, Paris

Müller-Eckhard E (1974) Äusserungslänge und Eindrucksbildung. Brockmeyer, Bochum

Neisser U (1967) Cognitive psychology. Appleton-Century-Crofts, New York

Nelson K (1974) Concept, word, and sentence: Interrelations in acquisition and development. Psychol Rev 81:267–285

Newmeyer FJ (1970) On the alleged boundary between syntax and semantics. Found Lang 6:178–286

Noble CE (1952) An analysis of meaning. Psychol Rev 59:421–430

O'Connell DC (1969) Nonsense strings, words, and sentences: Some cross-linguistic comparisons. Psychol Forsch 33:37–49

O'Connell DC, Kowal S (1972) Cross-linguistic pause and rate phenomena in adults and adolescents. J Psycholinguist Res 1:155–164

O'Connell DC, Kowal S, Hörmann H (1969) Semantic determinants of pauses. Psychol Forsch 33:50–67

Ogden CK, Richards IA (1923) The meaning of meaning. Kegan Paul, London

Oldfield RC (1966) Contribution to the discussion of Thorne JP (1966) On hearing sentences. In: Lyons J, Wales RJ (eds) Psycholinguistics papers. Edinburgh University Press, Edinburgh, pp 17–23

Oller JWJr (1972) On the relation between syntax, semantics and pragmatics. Linguistics 83:43–55

320

Olson DR (1970) Language and thought: Aspects of a cognitive theory of semantics. Psychol Rev 77:257–273

Olson DR, Filby N (1972) On the comprehension of active and passive sentences. Cogn Psychol 3:361–381

Osgood CE (1963a) On understanding and creating sentences. Am Psychol 18:735–751

Osgood CE (1963b) Psycholinguistics. In: Koch S (ed) Psychology: A study of a science, vol 6. McGraw-Hill, New York, pp 244–316

Osgood CE (1968) Toward a wedding of insufficiencies. In: Dixon TR, Horton DL (eds) Verbal behavior and general behavior theory. Prentice-Hall, Englewood Cliffs, pp 495–519

Osgood CE (1971a) Exploration in semantic space: A personal diary. J Soc Issues 27/4:5–64

Osgood CE (1971b) Where do sentences come from? In: Steinberg DD, Jakobovits LA (eds) Semantics, Cambridge University Press, Cambridge, England, pp 497–529

Osgood CE, Sebeok TA (eds) (1954) Psycholinguistics: A survey of theory and research problems. Indiana University Publications in Anthropology and Linguistics, Memoir 10. Waverly Press, Baltimore [2nd edn (1965) by Indiana University Press, Bloomington]

Osgood CE, Tannenbaum PH (1955) The principle of congruity in the prediction of attitude change. Psychol Rev 62:42–55

Osgood CE, Suci GJ, Tannenbaum PH (1957) The measurement of meaning. University of Illinois Press, Urbana, Ill.

Paivio A (1969) Mental imagery in associative learning and memory. Psychol Rev 76:241–263

Paivio A (1970) On the functional significance of imagery. Psychol Bull 73:385–392

Paivio A (1971) Imagery and verbal processes. Holt, Rinehart & Winston, New York

Paivio A, Begg I (1971) Imagery and comprehension latencies as a function of sentence concreteness and structure. Percept Psychophys 10:408–412

Paivio A, Csapo K (1973) Picture superiority in free recall: Imagery or dual coding? Cogn Psychol 5:176–206

Patzig G (1970) Sprache und Logik. Vandenhoeck & Ruprecht, Göttingen

Paul H (1909) Prinzipien der Sprachgeschichte. Niemeyer, Halle

Peirce CS (1960) Collected papers. Belknap Press of Harvard University Press, Cambridge, Mass.

Perfetti CA (1972) Psychosemantics. Psychol Bull 78:241–259

Piaget J (1953) The origin of intelligence in the child (translated by Cook M). Routledge & Kegan Paul, London

Piaget J (1954a) Le langage et la pensée du point de vue génétique. In: Revesz G (ed) Thinking and speaking: A symposium. (Special issue of Acta Psychol 10) North-Holland, Amsterdam

Piaget J (1954b) The construction of reality in the child. Basic Books, New York

Piaget J (1959) The language and thought of the child, 2nd edn (translated by Gabain M). Routledge & Kegan Paul, London

Pick A (1931) Aphasie. In: Bethe's Handbuch der normalen und pathologischen Physiologie, vol 15. pp 1416–1524, Springer, Berlin Heidelberg New York

Ploog D (1972) Kommunikation in Affengesellschaften und deren Bedeutung für die Verständigungsweisen des Menschen. In: Gadamer H-G, Vogler P (eds) Neue Anthropologie, vol 2, Biologische Anthropologie. Thieme, Stuttgart, pp 98–178

Polanyi M (1962) Tacit knowing: Its bearing on some problems of philosophy. Rev Mod Phys 34:601–616

Polanyi M (1966) The tacit dimension. Doubleday, Garden City

Polanyi M (1968) Life's irreducible structure. Science 160:1308–1312

Polzella D, Rohrmann N (1970) Psychological aspects of transitive verbs. JVLVB 9:537–540

Popper KR (1972) Objective knowledge: An evolutionary approach. Clarendon, Oxford

Popper KR, Eccles JC (1977) The self and its brain. Springer, Berlin Heidelberg New York

Porzig W (1934) Wesenhafte Bedeutungsbeziehungen. Beiträge zur Geschichte der deutschen Sprache und Literatur 58:70–97

Posner MI, Warren RE (1972) Traces, concepts, and conscious constructions. In: Melton AW, Martin E (eds) Coding processes in human memory, Winston, Washington, pp 25–43

Premack D (1970) A functional analysis of language. J Exp Anal Behav 14:107–125

Průcha J (1972a) Recent Soviet studies in psycholinguistics. Found Lang 8:41–61

Průcha J (1972b) Soviet psycholinguistics. Mouton, The Hague

Quillian MR (1967) Word concepts: A theory and simulation of some basic semantic capabilities. Behav Sci 12:410–430

Quillian MR (1969) The teachable language comprehender: A simulation program and theory of language. Commun Assoc Comput Machinery 12:459–476

Quine WV (1960) Word and object. MIT Press/Wiley, New York

Quine WV (1971) The inscrutability of reference. In: Steinberg DD, Jakobovits LA (eds) Semantics, Cambridge University Press, Cambridge, England, pp 142–156

Raskin V (1972) Review of Seuren PAM, Operators and nucleus: A contribution to the theory of grammar. Linguistics 83:89–96

Rickheit G (1975) Zur Entwicklung der Syntax im Grundschulalter. Schwann, Düsseldorf

Rips LJ, Shoben EJ, Smith EE (1973) Semantic distance and the verification of semantic relations. JVLVB 12:1–20

Robins RH (1973) The current relevance of the Sapir-Whorf hypothesis. Commun Cognition 6:37–44

Rommetveit R (1968) Words, meanings, and messages. Academic Press, London

Rommetveit R (1974) On message structure. Wiley, New York

Rommetveit R, Turner EA (1967) A study of "chunking" in the transmission of messages. Lingua 18:337–351

Romney AK, D'Andrade RG (1964) Cognitive aspects of English kin terms. Am Anthropol. 66/3 (Part 2):146–170

Rosch EH (1973) On the internal structure of perceptual and semantic categories. In: Moore TE (ed) Cognitive development and the acquisition of language. Academic Press, New York, pp 111–144

Rosenberg S, Jarvella RS (1970) Semantic integration and sentence perception. JVLVB 9:548–553

Rosenberg S, Jarvella RS, Cross M (1971) Semantic integration, age, and the recall of sentences. Child Dev 42:1959–1966

Rule C (1967) A theory of human behavior based on studies of non-human primates. Perspect Biol Med 10:153–176

Rumelhart DE, Lindsay PH, Norman DA (1972) A process model of long-term memory. In: Tulving E, Donaldson W (eds) Organization of memory. Academic Press, New York, pp 197–246

Russell B (1968) Autobiography, vol 2. Allen & Unwin, London

Ryle G (1949) The concept of mind. Barnes & Noble, New York

Sachs J (1967) Recognition memory for syntactic and semantic aspects of connected discourse. Percept Psychophys 2:437–442

Sachs J (1974) Memory in reading and listening to discourse. Mem Cognition 2:95–100

Sapir E (1949) Selected writings in language, culture and personality (edited by Mandelbaum DG). University of California Press, Berkeley

Saussure F de (1959) Course in general linguistics (translated by Baskin W). Philosophical Library, New York (orginal publication in French 1916)

Savigny E von (1969) Die Philosophie der normalen Sprache. Suhrkamp, Frankfurt

Savin HB, Bever TG (1970) The nonperceptual reality of the phoneme. JVLVB 9:295–302

Schaeffer B, Wallace R (1970) The comparison of word meanings. J Exp Psychol 86:144–152

Schaerlaekens AM (1973) The two-word sentence in child language development: A study based on evidence provided by Dutch-speaking triplets. Mouton, The Hague

Schaff A (1967) Specific features of the verbal sign. In: To honor Roman Jakobson, vol 3. Mouton, The Hague, pp 1745–1756

Schaff A (1962) Introduction to semantics. Pergamon Press, New York

Schank RC (1972) Conceptual dependency: A theory of natural language understanding. Cogn Psychol 3:552–631

Schiller F (1795) Über die ästhetische Erziehung des Menschen. Quoted from (1954) On the aesthetic education of man: In a series of letters (translated by Snell R). Routledge & Kegan Paul, London

Schlesinger IM (1967) A note on the relationship between psychological and linguistic theories. Found Lang 3:397–402

Schlesinger IM (1971a) On linguistic competence. In: Bar-Hillel Y (ed) Pragmatics of natural languages. Reidel, Dordrecht, pp 150–172

Schlesinger IM (1971b) Learning of grammar: From pivot to realization rule. In: Huxley R, Ingram E (eds) Language acquisition: Models and methods. Academic Press, London, pp 79–93

Schlesinger IM (1971c) Production of utterances and language acquisition. In: Slobin D (ed) The ontogenesis of grammar. Academic Press, New York, pp 63–101

Schlesinger IM (no date) Perceptual strategies and judgments of acceptability. Mimeographed paper

Schmidt R (1976) On the spread of semantic excitation. Psychol Res 38:333–353

Schmidt SJ (1973) Texttheorie. Fink, Munich

Schnelle H (1970) Zur Entwicklung der theoretischen Linguistik. Studium Generale 23:1–29

Schönbach P (1974) Soziolinguistik. In: Koch WA (ed) Perspektiven der Linguistik, vol 2. Kröner, Stuttgart, pp 156–177

Searle JR (1962) Meaning and speech acts. Philos Rev 71:423–432

Searle JR (1968) Austin on locutionary and illocutionary acts. Philos Rev 77:405–424

Searle JR (1969) Speech acts. Cambridge University Press, Cambridge, England

Seuren PAM (1972) Autonomous versus semantic syntax. Found Lang 8:237–265

Shafto M (1973) The space for case. JVLVB 12:551–562

Sinclair-de Zwart H (1969) Developmental psycholinguistics. In: Elkind D, Flavell JH (eds) Studies in cognitive development: Essays in honor of J. Piaget. Oxford University Press, New York, pp 315–336

Sinclair-de Zwart H (1971) Sensorimotor action patterns as a condition for the acquisition of syntax. In: Huxley R, Ingram E (eds) Language acquisition: Models and methods. Academic Press, London, pp 121–129

Sinclair-de Zwart H (1973) Language acquisition and cognitive development. In: Moore TE (ed) Cognitive development and the acquisition of language. Academic Press, New York, pp 9–25

Singer H (1973) Semantik. In: Koch WA (ed) Perspektiven der Linguistik, vol. 1. Kröner, Stuttgart, pp 80–104

Skinner BF (1957) Verbal behavior. Appleton-Century-Crofts, New York

Slobin DJ (1966) Grammatical transformations and sentence comprehension in childhood and adulthood. JVLVB 5:219–227

Slobin DJ (1970) Universals of grammatical development in children. In: Flores d'Arcais G, Levelt WJM (eds) Advances in Psycholinguistics. North-Holland, Amsterdam, pp 174–184

Smith EE, Shoben EJ, Rips LJ (1974) Structure and process in semantic memory: A feature model for semantic decisions. Psychol Rev 81:214–241

Snow CE (1977) The development of conversation between mothers and babies. J Child Lang 4:1–22

Sokolov AN (1967) Speech-motor afferentation and the problem of brain mechanisms of thought. Vopr Psikhol 13/3:41–54 (quoted from Sov Psychol)

Sokolov AN (1971) Internal speech and thought. Int J Psychol 6:79–92

Sokolov EN (1960) Neuronal models and the orienting reflex. In: Brazier MAB (ed) The central nervous system and behavior. Josiah Macy Jr. Foundation, New York, pp 187–276

Sokolov EN (1963) Perception and the conditioned reflex. Macmillan, New York

Solars AK (1960) Latency of instrumental responses as a function of compatibility with the meaning of eliciting verbal signs. J Exp Psychol 59:239–245

Sommer R (1965) Further studies of small group ecology. Sociometry 28:337–348

Sperry RW (1969) A modified concept of consciousness. Psychol Rev 76:532–536

Stalnaker RC (1970) Pragmatics. Synthese 22:272–289

Steinberg DD (1970) Analyticity, amphigory, and the semantic interpretation of sentences. JVLVB 9:37–51

Steinberg DD, Jakobovits LA (eds) (1971) Semantics, Cambridge University Press, Cambridge, England

Steinthal H (1855) Grammatik, Logik und Psychologie, ihre Prinzipien und ihr Verhältnis zueinander. Dümmler, Berlin

Steinthal H (1871) Einleitung in die Psychologie und Sprachwissenschaft. Dümmler, Berlin

Stemmer N (1973) Non-linguistic factors in language. Commun Cognition 6:45–52

Stern C, Stern W (1907) Die Kindersprache. Barth, Leipzig

Stern W (1924) Psychology of early childhood: Up to the sixth year of age (translated by Barwell A). Holt, New York

Stich SP (1971) What every speaker knows. Philos Rev 80:476–496

Stokoe WC Jr (1974) Motor signs as the first form of language. Semiotica 10:117–130

Strawson PF (1949) Truth. Analysis 9:81–97

Suci GJ, Hamacher JH (1972) Psychological dimensions of case in sentence processing: Action role and animateness. Int J Psycholing 1:34–47

Szalay LB, Bryson JA (1973) Measurement of psychocultural distance: A comparison of American blacks and whites. J Pers Soc Psychol 26:166–177

Szalay LB, D'Andrade RG (1972) Scaling versus content analysis: Interpreting word association data from Americans and Koreans. Southwest J Anthropol 28:50–68

Szalay LB, Maday BC (1973) Verbal associations in the analysis of subjective culture. Curr Anthropol 14:33–42

Taylor I (1969) Content and structure in sentence production. JVLVB 8:170–175

Terbuyken G (1976) Sprechform, Situationsstruktur und Verstehensprozess. Brockmeyer, Bochum

Tesnière L (1959) Eléments de syntax structurale. Klincksieck, Paris

Thorne JP (1966) On hearing sentences. In: Lyons J, Wales RJ (eds) Psycholinguistics papers. Edinburgh University Press, Edinburgh, pp 3–10

Thumb A, Marbe K (1901) Experimentelle Untersuchungen über die psychologischen Grundlagen der sprachlichen Analogiebildung. Engelmann, Leipzig

Thurber J (1974) Fables for our time and famous poems. Harper & Row, New York

Titchener EB (1909) A text-book of psychology. Macmillan, New York

Toulmin S (1971) Brain and language. Synthese 22:369–395

Trier J (1931) Der deutsche Wortschatz im Sinnbezirk des Verstandes. Winter, Heidelberg

Uexküll J von (1926) Theoretical biology (translated by Mackinnon DL). Kegan Paul, London

Uhlenbeck EM (1963) An appraisal of transformational theory. Lingua 12:1–18

Uhlenbeck EM (1967a) Language in action. In: To honor Roman Jakobson, vol 3. Mouton, The Hague, pp 2060–2066

Uhlenbeck EM (1967b) Some further remarks on transformational grammar. Lingua 17:263–316

Uhlenbeck EM (1971a) Recent developments in transformational generative grammar. Slovo a Slovesnost 32 [Quoted from Uhlenbeck (no date) pp 84–134]

Uhlenbeck EM (1971b) On the notion of completely novel sentences. Cahiers Ferdinand de Saussure 26:179–186 [Quoted from Uhlenbeck (no date) pp 76–83]

Uhlenbeck EM (no date) Critical comments on transformational generative grammar 1962–1972. Smits, The Hague

Ullman S (1962) Semantics: An introduction to the science of meaning. Basic Blackwell, Oxford

Ungeheuer G (1967) Die kybernetische Grundlage der Sprachtheorie von Karl Bühler. In: To honor Roman Jakobson, vol 3, Mouton, The Hague, pp 2067–2086

Ungeheuer G (1973) Aspekte sprachlicher Kommunikation. Linguistics 105:91–105

Vendler Z (1963) The grammar of goodness. Philos Rev 72:446–465

Vygotsky LS (1962) Thought and language (translated by Hanfmann E, Vakar G). MIT Press, Cambridge, Mass. (original publication in Russian 1934)

Wakefield JA, Doughtie EB, Yomb BHL. (1974) The identification of structural components of an unknown language. J Psycholinguist Res 3:261–270

Wales RJ, Marshall JC (1966) The organization of linguistic performance. In: Lyons J, Wales RJ (eds) Psycholinguistics papers. Edinburgh University Press, Edinburgh, pp 29–80

Wallace AFC, Atkins J (1960) The meaning of kinship terms. Am Anthropol 62:58–79

Wason PC (1965) The contexts of plausible denial. JVLVB 4:7–11

Wason PC, Johnson-Laird PN (1972) Psychology of reasoning. Batsford, London

Wasow P (1973) The innateness hypothesis and grammatical relations. Synthese 46:38–56

Watson OM, Graves TD (1966) Quantitative research in proxemic behavior. Am Anthropol 68:971–985

Watzlawick P, Beavin JH, Jackson DD (1967) Pragmatics of human communication. Norton, New York

Weinreich U (1963) On the semantic structure of language. In: Greenberg JH (ed) Universals of language. MIT Press, Cambridge, Mass., pp 114–171

Weinreich U (1971) Explorations in semantic theory. In: Steinberg DD, Jakobovits LA (eds)Semantics, Cambridge University Press, Cambridge, England, pp 308–328

Weisberg RW (1971) On sentence storage: The influence of syntactic versus semantic factors on intrasentence word associations. JVLVB 10:631–644

Weksel W (1965) Review of Bellugi U, Brown RW (eds) The acquisition of language. Language 41:692–709

Wenzl A (1937) Empirische und theoretische Beiträge zur Erinnerungsarbeit bei erschwerter Wortfindung. Arch Ges Psychol 97:294–318

Werner H (1957) Comparative psychology of mental development (translated by Garside EB). International Universities Press, New York

Wettler M (1970) Syntaktische Faktoren im verbalen Lernen. Huber, Bern

Wexler KN (1970) Semantic structure: Psychological evidence for hierarchical features. Paper read at Research Workshop on Cognitive Organization and Psychological Processes, California

Whorf BL (1957) Language, thought and reality: Selected writings of Whorf BL (edited by Carroll JB). MIT Press, Cambridge, Mass.

Wickens DD (1970) Encoding categories of words: An empirical approach to meaning. Psychol Rev 77:1–15

Wickler W (1967) Vergleichende Verhaltensforschung und Phylogenetik. In: Heberer G (ed) Die Evolution der Organismen, vol 1, 3rd edn. Fischer, Stuttgart, pp 420–508

Wiener M, Devoe S, Rubinow S, Geller J (1972) Nonverbal behavior and nonverbal communication. Psychol Rev 79:185–214

Witte W (1959a) Aktualgenese der Erinnerung. Z Exp Angew Psychol 6:508–518

Witte W (1959b) Mnemische Determination und Dynamik des reproduktiven Tatonnements. Psychol Beitr 4:179–205

Wittgenstein L (1953) Philosophical investigations. Blackwell, Oxford

Wunderlich D (1968) Pragmatik, Sprechsituation, Deixis. Paper No. 9, Lehrstuhl für Linguistik, Stuttgart

Wunderlich D (1970a) Die Rolle der Pragmatik in der Linguistik. Deutschunterricht 22/4:5–41

Wunderlich D (1970b) Pragmatik, Sprechsituation, Deixis. Z Literaturwiss Ling 1–2:153–190

Wunderlich D (1972) Sprechakte. In: Maas U, Wunderlich D (eds) Pragmatik und sprachliches Handeln. Athenäum, Frankfurt

Wundt W (1900) Völkerpsychologie, vol 1, 2, Die Sprache. Engelmann, Leipzig

Zhinkin NJ (1967) Internal codes of language and external codes of speech (in Russian). In: To honor Roman Jakobson, vol 3. Mouton, The Hague, pp 2355–2375

Ziff P (1972) What is said. In: Davidson D, Harmann H (eds) Semantics of natural language. Reidel, Dordrecht, pp 709–721

Author Index

327

Subject Index

Consciousness (awareness) 16, 31, 82, 117,
120, 164, 192, 193, 205, 207, 215, 237,
246, 247, 252, 257, 291, 301, 305, 306
Constancy, *see* Establishment of c., Sense
c., Size c.
Constructive processes, constructivist model (of language comprehension) 284,
285, 287, 292, 297, 298, 308
Context 9, 62, 81, 94, 105, 109, 159, 160,
189, 259, 266, 280, 285, 286, 288, 291,
304
Conventional phrases, *see* Automatic
speech

Decoding, *see* Coding
Deep structure 21, 34, 35, 37, 62, 125–129,
132, 133, 135, 144, 178, 185, 204, 209,
230, 274, 277, 284, 303
Deixis, deictic field, deictic words 223,
242–245, 251, 278, 284, 307
Dependence grammar 134
Depth of (language) processing 297–298,
308–309
Dictionary, lexicon 37–39, 40, 42–45,
47–50, 57, 60, 61, 64, 65, 68, 70, 73–76,
80–82, 88, 90, 91, 93, 95, 103, 110, 112,
125, 129, 130, 139, 144, 169, 221, 236,
283, 285, 303–304
Discourse 1, 142, 245
Dual coding hypothesis (Paivio) 283, 287

Ego, *see* Self
Egocentric speech (Piaget) 172, 173, 201
Elementary cognitive characteristics 79,
87
Elementary meaning units 63, 86, 88
Encoding, *see* Coding
Establishment of constancy 211, 213, 216,
226, *see also* Sense constancy, Size constancy
Evolution of language 255, *see also* Biological basis of language
Extralinguistic (contextual) clues 65, 189
Eye contact 200, *see also* Communication,
non-verbal

Factor analysis 43, 53, 71
Feature 42, 71, 73–76, 78, 79, 80, 81–88,
91, 92, 93, 95–98, 117, 139, 234, 236, 270,

275, 283, 285, 286, 300, 304, *see also* Semantic marker, Semantic feature
Feature hierarchy 64, 78, 99
Figure on ground 47, 203–205, 210, 211,
235, 240, 249, 252, 254, 261
Free association experiment, *see* Word association test
Functionalist approach to language 94,
172, 176
Functions of language 2, 8, 32, 151, 164,
173, 238, 305, 307

Generation (Chomsky) 12, 22, 23, 33
– (genesis) of utterance, *see* Microgenesis
Generative semantics 60, 95, 99, 109,
125–132, 135–139, 164, 182, 185, 203,
209, 223, 306, 307
Generative (transformational) grammar,
linguistics 8, 12–19, 21–29, 31, 33, 36,
39, 42, 50, 61, 80, 94, 103, 107, 108, 109,
124, 125–129, 133, 135, 139, 144, 147,
165, 171, 178, 195, 214, 231, 236, 257,
264, 274, 278, 303
Genetic determination of language 21, 49,
211, *see also* Biological basis of language
Gestalt psychology 33, 47, 48, 49, 57, 58,
74, 91, 211, 261, 287
Gesture(s) 21, 193, 201
Grammar, *see* Case g., Generative g., Psychological reality of g., Reference g.
Grammaticalness, grammaticality, wellformedness 13, 14, 16, 17, 19, 26, 29, 31,
32, 35, 94, 105, 133, 137, 139, 140, 182,
303

Hesitation, *see* Pauses in speech

Ideal speaker-hearer 14–15, 17, 19, 25, 28,
35, 45, 46, 51, 107, 303
Idiom(s) 101–102, 122, 144, 202, 212, 304
Illocutionary force 164–169, 242
Image, imagery 86, 87, 143, 177, 178, 184,
283, 285, 287
I-marker (Schlesinger) 214, 219
Indeterminacy of language 45, 97,
279–280, 304
Information theory 10–11, 118, 164
Inner (internal) speech 88, 173, 176–185,
202, 203

G. Hammarström

Linguistic Units and Items

1976. 17 figures. IX, 131 pages
(Communication and Cybernetics, Volume 9)
ISBN 3-540-07241-1

H. Hörmann

Psycholinguistics

An Introduction to Research and Theory
Translated from the German by H. H. Stern, P. Leppmann
2nd revised edition. 1979. 60 figures, 21 tables. IX, 342 pages
ISBN 3-540-90417-4

T. Kohonen

Associative Memory

A System-Theoretical Approach
Corrected printing 1978. 54 figures, 7 tables. IX, 176 pages
(Communication and Cybernetics, Volume 17)
ISBN 3-540-08017-1

B. Malmberg

Structural Linguistics and Human Communication

An Introduction into the Mechanism of Language and the Methodology of Linguistics
Reprint of the 2nd revised edition. 1976. 88 figures. VIII, 213 pages
(Kommunikation und Kybernetik in Einzeldarstellungen, Band 2)
ISBN 3-540-03888-4

Structure and Process in Speech Perception

Proceedings of the 'Symposium on Dynamic Aspects of Speech Perception' held at I.P.O., Eindhoven, Netherlands, August 4–6, 1975
Editors: A. Cohen, S. G. Nooteboom
1975. 62 figures, 21 tables. X, 353 pages
(Communication and Cybernetics, Volume 11)
ISBN 3-540-07520-8

K. Weltner

The Measurement of Verbal Information in Psychology and Education

Translated from the German by B. M. Crook
1973. 82 figures. XIII, 185 pages
(Kommunikation und Kybernetik in Einzeldarstellungen, Band 7)
ISBN 3-540-06335-8

Springer-Verlag
Berlin
Heidelberg
New York

Springer Series in Language and Communication

Editor: W. J. M. Levelt

Volume 1
W. Klein, N. Dittmar

Developing Grammars

The Acquisition of German Syntax by Foreign
Workers
1979. 9 figures, 38 tables. X, 222 pages
ISBN 3-540-09580-2

Volume 2

The Child's Conception
of Language

Editors: A. Sinclair, R. J. Jarvella, W. J. M. Levelt
1978. 9 figures, 5 tables. IX, 268 pages
ISBN 3-540-09153-X

Volume 3
M. Miller

The Logic of Language Development in Early Childhood

Translated from the German by R. T. King
1979. 1 figure, 30 tables. XVI, 478 pages
ISBN 3-540-09606-X

Volume 4
L. G. M. Noordman

Inferring from Language

With a Foreword by H. H. Clark
1979. 4 figures, 25 tables. XII, 170 pages
ISBN 3-540-09386-9

Volume 5
W. Noordman-Vonk

Retrieval from Semantic Memory

With a Foreword by J. C. Marshall
1979. 10 figures, 19 tables. XII, 97 pages
ISBN 3-540-09219-6

Volume 6

Semantics from Different Points of View

Editors: R. Bäuerle, U. Egli, A. von Stechow
1979. 15 figures, 7 tables. VIII, 419 pages
ISBN 3-540-09676-0

Volume 7
C. E. Osgood

Lectures on Language Performance

1980. 31 figures, 33 tables. XI, 276 pages
ISBN 3-540-09901-8

Volume 8
T. Ballmer, W. Brennenstuhl

Speech Act Classification

A Study in the Lexical Analysis of English Speech
Activity Verbs
1980. 4 figures. X, 274 pages
ISBN 3-540-10294-9

Volume 9
D. T. Hakes

The Development of Metalinguistic Abilities in Children

In collaboration with J. S. Evans and W. Tunmer
1980. 6 figures, 8 tables. X, 119 pages
ISBN 3-540-10295-7

Springer-Verlag
Berlin
Heidelberg
New York

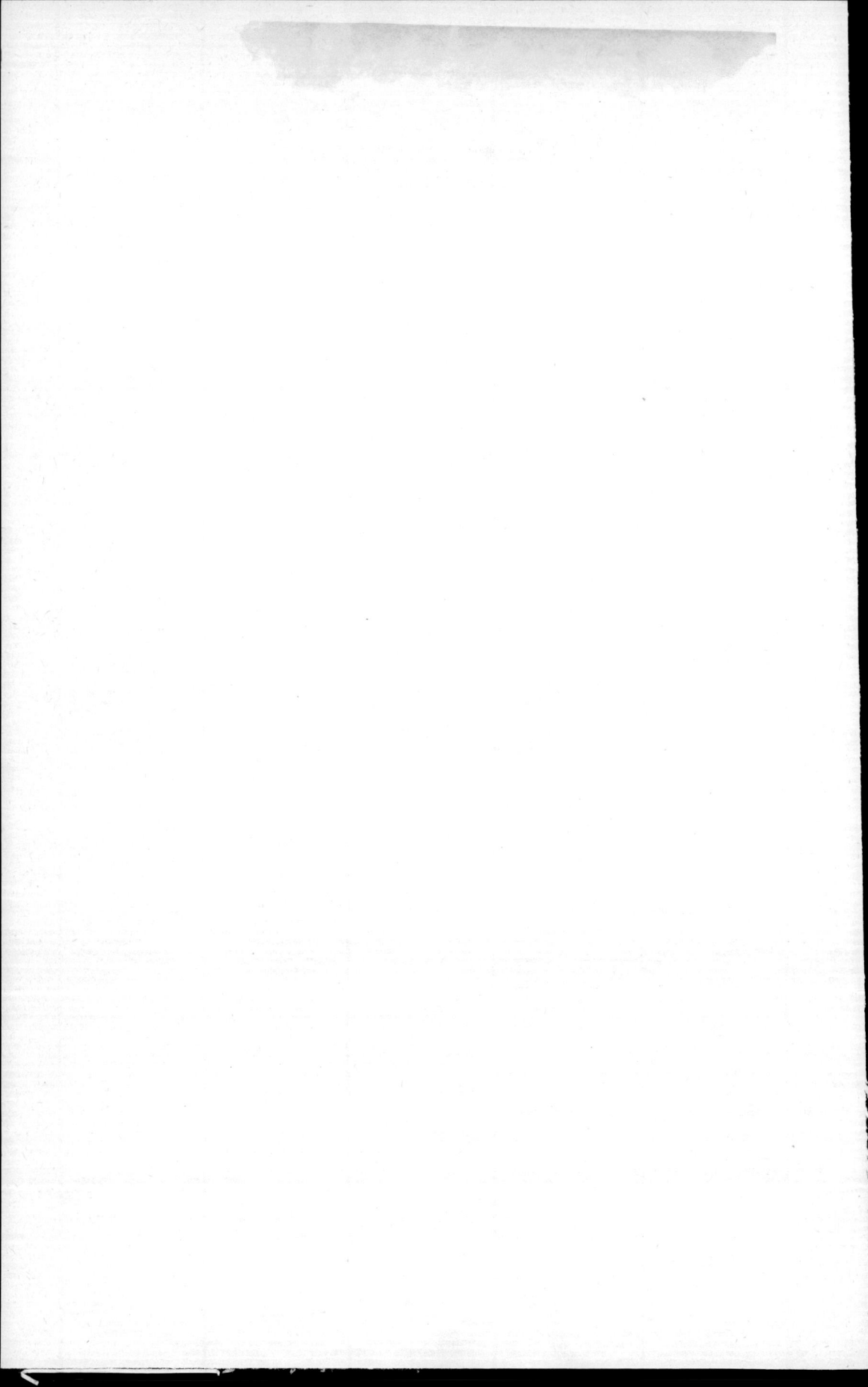